The Mahabharata in Global Political and Social Thought

The ancient Indian epic Mahabharata was first composed in Sanskrit and then rendered into Indian vernaculars as well as other Asian and European languages. *The Mahabharata in Global Political and Social Thought* positions the epic as an influential political text and explores its role in shaping the global history of ideas and modern social, political, and religious thought across India, Europe, Japan, China, Thailand, Iran, and the Arab world. Drawing on methodologies of global intellectual and religious history, contributing authors to this volume study how kings and peasants, statesmen and revolutionaries, intellectuals and activists have invoked the epic to forge their political visions over the past centuries. The epic has thus contributed to state formation, nationalism, as well as the decolonization and democratization of the modern world. This book helps us understand the non-Eurocentric roots of modern political and social ideas, in India and across Asia and Europe, and thereby the global origins of contemporary politics, society, and democracy.

Milinda Banerjee is a lecturer in the history of modern political thought and political theory at the University of St Andrews, Scotland. His research interests lie in intellectual history, global history, South Asian history, and political thought. He published *The Mortal God: Imagining the Sovereign in Colonial India* (2018) with the Press.

Julian Strube is a professor of religious studies at the University of Göttingen. He works from a global historical perspective about the relationship between religion and politics, as well as debates about the meaning of religion, science, and philosophy. He is the author of *Global Tantra: Religion, Science, and Nationalism in Colonial Modernity* (2022).

SOUTH ASIAN INTELLECTUAL HISTORY

This series aims to create a cohesive set of volumes on South Asian intellectual history which will set the paradigm for an emerging academic sub-discipline.

The series, about South Asian worlds of ideas, contributes in multiple ways to realms of scholarship beyond the niche of South Asian studies. It contributes to global history, and especially global intellectual history. South Asianist historians – of the premodern and early modern as well as colonial and postcolonial periods – have shown with remarkable clarity the problems with provincialized area studies approaches, and the necessity of studying intellectual-cultural production through transregional frames. This series therefore marks a pioneering development in intersecting transregional, transnational, and global history with intellectual history. It also facilitates interdisciplinary dialogue between established approaches to intellectual history and wider fields of studying subaltern, demotic, and vernacular thought, with their profound impact on South Asian history and politics. In doing so, it plays a profoundly transfigurative role, taking history of ideas beyond elite vocabularies and text-centrism.

Series Editors
Asad Q. Ahmed
University of California, Berkeley, USA

Milinda Banerjee
University of St Andrews, Scotland, UK

Farhat Hasan
University of Delhi, India

Anshu Malhotra
University of California, Santa Barbara, USA

Upinder Singh
Ashoka University, India

Books in the Series
Local Selfhood, Global Turns: Akshay Kumar Dutta and Bengali Intellectual History in the Nineteenth Century
Sumit Chakrabarti

The Mahabharata in Global Political and Social Thought

Edited by

Milinda Banerjee
Julian Strube

CAMBRIDGE
UNIVERSITY PRESS

Shaftesbury Road, Cambridge CB2 8EA, United Kingdom

One Liberty Plaza, 20th Floor, New York, NY 10006, USA

477 Williamstown Road, Port Melbourne, VIC 3207, Australia

314–321, 3rd Floor, Plot 3, Splendor Forum, Jasola District Centre, New Delhi – 110025, India

103 Penang Road, #05–06/07, Visioncrest Commercial, Singapore 238467

Cambridge University Press is part of Cambridge University Press & Assessment, a department of the University of Cambridge.

We share the University's mission to contribute to society through the pursuit of education, learning and research at the highest international levels of excellence.

www.cambridge.org
Information on this title: www.cambridge.org/9781009484688

© Cambridge University Press & Assessment 2024

First published 2024

Printed in India by Avantika Printers Pvt. Ltd.

A catalogue record for this publication is available from the British Library

ISBN 978-1-009-48468-8 Hardback

Contents

Acknowledgements

We are grateful to the Ludwig Maximilian University (LMU) Munich, where one of us (Banerjee) was a research fellow from 2017 to 2019, for generously funding the conference 'The Mahabharata in Modern Intellectual History: Perspectives from South Asia, Europe, and East Asia', held at LMU on 24 November 2018. The conference is the foundation for the present volume. We express our sincere gratitude to Robert Yelle and the Interfaculty Program for the Study of Religion at LMU for co-sponsoring this event. We are profoundly grateful to Klaus Vollmer and Andreas Renner for their generous encouragement that nourished this endeavour, and indeed made intellectually fruitful Banerjee's time in Munich. We are indebted to Michael Kinadeter, Ben Brücher, and Frieda Ottmann for their organizational cooperation and academic solidarity, without which this event would not have been possible. Simon Cubelic and Shuvatri Dasgupta presented at the conference, but could not eventually be part of the volume – their contributions tremendously enriched our brainstorming in Munich.

We are grateful to each author in this volume, some of whom presented in Munich and others who joined later, for engaging in intense dialectics with us, bringing their areas of expertise into dialogue with our questions about the Mahabharata. We would like to warmly thank the artist Shuvaprasanna for kindly allowing us to use his painting *Krishna* (2020) as our book's cover image. There could not be a better visual representation of how the Mahabharata and the globe shape each other – the volume's central theme. We are indebted to Cambridge University Press, and especially to Qudsiya Ahmed, Sohini Ghosh, Anwesha Rana, Saniya Puri, and Priyanka Das, for shepherding us through the publication process with their usual cheerful generosity and care.

Banerjee first heard the Mahabharata's tales from his parents, Sonali Chakravarti Banerjee and Alapan Bandyopadhyay, and his grandparents, Sushama and Nirendranath Chakravarti, and Tripti and Birendra Kumar Banerjee. Nirendranath and Birendra Kumar were inspired by the epic to author their own literary works, in poetry and prose. Thanks to all of them, Banerjee's was a childhood of stories, rooted in India but branching out beyond. In recent years, Shuvatri Dasgupta has not only offered camaraderie and companionship, but also shared with Banerjee the pleasures of discovering how Indian texts, politics, and the world have shaped each other across the millennia. Banerjee sees this book as an offering to all of them, but especially as a libation to his grandparents, who passed away in the years between the Munich conference and this volume's publication.

Strube would like to thank all his colleagues and friends, especially those in Bengal, who have opened up the rich world of Indian literature and art to him. The Mahabharata stands not only as a monument that should motivate us to rethink established literary canons around the world, but it also demonstrates, through its many transformations and forms, the vibrancy and fluidity of knowledge and beauty. The diversity of its reception in different cultural and historical contexts, so beautifully illustrated in this volume, is a testament to its value as a common good of humanity.

Milinda Banerjee
Julian Strube

A Note on Transliteration

The authors in this volume use sources in multiple languages, including Arabic, Bengali, Chinese, English, Hindi, German, Japanese, Marathi, Persian, Thai, and Urdu. Given this linguistic diversity, our general policy in relation to transliteration has been to avoid using diacritics, in order to enhance ease of reading for the non-specialist reader. Specialists in these languages would be easily able to guess the words being transliterated. Only in a few exceptional cases have we admitted diacritics, where the absence of these would compromise intelligibility.

Introduction

Milinda Banerjee and Julian Strube

Shri Krishna was a politician without parallel – accomplished as providence in building and dissolving empires – hence conceived to be the incarnation of God.... His aim was not merely to make the Pandavas [the] sole master. His aim was the unity of India.
                                —Bankimchandra Chattopadhyay, 'Krishnacharitra', 1875[1]

In the Mahabharata a very definite attempt has been made to emphasize the fundamental unity of India.... That war was for the overlordship of India ... and it marks the beginning of the conception of India as a whole, of Bharatvarsha.
                                —Jawaharlal Nehru, *The Discovery of India*, 1946[2]

The speech of the Mahabharata is same as ambrosia
In every era, it is interpreted in new ways
Interpreted in ever new ways.
                                —Shaoli Mitra, 'Nathavati Anathavat', 1983[3]

Arguably, the Mahabharata is India's most influential political text. Kautilya's *Arthashastra* may seem a close contender, but it never attained the epic's social depth and was, in any case, forgotten for a millennium before its rediscovery in 1905.[4] The Constitution of India certainly plays a more important role in shaping the modern Indian state, but, as a text, it hardly permeates popular consciousness in the way the Mahabharata does. For over two millennia, the Mahabharata has shaped Indian politics. It has nourished the statecraft of Hindu rajas and Mughal emperors, stirred anti-colonial nationalism and peasant rebellion, moulded Dalit–Bahujan and feminist activism. Beyond India, it has profoundly shaped political cultures across Southeast Asia, inspired pan-Asian thinking in China and Japan, activated the philosophical imagination of European and Arab thinkers, and conversed with Iranian nationalism.

Like one of its protagonists, the divine statesman Krishna, the Mahabharata exists in multiple avatars. The Sanskrit text, ascribed to Vyasa, coexists with versions in several Indian and extra-Indian languages. For many decades now, scholars have written about these textual traditions as well as about the popular appeal of Mahabharata stories. Historians, anthropologists, religious studies scholars, and philosophers have all written about the epic. Admittedly, much more has been said about the pre-modern lives of the Mahabharata than about its modern incarnations – but even on the latter the scholarship is rich and growing.[5]

In this milieu, why is a new book needed about the epic? We offer two compelling reasons. First, there exists no single volume that engages with the Mahabharata's role in shaping modern social, political, and religious thought. A monograph by Nagappa Gowda and an edited volume by Shruti Kapila and Faisal Devji address the role of the Bhagavadgita in shaping modern Indian political thought – but no comparable volume exists on the epic as a whole.[6] Second, scholarship on the Mahabharata has, by and large, with only a few exceptions, focused on India. We know far less about the epic's role in the global history of ideas.

Our volume addresses both research gaps. It studies the impact of the epic as a whole in shaping modern intellectual history. And, going further, our gaze extends beyond India to also focus on Japan, China, Thailand, Iran, the Arab world, Germany, and Britain. Our authors show how the Mahabharata helped connect India to much wider, pan-Eurasian, intellectual, and political networks. They also demonstrate how the Mahabharata became central to globally entangled debates about religion in general and Indian religion in particular.

Studying the Mahabharata on this global scale requires new methodological frameworks. All of our authors engage, in one form or another, with the history of ideas. Yet intellectual history, as it has been practised in the past, has two main limitations. First, intellectual historians have traditionally focused on 'great men'. Second, they often inordinately focus on metropolitan geographies. We shall not be able to appreciate the Mahabharata's role in shaping global thought if we continue with these limitations. After all, the epic has commanded such power and prestige precisely because it has gone beyond great men and big cities to stir the multitudes.

In expanding our gaze, we have been inspired by new directions in global intellectual and religious history. To overcome the limitations of older forms of intellectual history, global intellectual historians have made two major interventions. First, going beyond canonical intellectuals – Plato to Karl Marx, the Buddha to Jawaharlal Nehru, so to speak – they have started recognizing a much broader array of actors as intellectual agents. In a common-sense way, this should be obvious. Everyone can think, can generate new ideas – hence, anyone and everyone can be a subject matter of intellectual history. However, within the walls of academia, it still feels quite a revolution to claim that peasants and artisans, traders and tribesmen, women and working classes can all be intellectuals. Fortunately, there is a growing group of scholars who are precisely focusing on such actors, studying their ideas as intellectual history.[7]

Second, global intellectual histories have relentlessly emphasized transnational movements of ideas. Ideas seldom remain imprisoned within borders. Though intellectual historians had long recognized this, they – especially those studying the modern world – often remained content with studying the formation of modern ideas within Europe and North America. At most, they might study the 'diffusion' of these ideas to the non-Western world. In the wake of global intellectual history, there is an increasing impetus to also study other kinds of movements, connecting different parts of Asia and Africa to the wider non-white world.[8] Centring non-white actors, especially subaltern actors, can contribute in important ways to challenging Eurocentrism and thereby decolonizing intellectual history.[9]

These concerns also relate to recent debates in religious studies, where the approach of global religious history has been proposed as the basis of a decentred historiography of religion.[10] Indeed, the Mahabharata was in the spotlight within global debates about the origin and meaning of religion, not least with regard to the colonial context. The epic's antiquity could be invoked to ascertain the authority of Indian learning, which Orientalist scholarship often identified as the root of an 'Aryan' primordial civilization shared by Asia and Europe. This allowed for the contestation of colonial hierarchies within a complex tangle of exchanges, in which the role of the Mahabharata was elevated by anti-colonial nationalists and movements such as the Theosophical Society alike, which, in turn, shaped perceptions of the epic in India and elsewhere.[11]

Our volume draws inspiration from these debates. Our authors do analyse a range of canonical figures, such as the German philosopher G. W. F. Hegel, the Prussian statesman and thinker Wilhelm von Humboldt, the Japanese pan-Asianist Kakuzo Okakura, the Thai king Rama VI, the literary progenitors of anti-colonial Indian nationalism such as Bankimchandra Chattopadhyay and Kazi Nazrul Islam, and the statesmen M. K. Gandhi and Jawaharlal Nehru. Some of the actors we study are celebrated in their own countries but, unfortunately, are less-known outside, such as the Chinese revolutionary Zhang Taiyan and the Sino-Japanese poet Su Manshu.

Simultaneously, our authors go beyond the historiographical canon to illumine an oceanic multitude of charismatic figures – to name only a few among them, a commercial translator like Munshi Tota Ram Shayan; 'lower-caste' political leaders and intellectuals like Panchanan Barma and Jagat Mohan Devsimha Barman; the Chinese art collector Liu Jiping; the Arabic litterateur Wadi' al-Bustani; the pioneer Odia female writer Pratibha Ray.

From rural 'lower-caste' women's journals such as *Mahishya-Mahila* to the Constituent Assembly of India, the Mahabharata has been discussed and debated across the length and breadth of modern India. In the Constituent Assembly, the Indian Constitution was itself conceived of as a second Mahabharata. In the original illustrated edition of the Constitution, Part IV: 'Directive Principles of State Policy' begins with an image of Krishna and Arjuna in the battlefield of Kurukshetra – a despondent Arjuna urged into action by Krishna's sermon, known to us as the Bhagavadgita.[12]

When we thus expand our range of thinkers, we also expand the geographies we study. Intellectual histories of modern India tend to focus on specific regional clusters, such as Calcutta (present-day Kolkata) and, more broadly, southern Bengal; the larger cities of northern India, such as Aligarh, Allahabad, and Delhi; or cities of western India, such as Bombay (present-day Mumbai) and Pune. This volume studies in detail these metropolitan intellectual landscapes but also pays attention to lesser-known centres of political thought, such as sub-Himalayan northern Bengal, the princely states of Tripura and Manipur, and prisons in Belgaum and Dhule in south-western India. The authors in this volume often emphasize intellectual networks rather than only singular individuals.

In expanding our gaze transnationally, even beyond India, we are forced to ask: Why was the Mahabharata so attractive to political actors across Eurasia? What was its mystique that drew so many thinkers? We would argue that if one central rationale is to be suggested, it would be 'sovereignty'. Across the long nineteenth century, European states expanded their power across Asia. In the process, the modern European-origin form of sovereign state also got globalized. In Europe, as well as among anti-colonial Asian elites, nationalism became the hegemonic ideology.[13] This was closely related to religious identities. For instance, the elevation of the Gita to the 'Hindu Bible', as well as the socio-religious teachings contained in the Mahabharata more broadly, enabled universalist claims to equality between Christianity and Hindu *dharma*, or even claims to superiority of the latter over the religion of the colonizers.[14]

In this milieu, the epic form came to be seen as foundational to the birth of a nation. In other words, every nation needed an epic to describe its founding moment. In the age before the globalization of written constitutions, Romantic nationalism cast heroic literature as the constituent moment of a nation, when a nation came into self-consciousness and became a being-for-itself. In this volume, Philipp Sperner refers to Hegel's concept of *Nationale Grundbücher* (national origin-books) to conceptualize this role of the epic form and underlines how the Mahabharata played a significant role in the development of early German nationalism (Chapter 4). Milinda Banerjee and Sperner further show how across nineteenth- and early-twentieth-century Hindi-speaking northern India, Bengal, and the princely states of Cooch Behar, Tripura, and Manipur, the Mahabharata was shaped into the founding moment of the nation (Chapters 1 and 4).

For Hindu Indian nationalists, the war described in the Mahabharata culminated in the unification of the Indian nation. The epic gave them the hope that colonized India would, one day, recover its freedom and unity. Inspired by Italian and German nationalism, they saw Krishna as an ancient Cavour or Bismarck. They found the globally most ancient forms of social contract theory enunciated in the epic and used that to carve out modern Indian constitutionalism. At the same time, local polities in north-eastern India also rooted their origin moment of sovereignty in stories derived from the Mahabharata. In this volume, Alok Oak demonstrates, with particular reference to Maharashtra, that the chronology of the Mahabharata thus assumed paramount importance. Fixing the date of the Mahabharata amounted to nothing less than determining the antiquity of the Indian nation (Chapter 2).

This was not a process confined to India. As Amanda Lanzillo shows, Iranian nationalists, struggling against British and Russian dominance, saw Firdausi's *Shahnamah* (The Book of Kings) and the Mahabharata as comparable national epics (Chapter 6). In East Asia, as Egas Moniz Bandeira underlines, Chinese nationalists even rooted the very name 'China' in the Mahabharata. From a pan-Asianist perspective, they cast the Mahabharata as an Asian epic – for some comparable to and for others slightly less philosophical than the Buddhist canon (Chapter 8). The Mahabharata inspired Chinese and Japanese visions of turning away from the West to 'return to the East'. This was not the case in the Kingdom of Siam, as David M. Malitz shows. After a period of obscurity in the early modern period, the Mahabharata, once cherished at courts, was translated at the beginning of the twentieth century. However, it never gained the appeal that the epic had elsewhere or that the Ramayana had (and has) in Siam/Thailand (Chapter 9). In the Arab world, as Christopher Bahl and Abdallah Soufan highlight, Wadiʿ al-Bustani's translation project was similarly motivated by the desire to challenge the political and cultural hegemony of the West. Hence, the Mahabharata was posited against the Iliad and the Odyssey (Chapter 10).

However, 'sovereignty' is not a monolith; it is always liable to fracture. If 'high-caste' Hindu nationalist men crystallized their projects of nation-making around the epic, so did subalterns. Scholars associated with the Subaltern Studies Collective have alerted us to the fact that elites may often exercise political dominance, but they seldom enjoy hegemony. That is, they are often unable to control the minds of non-elite classes – peasants, artisans, and so on. Ranajit Guha, founder of the Subaltern Studies Collective, referred to this as dominance without hegemony.[15] Guha especially posited the Mahabharata as a narrative form that escapes top-down control by a narrator. Through a close reading of the Sanskrit version of the epic, Guha suggests that

> it will unfold in a retelling that works closely with its listeners as a conversational process. Called *kathāyoga* in the text (*MBh* 1.4.3), that process requires the bard to consult his audience about their preferences not only at the start of the narrative cycle but all throughout. At the end of an episode he will leave it to them to advise what they want to hear next, and an interlocutor who speaks for them will name an event or personality or sometimes even a moral or metaphysical topic around which to spin the next round of tales.[16]

Guha concludes: 'It is thus that provenance makes for a clear distinction between the two paradigms: in the West the narrative issues from the narrator's initiative, in South Asia from the listener's.'[17] We do not need to accept the radical distinction that Guha draws between Europe and India. Nevertheless, Guha stimulates us to think of the epic as exchange. This dovetails with the manner in which Sudipta Kaviraj encourages us to conceptualize a narrative as a social contract.[18] From our standpoint, a narrative embodies an exercise of sovereignty. To tell a story is to narrate 'what is' or at least 'ought to be' – that is, to narrate, shape, and control Being – the world in its total and ultimate reality. In practice, narratives always confront counter-narratives; sovereignties are fractured by counter-sovereignties. The Mahabharata has never been a singular text; it has always existed in multiple renditions. With the advent of print capitalism, as Lanzillo underlines, the Mahabharata rapidly circulated through the novel form of lithograph. Older modes of storytelling, assembly speech, and liturgy now coexisted with print versions of the epic (Chapter 6).

Across India, subaltern communities and individuals were quick to seize on the opportunities offered by print and, indeed, by new forms of modern public association. Banerjee explores how 'lower-caste' peasant and pastoral communities in India deployed the Mahabharata to proclaim their own sovereignty. In their association meetings and printed texts, they drew descent from the gods and heroes of the epic. Lucia Michelutti refers to this as the vernacularization of democracy.[19] Subaltern actors saw in the *dharma samsthapan* (establishment of *dharma*) of the Gita a prefiguring of their own constituent law-making power. Socialists used the Mahabharata to speak about working-class revolution (Chapter 1). Melanie J. Müller highlights the feminist afterlives of the epic, as women writers across India have drawn upon female characters of the epic to describe their own resistance to patriarchy (Chapter 5).

What explains this enormous political fecundity of the Mahabharata? Is it its ability to be both a text of state power and a weapon of subaltern resistance? Taking a cue from Paulus Kaufmann, we may say the Mahabharata is so powerful because it is a properly dialectical text. Kaufmann suggests that a work, to be truly philosophical, must create a dialogue between contradictory ideological positions. It cannot simply declare 'this is how things are'. Rather, it must allow a conversation between the opposing sides, between thesis and antithesis, so that a higher synthesis is reached through that dialogue. Dialogues, dialectical modes of argumentation – to use the Indian terms *vada, samvada, vichara, tarka* – are thus central to philosophy.[20] Kaufmann argues, against Hegel, that the Gita is a work of true philosophy in this sense. There is a genuine crisis, a moral dilemma, a philosophical struggle in the battlefield of Kurukshetra that is resolved through the dialogue between Krishna and Arjuna. Kaufmann compares the situation to dialogues between Socrates and his disciples in ancient Greece (Chapter 7).

The Mahabharata repeatedly says *dharma* is *sukshma* (subtle).[21] Since it is difficult to know what is right, there opens up space for contradiction. Philosophical contradiction and political contradiction are two sides of the same coin. Arkamitra Ghatak thus shows how the Gita, which was often used by militant Indian nationalists to justify anti-colonial violence, was transfigured by Gandhi into a text about non-violence. At the hands of Vinoba Bhave, the Gita became a blueprint for non-violent revolution to usher in an egalitarian society. That a text about war could be interpreted as a programme for non-violence demonstrates the protean magic of the Mahabharata (Chapter 3).

Taking a cue from Sperner but also departing from him, we may say the Mahabharata ultimately resists transcendental closure. As the Bengali dramatist Shaoli Mitra emphasized, every epoch will interpret the Mahabharata in its own way.

Global intellectual historians tend, in general, to be modernists. They explain the globalization of ideas by taking recourse to modern historical phenomena – attributing intellectual globalization to the operations of global capitalism,[22] mass violence,[23] or developments in high-velocity transportation and print media.[24] Similarly, religious studies scholars often focus on the modern colonial period, in which 'Western ideas' supposedly diffused into the rest of the world.[25] The story of the Mahabharata's globalization opens up a much deeper time frame – where ancient ideas inspire actors across distances of space and time. In David Armitage's words, this is transtemporal intellectual history.[26] Ideas refuse to die, to be immured in narrow historical contexts – they have millennial afterlives.[27]

Drawing together the insights of Guha and Kaufmann, we may see that the movement of a narrative does not only depend on the original narrator but rather also on those who listen. This is certainly true of the fundamentally dialogic structure of the Mahabharata. Given the many versions of the epic, as well as its wide spatial and temporal influence, we may say that the epic's dialectics span across vast distances of space and time. Perhaps this even endows the epic with a certain immortality. We may almost describe the Mahabharata in the way that its Gita episode (chapter 2, verse 20) describes the soul:

> Neither is this
> Born nor does it die at any time,
> Nor, having been, will it again come
> Not to be.
> Birthless, eternal, perpetual,
> Primaeval,
> It is not slain when the body is slain.[28]

If this volume underlines anything, it is that the Mahabharata has never been a narrowly Brahmanical tradition. The epic is protean and pluriform. If, in some avatars, it announces ruling-class hegemony, in other avatars it is a subaltern manifesto, a global palimpsest. The Mahabharata has been used to legitimate the Mughal and the British empires; it has also been used to justify rebellion against those very empires. It has been deployed to articulate 'high-caste' male dominance; it has also been used to question and dismantle these hierarchies.

Ultimately, the Mahabharata is perhaps simply what its listeners think it is. The audience is the author. Every act of listening can potentially turn into a constituent act, an act of political mobilization and transformation, of norm-making and lawgiving. *Dharma* may be subtle, but the Mahabharata continues to energize collective politics from the most ancient times until today. When Dalit–Bahujan actors, Adivasi thinkers, feminists, and Muslims voice and interpret the text, they announce their constituent power, they move the wheel of law. Democracy is perhaps just this – an unceasing renovation of constituent power, a relentless opening up of sovereignty by and to the multitudes. In this sense, the Mahabharata is, perhaps, the constituent text par excellence of India.

Notes

1. Bankimchandra Chattopadhyay, 'Krishnacharitra', in *Bankim Rachanavali*, vol. 2 (Calcutta: Sahitya Samsad, 1954), 903–04.

2. Jawaharlal Nehru, *The Discovery of India* (Delhi: Oxford University Press, 1994), 107.

3. Shaoli Mitra, 'Nathavati Anathavat', in *Nathavati Anathavat o Katha Amritasaman* (Calcutta: Mitra o Ghosh, 2012), 20.

4. Patrick Olivelle (trans.), *King, Governance, and Law in Ancient India: Kautilya's Arthasastra* (Oxford: Oxford University Press, 2013).

5. It is impossible to summarize scholarship on the Mahabharata here. See, for example, Bimal Krishna Matilal (ed.), *Moral Dilemmas in the Mahabharata* (Delhi: Motilal Banarsidass, 1989); Alf Hiltebeitel, *The Ritual of Battle: Krishna in the Mahabharata* (Albany, NY: State University of New York Press, 1990); Joyce Burkhalter Flueckiger and Laurie Sears (eds.), *Boundaries of the Text: Epic Performances in South and Southeast Asia* (Ann Arbor, MI: University of Michigan Press, 1991); John Brockington, *The Sanskrit Epics* (Leiden: Brill, 1998); Alf Hiltebeitel, *Rethinking India's Oral and Classical Epics: Draupadi among Rajputs, Muslims, and Dalits* (Chicago, IL: University of Chicago Press, 1999); Alf Hiltebeitel, *Rethinking the Mahabharata: A Reader's Guide to the Education of the Dharma King* (Chicago, IL: University of Chicago Press, 2001); Catherine A. Robinson, *Interpretations of the Bhagavad-Gita and Images of the Hindu Tradition: The Song of the Lord* (Abingdon: Routledge, 2006); Bradley L. Herling, *The German Gita: Hermeneutics and Discipline in the German Reception of Indian Thought, 1778–1831* (New York: Routledge, 2006); Simon Brodbeck and Brian Black (eds.), *Gender and Narrative in the Mahabharata* (Abingdon: Routledge, 2007); Pamela Lothspeich, *Epic Nation: Reimagining*

the *Mahabharata in the Age of the Empire* (Delhi: Oxford University Press, 2009); Emily T. Hudson, *Disorienting Dharma: Ethics and the Aesthetics of Suffering in the Mahabharata* (Oxford: Oxford University Press, 2013); Arindam Chakrabarti and Sibaji Bandyopadhyay (eds.), *Mahabharata Now: Narration, Aesthetics, Ethics* (Delhi: Routledge, 2014); Richard H. Davis, *The Bhagavad Gita: A Biography* (Princeton, NJ: Princeton University Press, 2015); Sibaji Bandyopadhyay, *Three Essays on the Mahabharata: Exercises in Literary Hermeneutics* (Hyderabad: Orient BlackSwan, 2015); Vrinda Dalmiya, *Caring to Know: Comparative Care Ethics, Feminist Epistemology, and the Mahabharata* (Oxford: Oxford University Press, 2016); Audrey Truschke, *Culture of Encounters: Sanskrit at the Mughal Court* (New York: Columbia University Press, 2016); Kevin McGrath, *Raja Yudhisthira: Kingship in Epic Mahabharata* (Ithaca, NY: Cornell University Press, 2017); Sibesh Chandra Bhattacharya, Vrinda Dalmiya, and Gangeya Mukherji, *Exploring Agency in the Mahabharata: Ethical and Political Dimensions of Dharma* (Abingdon: Routledge, 2018); Ding Choo Ming and Willem van der Molen (eds.), *Traces of the Ramayana and Mahabharata in Javanese and Malay Literature* (Singapore: ISEAS–Yusof Ishak Institute, 2018); Alf Hiltebeitel, *Freud's Mahabharata* (Oxford: Oxford University Press, 2018); Nell Shapiro Hawley and Sohini Sarah Pillai (eds.), *Many Mahabharatas* (Albany, NY: State University of New York Press, 2021); Kanad Sinha, *From Dasarajna to Kuruksetra: Making of a Historical Tradition* (Delhi: Oxford University Press, 2022).

6. Nagappa Gowda, *The Bhagavadgita in the Nationalist Discourse* (Delhi: Oxford University Press, 2011); Shruti Kapila and Faisal Devji (eds.), *Political Thought in Action: The Bhagavad Gita and Modern India* (Cambridge, UK: Cambridge University Press, 2013).

7. See, for example, Samuel Moyn and Andrew Sartori (eds.), *Global Intellectual History* (New York: Columbia University Press, 2013); Andrew Sartori, *Liberalism in Empire: An Alternative History* (Oakland, CA: University of California Press, 2014); Emma Hunter, *Political Thought and the Public Sphere in Tanzania: Freedom, Democracy and Citizenship in the Era of Decolonization* (Cambridge, UK: Cambridge University Press, 2015); Mia Bay, Farah J. Griffin, Martha S. Jones, and Barbara D. Savage (eds.), *Toward an Intellectual History of Black Women* (Chapel Hill, NC: University of North Carolina Press, 2015); Noenoe K. Silva, *The Power of the Steel-Tipped Pen: Reconstructing Native Hawaiian Intellectual History* (Durham, NC: Duke University Press, 2017); Milinda Banerjee, *The Mortal God: Imagining the Sovereign in Colonial India* (Delhi: Cambridge University Press, 2018);

Shuo Wang, *Negotiating Friendships: A Canton Merchant between East and West in the Early 19th Century* (Berlin: De Gruyter, 2020).

8. See, for example, Cemil Aydin, *The Politics of Anti-Westernism in Asia: Visions of World Order in Pan-Islamic and Pan-Asian Thought* (New York: Columbia University Press, 2007); Nico Slate, *Colored Cosmopolitanism: The Shared Struggle for Freedom in the United States and India* (Cambridge, MA: Harvard University Press, 2017); Adom Getachew, *Worldmaking after Empire: The Rise and Fall of Self-Determination* (Princeton, NJ: Princeton University Press, 2019).

9. Milinda Banerjee, 'Decolonize Intellectual History! An Agenda for the Capitalocene', *Journal of the History of Ideas Blog*, 19 May 2021, https://jhiblog.org/2021/05/19/decolonize-intellectual-history (31 January 2024).

10. See, most recently, Julian Strube, *Global Tantra: Religion, Science, and Nationalism in Colonial Modernity* (New York: Oxford University Press 2022); Giovanni Maltese and Julian Strube, 'Global Religious History', *Method and Theory in the Study of Religion* 33, nos. 3–4 (2021): 229–57; and the other contributions to the respective special issue.

11. See Michael Bergunder, 'Hinduism, Theosophy, and the Bhagavad Gita within a Global Religious History of the Nineteenth Century', in *Theosophy across Boundaries: Transcultural and Interdisciplinary Perspectives on a Modern Esoteric Movement*, ed. Hans Martin Krämer and Julian Strube, 65–107 (Albany, NY: State University of New York Press, 2020).

12. 'Part IV: Directive Principles of State Policy', Constitution of India, https://www.loc.gov/resource/llscd.57026883/?sp=41&r=0.084,0.307,0.881,0.319,0 (accessed on 31 January 2024).

13. Milinda Banerjee, 'Sovereignty as a Motor of Global Conceptual Travel: Sanskritic Equivalents of "Law" in Bengali Discursive Production', *Modern Intellectual History* 17, no. 2 (2020): 487–506.

14. For the role of anti-colonial nationalism in the emergence of comparative religion and the claim of the superiority of Hindu *dharma*, see Julian Strube, 'Rajnarayan Basu and His "Science of Religion": The Emergence of Religious Studies through Exchanges between Bengali and Christian Reformers, Orientalists, and Theosophists', *Method and Theory in the Study of Religion* 33, nos. 3–4 (2021): 289–320.

15. Ranajit Guha, *Dominance without Hegemony: History and Power in Colonial India* (Cambridge, MA: Harvard University Press, 1997).

16. Ranajit Guha, *History at the Limit of World-History* (New York: Columbia University Press, 2002), 58.

17. Ranajit Guha, *History at the Limit of World-History*, 59.

18. Sudipta Kaviraj, 'The Imaginary Institution of India', in *The Imaginary Institution of India: Politics and Ideas*, by Sudipta Kaviraj, 167–209 (New York: Columbia University Press, 2010).

19. Lucia Michelutti, *The Vernacularisation of Democracy: Politics, Caste and Religion in India* (Delhi: Routledge, 2008).

20. See, with special reference to the Mahabharata, Brian Black, *In Dialogue with the Mahabharata* (Abingdon: Routledge, 2021). See also Brian Black and Laurie Patton (eds.), *Dialogue in Early South Asian Religions: Hindu, Buddhist, and Jain Traditions* (Abingdon: Routledge, 2016); Brian Black and Chakravarthi Ram-Prasad, *In Dialogue with Classical Indian Traditions: Encounter, Transformation and Interpretation* (Abingdon: Routledge, 2019).

21. See, for example, the Mahabharata, 'Sabha Parva' (2.62.14–16), http://gretil. sub.uni-goettingen.de/gretil/1_sanskr/2_epic/mbh/sas/mahabharata.htm (accessed on 31 January 2024).

22. Andrew Sartori, *Bengal in Global Concept History: Culturalism in the Age of Capital* (Chicago, IL: Chicago University Press, 2008).

23. Shruti Kapila, *Violent Fraternity: Indian Political Thought in the Global Age* (Princeton, NJ: Princeton University Press, 2022).

24. Nile Green, 'The Waves of Heterotopia: Toward a Vernacular Intellectual History of the Indian Ocean', *American Historical Review* 123, no. 3 (2018): 846–74.

25. For a critical view on this diffusionist model, see Strube, *Global Tantra*, 12–28.

26. David Armitage, 'What's the Big Idea? Intellectual History and the Longue Durée', *History of European Ideas* 38, no. 4 (2012): 493–507.

27. Milinda Banerjee, 'Transversal Histories and Transcultural Afterlives: Indianized Renditions of Jean Bodin in Global Intellectual History', in *Engaging Transculturality: Concepts, Key Terms, Case Studies*, ed. Laila Abu-Er-Rub, Christiane Brosius, Sebastian Meurer, Diamantis Panagiotopoulos, and Susan Richter, 155–69 (Abingdon: Routledge, 2019).

28. Winthrop Sargeant (trans.), *The Bhagavad Gita* (Albany, NY: State University of New York Press, 2009), 105.

1

The Mahabharata and the Making of Modern India

Milinda Banerjee

Introduction

This chapter suggests that the Mahabharata has played a central role in the forging of concepts and practices of sovereignty in modern India. I argue that while British and Indian elites deployed the Mahabharata to legitimate the construction of centralized regimes of state sovereignty – imperial sovereignty and nation-state sovereignty – more socially marginal actors, such as 'lower-caste' and female activists, as well as sections of the middle-class literati, used the epic to express more democratic, polycentric models of sovereignty. These debates reverberated across state legislatures and princely courts, literary gatherings and peasant assemblies, theatres and secret revolutionary meetings. As Indians journeyed abroad, the Mahabharata came alive in political ritual and deliberation, uniting Indians with other anti-colonial Asians who were carving out their own projects of national sovereignty. The Mahabharata thus helped in decolonizing and democratizing sovereignty in South Asia. In every way, it fulfils the German philosopher G. W. F. Hegel's (1770–1831) definition of epics as embodying 'the spirits of peoples', 'the proper foundations of a national consciousness'.[1]

The Mahabharata and State Formation in Early Modern India

The Mahabharata was central to state formation in early modern South Asia. In the 1580s, the Mughal emperor Akbar (1542–1605) commissioned a Persian translation of the Mahabharata, called the *Razmnamah* (Book of War). There were earlier precedents of Indo-Muslim rulers and officials commissioning translations of the epic. The fifteenth-century ruler of Kashmir, Zayn al-Abidin, is said to have commissioned a translation into Persian, though the text has not survived.[2] Later, Laskar Paragal Khan, governor of Chittagong in eastern Bengal, driven by intellectual curiosity (*kutuhale puchhilek*), asked Kavindra Parameshvar Das to author a Bengali translation in the early sixteenth century. Parameshwar, in turn, eulogized his patron as an incarnation of righteousness (*dharma avatar*).[3] Translations of the Mahabharata legitimated regional state formation across South Asia.

However, the Mughal project had a wider pan-subcontinental legacy. Akbar aimed to create an Indo-Persian grammar of kingship that would enable mutual intelligibility and dialogue between Hindu and Muslim subjects across the empire. Audrey Truschke has argued that the translation occasionally abbreviated religious–philosophical discussions present in the epic, including criticisms of kingship and war, while emphasizing and expanding the discussions on just monarchy.[4] The Mahabharata combined themes of martial heroism and ethical kingship in a manner that eminently suited the Mughal ruling classes.

It helped that the Mughals could relate Indraprastha, the ancient Pandava capital described in the Mahabharata, with their own centre of power in Delhi. Indraprastha's name had been simplified over the ages into Indrapat. The Mughal courtier Abul Fazl (1551–1602) suggested in the *Ain-i-Akbari* (Akbar's Institutes) that Akbar's father, Humayun (1508–56), had 'restored the citadel of Indrapat and named it Dinpanah (asylum of the faith)'. Abul Fazl stressed the identity of Indraprastha and Delhi by arguing that Delhi was 'one of the greatest cities of antiquity. It was first called Indrapat'. The *Ain-i-Akbari* gave details about the Mahabharata story to strengthen this identification, concluding that the epic 'affords many instructive moral observations'.[5]

In the eastern frontier of the Mughal Empire, in the seventeenth-century Arakan (Rakhine) kingdom on the Bay of Bengal coast, Muslim writers like Daulat Qazi and Alaol invoked the Mahabharata to describe a cosmopolitan state capable of integrating the different communities which were assembling in the region due to Indian Ocean commerce. In *Lorchandrani o Satimayna* (Lor, Chandrani, and the Virtuous Mayna), composed in the 1630s, Daulat Qazi described the Buddhist king of Arakan, Sudharma, as *dharmaraj* (righteous king), a term used for the Pandava king Yudhishthira in the Mahabharata. His court resembled the court of Krishna in Dwarka, a city on the western coast of India; his people were the people of Dwarka (*dvarika samaj*). Qazi appreciated this multi-community (*nana jati*) ethos of Arakan, where Hindus, Muslims, and Buddhists coexisted in peace.[6] Alaol, in his mid-seventeenth-century Bengali-language verse epic, *Padmavati*, added various European nations, including the Dutch, the Danes, the English, the Spanish, and the Portuguese, who were all sheltered by the ruler of Arakan. Due, at least in part, to this commerce-protecting role, the ruler was seen as rivalling Yudhishthira in *dharma* (righteousness), Karna in generosity, and Bhima in strength.[7]

From the late seventeenth century through the eighteenth century, anti-Mughal agrarian rebellions erupted across India, causing the demise of the Mughal Empire. I have elsewhere contextualized these uprisings as part of a global age of revolutions.[8] Here, I would stress that the Sikh and Maratha revolutions were saturated with references to the Mahabharata. For the peasant–pastoral rebels against the empire, they, and not the Mughals, were the righteous heroes of the epic. They had fought just wars, like the Pandavas at Kurukshetra, and had founded new polities. Their leaders, like Guru Gobind Singh (1666–1708) and Shivaji (d. 1680), were imbued with *avatara* (divine incarnation)-like characteristics, as Krishna was in the Mahabharata.[9] As the Mughal Empire disintegrated, other regional potentates also staked a claim on the Mughal heartland, reclaiming the spaces of the Mahabharata. Rani Bhavani, the celebrated Bengali female landlord, thus excavated a Kurukshetra *talao* (tank) at Varanasi in the late eighteenth century.[10]

The Mahabharata and the British Empire

When the British stepped into the shoes of the Mughals, they would reuse the Mahabharata to justify their imperial policies. The trend was already visible during the rule of the English East India Company. For example, John Malcolm (1769–1833) – who was key to the British conquest of central and western India and rose to become the governor of Bombay – claimed that the epic had described the ancestor of the Bhil tribes of Central India as possessing an 'original depravity of ... nature'. Hence, he had been 'driven from the abodes of civilized men'.[11] (In fact, the epic speaks about the *nishada*s – a more generic Sanskrit term for frontier peoples – rather than the Bhils, as James Campbell (1846–1903), another British administrator, suggested later while correcting Malcolm.[12]) Malcolm thus (mis)read the epic to show the Bhils as inferior – part of a wider British project to condemn them as a criminal tribe.[13]

A different perspective was offered by fellow Scotsman James Tod (1782–1835), who had served as a political agent to the Western Rajput states.

Tod presented the British as the heirs of the Pandava rulers of Indraprastha, which he identified with Delhi: 'Britain has become heir to the monuments of Indraprest'ha ...; to the iron pillar of the Pandus.' Hence, Britain should rule India for India's 'national benefit'[14], working in partnership with Indian communities and, above all, with the Rajput princely states and clans of northern India. Reading the Mahabharata and other Indian texts in dialogue with Greek and Roman authors, Tod argued that Indians and Europeans indeed had a shared ancestry. Tod saw similarity, if not identity, between the Greek hero Hercules and the Mahabharata protagonists Krishna and Balarama. He quoted the Greek historian Diodorus Siculus to explore the possibility that Hercules was born in India and that democratic cities in ancient India had been founded by Hercules' descendants.[15] Tod observed that 'the families of Jessulmer and Cutch (the Bhatti and Jareja races)' derived their origin from the Lunar line of Krishna.[16] Ultimately, Indians and Europeans were kin. This explained 'the conformity of manners and mythology between the Scandinavian or German tribes and the Rajpoots'.[17] Tod concluded by urging King George IV to restore the 'independence' of the Rajputs so that they would be loyal 'tributaries' of the empire.[18] Over the next decades, the Rajputs would indeed become firm military pillars of the British imperial army.

In 1858, the British Crown took direct control of India, ending the rule of the East India Company. In 1876, Queen Victoria assumed the title of Empress of India. Regular *durbar*s (imperial assemblages) were held in Delhi to celebrate this British imperial monarchy in 1877, 1903, and 1911. To many British minds, the unified monarchy of the Mahabharata seemed to have found its rightful successor in the unified monarchy of the British Raj. Hence, in the course of his excavations in the 1860s, the British archaeologist Alexander Cunningham (1814–93) was thrilled to identify the site of Indraprastha, or Indrapat, with Purana Qila in Delhi.[19] More broadly, the Mahabharata comprehensively infiltrated the colonial mind – the writings of colonial administrators amply testify to this. At least in part this was because in the late nineteenth century, the Indian Civil Service examination syllabus prescribed studying sections of the Mahabharata, in Sanskrit as well as vernacular languages, and applicants were regularly asked questions on the epic.[20]

In the second half of the nineteenth century, high-caste Hindu Indian elites, in turn, often compared the British to the Pandava heroes in order to benefit from imperial support. Indians composed eulogies in Sanskrit, as well as in vernacular languages such as Bengali and Hindi, in prose and verse, portraying Victoria as the heir of the Pandavas. Raja Sourindro Mohun Tagore (1840–1914), member of a leading Bengali landed magnate family and himself a celebrated musicologist, is representative. In his Bengali, English, and Sanskrit compositions, he eulogized Queen-Empress Victoria as the successor of the Chandravamsha, or Lunar dynasty of rulers, described by the Mahabharata. The British were, in his eyes, the successors of the Kuru-Pandava kings.[21] Hence, in a text distributed during Victoria's golden jubilee in 1887, he referenced the Mahabharata extensively to urge Indians to be devoted to monarchy in general and to the British monarchy in particular. Devotion to monarchy was necessary, he felt, to protect life and property.[22] Tagore even used Mahabharata narratives to present earlier rulers of England as righteous heroes.[23] Similarly, Bharatendu Harishchandra (1850–85), considered the father of modern Hindi literature, invoked the Mahabharata's heroes and the epic's image of the Rajasuya (royal consecration) sacrifice in order to describe the welcome given by Indians to the Prince of Wales, future Edward VII, in 1875–76.[24] In general, during British royal visits to Indian towns, loyal elites often acclaimed the British monarchy by comparing it to Pandava kingship.[25]

In the discussions that accompanied the transfer of the imperial capital from Calcutta to Delhi in 1911, as well as during the building of New Delhi, Indraprastha was always in sight. In April 1911, the Government of India officially wrote to the Secretary of State for India about the plan to transfer the capital. The letter declared:

> The political advantages of the transfer it is impossible to over-estimate. Delhi is still a name to conjure with. It is intimately associated in the minds of the Hindus with sacred legends which go back even beyond the dawn of history. It is in the plains of Delhi that the Pandava Princes fought out with the Kurawas the epic struggle recorded in the Mahabharata, and celebrated on the bank of the Jumna the famous sacrifice which consecrated their title to Empire. The Purana Kila marks the site of the city which they founded and called Indraprastha, barely three miles from the south gate of the modern city of Delhi.[26]

Viceroy Lord Hardinge (1858–1944), in particular, felt that Delhi's association with Indraprastha and Mughal Shahjahanabad would endear it alike to Hindu and Muslims.[27] The Secretary of State, the Marquess of Crewe (1858–1945), concurred that

> the near neighbourhood of the existing city formed the theatre for some most notable scenes in the old-time drama of Hindu history, celebrated in the vast treasure-house of national epic verse. To the races of India, for whom the legends

and records of the past are charged with so intense a meaning, this resumption by the Paramount Power of the seat of venerable Empire should at once enforce the continuity and promise the permanency of British sovereign rule over the length and breadth of the country. Historical reasons will thus prove to be political reasons of deep importance and of real value in favour of the proposed change.[28]

The Mahabharata influenced the urban planning of the new capital. The King's Way (later Rajpath; recently renamed Kartavya Path, or the Path of Duty) that emerged from the Viceregal Palace (now Rashtrapati Bhavan, the presidential palace) was designed to culminate in Indrapat, or Purana Qila.[29] From the Pandavas to the Mughals to the British, Delhi was to be the eternal capital of the Indian Empire.

By the interwar years, however, the colonial romance with the Mahabharata had faded. The 1921–22 visit of the Prince of Wales, the future Edward VIII, was the last major royal occasion in India. The Prince, in his address to the Delhi Municipality, observed: 'From the days of the Pandavas to the times of the Prithwi Raj a Hindu Empire held sway here.' He observed how, following the transfer of capital, 'Delhi was to rise again as an imperial city'.[30] However, when one turns away from this imperial vision and focuses on Indian multitudes, we get a different portrait. In fact, owing to anti-colonial agitation across the subcontinent, uniting Hindus and Muslims in the Khilafat–Non-Cooperation Movement, the royal visit was a resounding failure.[31]

By now, it was clear to many Indians that the colonial state was nakedly instrumentalizing the Mahabharata to support authoritarian rule. Abd-ur-Rahim (1867–1952), a (Muslim) judge, politician, and member of the Executive Council of the Governor of Bengal, sarcastically noted in 1924 how

> some theorists ... would argue from the form of government which the people were used to from the days of the Mahabharata down to those of the Moghuls, indeed, in fact, until 1921 ... that government by means of a representative assembly can only lead to inefficiency and perhaps anarchy. And efficiency marks the limit of their ideas.[32]

Criticizing such voices, he championed greater devolution of powers to Indians.

There were other leaders now who, rather than British monarchs, deserved the Mahabharata's sanction. William Wayland (1869–1950), an English politician from the Conservative Party and member of parliament from Canterbury, thus confessed in a speech at the House of Commons in 1931:

Mr. Gandhi has been elevated to the position of a kind of Krishna of India, and, as long as he occupies that position, he will wield in the minds of the masses of India a power far greater than he is entitled to wield, and his influence upon the progress of our negotiations in connection with the future of Indian government must be greatly in advance of that which he himself is entitled to demand.[33]

Wayland would have been astonished to hear that, less than a century later, another Conservative Party member of the British parliament, Rishi Sunak (b. 1980), would not only swear his oath to parliament on the Bhagavadgita – the philosophical centrepiece of the Mahabharata – but go on to become Britain's first non-white (Indian-origin) prime minister in 2022.[34] The epic thus remains a presence in the British parliament.

The Mahabharata and the Princely States

Even as the British were conquering India, regional polities sometimes managed to evade annexation. They survived as princely states, islands of semi-autonomous Indian rule within the British Raj. I shall focus in this section on three princely states from north-east India: Cooch Behar, Tripura, and Manipur. Indigenous martial–peasant communities had forged these polities in the pre-colonial period; the royal families stemmed from these communities. When the British brought these states under their sway, they labelled the indigenous communities as civilizationally inferior 'tribes' or 'lower castes' – they were seen as non-Aryan and thus racially inferior to both the British and the high-caste Hindus who supposedly had shared Aryan ancestry. British conquest of these communities was brutal across the north-east. In reaction, and to justify their political survival, these states drew on the Mahabharata. The epic gave these states a glorious ancestry and patriotic identity, which would inspire resistance to conquest.

It is not that this necessarily guaranteed independence. In north-east India, the rulers of Cachar had evolved a sophisticated form of governance in the early modern era, whereby the different communities within the polity enjoyed a significant amount of self-governance. At least in part to legitimate themselves before their Hindu subjects, the rulers claimed descent from Ghatotkacha, son of the Pandava hero Bhima and his wife Hirimba (or Hirimbi) – hence, their state was called Heramba, and the rulers bore the title Herambeshvar. This royal status did not prevent the British from annexing the kingdom in the nineteenth century. While British ethnographers challenged the exalted ancestry of the

Cachar rulers, Indian scholarship sometimes counter-attacked these British views as being racially biased.[35]

Cooch Behar was politically far more successful. Though the Koch kings drew their lineage from the god Shiva, they also saw their polity as a successor of the kingdom of Bhagadatta, mentioned in the Mahabharata. From the sixteenth to the nineteenth centuries, successive Koch rulers patronized Bengali translations of the Sanskrit Mahabharata.[36] Radhakrishna Das, in the epic *Gosanimangal* (Sacred Tale of Gosani), composed in 1823–24, described Bhagadatta as the primal king of the state, who had fought with valour at Kurukshetra – his amulet (*kavacha*) continuing to bless the state across the centuries. Patronized by the ruler Harendra Narayan (1780–1839), the author clearly wanted to stress the ancient sovereignty and martial prowess of Cooch Behar at a time when the state had become militarily weak owing to British expansion and Bhutanese conquests.[37] That the Bhagadatta legend had wider traction in Cooch Behar is evident from its mention in Jayanath Munsi's (ca. 1771–1858) chronicle *Rajopakhyan* (Royal Narrative) (1823–33) as well.[38]

Under Nripendra Narayan (1862–1911), a Western-educated prince who enjoyed close relations with the British ruling classes, including with the British royal family, Cooch Behar acquired the image of an 'enlightened' monarchy that heavily invested in public works, education, and similar developmental acts.[39] Hence, though the British described the Koch–Rajavamshi people as civilizationally non-Aryan – 'a large Dravidian tribe' with 'some admixture of Mongolian blood', with 'the thick protuberant lips and maxillaries of the negro', 'the social status ... extremely low'[40] – the royal family itself was insulated from any racial criticism. The princely coat of arms carried as its motto a line from the Mahabharata: 'Yato dharmastato jayah' (Where there is *dharma*, there is victory).[41]

Nripendra Narayan's wife, Sunity Devi (1864–1932), was a pioneer female intellectual, promoter of women's education, and organizer of women's associations. Sunity was close to British and German royalty, and especially to royal women. In her political vision, enlightened princely rulers would take care of their subjects. The Indian female royalty would advise the British government, such as through service to the British queen.[42] She wrote about Indian legendary and historical figures, presenting them as role models for women. For example, she dwelt on Shakuntala, a powerful figure in the 'Adi Parva' (First Book) of the Sanskrit Mahabharata, of non-royal but genteel origin like Sunity herself. In the Mahabharata, Shakuntala had denounced her husband, Dushmanta, for abandoning her while also offering him political advice about the importance of wives in guaranteeing the well-being of the household and the state.[43] Sunity's Shakuntala is also a strong character, albeit less fiery than the Mahabharata version. The queen holds both family and state together through love: 'Maharani Sakuntala was loved by all his [Dushmanta's] subjects. She brought pure and unselfish love as the most priceless jewel to her husband's court, and she gave generously of her love to all his people.'[44]

Since the late nineteenth century, the British had cast the rulers and people of Tripura as inferior non-Aryans.[45] For example, H. H. Risley (1851–1911), the pre-eminent British ethnographer of eastern India, described the 'Tipperah tribe' as people with 'strongly-marked Mongolian features, with flat faces and thick lips' who practised 'a debased form of Hinduism'. Their rulers 'put forward an untenable claim to be Rajputs'.[46] In response to such racial discourses, the rulers patronized the publication of a modern edition of the *Rajmala* (Royal Garland) chronicle, edited by the Bengali scholar Kaliprasanna Sen. The volumes came out between 1926 and 1931.

Tripura's rulers claimed descent from the Chandravamsha to which the Kuru-Pandava line of the Mahabharata also belonged. Hence, they named Hastinapura the capital of the Kuru state, as their capital (*rajdhani*).[47] This genealogy was elaborated in the *Rajmala*, Tripura's state chronicle, reputed to have been composed in several stages from the fifteenth to the nineteenth centuries. Challenging European racial ideas, Sen added a historical apparatus to undergird this Kshatriya ancestry – from Chandra, the moon god, via Chandra's descendant Yayati and Yayati's son Druhyu. Reading the *Rajmala* in relation to the Mahabharata and other Sanskrit texts, Sen described a legendary encounter between Tripura's ancient ruler Trilochan and the Pandava king Yudhishthira.[48] From the 1920s to the 1940s, in continuation of this Kshatriya-izing discourse, Tripura's rulers pursued a wider scheme of endowing most of their indigenous subjects with a Kshatriya identity – pursuing various social reforms as well as building a constitutional apparatus of governance. This Kshatriya constitutionalism ultimately paved the way for the growth of a self-consciously indigenist politics in Tripura, which outlived the demise of princely rule and remains vibrant in Tripura until today.[49]

In neighbouring Manipur, too, the Mahabharata moulded political thought. From the eighteenth century onwards, the rulers of Manipur promoted Bengali Vaishnavism in their realm. Given that Bengali Vaishnavism centre-stages the worship of the Krishna incarnation of Vishnu, the Mahabharata, where Krishna is a theological centrepiece, naturally also acquired traction. In the local tradition, which draws on an episode of the Mahabharata, the ancestry of the Manipur royal family is traced back to Babhruvaha(na), the child of the Pandava warrior prince Arjuna and the princess of Manipur, Chitrangada. Thus, the chronicle *Bijay Panchali* (Victory Narrative) details how Babhruvaha was born from the erotic love (*shringara rasa*) between Chitrangada and Arjuna and how he subsequently became the king of Manipur and even defeated his father in battle.[50] Rabindranath Tagore (1861–1941), modern India's most famous littérateur, endowed the romance between Chitrangada and Arjuna with transregional literary fame by composing the Bengali-language verse drama *Chitrangada* (1892; *Chitra* [English version, 1914]).[51] Mainland Indian, and especially Bengali, scholars, such as the celebrated linguist Suniti Kumar Chatterji (1890–1977), underlined these connections and investigated translations and adaptations of the Mahabharata in Manipur. For Indian nationalists, these epic connections showed the region's potential to be integrated with the Indian nation.[52]

Today, however, this narrative is deeply contested in Manipur. Politicians belonging or aligned to the Bharatiya Janata Party (BJP), the Hindu nationalist ruling party of India, champion this tradition, emphasizing Manipur's and, more broadly, north-east India's historical connections to mainland Hindu India. However, those supporting greater political independence for Manipur, outside the control of the Indian state, denounce such arguments. They hold Hindu kingship as responsible for the subjugation of the indigenous population. Hence, when the chief minister of Manipur, N. Biren Singh (b. 1961), a BJP politician, gave a speech in 2018 emphasizing legendary marriage ties between the Mahabharata heroes and north-eastern India, and also asserted that Krishna had brought about the unity (*ekata*) of India in the ancient past, it created widespread controversy in the state.[53]

The Mahabharata and the Making of the Indian Nation

From the late nineteenth century, the Mahabharata assumed centre stage in anti-colonial Indian nationalism. Bankimchandra Chattopadhyay (1838–94), nineteenth-century India's most famous nationalist littérateur, was a pioneer here. The unification of Italy under the Savoy monarchy and the unification of Germany under the Hohenzollerns, which solidified across the 1860s and the early 1870s, was an immediate inspiration for him. In a short essay on Krishna written in 1875, Chattopadhyay argued that Krishna had used the Pandavas to unite India in antiquity under one royal parasol (*ekachhatradhin*). Since Krishna had helped establish the unity of India (*bharatvarsher aikya*), Indians regarded him as an incarnation of God (*ishvaravatar*). He compared Krishna to Cavour and Bismarck, and Arjuna to Garibaldi and Moltke – the political and military strategists behind the unification of Italy and Germany. He underlined that India's national unity was an absolute necessity if Indians were to be protected from war as well as to achieve progress (*unnati*).[54]

In a later, much longer essay on Krishna, 'Krishnacharitra' (1886, 1892), Chattopadhyay presented the 'Shanti Parva' (Book of Peace) of the Mahabharata as ancient India's constituent moment, when India was united through the establishment of rule of law (*vidhi sansthapan*).[55] Hence, it was important to underline the historicity (*aitihasikata*) of the epic, and especially the humanity (*manavikata*), and not just divinity, of its statesman Krishna.[56] In novels such as *Anandamath* (Monastery of Bliss) (1880–82) and *Devi Chaudhurani* (1884), Chattopadhyay invoked Krishna to create portraits of heroic male and female Indians who fought against Muslim and British rulers – for him, they were the new Krishnas of modern India.[57]

In essays like 'Krishnacharitra' and 'Dharmatattva' (Essence of Dharma) (1884–86, 1888), Bankimchandra drew on the Mahabharata to forge a nationalist ethic of character-building, whereby Indians would emulate Krishna to achieve both spiritual and worldly progress (*unnati*). He cited passages from the 'Vana Parva' (Book of the Forest) of the Mahabharata that suggested that the true Brahmin was not defined by birth but by moral behaviour, in order to offer limited critiques of caste hierarchy. Ultimately, reform of the individual, of the family, of the nation, and of the cosmos as a whole became interlinked in this epic-inspired vision. The Gita-inspired ideal of desireless action (*nishkama karma*) was the lynchpin of the programme.[58]

Meanwhile, the British imperial assemblage of 1877 in Delhi provoked Rabindranath Tagore to return to the Mahabharata. Tagore urged Indians not to bow to the British, but rather to remember their past, when they had been ruled by kings like Yudhishthira and witnessed heroes like Arjuna.[59] In 1911, in an angry reaction against the King-Emperor George V's visit to India and his *durbar* in Delhi, the poet composed a song whose first stanza would become the national anthem of independent India. It was first sung at the annual session of the Indian National Congress, held that year in Calcutta. Drawing on the imagery of Krishna as the charioteer in the Kurukshetra war, the song acclaimed God as the eternal charioteer (*chirasarathi*) of India.[60]

To turn to yet another major Indian nationalist littérateur, Nabinchandra Sen (1847–1909), in his trilogy *Raivatak–Kurukshetra–Prabhas* (1887–97), suggested that the Mahabharata represented the history of the Aryan conquest and unification of India under 'one *dharma*, one nation, one throne' (*ek dharma, ek jati, ek simhasan*). There was a clear programme of monotheistization here. Inspired in part by Advaita Vedanta philosophy and, above all, by modern Western nationalism, Sen argued that belief in a unitary God went hand in hand with a programme to create a unitary nation. Just as God was one, without a second (*param brahma ekamevadvitiyam*), so there would be 'one *dharma*, one nation, one kingdom, one ethics' (*ek dharma, ek jati, ek rajya, ek niti*).[61]

Hindu thinkers such as Chattopadhyay and Sen relied on the Mahabharata to imagine the nation as a Hindu *dharmarajya*, or a righteous rulership. However, they had no monopoly here. Late-nineteenth-century Bengali Muslim literary works, such as Mir Mosharraf Hossain's (1847–1912) novel *Vishad Sindhu* (Sea of Sorrow) (1886–91) and Kaikobad's (1857–1951) verse epic *Mahashmashan* (Great Cremation Ground) (1904), also deployed the *dharmarajya* concept, but to imagine a Muslim righteous state. Both went back to early Muslim history – to the glory days of Prophet Muhammad and the early Caliphate – to envision this *dharmarajya*. Like the Hindu writers, they, too, linked the unity of God to the unity of political sovereignty, merging Islamic and Advaita Vedanta concepts.[62]

When we think about intellectual history, we normally think about texts written by named individuals – in traditional intellectual history, often 'great men'. To understand the centrality of the Mahabharata in Indian nationalism, we have to shift our gaze to a far wider corpus of texts. From the late 1900s, revolutionary leaflets circulated across India, inciting violent insurrection against the British. Authored anonymously, they struck fear into the hearts of colonial administrators who kept close surveillance on their circulation. The British responded by forfeiting the leaflets and banning their circulation – taking recourse to laws such as the Indian Press Act of 1910 – and punishing those responsible for spreading the message. Frequently, the pamphlets referenced the Mahabharata, and especially the Gita, to urge Indians to become like Krishnas and Arjunas and fight against the British, who were now cast as the Kauravas.

For example, a revolutionary leaflet published in 1912 and circulated from Bengal to Agra, conceptualized the anti-colonial struggle as a mission to establish a righteous polity (*dharmarajya sansthapan*, a phrase that draws on the Gita's dictum of *dharma sansthapan* and combines it with the Mahabharata ideal of *dharmarajya*). The insurrection against the British was thus a *dharmayuddha*, or righteous war.[63] Another leaflet, which circulated in 1913 across Punjab, the United Provinces, the North-West Frontier Province, and Bengal, interpreted the Gita in a Hegelian light. It invoked Krishna's urging of Arjuna to fight, to suggest that the spirit, and especially the zeitgeist – the spirit of the times – impelled Indians to rise up in revolution. 'Nature will yoke you to your work.... Revolution has never been the work of men. It is always God's own will worked through instruments. Those who were commissioned to bring about mighty changes were full of the force of the Zeitgeist.'[64]

Another leaflet, circulated in Bengal in 1913, argued that the incarnation of divinity (*bhagavatshaktir avataran*) mentioned in the Gita did not refer to any specific individual (*vyakti*) or icon (*murti*) – rather, it was the collective awakening of the people (*janamandali*) of the nation. To instantiate this, every nationalist was urged to create a small revolutionary cell (*mandali*).[65] A notable feature of such leaflets was the collectivization of the Mahabharata's heroic ideal – the people themselves were the new Arjunas. One Bengali leaflet glorified Indians as the descendants (*vamshadhar*) of the Mahabharata heroes Bhima and Arjuna.[66] Another urged women to be like Kunti, mother of the Pandavas, so that they would dedicate their children to the revolution.[67]

The Gita ultimately helped in the construction of an extremely sophisticated model of revolutionary agency. God, or Krishna – variously identified with the spirit of the times, providence, nature, or revolution – expressed the laws of historical transformation, the general movement towards freedom, in the abstract. He was made concrete through the labour of Indian rebels, identified with Arjuna. In the words of one leaflet, God was the charioteer (*rathi, sarathi*), the one who held the horse's bridle – as Krishna had been in the Gita, driving Arjuna's chariot – while the human revolutionary was his instrument (*yantra*), who only had to carry out his duty (*kartavya*).[68] Another leaflet, from late 1916, expanded on the theme by arguing that it was the awakened power of the people (*jagrata prajashakti*) which embodied divinity. This power had incarnated (*avatirna*) in the past as the American and French revolutionaries of the eighteenth century, as the forces of Italian liberation that aided Giuseppe Mazzini and Giuseppe Garibaldi, and was now organizing revolution in China, Russia, and Turkey.[69] Indian revolutionaries had thus become the wheels of the chariot of world history.

By the 1910s, across India, the nationalist public sphere was thus saturated with the Mahabharata. Indian nationalist leaders, such as Bal Gangadhar Tilak (1856–1920) and Aurobindo Ghose (1872–1950), wrote lengthy commentaries on the Gita.[70] The historian Shruti Kapila observes that through his commentary, Tilak 'structured political thought under the categories of Hindu philosophy relating to action, the creation of the universe, spirituality, renunciation and devotionalism', thereby cogently 'linking action to the idea of freedom'.[71]

This trajectory was not surprising given that, as Sheldon Pollock argues, the Mahabharata had since pre-colonial times been 'preeminently a work of political theory'.[72] Thus, the war of Kurukshetra provided a fundamental template through which Indians conceived their militant uprising against the British. In the famous Rowlatt Committee report of 1918, the British officially admitted that one of the major influences on Indian militant nationalists was 'the teaching of the *Bhagavad Gita* or Lord's song of the Mahabharat epic'.[73]

M. K. Gandhi (1869–1948), famous for his doctrine of non-violence (*ahimsa*), himself evolved his thoughts on the Gita from this militant milieu. The power of *ahimsa*, despite its (partial) disavowal of violence, was inseparable from the spirit of revolution. Faisal Devji suggests: 'Violence occupied Gandhi not as a political, let alone a peculiarly Indian, problem, but as a problem of everyday life. Yet it was the battlefield that provided him with a site to think about such violence, specifically the battlefield of the Bhagavad Gita.'[74] Devji shows how Gandhi's understanding of morality was imbricated with consciousness of life as a continual battlefield.

I would also note that, like Indian militants, Gandhi repeatedly invoked the Gita to cast the anti-colonial struggle as a spiritual struggle. For example, in a leaflet written in 1919, Gandhi commented on the Gita:

> The poet has seized the occasion of the war between the Pandavas and the Kauravas on the field of Kurukshetra for drawing attention to the war going on in our bodies between the forces of Good (Pandavas) and the forces of Evil (Kauravas) and has shown that the latter should be destroyed.[75]

Again, in 1921, Gandhi observed that the Gita 'does not deal with an earthly war but it deals with the ceaseless spiritual war going on in the human Kurukshetra'.[76]

Gandhi thus comprehensively ethicized the epic, transforming its warriors into transhistorical ideal types. For example, in 1925, he wrote: 'Personally, I believe that Duryodhana and his supporters stand for the Satanic impulses in us, and Arjuna and others stand for God-ward impulses.' However, this spiritualization did not entail an absolute withdrawal from violence. Gandhi continued:

> In this world which baffles our reason, violence there will then always be. The *Gita* shows the way which will lead us out of it, but it also says that we cannot escape it simply by running away from it like cowards. Anyone who prepares to run away would do better, instead, to kill and be killed.[77]

Given this fundamental radicalism of Gandhi's reading of the epic, it is perhaps not surprising that anti-colonial militant multitudes, and especially peasant communities, conceptualized Gandhi as a messianic figure, including (like Krishna) as an incarnation of Vishnu. Such subaltern beliefs nourished violent insurrections against the British from the late 1910s to the 1930s and beyond.[78]

By the interwar years, across the Indian political spectrum, the Mahabharata was a seminal text. Jawaharlal Nehru (1889–1964), who would go on to become the first prime minister of independent India, eulogized the Mahabharata as an epic about the achievement of Indian national unity. 'In the Mahabharata a very definite attempt has been made to emphasize the fundamental unity of India.... That war was for the overlordship of India ..., and it marks the beginning of the conception of India as a whole, of Bharatvarsha.'[79] Further, the Mahabharata connected Congress leaders such as Nehru with the Indian multitudes, enabling the latter to understand nationalist politics in terms of epic ideals. As Nehru recalled: 'The old epics of India, the *Ramayana* and the *Mahabharata* and other books, in popular translations and paraphrases, were widely known among the masses, and every incident and story and moral in them was engraved on the popular mind and gave a richness and content to it.'[80]

On the radical right of the political spectrum, for a militant Hindu nationalist such as Vinayak Damodar Savarkar (1883–1966), the epic embodied a specifically Hindu national unity conceptualized in racial as well as civilizational lines. As he noted in his book *Hindutva* (1923): 'The story of Ramayan and Mahabharat alone would bring us together and weld us into a race even if we be scattered to all the four winds like a handful of sand.' Further, he observed their living valence: 'The giant struggle of the Kurus, the set duels of Arjun and Karna, of Bheem and Dusshasan that took place on the field of Kurukshetra thousands of years ago, are rehearsed in all their thrill from cottage to cottage and from palace to palace.'[81]

For Savarkar, the Mahabharata embodied a Hindu sovereignty that had been lost to foreigners. As he noted in *Hindu Pad-Padashahi* (Hindu Empire) (1925): '[H]ow can the mission of Shivaji of Hindavi Swaraj, of Hindu pad-padshahi, be said to have been fulfilled when the alien sat on the Hindu Throne of Yudhistir at Delhi?' When the Marathas had captured Delhi, in Savarkar's vision, they had returned the imperial city to Hindu control, continuing the legacy of the Pandavas. However, they had been defeated by the British, and hence, for Savarkar, the war to liberate the Hindu nation remained unfulfilled. In supporting a radically anti-Muslim vision of Hindu sovereignty, Savarkar gravitated towards support for a hyper-centralized national state, even a monarchic–authoritarian polity.

Inspired by Italian and German violent nationalism, Savarkar concluded: 'As the Italian kingdom of Piedmont, as the German Empire of Prussia, even so the Hindu Empire of Maharashtra constitutes ... a national and Pan-Hindu achievement.'[82]

The Mahabharata and the Democratization of Indian Politics

It was, however, not yet clear as to how the free Indian nation would be governed. Kashi Prasad Jayaswal (1881–1937) was a pioneer historian and political theorist who went back to the Mahabharata in search of Indian democracy. He demonstrated that the epic contained information about non-monarchic republics (*gana, sangha*) – this challenged British assumptions that India had traditionally been ruled by absolute monarchs and hence was unfit for democracy. Focusing especially on chapter 107 of the 'Shanti Parva', Jayaswal explained how the 'disquisition in the Maha-Bharata makes it clear that "*Gana*" refers to the whole body politic, the entire Political Community, and, in the alternative, the Parliament'.[83] Writing in the 1910s and the early 1920s, when democratic politics was fragile across the world, Jayaswal elaborated how the Mahabharata offered cautionary advice about the weaknesses besetting republics and suggested means of overcoming these through alliances and confederacies.[84]

Jayaswal presented Krishna himself as an ace republican politician operating within the Andhaka–Vrishni league. He cited chapter 81 of the 'Shanti Parva' to show how 'there were sharp discussions in their parliament or council, and Krishna was attacked, and he attacked others in return'.[85] Jayaswal also used the epic as evidence to argue that even under the rule of kings, constitutional norms persisted in ancient India – these polities were not absolutist in nature but rather constitutional monarchies.[86]

Other Indian scholars, such as Devadatta Ramakrishna Bhandarkar (1875–1950), Pramathanath Banerjea (1879–1960), and Upendra Nath Ghoshal (1886–1969), also interpreted the Mahabharata in a comparable light, seeing in the 'Shanti Parva' (especially chapters 59 and 67) social contract theories similar to those offered by the seventeenth-century English political philosophers Thomas Hobbes and John Locke. The broad argument made by these Indian constitutionalist thinkers was that the state originated from an original social contract – state authority was justified only as long as the rulers protected the people and looked after their welfare.[87] To Indian nationalists, the political implication was clear: the British were not ruling India for the welfare of Indians, and hence an independent Indian constitutionalism, rooted in ancient traditions, needed to be forged to build a free and democratic Indian nation.

In 1920, the Communist Party of India (CPI) was founded in Soviet Turkestan. Across the 1920s and 1930s, socialist ideas spread across India. Newspapers and journals now often spoke of Vishnu or Krishna fighting a revolutionary war on behalf of the poor – a socialist Kurukshetra.[88] In innumerable poems and songs, Kazi Nazrul Islam (1899–1976), the militant socialist poet, drew upon the Mahabharata war to conceptualize the revolutionary struggle of common Indians – peasants, pastoralists, industrial workers, women – against exploitation by British and Indian ruling classes. For example, in a song on the spinning wheel, Nazrul invoked the Mahabharata's famous description of Vishnu–Krishna supplying cloth to Draupadi to save her from sexual violence at the hands of the Kauravas. Nazrul compared the Indian nation to Draupadi and the British to the Kaurava villain Duhshasana. The spinning wheel saved the honour of the nation-Draupadi (*desha*-Draupadi) by protecting indigenous manufacture from domination by the British colonial-capitalist textile industry. Hence, the spinning wheel was like Vishnu's wheel-weapon, the Sudarshana Chakra.[89]

Nazrul saw in the revolutions sweeping across India, Ireland, and Turkey the awakening of a revolutionary humanity: 'There is no more any difference between Man and Narayana [Vishnu]. Narayana has become Man today.'[90] The multitudes were a collective Arjuna – 'in every age, God is his charioteer'.[91] In his Bengali translation of the communist hymn 'L'Internationale', published in 1927, Nazrul subtly transformed the proletariat (*sarvahara*) into a new Krishna who would break out of the prison of the demon (*daitya-kara*) Kamsha.[92]

The Mahabharata assumed importance in Indian women's movements too. This was perhaps inevitable, given the profusion of powerful women in the epic. Sarojini Naidu (1879–1949) was a pioneer here. She referenced characters such as Damayanti, Shakuntala, and Savitri to emphasize how Indian women could strengthen their nation by joining men in the anti-colonial struggle.[93] As Naidu noted in a speech given in 1916 to the Hindu Ladies' Social and Literary Club in Bombay, the reason behind invoking this epic ideal was that the 'work of nation-building must begin from the woman unit'.[94] 'Lower-caste' women's journals, such as the *Mahishya-Mahila* (published from southern Bengal), similarly invoked the Mahabharata to underline the dignity of the Mahishya caste as well as emphasize solidarities between women and men in bringing about communitarian social and political reform.[95] Reform of the household, of the community, and of the nation were thus linked together in these democratic struggles.

In the decades following Indian independence, this optimism about cross-gender solidarity perhaps faded a little in Indian feminist consciousness. However, Indian women writers such as Mahasweta Devi (1926–2016) and Shaoli Mitra (1948–2022) have continued to invoke characters from the Mahabharata – above all, the epic's heroine Draupadi – to arouse political consciousness against the male exploitation of women. Devi's short story 'Draupadi' (1978) is a ringing criticism of Indian state oppression of tribal (Adivasi) populations, and especially women – a demand for justice from a masculinist, high-caste state.[96]

When the Kauravas threatened Draupadi with sexual violence, she asked if their conduct was consonant with *dharma*. For Mitra, the same question assumes poignancy in contemporary India: after all the struggle against colonialism, has a *dharmarajya*, a polity of freedom and justice, truly been achieved for women in independent India? In her celebrated play *Nathavati Anathavat* (Woman with, and yet as though without, a Lord or Husband) (1983), written in the aftermath of several episodes of violence against women in Bengal, Mitra confessed: 'Ah, there was a lot of hope in Draupadi's mind/*Dharmarajya* would be established on this earth.' Instead, Draupadi could now only despair: '*Dharma*! Krishna, where is *dharma*? Where is justice (*nyaya*)?'[97]

In 'lower-caste' politics, too, the Mahabharata has played a central role. As scholars like Aishwary Kumar and Meera Nanda have observed, the Dalit statesman B. R. Ambedkar (1891–1956) saw the Gita as a text of counter-revolution. According to him, in reaction to Buddhism and other heterodoxies, the Gita created a Brahmanical ideology of caste difference.[98] The historian William Pinch shows that 'lower-caste' martial peasant–pastoralist groups, such as the Kurmis and the Goalas/Gops/Ahirs/Yadavs of late colonial northern India, turned to the warrior heroes of the Mahabharata in search of their ancestors. They saw in the epic a charter for their claims to be Kshatriya – justifying their bid for political authority as well as resistance to exploitation by landed high castes. Krishna worship often became central to these projects.[99]

For reasons of space, I shall only consider one case in detail here. The Rajavamshis are one of the biggest peasant communities of eastern India; in fact, they are the largest Scheduled Caste (Dalit) community in West Bengal today. Between the fifteenth and nineteenth centuries, they were the principal state-builders in sub-Himalayan northern Bengal; the Koch kingdom emerged from their midst – hence the salience of their caste name Rajavamshi, literally meaning 'of the royal lineage'. However, across the late nineteenth and early twentieth centuries, British colonial and Cooch Behar princely state policies of revenue maximization and bureaucratization resulted in high-caste Hindu Bengali immigration into the Rajavamshi heartland. Rajavamshis were now displaced from land control and administrative offices, with the Bengali gentry taking their place. This transformed them into caste subalterns in a way that had not been the case in the precolonial centuries. In response, they began a mass movement – its principal institution, the Kshatriya Samiti. Across the interwar years, Rajavamshis organized community education, healthcare, and finance; initiated programmes of economic aid for peasants; resisted high-caste Hindu social and political dominance; fought against caste discrimination and atrocities; and secured political representation in the Bengal legislature as well as state benefits for community members. From the interwar years until today, Rajavamshis exemplify the prowess of Dalit politics in combating high-caste Hindu dominance.[100] In this programme, the Mahabharata was central to their community mobilization.

The Kshatriya Samiti emphasized the formation of assemblies, called *milan-ghar* (house of union). To energize community members, the Gita was discussed here (*dharmalochana*).[101] Rajavamshi intellectuals invoked the Gita's concept of *buddhiyoga*, the yoga of intelligence, to conceptualize forms of social communication and union (*milan*). In their view, such bonds were instantiated through similar feeling, thought, and action (*samabhava, samachinta, samakarma*) – thereby manifesting divine power and creating a community of the whole people (*samasta janasamaj*).[102]

Further, the Kshatriya Samiti urged Rajavamshis to remember the Mahabharata hero Bhagadatta as their ancestor and thereby reignite their Kshatriya consciousness (*kshatrabuddhi*).[103] This was, indeed, part of a wider Rajavamshi project to claim themselves as Kshatriyas, the traditional Sanskritic *varna* (class) of kings and aristocratic warriors. Rajavamshi scholars such as Jagat Mohan Devsimha Barman referenced the Mahabharata story of Prithu, the first good king of Sanskrit legend, to emphasize how Kshatriyas pleased and protected the people – a duty that was felt to be incumbent on Rajavamshis too.[104]

A climax of this politics is visible in the Kshatriya Samiti meeting of 1927. By then Rajavamshis had acquired representation in the Bengal Legislative Council – it was possible for their leaders to imagine themselves as law-makers. In a celebrated speech in this meeting, Rajavamshi legislator Panchanan Barma (1866–1935) passionately invoked the Gita to argue that Kshatriyas were responsible for instituting *dharma* on earth (*dharma sansthapan*). Quoting the Gita, Barma argued that the qualities of the Kshatriya included heroism, fiery splendour, firmness, skill, battle readiness, generosity, and lordly spirit. Hence, Kshatriya-hood (*kshatriyatva*) was divinity (*bhagavan*). God incarnated on earth as Kshatriya heroes such as Rama and Krishna.[105] In that assembly, another Rajavamshi politician, Krishnakanta Barma Adhikari, invoked the same ideas in order to argue that Rajavamshis should therefore self-organize against immigrant high-caste elites; they should intensify the building of political cells (*mandali*).[106] The Mahabharata thus structured the heart of interwar Rajavamshi politics.

The Mahabharata and the Forging of Transnational Solidarities

In the interwar years, as Indians began to increasingly travel across Asia, the Mahabharata came in handy to forge nationalist solidarities. During Rabindranath Tagore's visit to Java in 1927, the local rulers of Java staged performances of the Javanese Mahabharata for him. This was part of a broader project to create convergences between Javanese and Indian nationalism: Tagore also met Sukarno (1901–70), anti-colonial leader and future first president of independent Indonesia, during this visit (Sukarno's name comes from Karna, a hero in the Mahabharata). Following a conversation about the epic with the raja of Gianyar (Bali), Tagore observed that 'the hearts of these people have made their nest in the stories of the Mahabharata. In their pleasure, joy, poetry, music, acting, and life, every character of the Mahabharata is strangely present. Arjuna is their ideal man.'[107] He quipped that the Dutch Indies might be better renamed the Vyasa Indies – Vyasa being the legendary author of the Mahabharata.[108]

The writings of the linguist Suniti Kumar Chatterji, who had accompanied Tagore on this tour, reveal how the epic fostered intimacy between the Indian visitors and their Southeast Asian hosts. Chatterji conversed with locals to discover how the Mahabharata had been reshaped over the centuries, in text, sculpture, and performance, across Java and Bali. Local rulers often requested, and eventually received, copies of the Mahabharata printed in India to supplement indigenous manuscripts. Chatterji praised the manner in which the Mahabharata was also entering the world of print publishing in Indonesia, including schoolbooks, nourishing the spread of modern education.[109]

Later, when the nationalist historian and parliamentarian Kalidas Nag (1892–1966) visited Indonesia in 1954, while the country was celebrating the birth anniversary of Sukarno, he too saw Balinese- and Old Javanese (Kawi)-language drama performances of the Mahabharata in Balinese temples. Nag saw in the resilience of Hindu traditions in Muslim-majority Indonesia cultural antidotes to the sectarian conflicts that had plagued both South Asia and Indonesia, pitting Muslims and non-Muslims against each other.[110] Nag praised Sukarno as 'a great champion of religious toleration in a democratic secular state'. He found hope in the fact that common Indonesians 'spend whole nights listening to and witnessing the shadow plays or actual dramas based on the Mahabharata'.[111]

The Mahabharata provided a lens for Indians to interpret even the decolonization of Iran. In the 1920s, under Iran's monarch, Reza Shah Pahlavi (1878–1944), the country began to gradually emancipate itself from Western, especially British, domination. The regime promoted social reforms, such as increased civil rights for women and minorities, as well as the spread of modern education and economic infrastructure. Reza Shah invited Rabindranath Tagore to visit Iran in 1932. Profoundly impressed by the Iranian achievement, the poet offered a temporally deep reading of this monarchic nationalism by suggesting that India and Iran had a shared ancestral heritage, where royal saints helped bring about reform and progress – Krishna in India and Zarathustra in Iran had brought about such national development, working in partnership with local rulers.[112] From this vantage point, Iran's monarch appeared almost as a second Krishna, bringing about national unification.

When Nag led an Indian delegation to Iran in 1950, he was impressed by the Naqsh-e Rostam monument, with its depiction of the defeat of the Roman emperor Valerian by the Sassanid ruler Shapur I. Hence, Nag compared the ancient Iranian monarch to 'a Mahabharata hero'. Writing in the age of decolonization, as Asian rebels overthrew European empires, Nag saw in this episode of antiquity the 'historic triumph of Asia over the Roman West'.[113]

The Mahabharata in the Constituent Assembly of India

With India's independence in 1947, the Mahabharata received recognition in several national institutions. It was invoked several times during debates in the Constituent Assembly of India (1946–50) that framed the Constitution of India. For example, Seth Govind Das (1896–1974) invoked the epic to justify the name 'Bharat' for independent India.[114] Several members cited the epic to advance points about political ethics. H. V. Kamath (1907–82) cited the Mahabharata to emphasize that wisdom, rather than gender differences, mattered in political assemblies.[115] Sarvepalli Radhakrishnan (1888–1975), celebrated philosopher and future president of India, cited lines from the epic to emphasize the importance of gentleness in political debate.[116] Ramnarayan Singh (1885–1964) referenced the epic to underline the importance of an opposition, which would limit the dominance of the ruling party.[117]

Guptanath Singh (1900–77) invoked a verse of the 'Shanti Parva' of the Mahabharata, which declared that people could amass riches only by killing others, just as fishermen killed fish. Singh related this to the logic of capitalism: 'Colossal money, big capital, cannot be amassed unless and until ... you commit heinous acts and kill others by entrapping the people just as the fishermen butcher fishes by entrapping them.' Singh also referenced the French philosopher Pierre-Joseph Proudhon's (1809–65) argument that property is theft. Condemning the accumulation of wealth by landlords and capitalists, Singh urged for the nationalization and socialization of property such that it would be used for the welfare of the common people.[118]

Given the importance of the Mahabharata in nourishing modern Indian political thought, it is to be expected that it would be compared to the Constitution itself. O. V. Alagesan (1911–92) suggested that Indians were 'used to the long epics, Ramayana and Mahabharata, and so it is in keeping with the traditions of this country that we are having this epic of a Constitution'.[119] B. Das (1889–1984) suggested that the Constitution itself 'is a Mahabharata'.[120] However, Kamlapati Tiwari (1905–90) dissented. He lamented that though India possessed ancient democratic traditions, and though the Mahabharata itself was a repository of political philosophy and constitutional ideas, these indigenous traditions had not been woven into the Constitution. This created a 'cultural divorce between the Constitution and the country'[121] and fostered a hyper-centralized state, aiding the concentration of political and economic power.

Tiwari lamented: 'Centralisation is a terrible curse of the present times. It was the centralisation of production which gave birth to capitalism which in its turn put an end to economic freedom in the world.' Inspired by Bhishma's advice to Yudhishthira in the epic, Tiwari argued that the people must be the centre of the polity, and the state only exists to take care of their material wants. Tiwari castigated the Constitution for ignoring Bhishma's advice and for failing to address Indian poverty – hence, the document 'appears to be quite futile and lifeless'.[122]

Through such debates, the Mahabharata found a way into Indian constitutional life and iconography. In fact, in the original illustrated edition of the Constitution, the section on the Directive Principles of State Policy begins with an image of Krishna and Arjuna on a chariot – the episode of the Gita, the iconography of the chariot of state, introducing that part of the Constitution dealing with the ethical principles governing the Indian polity.[123] The Supreme Court of India adopted as its motto the Mahabharata's dictum 'Yato dharmastato jayah' – the rule of *dharma* thus conversed with the constitutional norm of the rule of law.[124]

The Indian parliament house is adorned with a passage from the Mahabharata, affirming the relation between truth (*satya*), righteousness (*dharma*), and political assembly (*sabha*).[125] K. C. S. Paniker (1911–77) painted a mural in the parliament depicting Vyasa composing the Mahabharata, with a verse from the epic emphasizing the role of *dharma* in maintaining the world.[126] The Mahabharata was thus fashioned into a supporting pillar for the constitutional rule of law and parliamentarianism. Democracy was indigenized – rooted into Indian moral worlds.

The Mahabharata in Contemporary Indian Politics

The Mahabharata remains vibrant in Indian politics today. For example, Yadav politicians in Uttar Pradesh and Bihar assert that their pastoral-origin community members are descendants of Krishna. As heirs of the divine statesman, Yadavs claim a mantle of just rulership. Thus, Mulayam Singh Yadav (1939–2022), Samajwadi Party politician and former chief minister of Uttar Pradesh, drew inspiration from the way in which 'Krishna fought against injustice, against atrocities'. Laloo Prasad Yadav (b. 1948), Rashtriya Janata Dal politician and former chief minister of Bihar, suggests: 'If we silently see the atrocities going on, then we do not have any right to be called the heirs of Lord Krishna. Hence ... the Mahabharata and the Gita should be our sources of inspiration; they are our charters.' Lucia Michelutti demonstrates that such arguments are central to Yadav political empowerment in northern India, bolstering the vernacularization of democracy.[127] For Yadavs, the Mahabharata affirms the presence of democracy in ancient India. In Yadav discourse, '[t]he Mahabharata period which was the period of Yadavas is known for its republican and democratic government'.[128]

Similarly, the Greater Cooch Behar People's Association, which seeks political autonomy for Rajavamshis and other indigenous communities of northern Bengal, celebrates the Mahabharata-derived motto of the Cooch Behar princely house: 'Yato dharmastato jayah'. It suggests that the Koch kingdom had been a utopian kingdom (Ramarajya), where the kings loved the people like their own children. Hindus and Muslims lived there in harmony. The demise of this kingdom led to the decline of the indigenous communities; hence, the movement seeks to restore the kingdom's dharmic ideals and protect its subaltern communities.[129]

To move next to examples from national politics, prime minister Narendra Modi (b. 1950) urged Indians in 2020 to mobilize against the Covid-19 pandemic and defeat it, just as the Mahabharata war had been won.[130] Union finance minister Nirmala Sitharaman (b. 1959), in her budget speech in 2022, referenced a verse from the 'Shanti Parva' of the epic to suggest that state taxation policy must be in accordance with *dharma*.[131] The original passage, in fact, forms part of an elaborate argument about the responsibilities of rulership and places limits on the authority of kings to tax their subjects, suggesting that an avaricious state goes to ruin.[132]

BJP politician and chief minister of Assam, Himanta Biswa Sarma (b. 1969), argued in 2022 that the 'Shanti Parva' of the Mahabharata contained concepts about the assembly of the people that resemble parliamentary institutions and that the epic also mentions republican *janapada*s (city states).[133] The implication is that Indian democracy owes its origins not just to Western constitutionalism but to its own indigenous traditions – a theme that recurs in the speeches of other BJP politicians, including those of Modi.[134]

Meanwhile, opposition politicians have equally deployed the Mahabharata against the BJP. Arvind Kejriwal (b. 1968), Aam Aadmi Party (AAP) politician and chief minister of Delhi, sees his party as Arjuna and the BJP government as well as the Congress party as Duryodhana, the Kaurava prince and arch-villain of the Mahabharata.[135] The BJP government's alliance with big business capitalism has invited comparisons with the Kauravas. Thus, Congress politician and former union minister Jairam Ramesh (b. 1954) has accused Modi of 'behaving like Duryodhan of Mahabharat and ready to sacrifice interest of farmers and tribals to appease the corporates'. He envisions that a Mahabharata war will be fought against land acquisition policies directed against India's peasant–tribal populations.[136]

During the farmers' protest of 2020-21, the central BJP government was widely castigated for enacting agrarian legislation that was perceived as pro-corporate and anti-peasant. Large peasant assemblies, involving tens of thousands of people, gathered in Punjab and Haryana, finally converging in Delhi, thus straddling the landscape of the Kurukshetra war. Protesting peasants, as well as opposition politicians, such as Congress leader Randeep Singh Surjewala (b. 1967), compared the government to the Kauravas and the peasants to Pandavas. Finally, in 2021, the government repealed the legislation, leading to the withdrawal of the movement.[137]

Conclusion

From the reign of the Mughals through the British Raj to contemporary India, the Mahabharata has thus offered to the rulers and multitudes of India a shared lexicon for making political arguments, nevertheless provoking as much political contestation as any opportunity for consensus. Indians today remain deeply divided as to who the contemporary Pandavas and who the Kauravas are – as their ancestors have been through the ages. This is because, ultimately, the Mahabharata is India's paramount document of sovereignty. Hindus and Muslims, princes and peasants, high castes and Dalit–Bahujan–Adivasis, men and women – even those from outside India, such as British imperialists and Indonesian rulers – have appropriated the epic to articulate their visions of sovereignty. From Manipur to Maharashtra, from Punjab to Patna, the Mahabharata has sanctioned kingship as well as provided a longue durée foundation for Indian democracy.

Arguably, no other comparable epic poem – the Iliad, the Odyssey, the Aeneid, the Norse sagas – plays as important a political role in any modern nation as the Mahabharata and the Ramayana do in India.[138] This is an astonishing phenomenon with which scholars have not even begun to reckon yet. One may certainly argue that the Mahabharata provides to state-builders in India a long and glorious history of sovereignty – attractive, above all, to Hindu Indian nationalists.[139] That is, it offers a blueprint of Indian sovereignty, a manifesto for Indian nationalism. However, this would not explain the epic's enduring appeal to a much wider array of actors – to peasants, to women, to Muslims, to people in regions far away from northern India, where the bulk of the epic's action is set. To see the Mahabharata as a mere legitimating text for sovereignty, a device for imagining the nation as a community,[140] would make us lose sight of how it has, more importantly, shaped the very content of modern Indian democratic political thought. The epic is not a mere talisman of national sovereignty, a mere ornament that aestheticizes the hardcore business of politics. Rather, the Mahabharata structures the intellectual sinews of collective political action itself in India. The epic is a bustling agora – the political assembly of India crystallized into pure intellectual form.

I believe Hegel can offer us a vital clue as to why this should be the case. He argues that the epic form embodies a historical epoch when the individual is not yet alienated from their community, when the community's consciousness 'still remains a living attitude of mind from which no individual separated himself'. When this changes, when 'the individual's spirit becomes disentangled from the nation's concrete whole and its situations, deeds, fates, and attitudes of mind', the epic form gradually withers away. Hegel relates this to the rise of the state, or, in his words, the birth of 'a just and legal order, ... a prosaic arrangement of things, ... a political constitution'. With the birth of the state, a 'man's substantive obligations enter as a necessity external to him, not immanent in himself, and compelling him to recognize their validity'.[141]

It is this transformation which has not yet fully come about in India. Modern India does have a legal order, a political constitution, which confronts individuals as an external necessity and compulsion. Yet, even today, Indians live much of their social and political life in communities. This is especially true for Dalit–Bahujan–Adivasi actors. Subaltern politics is still largely community politics. State and capital have not fully devoured subaltern life-worlds. Hence, the epic form, too, remains alive, resisting its relegation to myth. Gods, ancestors, and heroes continue to inspire and exult subaltern resistance against the state and capital. Common people shape themselves every day as Mahabharata's warrior heroes, marching under the banner of the Pandavas, producing miraculous transformations in Indian politics. Indian democracy is epic democracy, where the individual and community remain immanent in each other.[142] Who shall be sovereign in this India? The battle over Indraprastha rages on.

In this sense, Indian politics is itself the perennial battlefield of Kurukshetra.

Notes

1. G. W. F. Hegel, *Aesthetics: Lectures on Fine Art*, vol. 2, trans. T. M. Knox (Oxford: Clarendon Press, 1975), 1045.

2. Audrey Truschke, 'Mahābhārata (Zayn al-'Ābidīn translation)', in *Perso-Indica: An Analytical Survey of Persian Works on Indian Learned Traditions*, ed. F. Speziale and C. W. Ernst (2019), http://www.perso-indica.net/work/mahabharata_%28zayn_al-abidin_translation%29 (accessed on 20 August 2022).

3. Kalpana Bhowmik, *Kavindra Mahabharata: Lipitattvik-Bhashatattvik Samiksha o Sanskrita Mahabharater sange Tulana*, vol. 2 (Dhaka: Bangla Academy, 1949), 12, 693.

4. Audrey Truschke, *Culture of Encounters: Sanskrit at the Mughal Court* (New York: Columbia University Press, 2018). See also Audrey Truschke, 'A Padshah Like Manu: Political Advice for Akbar in the Persian *Mahābhārata*', *Philological Encounters* 5, no. 2 (2020): 112–33; Michael Willis (ed.), *Translation and State: The Mahābhārata at the Mughal Court* (Berlin: De Gruyter, 2022).

5. Abul Fazl, *Ain-i-Akbari*, vol. 2, trans. H. S. Jarrett, ed. Jadunath Sarkar (Calcutta: Royal Asiatic Society of Bengal, 1949), 283–90.

6. Daulat Qazi, *Lorchandrani o Satimayna*, ed. Debnath Bandyopadhyay (Calcutta: Sahitya Samsad, 2017), 4–11.

7. Alaol, *Padmavati*, ed. Debnath Bandyopadhyay (Calcutta: West Bengal State Book Board, 2002), 10–14.

8. Milinda Banerjee, *The Mortal God: Imagining the Sovereign in Colonial India* (Delhi: Cambridge University Press, 2018), 52–55.

9. See, for example, Louis E. Fenech, *The Darbar of the Sikh Gurus: The Court of God in the World of Men* (Delhi: Oxford University Press, 2008), 21–22, 145–46, 151–52, 158, 221; Robin Rinehart, *Debating the Dasam Granth* (New York: Oxford University Press, 2011), 28–30, 84, 140, 154–55, 163, 166, 169–70; Louis E. Fenech, *The Cherished Five in Sikh History* (New York: Oxford University Press, 2021); James W. Laine, *Shivaji: Hindu King in Islamic India* (New York: Oxford University Press, 2003), 32–35, 53–54.

10. Rajani Ranjan Sen, *The Holy City (Benares)* (Chittagong: M. R. Sen, 1912), 196.

11. John Malcolm, *A Memoir of Central India*, vol. 1 (London: Kingsbury, Parbury, and Allen, 1824), 518. See also John Malcolm, 'Essay on the Bhills', *Transactions of the Royal Asiatic Society of Great Britain and Ireland* 1, no. 1 (1824): 65–91.

12. James M. Campbell, *Gazetteer of the Bombay Presidency*, vol. 12: *Khandesh* (Bombay: Government Central Press, 1880), 80.

13. Stewart N. Gordon, 'Bhils and the Idea of a Criminal Tribe in Nineteenth-Century India', in *Crime and Criminality in British India*, ed. Anand A. Yang, 128–39 (Tucson, AZ: University of Arizona Press, 1985).

14. James Tod, *Annals and Antiquities of Rajast'han*, vol. 1 (London: Smith, Elder & Co., 1829), 31–32.

15. Tod, *Annals and Antiquities*, vol. 1, 30, 51.

16. Tod, *Annals and Antiquities*, vol. 1, 45.

17. Tod, *Annals and Antiquities*, vol. 1, 65.

18. Tod, *Annals and Antiquities*, vi. For the Scottish gaze behind this reading of the Rajputs, see Milinda Banerjee, 'How "Dynasty" Became a Modern Global Concept: Intellectual Histories of Sovereignty and Property', *Global Intellectual History* 7, no. 3 (2022): 421–52.

19. Alexander Cunningham, *Archaeological Survey of India: Four Reports Made during the Years 1862-63-64-65*, vol. 1 (Simla: Government Central Press, 1871), 134–36.

20. See the reports of the Civil Service Commissioners in the House of Commons Parliamentary Papers, relating to the second half of the nineteenth century.

21. Sourindro Mohun Tagore, *Victoria Samrajyan, or Sanskrit Stanzas (with a Translation) on the Various Dependencies of the British Crown* (Calcutta: Sourindro Mohun Tagore, 1882), 8–17.

22. Sourindro Mohun Tagore, *Hindu Loyalty: A Presentation of the Views of Sanskrit Authorities on the Subject of Loyalty* (Calcutta: Sourindro Mohun Tagore, 1887).

23. Sourindro Mohun Tagore, *Victoria-Giti-Mala, or A Brief History of England* (Calcutta: Sourindro Mohun Tagore, 1887), 36.

24. Bharatendu Harishchandra, *Bhartendu Granthavali* (Varanasi: Nagari Pracharini Sabha, 1935), 699, 704.

25. See the following example on Varanasi: William Howard Russell, *The Prince of Wales' Tour: A Diary in India* (London: Sampson Low, Marston, Searle & Rivington, 1877), 386; on Delhi: *The Imperial Tour in India and Durbar, 1911–12* (Lahore: The Imperial Publishing Co., n.d.), 96.

26. Government of India, *The Historical Record of the Imperial Visit to India, 1911, Compiled from the Official Records under the Orders of the Viceroy and Governor-General of India* (London: John Murray, 1914), 317.

27. Robert Grant Irving, 'Indian Summer: Imperial Delhi', PhD dissertation, Yale University, New Haven, CT, 1978, 53.

28. Government of India, *The Historical Record*, 324.

29. Irving, 'Indian Summer', 144, 156, 172–74.

30. M. O'Mealey, *Programmes, Speeches, Addresses, Reports and References in the Press Relating to His Royal Highness the Prince of Wales' Tour in India, 1921–1922* (Delhi: Superintendent Government Printing, 1923), 345.

31. Banerjee, *The Mortal God*, 89–90.

32. Note of Abd-ur-Rahim, 19 July 1924, in House of Commons Parliamentary Papers, East India (Constitutional Reforms), Reforms Enquiry Committee, 1924, Views of Local Governments, on the Working of the Reforms, Dated 1924, 145.

33. 'India', Commons Sitting, 31 July 1931, series 5, vol. 255, https://api.parliament.uk/historic-hansard/commons/1931/jul/31/india-2 (accessed on 21 August 2022).

34. Sherwood Harriet, 'Rishi Sunak to Become First British PM of Colour and Also First Hindu at No 10', *The Guardian*, 24 October 2022, https://www.theguardian.com/politics/2022/oct/24/rishi-sunak-becomes-first-british-pm-of-colour-and-also-first-hindu-at-no-10 (accessed on 26 October 2022).

35. See Padmanath Bhattacharya (ed.), *Heramba Rajyer Dandavidhi* (Calcutta: Gauhati Bangasahityanushilani Sabha, 1911), 21–22, for the critique of British ethnography; Upendrachandra Guha, *Cachharer Itivritta* (Dhaka: Sadhana Library, n.d.).

36. Swapan Kumar Ray, *Kochbihar Rajdarbarer Sahityacharcha* (Calcutta: Books Way, 2011); Sachindra Nath Roy, *Sahitya Sadhanay Rajanya Shasita Kochbihar* (Siliguri: N. L. Publishers, 2013), 128–62.

37. Radhakrishna Das, *Gosanimangal*, ed. Harishchandra Paul (Cooch Behar: Chandrashekhar Paul), 1977, 2, 53–58.

38. Jayanath Munsi, *Rajopakhyan*, ed. Bishwanath Das (Calcutta: Mala Publications, 1989), 5.

39. Banerjee, *The Mortal God*, 127–30.

40. H. H. Risley, *The Tribes and Castes of Bengal*, vol. 1 (Calcutta: Bengal Secretariat Press, 1891), 491–500.

41. Harendra Narayan Chaudhuri, *The Cooch Behar State and Its Land Revenue Settlements* (Cooch Behar: Cooch Behar State Press, 1903), 438.

42. Banerjee, *The Mortal God*, 202–03.

43. For an English translation of the Sanskrit text, see Manmatha Nath Dutt, *A Prose English Translation of the Mahabharata: Adi Parva* (Calcutta: Manmatha Nath Dutt, 1895), 106–111.

44. Sunity Devi, *Nine Ideal Indian Women* (Calcutta: Thacker, Spink & Co., 1919), 80.

45. Banerjee, *The Mortal God*, 299–300.

46. Risley, *The Tribes and Castes of Bengal*, 323–27.

47. Dwijendrachandra Datta and Suprasanna Bandyopadhyay (eds.), *Rajgi Tripurar Sarkari Bangla* (Agartala: Government of Tripura, 1976), especially 14.

48. Kaliprasanna Sen (ed.), *Shrirajmala*, vol. 1 (Agartala: Government of Tripura, 2020), especially i–xciv, 5–10, 33, 161–70.

49. Banerjee, *The Mortal God*, 298–312; Milinda Banerjee, 'A Non-Eurocentric Genealogy of Indian Democracy: Tripura in History of Political Thought', in *Vernacular Politics in Northeast India: Democracy, Ethnicity, and Indigeneity*, ed. Jelle J. P. Wouters, 83–109 (Oxford: Oxford University Press, 2022).

50. Laishram Mangi Singh and Longjam Mani Singh (eds.) *Manipur Itihas Bijay Panchali Garibniwaz Charit*, vol. 1 (Imphal: Mahabharat Press, 1966), 10–11.

51. Rabindranath Tagore, *Chitrangada* (Calcutta: Viswa-Bharati Granthalaya, 1955).

52. Suniti Kumar Chatterji, *Kirata-Jana-Krti, The Indo-Mongoloids: Their Contribution to the History and Culture of India* (Calcutta: The Asiatic Society, 1998), 142–66.

53. Deepak Naorem, 'Myth Making and imagining a Brahmanical Manipur since 18th century CE', *Raiot*, 2 April 2018, https://raiot.in/myth-making-and-imagining-a-brahmanical-manipur-since-18th-century-ce (accessed on

22 August 2022); Sudeep Chakravarti, 'Biren Singh: The Mahabharat Man Returns', *Open*, 11 March 2022, https://openthemagazine.com/cover-stories/biren-singh-the-mahabharat-man-returns (accessed on 22 August 2022); Khelen Thokchom, 'Biren Sparks Storm with Krishna Remark', *Telegraph*, 30 March 2018, https://www.telegraphindia.com/north-east/biren-sparks-storm-with-krishna-remark/cid/1445535 (accessed on 22 August 2022); NE Now News, 'Manipur Chief Minister still feeling heat of controversial statement', 1 April 2018, https://nenow.in/north-east-news/manipur-chief-minister-still-feeling-heat-controversial-statement.html (accessed on 22 August 2022).

54. Bankimchandra Chattopadhyay, *Bankim Rachanavali*, vol. 2 (Calcutta: Sahitya Samsad, 1954), 902–06.

55. Chattopadhyay, *Bankim Rachanavali*, vol. 2, 574–75.

56. Chattopadhyay, *Bankim Rachanavali*, vol. 2, 410–24, 506–08. See also Sudipta Kaviraj, *The Unhappy Consciousness: Bankimchandra Chattopadhyay and the Formation of Nationalist Discourse in India* (Delhi: Oxford University Press, 1995).

57. Bankimchandra Chattopadhyay, *Bankim Rachanavali*, vol. 1, 715–872 (Calcutta: Sahitya Samsad, 1957).

58. Chattopadhyay, *Bankim Rachanavali*, vol. 1, 407–679.

59. Rabindranath Tagore, 'Dilli Darbar', in *Ravindrarachanavali*, vol. 3, 1110–11 (Calcutta: Government of West Bengal, 1983).

60. Rabindranath Tagore, *Ravindrarachanavali*, vol. 4 (Calcutta: Government of West Bengal, 1987), 347–48; Banerjee, *The Mortal God*, 165.

61. Nabinchandra Sen, 'Raivataka', in *Navinachandrer Granthavali*, vol. 1, 757–1055 (Calcutta: Ashvinikumar Haldar, 1904); 'Kurukshetra' and 'Prabhas', in *Navinachandrer Granthavali*, vol. 2, 1061–512 (Calcutta: Ashvinikumar Haldar, 1904). The quoted phrases in italics are from Sen, 'Raivataka', 795, 1006–07.

62. Mir Mosharraf Hossain, *Vishad Sindhu* (Calcutta: Haraf Prakashani, 2005); Kaikobad, *Mahashmashan* (Dhaka: Student Ways, 2006); Banerjee, *The Mortal God*, 184–85.

63. Intelligence Branch, Criminal Investigation Department of Police, Bengal, File No. 37/1913, Sl. No. 17/1913, 'Jugantar Leaflet Enquiries Regarding Which Appeared in November 1912'. This and other Intelligence Branch (IB) files subsequently cited are kept at the West Bengal State Archives, Kolkata.

64. Intelligence Branch, Criminal Investigation Department of Police, Bengal, File No. 663/1913, Sl. No. 5/1913, 'Liberty, by Karmajog's Press, Howrah'.

65. Intelligence Branch, Criminal Investigation Department of Police, Bengal, File No. 404/1913, 'Seditious Leaflet Received by Amarendra Nath Ghosh, Muktear of Tangail, Mymensingh'.

66. Intelligence Branch, Criminal Investigation Department of Police, Bengal, File No. 1340/1913, Sl. No. 56/1913, 'Jugantar Leaflets. Typed Copies Circulated to European and Indian Residents of Calcutta'.

67. Intelligence Branch, Criminal Investigation Department of Police, Bengal, File No. 191/1910, Sl. No. 35/1910, 'Swadhin Bharat, Found in Jagannath College, Dacca'.

68. Intelligence Branch, Criminal Investigation Department of Police, Bengal, File No. 2223/1916, Sl. No. 115/1916, 'Leaflet Jugantar in Bengali (New Issue)'.

69. Intelligence Branch, Criminal Investigation Department of Police, Bengal, File No. 2223/1916, Sl. No. 115/1916, 'Leaflet Jugantar in Bengali (New Issue)'.

70. Shruti Kapila, 'Self, Spencer and *Swaraj*: Nationalist Thought and Critiques of Liberalism, 1890–1920', *Modern Intellectual History* 4, no. 1 (2007): 109–27; Andrew Sartori, 'The Transfiguration of Duty in Aurobindo's *Essays on the Gita*', *Modern Intellectual History* 7, no. 2 (2010): 319–34.

71. Kapila, 'Self, Spencer and *Swaraj*', 117, 120.

72. Sheldon Pollock, *The Language of the Gods in the World of Men: Sanskrit, Culture, and Power in Premodern India* (Berkeley, CA: University of California Press, 2006), 17.

73. House of Commons Parliamentary Papers, East India (Sedition Committee, 1918), Report of Committee Appointed to Investigate Revolutionary Conspiracies in India, 1918, 16. See also Nagappa Gowda, *The Bhagavadgita in the Nationalist Discourse* (Delhi: Oxford University Press, 2011); Shruti Kapila and Faisal Devji (eds.), *Political Thought in Action: The Bhagavad Gita and Modern India* (Cambridge, UK: Cambridge University Press, 2013).

74. Faisal Devji, 'Morality in the Shadow of Politics', *Modern Intellectual History* 7, no. 2 (2010): 373–90, 375.

75. Mahatma Gandhi, *The Collected Works of Mahatma Gandhi*, vol. 15 (Delhi: Government of India, 1998), 288.

76. Mahatma Gandhi, *The Collected Works of Mahatma Gandhi*, vol. 20 (Delhi: Government of India, 1966), 130.

77. Mahatma Gandhi, *The Collected Works of Mahatma Gandhi*, vol. 28 (Delhi: Government of India, 1968), 320.

78. Banerjee, *The Mortal God*, ch. 5.

79. Jawaharlal Nehru, *The Discovery of India* (Delhi: Oxford University Press, 1994), 107.

80. Nehru, *The Discovery of India*, 67.
81. Vinayak Damodar Savarkar, *Hindutva: Who Is a Hindu?* (Bombay: Veer Savarkar Prakashan, 1969), 94.
82. Vinayak Damodar Savarkar, *Hindu Pad-Padashahi, or a Review of the Hindu Empire of Maharashtra* (Madras: B. G. Paul & Co., 1925), 26, 254.
83. K. P. Jayaswal, *Hindu Polity: A Constitutional History of India in Hindu Times*, vols. 1–2 (Calcutta: Butterworth & Co., 1924), 125.
84. Jayaswal, *Hindu Polity*, vol. 1, 125–30.
85. Jayaswal, *Hindu Polity*, vol. 1, 191.
86. Jayaswal, *Hindu Polity*, especially vol. 2.
87. D. R. Bhandarkar, *Lectures on the Ancient History of India: On the Period from 650 to 325 BC* (Calcutta: University of Calcutta, 1919), 119–24; Pramathanath Banerjea, *Public Administration in Ancient India* (London: Macmillan & Co., 1916), 34–37, 72; U. N. Ghoshal, *A History of Hindu Political Theories: From the Earliest Times to the End of the First Quarter of the of the Seventeenth Century AD* (Calcutta: Oxford University Press, 1923), 65–66, 271–78.
88. For example, Report on Native Newspapers of Bengal, West Bengal State Archives, *E. B. Railway Labour Review*, June 1930 and October 1932.
89. Kazi Nazrul Islam, *Kazi Nazrul Islam Rachanasamagra*, vol. 1 (Calcutta: Pashchimbanga Bangla Akademi, 2005), 119–21.
90. Islam, *Kazi Nazrul Islam Rachanasamagra*, vol. 1, 415.
91. Islam, *Kazi Nazrul Islam Rachanasamagra*, vol. 3 (Calcutta: Pashchimbanga Bangla Akademi, 2002), 3–5.
92. Islam, *Kazi Nazrul Islam Rachanasamagra*, vol. 3, 31–32.
93. Sarojini Naidu, *Speeches and Writings* (Madras: G. A. Natesan & Co., n.d.).
94. Naidu, *Speeches and Writings*, 59.
95. See, for example, *Mahishya-Mahila* 1, no. 1 (1911), ed. Krishnabhavini Biswas.
96. Mahasweta Devi, 'Draupadi', in *Agnigarbha*, 100–111 (Calcutta: Karuna Prakashani, 1996).
97. Shaoli Mitra, *Nathavati Anathavat o Katha Amritasaman* (Calcutta: Mitra o Ghosh, 2012), 62.
98. Aishwary Kumar, 'Ambedkar's Inheritances', *Modern Intellectual History* 7, no. 2 (2010): 391–415; Meera Nanda, 'Ambedkar's Gita', *Economic and Political Weekly* 51, no. 49 (2016): 38–45.
99. William R. Pinch, *Peasants and Monks in British India* (Berkeley, CA: University of California Press, 1996).
100. Banerjee, *The Mortal God*, ch. 4.

101. I shall refer here and subsequently to meeting proceedings of the Kshatriya Samiti, which were annually published by the organization. Kshatriya Samiti, *Tritiya Varsher Vrittavivarani, Chaturtha Varsher Adhiveshan* (n.p., 1913), 13–14.

102. Kshatriya Samiti, *Chaturdash Varsher Arthat San 1329 Saler Vrittavivaran* (n.p., 1923), 32–33.

103. Kshatriya Samiti, *Ekadash Sammilani, Karyavivarani* (n.p., 1919), 29.

104. Jagat Mohan Devsimha Barman, *Kshatriya Rajavamshi Kula Kaumudi, Arthat Paundra Kshatriya Rajavamshi Jatir Itivritta* (Hatibandha, Rangpur: n.p., 1911), 34–36.

105. Kshatriya Samiti, *Ashtadash Varshik Adhiveshan, Karya-Vivaran* (n.p., 1927), 23–24.

106. Kshatriya Samiti, *Ashtadash Varshik Adhiveshan, Karya-Vivaran*, 58-59.

107. Rabindranath Tagore, *Java-Yatrir Patra* (Calcutta: Viswa-Bharati, 1986), 60.

108. Tagore, *Java-yatrir Patra*, 94.

109. Suniti Kumar Chatterji, *Dvipamay Bharat* (Calcutta: Book Company, 1940), 157–58, 183, 208–09, 219–20, 228–31, 251–52, 258–59, 321–23, 332–36, 348.

110. Kalidas Nag, *Discovery of Asia* (Calcutta: Institute of Asian African Relations, 1957), 720, 729.

111. Nag, *Discovery of Asia*, 725.

112. Rabindranath Tagore, *The Religion of Man* (London: George Allen & Unwin, 1931), 74–89; Rabindranath Tagore, *Parasya-Yatri* (Calcutta: Viswa-Bharati, 1963).

113. Nag, *Discovery of Asia*, 155.

114. 'Constituent Assembly Debates', vol. 9, 18 September 1949, https://www.constitutionofindia.net/constitution_assembly_debates/volume/9/1949-09-18 (accessed on 21 August 2022).

115. 'Constituent Assembly Debates', vol. 8, 18 May 1949, https://www.constitutionofindia.net/constitution_assembly_debates/volume/8/1949-05-18 (accessed on 21 August 2022).

116. 'Constituent Assembly Debates', vol. 1, 11 December 1946, https://www.constitutionofindia.net/constitution_assembly_debates/volume/1/1946-12-11 (accessed on 21 August 2022).

117. 'Constituent Assembly Debates', vol. 8, 20 May 1949, https://www.constitutionofindia.net/constitution_assembly_debates/volume/8/1949-05-20 (accessed on 21 August 2022).

118. 'Constituent Assembly Debates', vol. 9, 10 September 1949, https://www.constitutionofindia.net/constitution_assembly_debates/volume/9/1949-09-10 (accessed on 21 August 2022). For the Sanskrit lines, see chapter 15 in

'The Mahabharata in Sanskrit', book 12, https://www.sacred-texts.com/hin/mbs/mbs12015.htm (accessed on 21 August 2022).

119. 'Constituent Assembly Debates', vol. 11, 23 November 1949, https://www.constitutionofindia.net/constitution_assembly_debates/volume/11/1949-11-24 (accessed on 21 August 2022).

120. 'Constituent Assembly Debates', vol. 11, 17 November 1949, https://www.constitutionofindia.net/constitution_assembly_debates/volume/11/1949-11-17 (accessed on 21 August 2022).

121. 'Constituent Assembly Debates', vol. 11, 23 November 1949, https://www.constitutionofindia.net/constitution_assembly_debates/volume/11/1949-11-23 (accessed on 21 August 2022).

122. 'Constituent Assembly Debates', vol. 11, 23 November 1949.

123. 'Image 41 of The Constitution of India', photolithographed at the Survey of India Offices, Dehra Dun, https://www.loc.gov/resource/llscd.57026883/?sp=41&r=-0.005,0.186,1.124,0.449,0 (accessed on 21 August 2022).

124. 'Judgments', Supreme Court of India, https://main.sci.gov.in (accessed on 21 August 2022).

125. 'Inscriptions in Parliament, Lok Sabha Secretariat, New Delhi', http://164.100.47.194/our%20parliament/Increptions%20in%20parliament%20house.pdf (accessed on 21 August 2022).

126. *Paintings in Parliamanet House* (New Delhi: Lok Sabha Secretariat), http://loksabhaph.nic.in/PhotoGal/PhotoGalleryPicture.aspx?GalID=2 (accessed on 21 August 2022).

127. Lucia Michelutti, *The Vernacularisation of Democracy: Politics, Caste and Religion in India* (Delhi: Routledge, 2008), 167.

128. Michelutti, *The Vernacularisation*, 164.

129. See the pamphlet 'Dangar Koch Biharbasir Kayta Katha', written by Bangshi Badan Barman and published by the Greater Cooch Behar People's Association (GCPA) from Dinhata on 13 December 2003, kept in the Office of Intelligence Branch, Government of West Bengal under section 'Communal, File on GCPA'.

130. 'Mahabharata Battle Won in 18 Days, War against Coronavirus Will Take 21 Days', *Times of India*, 25 March 2020, https://timesofindia.indiatimes.com/india/mahabharata-battle-won-in-18-days-war-against-coronavirus-will-take-21-days-pm-modi/articleshow/74813107.cms (accessed on 21 August 2022).

131. 'Budget 2023–2024: Speech of Nirmala Sitharaman, Minister of Finance', 1 February 2023, https://www.indiabudget.gov.in/doc/budget_speech.pdf (accessed on 21 August 2022).

132. Chapter 72 in 'The Mahabharata in Sanskrit', book 12, https://www.sacred-texts.com/hin/mbs/mbs12072.htm (accessed on 21 August 2022).

133. Himanta Biswa Sarma (@himantabiswa), 11 April 2022, https://twitter.com/himantabiswa/status/1513495146163171331 (accessed on 21 August 2022).

134. 'India Mother of All Democracies: Modi at Bihar Assembly Centenary Celebrations', *Times of India*, 12 July 2022, https://timesofindia.indiatimes.com/india/india-mother-of-all-democracies-modi-at-bihar-assembly-centenary-celebrations/articleshow/92832893.cms (accessed on 21 August 2022).

135. Nivedita Khandekar, 'In Kejriwal's Mahabharat, AAP Is Arjun', *Hindustan Times*, 7 April 2014, https://www.hindustantimes.com/india/in-kejriwal-s-mahabharat-aap-is-arjun/story-8Pq4UGb8f49urQj2XuFF8L.html (accessed on 20 August 2022).

136. '"Mahabharata" Will Be Fought over Land Act Amendments: Jairam Ramesh', *Indian Express*, 6 April 2015, https://indianexpress.com/article/india/india-others/mahabharata-will-be-fought-over-proposed-land-act-amendments-jairam-ramesh/ (accessed on 21 August 2022).

137. G. N. Devy, 'Epic Markers: The Return of the Mahabharata', *Telegraph*, 16 December 2020, https://www.telegraphindia.com/opinion/the-return-of-the-mahabharata/cid/1800628 (accessed on 21 August 2022); ETV Bharat, 'This Is Mahabharata and Modi Government Is Behaving Like Kaurava: Congress', 23 September 2020, https://www.etvbharat.com/english/national/bharat/bharat-news/this-is-mahabharat-and-modi-government-is-behaving-like-kaurava-says-congress/na20200923053554789 (accessed on 21 August 2022); 'PM Modi Goes on Offensive against Opposition, Calls Agri Bills "Pro-Farmer"', *Times of India*, 19 September 2020, https://timesofindia.indiatimes.com/india/pm-goes-on-offensive-against-opposition-calls-agri-bills-pro-farmer/articleshow/78196662.cms (accessed on 21 August 2022).

138. Due to lack of space in this chapter we are not going to discuss the role of the Ramayana in India. But see, for example, Paula Richman (ed.), *Many Ramayanas: The Diversity of a Narrative Tradition in South Asia* (Berkeley, CA: University of California Press, 1991).

139. Pamela Lothspeich, *Epic Nation: Reimagining the Mahabharata in the Age of the Empire* (Delhi: Oxford University Press, 2009).

140. Benedict Anderson, *Imagined Communities: Reflections on the Origin and Spread of Nationalism* (London: Verso Books, 2006 [1983]).

141. Hegel, *Aesthetics*, vol. 2, 1045–46.

142. Milinda Banerjee and Jelle J. P. Wouters, *Subaltern Studies 2.0: Being against the Capitalocene* (Chicago, IL: Prickly Paradigm, 2022).

2

'Epic' Past, 'Modern' Present

The Mahabharata and Modern Nationalism in Colonial Western India*

Alok Oak

Introduction

Ancient epics have played a significant role in the growth of modern nationalism. At the time of their conception, epics possessed no notion of nationalism. However, over the past three centuries, they have been routinely invoked in many parts of the world for fulfilling modern nationalist claims and aspirations. Political and cultural unity, key features of modern nationalism, were found to be described in ancient epics. Therefore, epics were routinely invoked either as repositories of a nation's past frozen in time (as with Homer or Virgil) or as a genealogical exercise meant to reconstruct an unbroken national–cultural lineage (as with the Ramayana and the Mahabharata).[1] Both processes helped in nationalist revival.

The two epics, the Ramayana and the Mahabharata, were used by Indian subcontinental nationalists during the colonial and post-colonial periods to imagine a politically and ethnically (Hindu) unified image of the country.[2] The study of Indian epics was facilitated by modern European Indology and the 'discovery' of India's ancient (largely Hindu and Buddhist) heritage during the late eighteenth century. Therefore, unlike the absolute devotional reverence and eschatological infallibility accorded to the epics during pre-modernity,[3] Indians were open to investigating their historical context and using them for

* I thank the editors of this volume for their insightful comments and suggestions on previous drafts of the chapter.

didactic–political purposes. History, coming to the aid of religious reverence, produced a strange concoction of nationalist rectitude and a strong antidote to colonial cultural hegemony. The fratricide depicted in the Mahabharata was seen as an act of reclaiming the unjust seizure of territory, rendering the epic's moral lesson 'analogous to the colonial occupation of India'.[4]

Epic studies developing during the nineteenth century drove European Indologists' primary interest – namely, determining the remote antiquity of the Mahabharata, deciphering the urtext from latter recensions, and granting it lesser value in comparison to the Greco-Roman classics. European Indological discourses posited India as the opposite of 'the West' and hence inferior in character. Indian thought was presented as mythical and symbolic and therefore unworthy of the cold rationality articulated through logical arguments.

Indians attached multifarious significance to its epics. If the Ramayana was the *adi-kavya* (the original poem), the Mahabharata was varyingly rendered as an *itihasa* (history) and the 'fifth Veda' and even garnered equivalency to a *Dharmashastra* text.[5] The Mahabharata also carried a powerful moral sermon on righteous violence (the Bhagavadgita), delivered by Krishna, the personification of the Absolute. Colonized Indians, fearful of losing their subjectivity, latched upon any and every resource which could provide them with a historical and cultural 'authenticity'. The Mahabharata, being an *itihasa*, provided nationalist historians with the historical–textual space to investigate the origin of the 'Indian nation', locate it in the remote past, and showcase India's political and cultural (largely Hindu) unity.

Partially using the European hermeneutical-historicist method, the Indian nationalist historians struggled to weave competing textures of interpretation and drew radically different lessons. In other words, Indian nationalist thinkers were appropriating the European Orientalist discourse and situating it within a traditional–indigenous textuality found within *Dharmashastra-itihasa* tradition. My purpose in this chapter is to primarily look at the use, reception, and deployment of the Mahabharata during the early twentieth century in western India (Maharashtra) for India's nationalist movement. I will be focusing on the 'epic trilogy' written by 'Bharatacharya'[6] Chintaman Vinayak Vaidya (1861–1938). I argue that Vaidya did not eschew the dominant European critical method, not for the lack of alternatives[7] but precisely due to the ideological avenues it opened for him.

Concentrating on a Marathi intellectual for such an exercise has its own merits. The commentarial tradition on the Mahabharata and the *Dharmashastras* and historical consciousness in western India could be traced to early modernity.

A rich lineage of Marathi pundits and *shastris* (religious scholars), from the early twelfth century CE onwards, had developed keen insights into Sanskrit *Dharmashastra* and scholastic traditions through numerous commentaries.[8] By the early sixteenth century, numerous Marathi Brahmin families had migrated to different parts of India, including the holy city of Benares, and created transregional networks of state power and religious authority.[9] Amongst them was Nilakantha Chaturdhara, a Deshastha Brahmin from Ahmednagar district in Maharashtra, who wrote an authoritative commentary on the Mahabharata called *Bharatabhavadipa*.[10] It offered an Advaita-based[11] metaphysical rendering of the Mahabharata and was widely circulated. The Bombay edition of the Mahabharata (1862–63), developing upon the epic's maiden publication in the 1830s at Calcutta, carried *Bharatabhavadipa* in its appendix.[12] Thus, the rich commentarial tradition on the Mahabharata in nineteenth-century Maharashtra followed a longer and continuous lineage dating a few centuries in the past.

Apart from the *Dharmashastra* textual lineage, Maharashtra boasted of a sophisticated understanding of history and its close association with statecraft. Starting from the early seventeenth century, influential Maratha chieftains commissioned learned poets to write historical accounts of the reigning king and genealogies of prominent families and document significant events. The chronicles of their feats were preserved in texts known as *bakhar*. Although hagiographical, the *bakhars* were 'fact-based chronicles' often showcasing profound awareness of historical temporality[13] and were remarkably secular in the treatment of their subject. These *bakhars* granted historical consciousness to the Marathi-speaking population while invoking militant pride. Their (re) discovery during the nineteenth century played no small role in adducing a strong foundation for nationalism in the region.

In what follows, I will pursue two principal lines of exploration. I will (*a*) briefly explore the use of ancient Greek and Roman cultures in Europe (in general) and Britain (in particular) during the nineteenth century in establishing colonial hegemony over India and (*b*) analyse the appropriation of European Enlightenment historiography and the use of the hermeneutical method used by Vaidya for his 'epic studies'. Vaidya's studies on the Mahabharata, I argue, provided definite reasons for the colonized to reimagine the notion of linear temporality and abjure Puranic cosmologies of temporal circularity. This, I suggest, had a bearing upon and was necessitated by India's quest for modern nationalism. In what way did Indian nationalist historians such as Vaidya, when confronted with these two interrelated thematic and historical meta-questions, resolve the ambiguous correlation between the past and the present by referring to India's foremost *itihasa* text – the Mahabharata? What was the nature of an 'idealized past' promoted by him through the Mahabharata? I conclude by drawing attention to the critical edition of the Mahabharata and the ways in which it utilized different exegetical methods vis-à-vis nineteenth-century Mahabharata scholarship.

Visions of an Ancient Past: Epics and Nationalism in Europe

Modern nationalist imaginaries, in search of a subjectivity, have regularly invoked history.[14] Post-Renaissance European thinkers took cognisance of their nationalist and pan-Continental pasts in numerous ways. The Scottish Enlightenment thinkers, for instance, produced outstanding histories of England and recreated the history of late antiquarian Europe, such as David Hume's *History of England* (in six volumes, 1754–61). Edward Gibbon's *The History of the Decline and Fall of the Roman Empire* (in six volumes, 1776–88) is another exemplary case study.[15] Such exercises were followed in other parts of Western Europe, subsequently laying the foundation of Enlightenment historiography.

Comparativist methods used in philology, philosophy, and mythology developing during this period facilitated the study of ancient Occidental civilizations, juxtaposing them against those of the Orient. Philosophical schools such as utilitarianism, neo-Hegelian phenomenology, and Comtean positivism also influenced these studies. Enlightenment historiography 'probed the past actions of mankind to establish a normative behaviour code for the contemporary political man'.[16] The historian was expected to collect information, stored in ancient texts and artefacts, in order to shed light on contemporary political, religious, and philosophical debates. Historians probed into antiquarian human experiences and dwelt upon the rise and fall of great civilizations. Such explorations were meant to instruct contemporary statesmen about their political and moral responsibilities.

European historians of the late eighteenth and early nineteenth centuries were eager to trace the origins of their respective nation states to the Greco-Roman period. 'Hellenomania', a term coined by Martin Bernal, covers the incredible efforts undertaken by modern Europeans to concoct a 'pure' and 'original' vision of Greece and fabricate evidence to justify their ancient heritage.[17] From the eighteenth century onwards, agents of newly evolving European nation states derived nationalist aspirations from antiquarian or medieval epics (the discovery of the *Nibelungenlied* in Germany, the *Chanson de Roland* in France, and the *Kalevala* in Finland are a few examples). The epics were cast as the 'expressions of the national spirit'[18] with respect to each country, whether 'self-respecting or aspirant',[19] assuming certain completeness in its idealized qualities through national epic(s). The archaic nature of the epic did not obstruct its co-option by modern formulations of nationalism. Rather, racial homogeneity and continuity in civilizational ethos, supposedly preserved through epic texts, were seen as advantageous to modern nationalism. In Germany, admiration towards Greek culture spilt over to an enchantment with the Orient. The Oriental world (and India in particular) displayed (allegedly) exemplary visions of purity, simplicity, courage, and racial homogeneity preserved in its religious scriptures.[20] Thus, Friedrich Schlegel's *Über die Sprache und Weisheit der Indier* (On the Language and Wisdom of the Indians) (1808), for instance, carried a long essay on ancient Indian culture, languages, and philosophy followed by translations from a few Sanskrit texts, including the Ramayana and Kalidasa's *Shakuntala*. Schlegel's approach to Sanskrit texts, similar to most Romantic and post-Romantic European Sanskritists of the nineteenth century, was largely based upon his reading of the Homeric epics and ancient Greek literature.[21] Nevertheless, Schlegel laid the foundation of epic studies in Germany, which grew exponentially in the subsequent decades.[22]

The Epic and the British Empire: Primitive Past and Continuous Present

Hellenic culture was presented in Victorian Britain through paintings and music, architecture and sculpture,[23] and Homeric epics. Not only were the Homeric epics translated and widely read in Britain, they inspired modern British poets and novelists to adopt the 'epic form' to construct and narrate their stories.[24] However, the reception of Rome also opened the floodgates of discussions and debates about republicanism, historicism, and the role of antiquity in modern times.[25] British littérateurs were therefore caught in a strange fix. British predecessors (historical and mythical) belonged, supposedly, either to the Celtic or the Germanic races. The Arthurian legend, exhibiting anti-Saxon sentiments, was found unpalatable and counterproductive to the strong British nationalism of the modern era. Therefore, British writers embarked upon constructing new epics, prominently Alfred Tennyson's *Idylls of the King*, in the nineteenth century.[26]

The British classicists, although engaged in a similar pursuit of Romantic primitivism, were confronted with challenges of a different kind.

The only resource available to them in excavating and recreating their antique past was through archaic texts. Antiquarian disciplines such as archaeology were yet to evolve into advanced sciences.[27] The Bible and the Christian faith, too, significantly influenced modern imaginations of the ancient past. As such, most of the British historical narratives built during the eighteenth and early nineteenth centuries were largely conjectural in character.[28] Subsequently, under the growing influence of Comtean positivism, large tracts on ancient Greece and Rome came to be written by British philosophers and historians.[29]

The Greco-Roman past and its philosophical and epic traditions were simultaneously used to justify modern imperialism. During the eighteenth century, British classicists were interested in comparing the Roman Empire with overseas British imperial expansion. The British imperialists were cautious to avoid the mistakes of imperialist Romans (sharply brought forth through Gibbon's *History*). At the same time, it provided the British colonial state the moral–historical locus standi to oppose anti-imperialist and socialist sentiments growing in Britain. The British conception of 'civilizing mission' was borrowed from the Roman notion of *civilis* (civic), and unlike the virtuous Greco-Roman civilization, which supposedly faltered under the weight of rising barbarism and tyranny, the British statesmen wished to perfect the realpolitik of empire.[30]

Colonial expansion in South Asia during the eighteenth century opened the vast pool of ancient Sanskrit texts to European classicists and bolstered existing European claims to ancient heritage. The first phase of Indological studies exhibited remarkable excitement about the new discoveries of Hindu religious traditions through its classical Sanskrit canon. Numerous scholars in Europe and, particularly, in Britain and Germany took great pains in 'deciphering' the Sanskrit language and partially translating Sanskrit treatises into European languages. This resulted in the birth of Indo-European language studies coupled with the search for a common homeland for the so-called Aryan civilization pioneered by William Jones. Jones read the flood myth found in the Puranic literature reminiscent of the Biblical stories so that the two civilizations (British and Indian) were construed in fraternal terms, sharing a common homeland and language.[31] Peter van der Veer, commenting on Jones' comparative methodology, suggests that '[t]he main thrust of this monogenetic line of thought was that Indians were not essentially different from the British nor [sic] significantly inferior'.[32] Trained into Enlightenment historiography, which considered linear historical temporality as a mark of civilizational progress, early British Indologists wanted to get rid of 'temporal cyclicity' exhibited in epic–Puranic literature.

For most of them, a historical fact carried 'an ontology of its own'.[33] Unsurprisingly, for them, an *itihasa* text such as the Mahabharata carried tremendous purport.

Jones' claims about fraternal relations between ancient Indians (Aryans) and Europeans ran counter to British imperial ambitions, forcing British administrators and Indologists to recast the antiquarian discourse. Thomas Babington Macaulay, for instance, believed modern Britain to be a successor of the Roman Empire and was vocal about the need to anglicize India. Consequently, the first three modern universities set up in India by the colonial state in 1857 taught ancient Greek and Latin texts, with modern European scholars drawing inspiration from them.[34] Compulsory papers on ancient Greece and Rome were taught to history graduates using Macaulay, Gibbon, Henry Thomas Buckle, Voltaire, and Edmund Burke.[35] The focus on Roman history in Indian university curricula was defended by Charles Trevelyan by arguing that since the Romans were the original civilizers of Europe, knowledge about Roman arts and literature would, at once, turn Indians docile towards their colonial masters.[36]

The British were merely following their imperial predecessors in establishing colonial hegemony by celebrating European heritage and denigrating the past of the colonized. An outstanding example of this process was Monier Monier-Williams' lectures on Indian epics. Comparing the two Homeric epics with the Mahabharata and the Ramayana, Monier-Williams wrote:

> Though the Ramayana and Mahabharata are no less wonderful than the Homeric poems as monuments of the human mind, and no less interesting as pictures of human life and manners in ancient times, they bear in a remarkable degree that peculiar impress ever stamped on the productions of Asiatic nations and separating them from European. On the side of art and harmony of proportion, they can no more compete with the Iliad and the Odyssey than the unnatural outline of the ten-headed and twenty-armed Ravana can bear comparison with the symmetry of a Grecian statue. While the one commends itself to the most refined classical taste, the other by its exaggerations only excites the wonder of the Asiatic mind, or if attractive to the European, can only please an imagination nursed in an Oriental school.[37]

For the Hindus, he further claimed that 'quality is nothing compared to quantity'[38] even if the latter did not lend itself to 'taste, unless seasoned with exaggeration'.[39] In Monier-Williams' judgement, the two Indian epics (and Indians) lacked high literary sensibilities and hence proved mediocre when compared to the Homeric epics.

Early Mahabharata Studies: The Search for the Urtext and the Date of the Text–War

The epics may have exhibited inferior literary character for British Indologists, but they were not utterly useless. Moritz Winternitz, the Viennese scholar, writing four decades after Monier-Williams, reflected on Sanskrit literature and observed that 'the division between "belle lettres" and didactic literature is not really possible in India. What appears to us [Europeans] a collection of fairy tales and fables is regarded by the Indians as a manual of political and moral instruction.'[40] Winternitz thought that the Sanskrit literature 'form[ed] a necessary complement to the classical literature of ancient Greece and Rome'[41] but when compared on artistic merit, found it inferior.

The inability of Indians to archive their own past upset European Indologists. Any reconstruction of the Indian ancient past and its precise chronology, they believed, would have to depend upon foreign resources – the Greek and Chinese travel accounts – which were widely considered 'wonderfully exact and reliable'.[42] The American philologist William Dwight Whitney famously stated in his *Sanskrit Grammar* (1879) that dates given in Sanskrit literature were like 'pins set up to be bowled down again'.[43] The Puranic cosmology, which imagined time in a cyclical fashion with remarkable intertextual differences, was, for European historians, emblematic of the primitive and archaic nature of Hindu civilization.[44] The Mahabharata carried these variegated notions of Puranic time. Therefore, methodologically borrowing from the Biblical hermeneutics, the European Indologists exposed the Mahabharata to intra-textual historical exegesis.

Consequently, nineteenth-century European scholarship on the Mahabharata revolved around five important axes of investigation: (*a*) differentiating the urtext of the Mahabharata from its interpolations; (*b*) determining the dates for the compositions of the urtext and its interpolations; (*c*) finalizing its authentic author(s); (*d*) establishing the precise date of the Mahabharata war; and (*e*) probing the influence of Vaishnavism on the epic. Consensus amongst nineteenth-century European scholars pointed towards an urtext of the Mahabharata, consisting of a detailed description of the conflict between the Pandavas and the Kauravas. Other portions of the text, such as lengthy didactic dialogues on morality and religion, were believed to have been added later.

The story of the Mahabharata, or the 'Bharati katha' (folktales about the Bharat war), was quite old and believed to be popular between 1700 and 700 BCE.[45] The 'Bharati katha' was orally transmitted during the so-called 'Mnemonic period of literature'[46] when Sanskrit alphabets and script were unformed. Consequently, the urtext (consisting of the poem's nucleus) may have been of short length (roughly around 8,000 verses according to the Danish Indologist Søren Sørensen).[47] The number of recensions which the epic's text underwent in subsequent centuries were few (only two, according to the Norwegian-German Indologist Christian Lassen) and must have occurred in the post-Buddhist period.[48] Since the origin of the epic narrative was believed to be in ancient lore and the urtext underwent multiple recensions over many centuries, European Indologists doubted the existence of Vyasa, and even if he did exist, there were bound to be multiple authors bearing (or writing under) his name.[49] Furthermore, the Mahabharata could not be an eyewitness account of the conflict (despite the text's explicit suggestions) but must have been a post-facto construction, separating the actual event (the war) and the text by numerous centuries. It was therefore extremely difficult to ascertain the precise date of the war (if at all it ever occurred), resulting in apprehensions about the authenticity of the characters of the text in terms of their historicity. The large coalescence of multiple theological schools into a singular grand narrative represented a successful transition from the Vedic to the post-Vedic period. The inclusion of Krishna (the symbol of the Vaishnavite cult), numerous sectarian deities, discussions around Hindu *darshana-shastras* (philosophical systems), and auxiliary sciences (such as Vedic astronomy) transformed the 'Bharati katha' into the Mahabharata, serving, indirectly, as an encyclopaedia on ancient India. In the process, the epic poem neglected to tell the tale of a heroic battle and thus lost its core 'epic character'.[50]

Since clear references to the Mahabharata were not found in Buddhist and Greek texts, some Indologists claimed the earliest portions of the text as post-Buddhist. Starting with the addition of the Pandavas and other heroes between 400 and 200 BCE, the epic absorbed Vaishnavism in subsequent centuries (100 BCE and 400 CE).[51] While some Western Indologists vehemently denied remote antiquity to the Mahabharata (the German philologist Adolf Holtzmann placed its final redaction between 900 and 1100 CE), most agreed that it recorded nothing of historical value[52] and hence was deemed futile for antiquarian pursuits.

The Mahabharata as India's 'National' Past: Historicism and Nationalism

Colonial pedagogy granted Indians access to European knowledge systems bolstering their historical consciousness. In Maharashtra, Ramkrishna Gopal

Bhandarkar (1837–1925) was the first to apply tools of modern historiography to discover epic primitivism. Using his expertise in the Sanskrit language and training in European methods of comparative philology and the German method of historicist text critique,[53] Bhandarkar pioneered critical exegesis of the Mahabharata in India. He owed much to the disciplinary paradigms developed in post-Enlightenment Europe, what he classified as 'critical, comparative, and historical method',[54] which he used to great effect in suggesting a chronology of the epic's interpolations. Speaking before the Bombay branch of the Royal Asiatic Society in September 1872, Bhandarkar established the earliest version of the Mahabharata to be from around Panini's era (c. fifth century BCE).[55] However, he was apprehensive in treating Indian epics 'as books of sober and authentic history',[56] and their use in reconstructing some aspects of India's ancient past had to be undertaken with great caution. Therefore, any study of the Mahabharata, Bhandarkar instructed on another occasion, 'should be thoroughly impartial. Our [sic] aim should be to find out the truth, whether it is flattering to our racial pride or otherwise.'[57] Bhandarkar, known for his Westernized liberal politics, wanted Indian scholars to imbibe European attitudes of non-partisanship towards history.

However, his compatriot and moderate Congress leader Justice K. T. Telang showed greater apprehension about the European 'non-partisan' approach towards Indian epics. European classicists such as Albrecht Weber had claimed that the Ramayana was copied from Homer. Telang felt that such claims not only demeaned the achievements of ancient Sanskrit literature but also went against popular perception held by Indians. Not only were the Ramayana and the Mahabharata 'the national epics of India'[58], the latter was the earliest document of recorded history (*itihasa*). He argued:

> To be told that the Ramayana – that noble work with which so many of one's pleasing and exalting associations are bound up – that work which sings the superhuman exploits of a deified man, who, beyond almost any other Deity in their Pantheon, is the greatest favourite of the Hindus of this day – that work which has ingrained itself into the very life of the nation, so that there is scarcely a Hindu who is not more or less acquainted with its plot – to be told that after all that work is more than a Buddhist saga dovetailed to the Homeric story of the Trojan War, that causes a shock to one's notion under which not many will find it easy to be stoical.[59]

Indian nationalist historiography developing during the late nineteenth century was thus confronted with a fundamental paradox – namely, who possessed the legitimate *right* to write Indian history? Ranajit Guha has addressed this issue by suggesting that the quest for a historical past was more than a nostalgia for primitivity.[60] Rather, it was informed by a notion of a temporal and culturalized 'other'. Guha explains that the Indian conception of the past broke away from a linear measurement of time as practised in European historiography. Thus, Indian historians reclaimed history 'not so much as a point of the path of time's arrow but as a moment of cyclical return'.[61]

The 'cyclical return' to the ancient past in modern Indian historiography, I would suggest, emerged out of a sociocultural milieu of race- and caste-based supremacy accorded to a Hindu section severely challenged by political institutions (the colonial state) and other ethnocultural groups (Muslim and non-Brahmin), fearing its loss of identity in the face of loss of political power which it enjoyed for many centuries.[62]

Closely aligned therefore was the issue of historical narrativity and the (ab) use of myths in antiquarian studies. For the historians trained under the auspices of Enlightenment historiography, fragments of the past, buried under the hubris of myths and legend, had to be thrashed out. This involved a concerted effort at demystification and demythologization. Modern Western historiography expected a perfect semblance between history and the construction of the past, which is to say that the past was seen to be entirely dependent upon history. 'History', viewed from the metropolitan centre, claimed universal fraternity between peoples and civilizations and was eager to render no culture alien and therefore unrecognizable. Indian perception of history, though seemingly different in a formal sense, worked on similar principles. The past was not just a fragment of memory but alive in the linear theological and cultural lives of its communities. Tradition, in this sense, became something which existed in the present while making claims about the past. Reflecting upon the peculiarity of Indian civilization, Ramesh Chandra Majumdar observed:

> The icons discovered at Mohenjo-daro are those of gods and goddesses who are still worshipped in India, and Hindus from the Himalaya to Cape Comorin repeat even today the Vedic hymns which were uttered on the banks of the Indus nearly four thousand years ago.[63]

The historical consciousness of Indian nationalists was bred upon *Dharmashastra*-based perception of the past. Rather than a dry record, the past was expected to carry moral lessons guiding future generations.[64] Thus, any understanding of the Indian tradition of 'history writing', ideally speaking, would have to eschew the Hegelian schemata and be established upon epistemic differences.[65] In such a case, a metaphysical commentary on the Mahabharata (à la Nilakantha Chaturdhara) proved hopeless in India's search for nationhood. Therefore, Indian nationalist historians tried to interrogate and negotiate their relationship with tradition while simultaneously enforcing tools of historiography upon it. In their anachronistic readings of the epics, they viewed pre-existing formulations with suspicion.[66] Of foremost importance for them, was the fulfilment of nationalist polemic, even if it meant delimiting the scope of their historical enquiry.

Vaidya and the Epic Studies: Authenticating the Mahabharata as *Itihasa*

Chintaman Vinayak Vaidya's epic trilogy,[67] written during the heydays of the Swadeshi movement (1905–07), is a classic example of Indian nationalist historiography. Unfortunately, he awaits a critical scholarly biography.[68] Unlike his predecessors, Vaidya's ambitious reading of the Mahabharata was interested in deciphering the relationship between the text, the battle, and its historical–theological ramifications for Indian civilization. Vaidya's interest in tracing the textual genealogy of the Mahabharata is a peculiar exercise. While he was eager to expose the text to historical hermeneutics, he found Western Indological studies inconclusive. Since the Mahabharata was an *itihasa*, the three recensions of the Mahabharata, narrated by Sauti, could have been the only interpolations ever made to the text. Vaidya found attempts at establishing further interpolations by Western Indologists revolting against Hindu tradition and therefore flawed.[69]

Vaidya accepted the traditional belief that Vyasa was the original author of the Mahabharata's first recension, varyingly called 'Jaya' or 'Bharat'. There could not have been more than one Vyasa since, Vaidya suggested, the work 'evidently bears the impress of a narration by one who had an intimate acquaintance with the events it describes. Characters and people are described with a vivacity and truthfulness which can only belong to the evidence of an eye-witness.'[70] The later recensions to the Mahabharata resembled 'fossils not yet obliterated, giv[ing] a clue to a real bygone era'.[71] Vaidya found remarkable resemblance between the writing style of some portions of the epic and the *Yajurveda* (the 'black' portion), granting additional mileage to the claim that Vyasa, the arranger of the four Vedas, was indeed the primal author of the epic. Nonetheless, even if the Mahabharata was an imagination of Vyasa, Vaidya argued, the diversity of characters and events knit together in a gigantic plot pointed to 'an imagination which is higher than that of Shakespeare'.[72]

A small chronicle of the Bharata war written by Vyasa was handed over to his disciple Vaishampayana. The latter, Vaidya argued, being a devout Vaishnavaite added some elements of Vaishnava devotionalism found in the Pancharatra system, elevating the text (Bharata) to the status of a *Dharmashastra*.[73] Sticking to the traditionally accepted text genealogy, Vaidya stated that the 'ambitious' Sauti wanted to transform the 'Bharata' into an 'all-embracing repository of legendary lore'.[74] Sauti therefore added numerous smaller legends (Akhyanas) to the Bharata text, transforming the chronicle into an epic. Ipso facto, the Mahabharata became a storehouse of 'old Aryan legends in a slightly modified form made for the purpose of invigorating the current cries of Aryanism, confronted as it was by Buddhism'.[75] Sauti's final redaction also introduced Shaiva elements into the epic. Therefore, in Vaidya's formulation, the Mahabharata had three components: *itihasa* (chronicle), *Dharmashastra*-sanctioned Vaishnavism (devotionalism or ritualism), and other minor sect-based regional variations. While the European Indologists found such a concoction of diverse religious elements unpalatable, Vaidya believed that the text exemplified perfect harmony and reflected conflict-free cohabitation of Aryan puritan-ritualism with non-Aryan religious traditions.

At the heart of the epic was the story of the Bharata war, declared by Vaidya as 'the first authentic event in the ancient history of India'.[76] The chief characters of the epic conflict, the Kauravas and the Pandavas (along with the divine avatar Krishna), acted as 'models of greatness and virtue, ever inspiring the Aryan mind in India to deeds of self-sacrifice in the performance of duty'.[77] The essence of the Mahabharata, Vaidya emphatically stated, was in the observance of *dharma* (righteous duty) under all conditions and in the face of adversity. *Dharma* was essentially the highest duty which every human ought to perform towards the Almighty and his or her compatriots.[78]

Since the Bharata war was a 'historical event', captured by Vyasa and chronicled by his disciples, it could be easily dated using the Mahabharata text. For such an exercise, Vaidya had to reject Puranic notions of cosmic time, neglect various Muslim frameworks of 'universal time' developed during early modernity,[79] and work his way through the *yuga* (aeon)-based cyclical transitions. Vaidya's (elderly) peers from Maharashtra had suggested that five thousand years had elapsed since the beginning of the Kali Yuga.[80] Taking a cue from them, Vaidya put 1899 CE as the base year and subtracted five thousand years from it, arriving at 3101 BCE. Megasthenes had referred to Heracles (the supposed Greek name for Krishna), who was removed from Chandragupta (king of the ancient Mauryan dynasty) by 137 generations. Vaidya took the average reign of each king to be 20 years so that Krishna must have been the monarch of Dwarka around 3052 BCE.[81] Defending his calculations, Vaidya pointed out that if Europeans were ready to place the constructions of the Egyptian pyramids in 2500 BCE, grant high antiquity to the Babylonian civilization (2458 BCE), and trace the reign of a certain ancient Chinese king, Hangtwi (or Huang Di), to 2332 BCE, then 'it is not at all strange that the historical memories of the Indian Aryans, like those of the other great nations of antiquity, go so far back as 3101 BC'.[82]

Such notions of linear history, used by Vaidya, went against the dominant trend of cyclical and aeon-based temporality sacrosanct to Hindu Brahmin orthodoxy and stored in the Puranas,[83] *jyotishashastra* (astronomy),[84] and the Smriti literature. The *Manusmriti* (Manu's Code of Law), for instance, provides a division of the four *yuga*s in divine and human years. The four *yuga*s in the eyes of Brahma appear to be 4,800, 3,600, 2,400, and 1,200 years, corresponding to Kreta, Treta, Dvapara, and Kali Yuga, respectively (*Manusmriti*, 1.61–73).[85] Thomas Trautmann has calculated these divine years in human terms (following the *Manusmriti*) and has provided the following numbers: 1,728,000 (Kreta), 1,296,000 (Treta), 864,000 (Dvapara), and 432,000 (Kali).[86] Vaidya's calculations fail to explain the enormous time interval between the existence of Rama and Krishna, each belonging to different aeons and hence presumably separated by thousands of years.[87] The Kali Yuga, on the other hand, made his efforts quite easy. Since the Kali Yuga was to be made up of 432,000 years in total, all the Brahmin texts (especially the Brahmana, Upanishads, *Jyotisha* texts, and Puranas) written in the post-Vedic period could be easily grouped together as belonging to the Kali age.

The Mahabharata as the Source of Hindu Nationalism: Vaidya's Quest for Aryan Racial Superiority

By the late nineteenth century, 'Indian history had been effectively eclipsed by Indian anthropology',[88] which is to say that the colonial rulers were not any more interested in asking historical questions but were rather content in 'thinking about India anthropologically'. In the official and Orientalist descriptions, Indians were classified according to their caste, character, and custom.[89] In the third book of his Epic Trilogy, Vaidya returned to the Mahabharata. Invoking the methodology of classical positivism, Vaidya treated the epic as a repository of various data, information, and facts about the antiquarian past. Moreover, the modern social categories and imaginaries (about race, caste, class, gender), customs and mannerisms (marriage, rituals) were juxtaposed against the epic, the latter acting as the primary source of validation. Vaidya's analysis was primarily premised upon the dominant Indo-Aryan racial theory pertaining to the so-called allochthonous origins of the Aryan race. Vaidya agreed with Bal Gangadhar Tilak's claim that the Aryans migrated to the Indian subcontinent from the Arctic Circle.[90] However, their migration via invasions, Vaidya argued, occurred in two phases. The Ramayana described the first phase of Aryan invasion. Rama's attack on Ravana (dated by Vaidya to c. 3500 BCE) represented a stable Aryan civilization in northwest India eager to expand amongst the indigenous 'cannibals'.[91] The Pandava–Kuru conflict, occurring a few centuries later, represented the second phase of Aryan invasions. The Aryans entered India via the Himalayas not 'as regular invaders bent upon conquest but as kindred races wishing to enjoy opportunities which the country afforded, in equal degree with their brethren previously settled upon the soil'.[92] Therefore, the socio-ritual customs of the Pandavas were different from their 'racial' Aryan cousins, the Kauravas (the former, for instance, practised polyandry). The Pandava–Kaurava conflict was a 'civil war'[93] between the two clans. The Kurus, who 'occupied the country between the Ganges and the Himalayas and who still kept up their marriage relations with the Aryans of the Punjab were supported in this conflict by these brethren of theirs'.[94] The Pandavas, in contrast, were the 'new Aryans'[95] who were supported by the people of 'mixed races and by their Dravidian relations'.[96] Vaidya compared the Pandava–Kaurava conflict with the American War of Independence, 'the local Americans fighting against those Englishmen who tried to rule America from England and to continue England's supremacy in America'.[97]

For Vaidya, the Pandavas, steeped in religious rituals, followed high morality, peculiar to the Aryan race. Institutions such as polygamous and polyandrous marriages, found abhorrent by modern Europeans, were widely followed by ancient Aryans since it was sanctioned by ritual.[98] Ancient Aryan womenfolk experienced great social freedom (for example, Draupadi's *swayamvara*-style marriage with the Pandavas or Kunti's *niyoga*-style marriage with Vyasa).[99] Such claims by Vaidya were meant to chastise his contemporary social reformers who lamented the loss of freedom and agency to Hindu women under the *Dharmashastra* customary laws.

The Aryans of the epic age showed remarkable advances in political culture, civil administration, and revenue system. Vaidya went to great lengths in establishing similarities between Aryan and Greek governing systems. Aryans were 'freedom-loving peoples or clans settled in small patches of territory'.[100] These city states were independent and respected each other's autonomy, but often fought without the slightest desire of effacing the clan altogether.[101] Invoking Herbert Spencer, Vaidya argued that respectful animosity was the hallmark of most ancient civilizations,[102] and recounted emperor Yudhishthira's *digvijay* (conquest of eight directions) ceremony in which smaller and weaker kingdoms were usurped into the larger empire. And yet the conquered territory was made to pay only a small tribute, and in case of the death of the king in battle, his heir apparent was immediately made king. It is clear that Vaidya was commenting upon the modern imperial British regime, which had betrayed the ancient customs of morally bounded imperial expansion, found in its own Indo-European civilizational lineage. Vaidya wrote:

> We see the existence of a similar feeling [of fraternity] operating even in Greece. Although the several states fought with one another they did not try to annihilate them. The several Christian states of modern Europe are visibly actuated by the same sentiment. Portugal and Belgium small though they are, are still guaranteed continued existence by that feeling of brotherhood which animates the Christian nations of Europe though their attitude towards Turkey may be due to quite different causes.[103]

What those 'quite different causes' are, we are not told. Possibly he might be referring to the Muslim culture in Turkey and the long-standing 'clash of cultures' between Christendom and Islam.

Congress extremist ideologues such as Tilak and Aurobindo Ghose were lamenting the loss of Hindu India's ancient glory and the material and spiritual weakening of the Aryan race. Vaidya found it important to highlight the supposed virtues of the ancient Aryan race: its courage, masculinity, and vitality. Vaidya portrayed the princes from the epic period as bejewelled, with extraordinary wealth and power and protectors of the subjects. Overcoming lethargy, the Aryan subjects 'relied on individual exertions far more than their [Aryan] descendants do [today]'.[104] Fate (*prarabdha*) was considered secondary to individual action, the latter emerging from relative free will guaranteed to all human beings. The Mahabharata contains numerous discussions on the supposed contradiction between fate and individual free will. For instance, Vaidya observed, Bhishma in the 'Anushasana Parva' (Book of Instructions) relies upon human effort and points out that both gods and humans have achieved great wealth, prosperity, and happiness through effort. Vaidya romantizised the Aryan life during the early epic period by stating that the 'Indo-Aryans were ... like all young and free peoples energetic and active, truthful and outspoken. They were a free people emphatically and treated none as slaves, neither foreigners nor any of their own people.'[105] The general Aryan population lived a 'frugal and simple life ... theft was almost unknown among the Indians'.[106] Nobility and high moral character were exhibited by the ancient Aryans.

However, at the end of the epic period, 'the extreme heat of the country and the abundance of produce from the land' coupled with 'the poverty of a section of the teeming population of the plains' may have resulted in apathy towards human effort and resignation to fate, as can be gauged from the 'Yaksha Prashna' (Yaksha's Questions) interpolated by Sauti.[107]

Vaidya's political ideology was Hindu nationalist with a tinge of Brahminical pride. The 'national epic', as he routinely referred to the Mahabharata, should be brought to serve India's anti-colonial movement as well as in establishing the foremost status for the Indian (Hindu Aryan) civilization amongst the great civilizations of the world. Vaidya's was one amongst many other voices in colonial India which propounded Aryan supremacy and Vedic antiquity for nationalist purposes.[108]

By the second decade of the twentieth century, however, the tide began to shift in favour of a robust and critical reception of the epic. The focus of the new research was towards excavating archival resources, collecting massive data, and using the tools of critical hermeneutics to arrive at definite and scientific conclusions. The Bhandarkar Oriental Research Institute (BORI) at Pune was at the forefront of the endeavour.

Conclusion: The Critical Edition of the Mahabharata and the Decline of the Nationalist Rhetoric

In the early twentieth century, the BORI started publishing a critical edition (CE) of the Mahabharata. The project, initiated under the general editorship of Vishnu Sitaram Sukthankar,[109] took 48 years to complete (1919–66). A team of scholars (Indian and foreign) consulted about 1,259 manuscripts and ended up publishing 19 volumes of the Mahabharata, comprising over 89,000 verses compiled from various manuscripts lodged in different libraries and private collections from around the world.[110]

Sukthankar considered the reconstruction of the Mahabharata's urtext an 'ideal but impossible desideratum'.[111] The CE, as Sukthankar declared in the prolegomena attached to it, was rather 'a modest attempt to present *a version of the epic as old as the extant manuscript material will permit us to reach* with some semblance of confidence'.[112] The CE was not a replica of any traditionally accepted versions supposedly recited by Vaishampayana or Sauti, but it endeavoured to be *the most ancient one according to the direct line of transmission*, purer than the others in so far as it is free from obvious errors of copying and spurious additions'.[113] Having been trained in the Rankean method of historical enquiry, he was also conscious of the ideological nature of European humanistic disciplines (*Geisteswissenschaften*). European scholars were obsessed with differentiating the didactic portions of the epic from the 'historical core', or, as Sukthankar put it, with 'cutting away what they regarded as the asphyxiating parasite and exposing the old primitive saga in its pristine purity and glory'.[114] Indian nationalist historians, on the other hand, were determined to showcase the epic in grand proportions, irrespective of whether it met critical historical criteria. In short, all attempts at searching for 'layers' or 'interpolations' within the Mahabharata, Sukthankar suggested, were faulty and/or sullied by ideological motivation. In preparing the CE, Sukthankar (and his successors to the position of general editor) rejected 'higher criticism' (which involved extracting the 'epic nucleus' from spurious interpolations) and followed the method of 'unity of the text' (which involved reconstructing the text by remaining faithful to the literary ethos and retaining its multiple redactions as indifferentiable to the text) or lower criticism.[115]

In his review of the prolegomena to Sukthankar's work, Vaidya lamented the assistance offered by European scholars in preparing the CE. Not that the European scholars lacked in 'high proficiency and the critical spirit',[116] but they could never compete with the 'erudition with the learned Pandits [*sic*] of India'.[117] The Indian *shastris*, carriers of centuries-old Hindu customs, could 'never commit strange mistakes as sometimes crop into the works of the greatest European scholars'.[118] Unhappy with the CE's ongoing work, Vaidya embarked upon translating the entire Mahabharata into Marathi along with a brief commentary. Before his death in 1938, Vaidya published eight volumes consisting of translations and commentary on six of the eighteen *parvas* (books) of the Mahabharata.

By the middle of the twentieth century, the search for the 'mythic origins of the Aryan race' in Europe took the form of the Nazi state and ideology, while European socialism was more interested in a grand utopia of the future.[119] In the late colonial period in India (or what is popularly remembered as the 'Gandhian era'), on the other hand, works on the Mahabharata with a strong emphasis on nationalist rhetoric coupled with dodgy historical proof rapidly declined. This is not to suggest that Indian nationalists ceased to care for the Mahabharata. The Mahabharata was used to conceptualize a secularised vision of India.[120] In any case, the strong correlation between European Indology and its (ab) use in popular Indian nationalist narrative was substantially curtailed. The Mahabharata was transformed into a historical–cultural textual artifice and a tale of moral rectitude. As the sun on the British Raj began to set, Indian nationalists competed to impose their ideological vicissitudes upon differing visions of independent India, turning the Mahabharata into a hermeneutical battleground. In the struggle between nationalist polemical and *dharmic* resurrections of the Mahabharata, à la Vaidya, against the historicist academic version presented through the CE, the former was found more palatable to the majoritarian impulse (through its televized version during the 1990s, for instance).[121] In the process, the Hindus were made self-conscious of their collective identity, which helped shape the post-colonial Indian public culture.

Notes

1. Romila Thapar, 'Epic and History: Tradition, Dissent and Politics in India', *Past and Present* 125, no. 1 (1989): 3–26.
2. The growth of the Ram Janmabhoomi movement in the late 1980s, under the auspices of the Hindu nationalist 'Sangha Parivar', fanned communal tensions in its quest for the birthplace of Rama, the mythic hero of the epic Ramayana and a Hindu deity. The movement culminated into an attack and demolition of the sixteenth-century Babri Mosque, supposedly built on the birthplace of Ram. See, among others, Sheldon Pollock, 'Rāmāyaṇa and Political Imagination of India', *Journal of Asian Studies* 52, no. 2 (1993): 261–97.
3. Ajay K. Rao, *Re-Figuring the Rāmāyaṇa as Theology* (London and New York: Routledge, 2015).
4. Pamela Lothspeich, *Epic Nation: Reimagining the Mahābhārata in the Age of Empire* (New Delhi: Oxford University Press, 2009), 4.
5. There is some debate over this distinction. The Mahabharata calls itself a *kavya* in its opening passage whereas the Ramayana has the potential to be considered an *itihasa*. For more discussion see, Robert Goldman (ed.), *The Rāmāyaṇa of Vālmīki: An Epic of Ancient India*, vol. 1: *Bālakāṇḍa* (Princeton, NJ: Princeton University Press, 1984), 1–59.
6. The epithet, literally meaning the 'learned teacher of the Mahabharata', was first used by Bal Gangadhar Tilak in 1905.
7. The most significant alternative available to the Indian commentators was a metaphysical reading of the Mahabharata, using the traditional school of hermeneutics named the *Mimamsa Shastra*.

8. R. N. Dandekar (ed.), *Sanskrit and Maharashtra: A Symposium* (Poona: University of Poona, 1972).

9. Rosalind O'Hanlon, 'Letters Home: Banaras Pandits and the Maratha Regions in Early Modern India', *Modern Asian Studies* 44, no. 2 (2010): 201–240.

10. Christopher Minkowski, 'What Makes a Work "Traditional"?: On the Success of Nīlakaṇṭha's *Mahābhārata* Commentary', in *Boundaries, Dynamics and Construction of Traditions in South Asia*, ed. Federico Squarcini, 225–52 (Florence: Firenze University Press, 2005).

11. Advaita (non-dualism or monism) is a Hindu philosophical discourse which believes in the existence of an objectless, all-pervading, and universal consciousness. The liberation (*mukti*) of an individual from the cycles of rebirth lies in the identification of their self with the universal consciousness. The Advaita thought was explicated through the principal Upanishads (c. 400–300 BCE), and Shankaracharya (c. eighth century CE) was its great systematizer.

12. John Brockington, *The Sanskrit Epics* (Leiden: Brill, 1998), 42.

13. *Bakhar*s had a great sense of history. While recounting battles and campaigns of kings (both contemporary and of yesteryears), the *bakhar* writers gave precise dates culled from Hindu calendars and astronomical charts. See Prachi Deshpande, *Creative Pasts: Historical Memory and Identity in Western India, 1700–1960* (Ranikhet: Permanent Black, 2007).

14. See, for instance, Nicholas Dirks, 'History as a Sign of the Modern', *Public Culture* 2, no. 2 (1990): 25–32; Prasenjit Duara, *Rescuing History from the Nation: Questioning Narratives of Modern China* (Chicago [IL] and London: University of Chicago Press, 1995); Anthony D. Smith, *The Nation in History: Historiographical Debates about Ethnicity and Nationalism* (Cambridge, UK: Polity Press, 2000).

15. Karen O'Brien, *Narratives of Enlightenment: Cosmopolitan History from Voltaire to Gibbon* (Cambridge, UK: Cambridge University Press, 1997); Hugh Trevor-Roper, *History and the Enlightenment* (New Haven [CT] and London: Yale University Press, 2010).

16. Ataç C. Akça, 'Roman Historiography of Eighteenth-Century Britain beyond Gibbon: Ancient Norms of Empire for Moderns', in *A Companion to Enlightenment Historiography*, ed. Sophie Bourgault and Robert Sparling, 469–504 (Leiden and Boston [MA]: Brill, 2013), 469.

17. Martin Bernal, *Black Athena: The Afroasiatic Roots of Classical Civilization*, vol. 1: *The Fabrication of Ancient Greece, 1785–1985* (New Brunswick, NJ: Rutgers University Press, 1987), 281–336.

18. Simon Dentith, *Epic and Empire in Nineteenth-Century Britain* (Cambridge [UK] and New York: Cambridge University Press, 2006), 67.

19. Dentith, *Epic and Empire*, 67.

20. Suzanne L. Marchand, *German Orientalism in the Age of Empire: Religion, Race, and Scholarship* (Cambridge, UK: Cambridge University Press, 2009), 53–101.

21. Gary Handwerk, 'Envisioning India: Friedrich Schlegel's Sanskrit Studies and the Emergence of Romantic Historiography', *European Romantic View* 9, no. 2 (1998): 231–42.

22. Vishwa Adluri and Joydeep Bagchee, *The Nay Science: A History of German Indology* (Oxford: Oxford University Press, 2014).

23. Katherine Harloe, Nicoletta Momigliano, and Alexandre Farnoux (eds.), *Hellenomania* (London and New York: Routledge, 2018).

24. Herbert R. Tucker, *Epic: Britain's Heroic Muse, 1790–1910* (Oxford: Oxford University Press, 2008); Isobel Hurst, 'Victorian Literature and the Reception of Greece and Rome', *Literature Compass* 7, no. 6 (2010): 484–95.

25. Jonathan Sachs, *Roman Antiquity: Rome in British Imagination, 1789–1832* (Oxford: Oxford University Press, 2009), 4–49.

26. Dentith, *Epic and Empire*, 69–71.

27. Margarita Díaz-Andreu, *A World History of Nineteenth-Century Archaeology: Nationalism, Colonialism, and the Past* (Oxford: Oxford University Press, 2007).

28. Frank Palmeri, *State of Nature, Stages of Society: Enlightenment Conjectural History and Modern Social Discourse* (New York: Columbia University Press, 2016).

29. I have in mind, particularly, George Grote's *History of Greece*, written in 12 volumes (1846–56).

30. Jerry Toner, *Homer's Turk: How Classics Shaped Ideas of the East* (Cambridge [MA] and London: Harvard University Press, 2013), 29–36.

31. Raj K. Kaul, *Studies in William Jones: An Interpreter of Oriental Literature* (Shimla: Indian Institute of Advanced Study, 1995).

32. Peter van der Veer, *Imperial Encounters: Religion and Modernity in India and Britain* (Ranikhet: Permanent Black, 2006), 137.

33. Thomas R. Trautmann, *Aryans and British India* (Berkeley, CA: University of California Press, 2004), 226.

34. Latin was offered as an optional course at Bombay University. See Narhar Raghunath Phatak, *Nyayamurti Mahadev Govinda Ranade Yanche Charitra* (Mumbai: N. R. Phatak, 1924), 22.

35. Phatak, *Nyayamurti Ranade*, 47–48.

36. Charles Trevelyan, *On the Education of the People of India* (London: Longman, 1838), 196–97.

37. Monier Monier-Williams, *Indian Epic Poetry, Being the Substance of Lectures Recently Given at Oxford with a Full Analysis of the Ramayana and of the Leading Story of the Maha-Bharata* (London and Edinburgh: Williams & Norgate, 1863), 42.

38. Monier-Williams, *Indian Epic Poetry*, 43.

39. Monier-Williams, *Indian Epic Poetry*, 43.

40. Moritz Winternitz, *A History of Indian Literature*, vol. 1, trans. S. Ketkar, rev. Moritz Winternitz (Calcutta: University of Calcutta Press, 1927 [1905]), 3.

41. Winternitz, *A History of Indian Literature*, 6.

42. Winternitz, *A History of Indian Literature*, 29.

43. William Dwight Whitney, *Sanskrit Grammar, Including Both the Classical Language, and the Other Dialects, of Veda and Brahmana* (Cambridge, Ma.: Harvard University Press, 1889 [1878]), xix.

44. Romila Thapar, *Time as a Metaphor of History: Early India* (New Delhi: Oxford University Press, 2011 [1996]).

45. Edward Washburn Hopkins, *The Great Epic of India* (New Haven, CT: Yale University Press, 1901), 386.

46. Friedrich Max Müller, 'Introduction', in *Maha-Bharata: The Epic of Ancient India Condensed into English Verse*, by Romesh Chunder Dutt, v–viii (London: J. M. Dent & Co., 1899), vii.

47. Vishnu Sitaram Sukthankar, *On the Meaning of the Mahābhārata* (Bombay: Asiatic Society of Bombay, 1957), 7–8.

48. Sukthankar, *On the Meaning*, 6–7.

49. The idea that multiple authors wrote epic texts was applied to Homer's *Iliad* and *Ulysses* as well, a claim first made by the German classical scholar Friedrich A. Wolf in his *Prolegomena to Homer* (1795).

50. Winternitz, *A History of Indian Literature*, 316–21.

51. Hopkins, *The Great Epic*, 386–402.

52. Hopkins, *The Great Epic*, 396.

53. The Deccan College in Poona (now Pune) had employed two German Indologists – Martin Haüg and Lorenz Franz Kielhorn – who laid the foundation of the German school of textual exegesis in the Bombay Presidency during the 1860s. Bhandarkar was their colleague and a collaborator. See Sumit Guha, *History and Collective Memory in South Asia, 1200–2000* (Seattle, WA: University of Washington Press, 2019), 136.

54. Ramakrishna Gopal Bhandarkar, 'The Critical, Comparative and Historical Method of Inquiry', in *Collected Works of Sir R. G. Bhandarkar*, vol. 1, ed.

Narayan Bapuji Utgirkar and Vasudev Gopal Paranjpe, 362–92 (Poona: Bhandarkar Oriental Research Institute, 1933).

55. Ramakrishna Gopal Bhandarkar, 'Consideration of the Date of the Mahābhārata', in *Collected Works of Sir R. G. Bhandarkar*, vol. 1, ed. Narayan Bapuji Utgirkar and Vasudev Gopal Paranjpe, 79–93, (Poona: Bhandarkar Oriental Research Institute, 1933).

56. Ramakrishna Gopal Bhandarkar, 'Lines for Fresh Research in Sanskrit Literature and Indian Antiquities', in *Collected Works of Sir R. G. Bhandarkar*, vol. 1, ed. Narayan Bapuji Utgirkar and Vasudev Gopal Paranjpe, 394–415 (Poona: Bhandarkar Oriental Research Institute, 1933), 395.

57. Ramakrishna Gopal Bhandarkar, 'The Mahābhārata', in *Collected Works of Sir R. G. Bhandarkar*, vol. 1, ed. Narayan Bapuji Utgirkar and Vasudev Gopal Paranjpe, 422–26 (Poona: Bhandarkar Oriental Research Institute, 1933), 425.

58. Kashinath Trimbak Telang, 'Introduction', in *The Bhagavadgītā, with the Sanatsujātīya and the Anugītā*, trans. Kashinath Trimbak Telang, *Sacred Books of the East*, vol. 8, ed. F. Max Müller, 1–36 (Oxford: Clarendon Press, 1882), 2.

59. Kashinath Trimbak Telang, 'Was the Ramayana Copied from Homer?' in *Selected Writings and Speeches*, with an introduction by D. E. Wacha, 4–93 (Bombay: G. S. B. Mitra Mandal, 1916), 4–5.

60. Ranajit Guha, *Dominance without Hegemony: History and Power in Colonial India* (Cambridge, MA: Harvard University Press, 1997), 154.

61. Guha, *Dominance Without Hegemony*, 155.

62. I thank Polly O'Hanlon for clarifying this point.

63. Ramesh Chandra Majumdar, 'Indian History: Its Nature, Scope and Method', in *The Vedic Age*, ed. R. C. Majumdar and A. D. Pusalker, 37–46 (London: George Allen & Unwin Ltd, 1951), 38.

64. Troy Wilson Organ, *The Hindu Quest for the Perfection of Man* (Athens, OH: Ohio University Press, 1970), 30–31.

65. Ranjan Ghosh, 'India, Itihāsa, and Inter-Historiographical Discourse', *History and Theory* 46, no. 2 (2007): 210–17.

66. Romila Thapar, 'Ideology and the Interpretation of Early Indian History', in *Cultural Pasts: Essays in Early Indian History*, 3–20 (New Delhi: Oxford University Press, 2000).

67. The three books are *Mahābhārata: A Criticism* (Bombay: A. J. Combridge & Co., 1905); *The Riddle of the Rāmāyaṇa* (London: Kegan Paul, 1906); and *Epic India: India as Described in Mahābhārata and Rāmāyaṇa* (Bombay: Mrs. Radhabai Atmaram Sagoon, 1907).

68. Vaidya graduated from the University of Bombay (1880) and later studied law at Deccan College in Pune. He was appointed the chief justice of the princely state of Baroda for some time but chose to quit his job and divert his energies towards anti-colonial agitation. He joined the Indian National Congress in 1904 and became a close associate of the extremist Congress leader Bal Gangadhar Tilak. Vaidya presided over the Marathi Sahitya Sammelan (Marathi Literary Festival) held at Pune in 1908. Apart from the epic trilogy, Vaidya wrote voluminous histories of Sanskrit literature and medieval India. To the best of my knowledge, the only major Indologist who has engaged with Vaidya's epic trilogy is Alf Hiltebeitel. See his *Rethinking the Mahābhārata: A Reader's Guide to the Education of the Dharma King* (London and Chicago [IL]: University of Chicago Press, 2001).

69. Vaidya, *Mahābhārata: A Criticism*, 3.

70. Vaidya, *Mahābhārata: A Criticism*, 9.

71. Vaidya, *Mahābhārata: A Criticism*, 10.

72. Vaidya, *Mahābhārata: A Criticism*, 49.

73. Vaidya, *Mahābhārata: A Criticism*, 39–40.

74. Vaidya, *Mahābhārata: A Criticism*, 22.

75. Vaidya, *Mahābhārata: A Criticism*, 23.

76. Vaidya, *Mahābhārata: A Criticism*, 65.

77. Vaidya, *Mahābhārata: A Criticism*, 51.

78. Vaidya, *Mahābhārata: A Criticism*, 52–2.

79. Rosalind O'Hanlon, '"Premodern" Pasts: South Asia', in *A Companion to Global Historical Thought*, ed. Prasenjit Duara, Viren Murthy, and Andrew Sartori, 107–121 (Chichester: Wiley Blackwell, 2014).

80. Balaji Janardan Modak, *Chronological Tables Containing Corresponding Dates of Hindu, Mohammedan and Christian Eras* (Poona and Kolhapur: Chitrashala and Vidyavilas Press, 1889); Shankar Balkrishna Dikshit, *History of Indian Astronomy* (Poona: Aryabhushan Press, 1896).

81. Vaidya, *Mahābhārata: A Criticism*, 67–90.

82. Vaidya, *Mahābhārata: A Criticism*, 90.

83. Vaidya considered the genealogy found in the *Vishnu Purana* to be flawed. If only 1,065 years had passed between the reign of king Nanda and the Mahabharata war, as stated in the *Vishnu Purana*, then the war had to be dated around 1400 BCE. But in another place the *Vishnu Purana* stated that the Kali Yuga began 1,200 divine years ago, which, when translated into mortal terms, would mean 360,800 years. Vaidya believed that the Puranas must have been written by overzealous and ignorant men eager to revive Hinduism. See Vaidya, *Mahābhārata: A Criticism*, 77–79.

84. Astronomical, or *jyotisha*-based, statements found in the epic were equally wrong. They must have been added, Vaidya believed, during the final redaction of the Mahabharata, predisposed to 'fanciful and absurd' propositions and lacking 'authenticity'. See Vaidya, *Mahābhārata: A Criticism*, 83. According to David Pingree, traditional *jyotishshastra* is formed of three components: *samhita* (omens), *ganita* (astronomy), and *hora* (astrology). However, the nomenclature among the nineteenth- and early-twentieth-century Indologists was to translate *jyotishshastra* as astronomy. See David Pingree, *Jyotiḥśāstra: Astral and Mathematical Literature* (Weisbaden: Otto Harrassowitz, 1981), 1–3.

85. Patrick Olivelle, *Manu's Code of Law: A Critical Edition and Translation of the Mānava-Dharmaśāstra* (Oxford and New York [NY]: Oxford University Press, 2005), 90.

86. Thomas R. Trautmann, 'Indian Time, European Time', in *Time: Histories and Ethnologies*, ed. Diane Owen Hughes and Thomas R. Trautmann, 167–200 (Ann Arbor, MI: University of Michigan Press, 1995), 169.

87. Vaidya suggests elsewhere that while the exact date for Valmikī's poem was unknown, the 'present edition' of the Ramayana could be dated to the second century BCE and written well after Sauti's redaction to the Mahabharata. See Vaidya, *The Riddle of the Rāmāyaṇa* (London: Kegan Paul, 1906), 11–20.

88. Dirks, 'History as a Sign', 27.

89. Bernard S. Cohn, *Colonialism and Its Forms of Knowledge: The British in India* (Princeton, NJ: Princeton University Press, 1996).

90. Bal Gangadhar Tilak, *The Arctic Home in the Vedas, Being Also a New Key to the Interpretation of Nany Vedic Texts and Legends* (Pune: Tilak Brothers, 2008 [1903]); Alok Oak, 'Political Ideas of Bal Gangadhar Tilak: Colonialism, Self and Hindu Nationalism', PhD dissertation, Institute for Area Studies, University of Leiden, 2022.

91. Vaidya, *Epic India: India as Described in Mahābhārata and Rāmāyaṇa* (Bombay: Mrs. Radhabai Atmaram Sagoon, 1907), 5.

92. Vaidya, *Epic India*, 14.

93. Vaidya, *Epic India*, 19.

94. Vaidya, *Epic India*, 19.

95. Vaidya, *Epic India*, 19.

96. Vaidya, *Epic India*, 19.

97. Vaidya, *Epic India*, 19.

98. The two chief characters of the Ramayana – Dasharatha and Ravana – had 350 and 1,000 wives, respectively. Krishna, too, born possibly of a 'mixed marriage' and hence dark skinned, had 16,000 wives. For Vaidya, access to plentiful resources along with a desire to rapidly spread the Aryan culture

amongst the tribals, Dravidians, and other cannibals explains the practices of polygamy and polyandry widespread amongst the Aryans invaders. The conquering Aryans were 'influenced by the natural desire to appropriate to themselves desirable women from among the conquered'. See Vaidya, *Epic India*, 85.

99. *Swayamvara* means 'self-chosen'. *Niyoga* refers to marriage commissioned specifically for procreation; the word 'niyoga' means 'commissioned'. Vaidya, *Epic India*, 84–92.
100. Vaidya, *Epic India*, 180.
101. Vaidya, *Epic India*, 181.
102. Vaidya, *Epic India*, 244.
103. Vaidya, *Epic India*, 245.
104. Vaidya, *Epic India*, 161.
105. Vaidya, *Epic India*, 163.
106. Vaidya, *Epic India*, 163.
107. 'Yaksha Prashna' was a section of the 'Vana Parva' (Book of Forest, the third chapter of the Mahabharata). It is a dialogue in the form of questions and answers between Yudhisthira and a *yaksha* (nature spirit). Vaidya, *Epic India*, 161–63.
108. Bal Gangadhar Tilak, 'Mahābhārata–1 to 8', in *Samagra Lokmanya Tilak*, vol. 5: 698–744 (Pune: Kesari Prakashan, 1976).
109. Sukthankar obtained his BA degree with Mathematical Tripos from Cambridge University (1906), completed his MA from University of Edinburgh (1909), and wrote his PhD dissertation on Indian philology under the supervision of Heinrich Lüders at Humboldt University, Berlin (1914). See S. M. Katre, 'Vishnu Sitaram Sukthankar: And His Contribution to Indology', *Bulletin of the Deccan College Post-Graduate and Research Institute* 5 (1943–44): vii–lvi.
110. While announcing the completion of the project, the then president of India and eminent philosopher, S. Radhakrishnan, is reported to have said: 'The Critical Edition of the *Mahābhārata* is a monument to Indian scholarship. I am inclined to feel that Maharṣi Vyāsa himself would have hesitated to embark on this stupendous project.' See 'The Completion of the Critical Edition of the Mahābhārata', *Annals of the Bhandarkar Oriental Research Institute* 47, nos. 1–4 (1966): i–xiv, ix (emphasis original).
111. Vishnu Sitaram Sukthankar, 'Prolegomena', in *Critical Studies in the Mahābhārata*, by Vishnu Sitaram Sukthankar, 10–140 (Poona and Bombay: V. S. Sukthankar Memorial Edition Committee and Karnataka Publishing House, 1944), 129.
112. Sukthankar, *Prolegomena*, 129 (emphasis original).
113. Sukthankar, *Prolegomena*, 129 (emphasis original).

114. Sukthankar, *On the Meaning*, 4.
115. The CE of the Mahabharata has received its fair share of adulation and criticism over the years. See M. A. Mehendale, 'The Critical Edition of the Mahābhārata: Its Achievements and Limitations', *Annals of the Bhandarkar Oriental Research Institute* 88 (2007): 1–16; Narhar Kurundkar, *Vyasanche Shilpa* (Pune: Deshmukh & Company, 2002). In recent years, Vishwa Adluri has denounced the nineteenth-century European studies on the Mahabharata for their neo-Protestantism and lacking genuine historical curiosity, and has defended Sukthankar's exegetical method. See Vishwa Adluri, 'Introduction', in *Ways and Reasons for Thinking about the Mahābhārata as a Whole*, ed. Vishwa Adluri, vii–xxxii (Pune: Bhandarkar Oriental Research Institute, 2013).
116. Chintaman Vinayak Vaidya, 'A Prospectus of a New and Critical Edition of the Mahābhārata, Undertaken by the Bhandarkar Oriental Research Institute, Poona: A Review', *Journal of the Bombay Branch of the Royal Asiatic Society* (New Series) 35, no. 2 (1918–19): 364–372, 365.
117. Vaidya, 'A Prospectus', 365.
118. Vaidya, 'A Prospectus', 366.
119. Sheldon Pollock, 'Deep Orientalism? Notes on Sanskrit and Power beyond the Raj', in *Orientalism and the Postcolonial Predicament*, ed. Carol A. Breckenridge and Peter van der Veer, 76–133 (Philadelphia, PA: University of Pennsylvania Press, 1993).
120. Pandit Jawaharlal Nehru, *Discovery of India* (Delhi: Oxford University Press, 1946).
121. Arvind Rajagopal, *Politics after Television: Hindu Nationalism and the Reshaping of the Public in India* (Cambridge, UK: Cambridge University Press, 2001).

3

The Bhagavadgita and the Gandhian Hermeneutic of Non-Violence

Globalizing Selfless Action

Arkamitra Ghatak

Thus the author of the Gita, by extending meanings of words, has taught us to imitate him ... after forty years' unremitting endeavor fully to enforce the teaching of the Gita in my own life, I have in all humility felt that perfect renunciation is impossible without perfect observance of ahimsa in every shape and form.

—M. K. Gandhi, *Anasaktiyoga*[1]

Introduction

The Bhagavadgita is an 18-chapter philosophical dialogue between Arjuna, the despondent warrior hero reluctant to raise arms against his kin, and his divine charioteer, Krishna, who exhorts him to wage war with detachment as an instrument of divine will. It is set on the battlefield in the Sanskrit epic, the Mahabharata, moments before the beginning of a war. The Bhagavadgita (henceforth Gita), as Richard H. Davis elucidates in his 'short biography' of the text, intrigued scholars with its 'doubleness' – 'its historical specificity and its continuing, even eternal, life'. Its ambiguities and accommodation of multiple theological currents made it possible (and continues to do so) for the text to appeal to diverse groups of readers and commentators in medieval, pre-colonial, and colonial India and beyond.[2] It gained a transnational community of readers in Europe and America, as colonial commentators, Christian missionaries, Romantic philosophers, and Indologists popularized it as a Hindu philosophical text at par with the Quran and the Bible. By the early twentieth century, it came to provide a wide range of Indian political thinkers, from Aurobindo Ghose to Bal Gangadhar Tilak, who were occupied in anti-colonial struggle with an opportunity to 'rethink politics in a novel language of action without consequence'.[3] Among such engagements, M. K. Gandhi's approach to the Gita as a guide to moral action in the realm of politics has attracted maximum scholarly attention. Such works have accorded due focus to the genealogies of (mostly Western) political and religious thought that informed his readings and the innovative agency of Gandhi himself.[4]

This chapter, however, shifts the optic from Gandhi to the Gandhian(s) to draw attention to the hermeneutics of reading the Gita through the prism of non-violence (*ahimsa*) that Gandhi introduces in Indian sociopolitical thought and constructs an intellectual history of such hermeneutical exercises. Through this, I wish to move beyond the individual centricity that has characterized the global intellectual history of Gandhian thought. I do so by highlighting the intellectual agency of the followers of Gandhi, notably Mahadev Desai (1892–1942) and the ascetic philosopher and mathematician Vinoba Bhave (1895–1982), in informing, elaborating, and globalizing Gandhian philosophy, especially Gandhi's interpretation of the Gita as a 'gospel of selfless action'.[5] Works that have already traced possible sources of influence on Gandhian thought have somehow overlooked the roles played by his political companions, who were notable intellectuals in their own right, in shaping his philosophy. This can be attributed to the fact that such associates like Desai and Vinoba identified themselves as 'followers' and 'disciples' of Gandhi, therefore casting Gandhi and themselves into a guru–*shishya* (disciple) relationship. This relationship tends to imply a hierarchical, unilateral process of knowledge transmission from the guru to the disciple. Such claims seem to have occluded from existing historiographies, the pivotal roles such 'followers' played as intellectual collaborators in the Gandhian project of promoting *satyagraha*[6] as non-violent political and social action.

By highlighting their involvement in expanding Gandhian thought, I argue that global intellectual history of Gandhian ideology needs to acknowledge the multi-vocality that characterized its production and dissemination in the context of sociopolitical action, especially in the aftermath of Gandhi's assassination in 1948. Multiple research works in recent years have iterated the poly-vocality evident in the transnational reception and appropriations of the Gita variously as a resource for the colonial Orientalist project, German Romanticism, Indological historical-critical enquiry, universalist aspirations of perennial philosophists,

Theosophists, and neo-Vedantins. The contrasting moralities of political and social action that nationalist thinkers – ranging from Lala Lajpat Rai and Bal Gangadhar Tilak to Aurobindo Ghose, Vinayak Damodar Savarkar, and Gandhi – derived from the theological premise of the Gita have been underscored by many intellectual histories written on the text. This multi-vocality highlighted by such academic projects, I believe, underscores the significance of the contexts and the 'interpretive community' at large rather than individual thinkers in the construction of the Gita as an eminent global text.[7] Yet the role of the 'interpretive community' of Gandhians in producing the Gita as a Gandhian text has been overlooked in the large body of scholarship on the Gita and its relationship with Gandhian thought, leaving a lacunae I wish to address through this chapter.

The chapter primarily engages with three texts: Gandhi's translation of the Gita from Sanskrit into Gujarati as *Anasaktiyoga* in 1929 (which was published on 12 March 1930, on the historic occasion of the beginning of his salt march to Dandi), Mahadev Desai's commentary, or 'Submission', on *Anasaktiyoga*, which he translated into English as *The Gospel of Selfless Action* in 1933–34, and Vinoba Bhave's *Talks on the Gita*, which he delivered in the course of his imprisonment at Dhule Jail in 1932. In the first section of the chapter, I explain how the Gandhian mode of reading the Gita as a treatise on non-violent action had to compete with Tilak's rival interpretation, which endorsed violence when performed for the sake of collective good. Gandhi and subsequently the 'interpretive community' of Gandhians came to constitute an alternative hermeneutic space where they claimed their authority to comment on the Gita not via scholarly rigour but from their experience of living in accordance with the teachings of the Gita. In the second section, I highlight how the followers of Gandhi, particularly Desai, in contrast to Gandhi himself who translated the Gita into Gujarati for an 'unlettered' population, were driven by the agenda of expanding their 'interpretive community'. Desai self-professedly sought to do so by disseminating and defending Gandhi's interpretation of the Gita as a text advocating truth and non-violence in the domain of action among a global readership. Such an enterprise involved the defence of Gandhi's allegorical approach to the Gita, which in turn required an intertextual polemical engagement with contemporary Indological scholarship on the historicity of the *Mahabharata* and the war it depicts. The third section shows how Gandhi and his followers developed a dialectical historicism of their own, with *anasaktiyoga*, or selfless action, taught by the Gita, representing individual and collective 'experiments' towards the unfolding of a non-violent social order. In the final section, I discuss how Bhave's conceptualization of *samyayoga*[8] derived from the Gita represented a semantic shift in Gandhian action as the very nature of *satyagraha* shifted from individual to collectivistic, in keeping with the pressures of social inequities in post-colonial India and the looming nuclear threat in the Cold War world.

By highlighting the global underpinnings of the efforts of Gandhians to elaborate Gandhi's philosophy in the domain of ethical action through their engagement with the Gita, I am embarking on a global intellectual history which treats Gandhian ideology as a collaboratively produced project rather than an individual-centric one. I also show how this process involved the constitution of a Gandhian hermeneutic space in which the Gita and the Mahabharata were transformed into dialectical histories of progressive non-violence.

Recent years have seen a renewed interest in the application of literary hermeneutics to the Mahabharata and the Gita and the production of novel concept histories through such enterprises. Angelika Malinar reads in the Gita a new political theology of ideal kingship and sovereignty.[9] Sibaji Bandyopadhyay's *Three Essays on the Mahabharata* studies the afterlives of specific themes derived from the text, like the semantic shifts through which verse 2.47 of the Gita acquired a context-neutral mantra-like status in (anti)-colonial discourses, becoming a 'national motto', as well as the account of the war-reporting, the overlapping of *anrishamsya* (non-cruelty) and *aparigraha* (self-restraint from greed and possessiveness), and the implications of such conceptualizations of non-violence in the face of a globalized Freudian *thanatos* (death instincts).[10] More recently, Kanad Sinha has excavated reflections of changing notions of historical consciousness from the hermeneutic shifts associated with the Mahabharata.[11] This chapter also concerns itself with the construction of a specific hermeneutic, that of reading the Gita in terms of Gandhian non-violence, and attempts to underscore the globalizing instincts operating within the Gandhian community, especially after Gandhi.

Lived Experience as a Gandhian Hermeneutic

I begin the chapter with a brief ideological backdrop in which Gandhi encountered and formulated his views on political action endorsed by the Gita. I also state how Gandhi and his followers came to constitute an alternative hermeneutic space by reading the Gita through the prism of non-violence, especially in the face of the popularity enjoyed by Tilak's interpretation of the Gita, which justified violence when committed for collective good.

Non–Violence as (Alternative) Hermeneutic Space

Gandhi first read the Gita with the Theosophists Bertram and Archibald Keightley in London in 1888–89. Keightley introduced him to Edwin Arnold's verse translation, *The Song Celestial* (1885). Subsequently, the Gita was to become Gandhi's moral encyclopedia, offering him answers to his queries on ethical action, ultimately providing the foundation for his doctrine of *satyagraha*. In the early years of the twentieth century, it had become commonplace for Indian political thinkers and Hindu socio-religious reformers to derive moral support from the Gita. By the late nineteenth century itself, it had acquired a special ideological status in anti-colonial protests and the nationalist response of Indian Theosophists and other religious thinkers to the hegemonic claims of European Indology.[12] However, Gandhi's reading was made unique by his insistence that the Gita, a discourse meant to motivate a recalcitrant warrior to wage war, implied the futility of violence and enjoined the means of non-violence or *ahimsa*.

Such a claim contradicted contemporary interpretations, most notably Tilak's Marathi commentary, *Shrimad Bhagavad Gita Rahasya* (1915), which had, since its publication, garnered immense popularity as a treatise on ethical action or *karma-yoga* (selfless action).[13] It was primarily targeted against Sanskrit doxographies, especially the *Gitabhashya* of Shankara, which argued that one who has attained *gnana*, or self-knowledge, was no longer compelled to participate in action. Tilak's work claimed that the Gita 'advocates the performance of action in this world even after the actor has achieved the highest union with the Supreme Deity by *gnana* (knowledge) or bhakti (devotion) provided such action ensures 'the world's welfare' (*lokasamgraha*).[14] Tilak went further to concede that the 'mentally stabilized' *sthitapragya* (individual with steadfast wisdom), in complete control of his senses, was 'by definition, sinless and is even, by example, a basis for the laws of behavior for others ... [In] his case, the motive, not the act itself, is the criterion by which an act is to be judged'.[15] This was the premise through which he justified the assassination of Mughal general Afzal Khan by the Maratha ruler Shivaji as an act committed 'for the good of others' in his journal *Kesari*. 'No blame,' claims Tilak, 'attaches to any person who ... is doing deeds without being motivated by a desire to reap the fruit of his deeds'; the actions of great men should be judged not in terms of the penal code but the 'high atmosphere of the Bhagavat Gita' where Krishna's teaching 'is to kill even our teachers and our kinsmen'.[16]

Gandhi's emphasis on non-violent action was in stark contrast to such a reading of the Gita as a text condoning violence when committed for the greater good. The *Gita Rahasya*, nevertheless, enjoyed widespread authority as a treatise on political action due to Tilak's stature as a reputed scholar and nationalist leader. It played a significant role as the ideological motivation behind militant nationalism in Maharashtra and Bengal, which took the form of bombings and assassinations of colonial officials. The very popularity of Tilak's interpretation therefore necessitated that Gandhi clarified his stance on the Gita in greater detail. In his introduction to *Anasaktiyoga*, Gandhi quotes Swami Anand, who had reportedly entreated him in the non-cooperation days that his followers 'shall be able to appreciate [his] meaning of the message of the Gita, only when [they] are able to study a translation of the whole text by [himself]'. The anxiety and need for such a systematic interpretation of the text is evident from the Swami's remark to him: 'I do not think it is just in your part to deduce ahimsa etc. from stray verses.'[17] It is noteworthy here that many among Gandhi's disciples, including Bhave who used to read out the *Kesari* to his mother, were erstwhile followers of Tilak's ideological position and aspired to become revolutionary nationalists. As is evident from his memoir cited here, he later converted to the Gandhian principle of non-violence and became a member of his Sabarmati Ashram, where he found the combined 'peace of the Himalayas and the revolutionary spirit of Bengal'.[18]

> Only I can know what I have got in the Ashram. It was an early ambition of mine to distinguish myself by a violent deed in the service of the country. But Bapu cured me of that ambition. It is he who extinguished the volcano of anger and other passions in me.[19]

Gandhi established his position by repudiating the notion that 'the end justifies the means' as he had already done in *Hind Swaraj*, where he had stated that violence led one farther from the pursuit of truth or self-realization. He justified his stance on the grounds that 'there is just the same inviolable connection between the means and the end as there is between the seed and the tree'.[20] In *Anasaktiyoga*, he reiterates that self-realization, which was the ultimate aim of a devotee, was but 'the extreme of means', which he identified as *anasakti*, or 'renunciation of fruits of action'.[21] According to Gandhi, since all acts of violence are prompted by the 'desire to attain the cherished end', and the Gita forbids such acts which are incapable of being performed without such attachment, he had 'felt that in trying to enforce in one's life the central teaching of the Gita, one is bound to follow truth and ahimsa'.[22]

Gandhians as Interpretive Community

Gandhi was acutely aware of the question of authority and what qualified (*adhikar*) him to produce an authoritative interpretation of the Gita.[23] Tilak was a learned Brahmin whose views in the *Gita Rahasya* were substantiated by a detailed 'study of the *Mahabharata*, the *Vedanta-Sutras*, the *Upanishads* and other Sanskrit and English treatises on Vedanta'.[24] Gandhi, on the other hand, was the son of a *Baniya*, whose knowledge of Sanskrit was limited and whose Gujarati was 'in no way scholarly'. Instead, his authority came from experience and 'the claim of an endeavor to enforce the meaning in [his] own conduct for an unbroken period of forty years', a claim he believed other translators have not made.[25] Nevertheless, concerned about the authenticity of his translation, Gandhi got his associates who were better-versed in scriptures or more adept in Sanskrit or Gujarati to cross-verify his work.

Desai and Bhave were two of these companions of Gandhi who were known for their erudition and were involved in the literary activities of the Gandhian movement. Desai, who was born in Surat, was well read in Gujarati and English literature, as well as the Gita and the Upanishads, which he had studied with the help of commentaries. He was an associate of Gandhi since his campaign at Champaran (1917) and in subsequent *satyagraha*s and also courted imprisonment alongside him. Gandhi sent him to run Motilal Nehru's paper, *The Independent*, in Allahabad. Since 1924 he edited the *Navjivan*, the newspaper propagating Gandhian ideologies and also translated Gandhi's autobiography, *The Story of My Experiments with Truth*, into English for serial publication in *Young India*. In 1933, he wrote *The Gita According to Gandhi* while imprisoned in Belgaum Jail, but it was published posthumously after his death in 1942.[26]

Vinayak Narahari (Vinoba) Bhave, like Gandhi, received a Western education, excelling in mathematics and, subsequently, philosophy. At a young age, he became a renunciant and studied Sanskrit scriptures in Banaras with the pandits. Inspired by Gandhi's speech at Banaras Hindu University, he joined the Sabarmati Ashram. In Gandhi's lifetime, Bhave mostly stayed away from political limelight, focusing on teaching, spinning, and Harijan uplift through the Gram Seva Mandal as the head of Gandhi's Wardha Ashram. While in Dhule Jail, where he was imprisoned for leading a *satyagraha*, he gave a talk on each chapter of the Gita every Sunday from 21 February to 19 June 1932, which came to be published later as *Talks on the Gita*.[27] After Gandhi's death, Bhave, widely recognized as his 'spiritual heir' after his assassination, formed the Sarvodaya Samaj and worked briefly for the uplift of the refugees from Pakistan and *karchan-mukti* (freedom from gold). From 1951 he came into prominence for the Bhoodan Movement (land gift mission) to which he devoted the rest of his career. He undertook *padayatras* (foot marches) across India, garnering around four million acres of land for redistribution among the poor.[28]

While Gandhi valued the scholarly insights of his companions, such as Desai and Bhave, who subsequently also wrote or delivered commentaries on the Gandhian approach to the Gita, it is the autobiographical component through which Gandhi claimed hermeneutic authority over the Gita. Gandhi's *Anasakatiyoga*, which is not based on 'mere intellect' but a life-long attempt to shape or write his own self in terms of its teachings, is as much a translation as it is his autobiography, another narrative of his 'experiments with truth' and non-violence. This hermeneutic peculiarity of writing the Gandhian self into the Gita becomes a standard Gandhian practice. It is more clearly visible in the case of Bhave, who calls his *Talks on the Gita* 'the story of my life, and ... also my message'.[29] Unlike Gandhi, Bhave is an erudite scholar, fluent in Sanskrit and efficient in Vedantic and Bhakti philosophies. Yet, in the fashion of Gandhi, he emphasizes his intimate relationship with the Gita at the beginning of his *Talks on the Gita*:

> Moving beyond the intellect, I therefore soar high in the vast expanse of the Gita on the twin wings of faith and experimentation. Most of the time I live in the ambience of the Gita. The Gita is my life-breath. I am as if afloat on the surface of this ocean of nectar when I am talking about the Gita with others, and when alone, I dive deep into this ocean and rest there.[30]

The purpose of highlighting this similarity is to draw attention to the 'interpretive community'[31] that Gandhians constituted and the role they played in the production of the Gita as a Gandhian text endorsing an ideology of selfless action.

As Karline McLain has shown, Gandhi's ashrams comprised such 'intentional communities', which Gandhi constituted with the intention to shape the daily lives of the residents through intense engagement with the Gita. This involved daily rituals like regular recitals of passages from it during morning and evening prayer sessions and contemplation on their application not only in political but also quotidian actions. The essential observances of the ashram designed for a Gandhian ashramite, involved a lifelong *karma-yoga*, marked not only by non-violence and truth but also 'daily discipline in the form of physical work, such as cleaning the lavatory and time spent at the spinning wheel, as well as practicing diet control, celibacy, and meditating upon scripture' and 'voluntary suffering on behalf of the nation'.[32] Bhave was one among such Gandhians shaped by the 'experiments' in *karma-yoga*, distinguishing himself by his dedication to physical labour, voluntary suffering, and erudition in scriptures, which earned him Gandhi's appreciation. Moreover, it was this endeavour of Gandhi to transform the Gita into a lived reality that had drawn Bhave to Gandhi, in whom he found somebody 'who came very near to' the ideal of 'Sthitaprajna, [or] one who lives in steadfast wisdom' described in the Gita.[33, 34]

As will be shown in subsequent sections of this chapter, the hermeneutic of experiment in Gandhian discourse did not merely constitute interpretive authority but also informed the production of new meanings of selfless action from the Gita. The role of Gandhians in such an intellectual project was far from merely derivative of Gandhi's opinion.

The Gandhian Gita and a Globalizing Impetus

Having established how Gandhi and his followers comprised an interpretive community, I now proceed to underscore how the Gandhian commentaries on the Gita mark 'global moments'. I do so by highlighting how they were informed by and often framed in response to the historical-critical readings of the Gita predominant among contemporary Western Indological–Orientalist scholarship. As I will show, the very necessity of fashioning the Gita into a handbook on non-violence required, on the part of Gandhi and his companions, the simultaneous denial of the historicity of its contents and the construction of an alternative historicality for it.

Anasaktiyoga as a Global Text

Gandhi's first encounter with the Gita in the form of *The Song Celestial* can be perceived, following the example set by Michael Bergunder, as a 'global moment' of 'historical entanglement'.[35] It was mediated through his attempts to reconcile its teachings with *The Light of Asia*, another verse by Edwin Arnold on the life of the Buddha and the Sermon on the Mount, a series of sayings attributed to Jesus Christ by the New Testament of the Bible. As Bergunder shows in his insightful work, Gandhi's extensive encounters with Theosophy strongly shaped his engagement with the Gita and Christianity as well. He derived the idea of Christianity as a 'system of religion which teaches universality'[36] from the Esoteric Christian Union based on the teachings of the Theosophists Anna Kingsford and Edward Maitland while residing in South Africa. On the other hand, like other English-educated Hindu elites in the late nineteenth century, he imbibed the Orientalist 'idea of Hinduism with Advaita Vedanta and the Bhagavad Gita at its core'.[37] Like many others, his entry into such Orientalist conceptions of an inclusive Hinduism was facilitated by the Theosophists via whom, as mentioned before, he first encountered the Gita and other texts on Advaita Vedanta and Raja Yoga. This is evident from the fact that in 1905 he got Annie Besant's translation of the Gita reprinted and circulated for the 'religious instruction of Indian youth in South Africa'.[38] The exercise of putting different religions in a comparative framework in the pursuit of a universal truth, which seems to have been inspired by the Theosophists, left him convinced that 'renunciation was the highest form of religion'.[39]

In *Anasaktiyoga*, however, Gandhi refrains from any mention of the Upanishads, or references beyond the Gita itself, despite his own admission of the number of Western thinkers who influenced his political philosophy of non-violence. This was because he explicitly addressed as his targeted readership the Gujarati-speaking 'women, the commercial class, the so-called Shudras and the like who have little or no literary equipment, who have neither the time nor the desire to read the Gita in the original yet who stand in need of its support'.[40]

The commentaries of the Gandhians, in contrast, are replete with references which reveal anxieties to cater to a more diverse yet erudite readership. This shift is apparent in Desai's *Submission*, the prologue to his English translation of *Anasaktiyoga*. He explains that the 'unsophisticated' and 'unlettered' nature of Gandhi's intended readership prevented him from addressing issues of scholarly concern like the 'date of the Gita, the text of the Gita' and the 'question of the Krishna Vasudeva cult'.[41] Desai's translation, on the other hand, was meant to cover this gap for the sake of the 'English-knowing youths in India [who] will like to have Gandhiji's interpretation of the Gita' and those 'outside India who are interested in Gandhiji's life and thought'.[42] His work was therefore addressed to a group which he assumed would be deeply immersed in the global episteme of early twentieth-century Indology and interested in the questions that were of crucial importance to the scholars of the field.

Such an intention to globalize the 'interpretive community' of readers aligned with the Gandhian way of reading the Gita as a political philosophy endorsing non-violence required Desai to underscore the universal applicability of such selfless action. The process of transforming the Gita into the 'Bible of humanity' therefore made it imperative that Desai diversify his choice of exemplars while arguing in favour of selfless action. This is evident from the list of exemplary figures who, Desai believed, 'had lived and moved in conformity with the essential law' and made 'ashes of all action' through 'the sovereign alchemy of selflessness'. His list includes the lives of Job and Harishchandra; ... Janaka and Marcus Aurelius, and Jalaluddin Rumi; of Plotinus and Epictetus; of St. Paul, St. Augustine and St. Ignatius; of Vidyaranya, of Shankaracharya and Eckhart; of St. Francis and St. Catherine of Siena, ... of Chaitanya, Kabir, and Tulsidas; of Jnaneshvar, Ramdas and Tukaram; of Mirabai and Andal; ... of Spinoza and Lessing and Savonarola; of Pascal and Fenelon; ... Pasteur and Madame Curie; of Father Damien and Cardinal Newman ... Lincoln and General Gordon.[43]

It is noteworthy to reiterate that the relationship of the Gita with projects that claimed to be the 'Bible of mankind' predates Desai. The Gita found a place in such encyclopedic projects as well as canons of second-generation American transcendentalists like James Freeman Clarke, Samuel Johnson, and Moncure Conway. These thinkers considered it a seminal treatise from the Orient which could represent the philosophical component of Hinduism alongside other Eastern philosophies such as Laozi, Confucius, and the Dhammapada of the Pali Buddhist canon in anthologies of comparative religion. For the early Theosophists, the Gita was one among the many doctrines like Esoteric Buddhism, which embodied the 'ancient wisdom'. However, as Bergunder shows, by the 1880s the Indian Theosophists alongside a few American members, such as W. Q. Judge, had upgraded it to the core text of Theosophical wisdom which possessed '*all the doctrines given in Esoteric Buddhism* and far more yet untouched'.[44] The Gita therefore transformed from *one* of the principal texts from the Orient to the timeless and universal 'Bible of humanity'. For Gandhians like Desai who functioned in an intellectual atmosphere saturated with Theosophical ideas, the Gita came to represent the 'essential law', the universal blueprint of 'selfless action', within which the actions of everyone who had acted out of the 'sovereign alchemy of selflessness', irrespective of time and space, could be fitted in.

Desai's list, however, includes 'Lincoln, who directed one of the fiercest, civil wars in history ... Gordon, whose hands may be said to be dripping, with blood for the best part of his life, and ... Pasteur much of whose work for humanity depended on his experiments involving vivisection'.[45] He is not unaware of the irony of including such figures in what was a polemic in defence of Gandhi's stance that 'perfect renunciation ... is impossible without perfect observance of truth and non-violence'.[46] He justifies his choice on the grounds of the '*selfless*'[47] dedication to 'truth and non-violence', divine will, and 'service to humanity' that marked the private and public actions of these individuals. Such a claim, however, came with a caveat that Desai was all too aware of. If any form of action undertaken 'in a spirit of complete self-surrender ... in the interests of the Self of all mankind' was justified, were the actions of Hitler, 'who declare[d] that by fighting against the Jews I am doing the Lord's work' to be condoned as well? Underscoring that the latter was motivated by 'nothing better than an implacable hatred for Jews', Desai ultimately leaves the task of passing judgement on him to 'History'.[48]

Desai's evaluation, which accords primacy to the intention of the actor in determining the ethical value of his action, irrespective of the degree of violence involved, reveals the pressures and tensions that the imperative to globalize brought into the Gandhian discourse. Such an interpretation borders closer to Tilak's legitimation of 'ends justifying the means' than Gandhi's insistence on the complete identification of means and ends. In the process of expanding the 'interpretive community' who could share Gandhi's ideology of *karma-yoga* as renunciatory selfless action, Gandhians, unlike Gandhi, were therefore compelled to respond to Tilak's interpretation.

The influence of Tilak on the readership Desai intended to attract and the prisoners to whom Bhave addressed his *Gita Pravachane* (*Talks on the Gita*), as well as on Desai and Bhave themselves, is evident from their allusions to the *Gita Rahasya,* especially in the course of comparing the paths of *karma-yoga* and *sannyasa* (renunciation). Desai attempts to resolve Tilak's complaints against Shankaracharya, whom he accused of denying the necessity of action on the part of the *jnani* (one who has attained knowledge). He does so by underscoring that Shankaracharya had argued for the renunciation of 'Vedic ritualism' and such actions that generated bondage, and not all activities, while also suggesting that the real object of Tilak's attack was not Shankaracharya as such but the 'soi-distant jnanis of the present-day, reveling in intellectual jugglery and shunning all action'.[49] Bhave, who was better known as a scholarly ascetic than a political activist by fellow Gandhians, 'whole heartedly [*sic*] endorse[s] Tilak's view that the Gita is for ordinary people engaged in worldly life' meant as it was to teach 'how worldly life can be purified'.[50] He nevertheless opposes Tilak's treatment of the paths of *karma-yoga* and *sannyasa* as 'mutually exclusive' by highlighting that Yajnavalkya, a *sannyasi* (renunciant), accepted Janaka, a *karma-yogi* (selfless actor), as his disciple. This, Bhave argues, proves that '[y]oga and *sannyasa* are two modes of the same reality',[51] but for the seeker, *karma-yoga*, being both 'the way and the goal', is superior.[52] Desai, meanwhile, attempts to resolve the Tilak–Shankaracharya disagreement over the culmination of selfless action by resorting back to the Gandhian emphasis on means, claiming that an 'earnest aspirant will throw all the energies in the pursuit of the goal, absorbed in the means and not even thinking of the goal'.[53] Both Bhave's defence of *karma-yoga* and Desai's argument therefore reiterate Gandhi's insistence on the identity of the means and end, even though Bhave and Desai conspicuously refrain from commenting on Tilak's approval of violence undertaken in a spirit of selfless detachment.

Desai, nevertheless, is compelled by his own agenda of globalizing to respond to contemporary scholars of Indology like the historian of religion, Robert Ernest Hume. Hume had argued that the Gita, under the influence of Upanishads, teaches that 'moral distinctions do not obtain for the man who has metaphysical knowledge'.[54] Desai states that Hume's 'misinterpretation' was 'due to the unfortunate English word "Knowledge" which has not the content of Jnana which far from meaning mere metaphysical knowledge means a new vision' but rather, like the Greek word *gnosis*, which 'means a full unification with the Universal Self'.[55] He returns to the figure of Hitler, whom he contrasts with a man, rare like Arjuna, who 'had cleansed himself of all desire for sovereignty, enjoyment and life' and therefore was entitled to take up arms as an instrument of divine will.[56]

He proceeds to quell the fears of 'Christian friends' that the Gita could be used in the defence of murder by suggesting that the 'Hindu' has examples of 'many Christs' (like King Shibi who risked his life for a dove) to follow while conceding that the 'test, after all, is not the claim advanced by the doer of the deed, but how the world judges him'.[57]

The Mahabharata as (Non-)History

Desai reverts to Tilak while addressing a concern that eludes Gandhi but is of pivotal importance, he assumes, to his target readership: the dating of the Gita. He cites the position of Tilak, who had used Pali texts to show that the current redaction of the Gita can be traced back to the fifth century BCE since it predated the development of Mahayana Buddhism. He also refers to the scholarship of S. Radhakrishnan and the British Indologist W. D. Hill, who date the Gita to the fifth century BCE and the second century BCE, respectively, to highlight how theories of Christian origins of the Gita are 'universally discredited'.[58] It is noteworthy that Desai feels the need to deliberate and repudiate the theories on possible Christian influence on the Gita, which had been proposed by scholars such as Albrecht Weber and the Catholic clergyman Franz Lorinser in his 1869 verse translation of the Gita in the middle half of the nineteenth century. As Bergunder has shown, such theories had been debunked by European Indologists such as Max Muller and Richard Garbe early on, even as in India they had generated a nationalist outcry, prompting scholars such as

Kashinath Trimbak Telang to provide public lectures in repudiation of the text in 1874.[59] That Desai felt the need to address this issue, which had already been rejected in the domain of European Indology while writing in 1933, reflects the endurance of the controversy and associated nationalist angst among English-educated Indians such as him and his readership. While the idea of Christian origins had been discarded, tracing parallels between the New Testament and the Gita remained a steady component of European Indological scholarship in the early twentieth century, appearing in works of E. W. Hopkins (1895, 1901), Paul Deussen (1906, 1911), and Richard Garbe (1914).[60] It is perhaps the ambivalent implications generated by such modes of scholarship which caused a certain intellectual discomfort for Indian nationalist scholars. Tilak responds by making a counterclaim that 'the principles of Self-Identification, Renunciation, Non-Enmity, and Devotion, to be found in the New testament of the Bible, must have been taken into the Christian religion from Buddhism, and therefore indirectly from the Vedic religion'.[61] While Desai does not reiterate Tilak's claim, the fact that he feels the need to reiterate the repudiation of the 'Christian influence' theory and his insistence that Hindus have had 'many Christs' to model their conduct on reflect the concern to universalize the Gita which subsumes and simultaneously supersedes Christian values. This particular case also drives home Bergunder's argument about the need to adopt an entangled approach to the development of global Indological knowledge production,[62] by underscoring how the Indian scholars played crucial interjectory roles in the endurance, appropriation, and reframing of Indological agendas.

Nevertheless, while Gandhi himself, like the Theosophists, read the Gita as an allegory, the project of globalizing the Gandhian interpretation could not proceed without acknowledging, if not addressing, the question of the historicity of the text or the figure of Krishna. As shown earlier, an intertextual engagement with contemporary Indological scholarship, which Desai's presumed readership of Western-educated Indian youth were well-versed in, was crucial to the exercise. In the *Gita Rahasya*, Tilak meticulously situates the historical Krishna of the Bhagavata cult and the Bharati war, as well as the ur-epic *Bharata* inspired by it in 1400 and 900 BCE, respectively.[63] Desai, in contrast, briefly assures his readers that Gandhi shares their (assumed) interest in historical details about Krishna and 'Krishna Vasudeva worship, i.e. the Bhagawat Dharma'.[64] However, he then proceeds to underscore the irrelevance of historicity in the Gandhian approach to the Gita, claiming that the discovery of the historical Krishna or the original Gita will not alter the 'essence or universality of the message'[65] Gandhi had extracted from it.

Tilak, in the fashion of contemporary Indologists, assumes the historicity of the Bharati war and, using historical-critical arguments, refutes theories of the Gita being a later interpolation to the Mahabharata. In his opinion, *Jaya*, an earlier 'historical book' which chronicled the historical victory of the Pandavas, was later expanded into the Mahabharata 'which dealt both with history and with Ethics'. The Gita, as the ethical compendium within the epic, 'expound[ed] the Energistic Bhagavata religion [without which] it was not possible to justify the deeds ... of the heroes of the Mahabharata'.[66] The very centrality of the Gita as a measure against which the morality of the actions of the protagonists could be judged implied for Tilak the inseparability of the Gita from the rest of the 'historical narrative' of the war in the Mahabharata.

The Gandhian hermeneutic imperative of reading the Gita as a text on non-violence, on the other hand, necessitated the disavowal of the Mahabharata as a historical narrative. At the very outset of his *Anasaktiyoga*, Gandhi states that the Mahabharata 'was not a historical work' but a 'religious poem', physical warfare being an allegory for the 'duel that perpetually went on in the hearts [of] mankind' with 'Krishna of the Gita [being] perfection and right knowledge personified'.[67] This he substantiates by underscoring the 'superhuman or subhuman origins' ascribed to the protagonists in the 'Adi Parva' through which he felt 'the great Vyasa made short work the history of kings and their peoples'.[68] Gandhi infers that the Mahabharata teaches the futility of warfare since 'the victors shed tears of sorrow and repentance' and 'the characteristics of the perfected man of the Gita' are 'inconsistent with the rules of conduct governing the relations between warring parties'.[69] Desai, in a similar fashion, attempts to support Gandhi's argument against the 'description of the Mahabharata as a historical war-epic' by underscoring the historical improbability of Sanjaya replying to a question on the events of the battlefield with an 'intensely philosophical dialogue'.[70] He then proceeds to highlight the allegorical implications already drawn by other interpreters with Dhritarashtra, the blind king, as 'the individual ego blindly holding on to the flesh ... listening to the dialogue between Krishna, the In-dweller, and Arjuna ... pure intellect obeying His behest and fighting the forces of darkness and winning the victory'.[71] As Desai's reference, which resembles the symbolic interpretation of Annie Besant,[72] the leader of the Theosophical Society, implies, the Gandhians were well aware of other 'interpretive communities' who read the warfare alluded to in the Gita as allegory. Theosophical discourses, in fact, introduced the allegorical approach to the reading of the Gita while popularizing it as 'a universal text acclaimed by all nations and a mirror of the complex history of the world'.[73]

However, the Mahabharata, Desai concedes, could still be considered a legitimate work of history without accepting the historicity of the Gita following the example of 'Thucydides, the most conscientious historian known to antiquity, [who] did not hesitate to introduce such imaginary dialogues between ... historical characters in order to elucidate situations'.[74] The Gita, nevertheless, was 'a profoundly meaningful poem' of the sort that employs 'semi-historical incidents ... for depicting imperishable visions of the soul of man' that transcend historical particularities of context. Desai establishes this by mapping the Gita onto a global comparative framework where the author of the Gita is posited against the English playwright William Shakespeare. Arjuna's mind, like Lady Blanch in *King John* and Brutus in *Julius Ceasar*, suffers 'the nature of an insurrection', and Vyasa 'put him face to face with God – as Shakespeare put Brutus face to face with his self – and made God quell the insurrection and surround him with ... peace and bliss'. The central teaching of the Gita therefore is a universal method for the resolution of doubts by way of an 'internal conversation' with the 'Divine [in Arjuna and] in every one of us',[75] which justifies its projection as the 'Bible of humanity'.[76]

The interpretation of the Gita as a Gandhian text thus involved a reconceptualization of the historicity that could be safely associated with the Gita as well as the Mahabharata narrative without reducing it to a proponent of warfare. From a treatise on ethical action retrospectively added to legitimize the 'historical' actions of the protagonists within a chronicle of history as Tilak saw it, the Gita in Gandhian thought becomes the 'jewel ... set in the field of gold of the great epic'.[77] An ahistorical poem of universal significance, the Gita in Gandhian hermeneutic could be meaningfully interpreted by reducing its battlefield setting to an allegory and without reference to the particularities of a historical Krishna or the Bharati war.

While Gandhi was sceptical about the historicity of the war depicted in the Mahabharata, he was not averse to reading a different history into the epic. He rejected conventional historiography as a chronicle of acts of unreason like violent revolutions, social injustice, and 'wars of the world', which comprised, in his opinion, a 'record of every interruption of the working of the force of love or of the soul'.[78] Instead, the 'real history of mankind' reflects the 'progress of man along the steep and narrow spiritual path through the practice of truth and non-violence' till he 'has become like unto God'.[79] Such a 'real history' of the inner moral and spiritual progress of man, Gandhi believed, was to be found in the Mahabharata, which underscored the futility of war in comparison to which 'Gibbon and Morley ... [with their chronicle of expansion of man's power over nature or territories, were] inferior editions'.[80] The 'names and forms' in the Mahabharata 'come and go', but the permanent 'truth [which] transcends history' and which the 'Hindu ancestors' recorded within the epic narrative 'by ignoring history ... and by building on slight events their philosophical structure ... eludes the historian of events'.[81] Building upon this premise set forth by Gandhi, Desai elaborates that the author of the Mahabharata was not a mere reporter but a poet who *lived* the 'doctrine of detachment ... or work in the spirit of sacrifice' and 'left his experience as an abiding heritage of mankind' through the Gita.[82]

Bhave, however, while admitting that the Gita was where Vyasa has 'presented the central message of the whole epic',[83] did not find the events depicted in the Mahabharata as dispensable as they were for Gandhi. This is evident from what he has to say about the nature of Vyasa's writing: 'With perfect detachment Vyasa, the great sage, graphically depicts ... the complex reality of the vast web of worldly life' which is like 'a fabric woven with ... threads of good and evil' from which everybody can 'take freely as much as he wants'.[84] It is this encyclopedic quality which made the Mahabharata 'a comprehensive treatise on the working of society'[85] for Bhave. Consequently, he reverted to the Mahabharata as a cautionary tale of social strife that would inevitably follow inequality in the distribution of land, when he was campaigning for the Bhoodan Movement. This is evident from the eyewitness account of Hallam Tennyson, a British associate who accompanied Bhave on his *padayatra* across the country:

> the Pandavas ... fought the classic battle ... [because] [t]heir relatives refused to let them inherit their rightful share of land.... So will the poor of to-day, says Vinoba, if we continue to whittle down their rights.... Finally there is the forgotten brother, Korana, ... the sixth son who had been hidden away at birth and whom Vinoba sees as symbolic of the submerged sixth in modern society. He it was who poisoned the ears of one branch of the family against the other, and who, armed with the bracelet which his mother had given him, became all-powerful in battle. Do we want, Vinoba asks, to forget our sixth brother like the Pandavas did and so stir up hatred and strife?[86]

Bhave's analogy, which linked the war in the Mahabharata with an impending social unrest arising out of the denial of land rights in modern India, hints at the context of conflict in which the Bhoodan Movement came to be launched. The communist-led agitation in Telengana against the landed classes in 1951 prompted Bhave to walk on foot to bring about a change of heart by convincing communists to give up violence. At the Pochampalli village, the Harijans told him that they supported the communists because they required 80 acres of land to make a living, which they believed the communists could provide for them. A member of the landed elite then voluntarily donated a hundred acres of land, prompting Bhave to launch the Bhoodan Movement to bring about a systematic non-violent redressal of the inequality in land distribution. In the course of his campaign, Bhave repeatedly reverted to the metaphor of five sons and the 'submerged sixth', requesting that a family of five sons accept him as 'the sixth son, the representative of the poor, and donate to [him] one sixth of [their] land to share with the landless'.[87] The 'submerged sixth' notably was more than a metaphor in the Bhoodan discourse and served as a concrete figure. Bhave demanded of his donors one-sixth of their land on the basis of his own 'mathematical' calculation that a 'complete redistribution of land and property, as also of power' required the reallocation of 50 million acres, which comprised about one-sixth of the arable land in India.[88]

The Gita as a Dialectical History of Non-Violence

Having explored the varying degrees to which Gandhi and the Gandhians were willing to accord historicity to the narrative of the Mahabharata and the Gita, I now proceed to disentangle the alternative history Gandhi and, subsequently, Bhave retrieved from them. This comprised a narrative of dialectical interplay through which mankind progressed towards a state of complete non-violence.

The Gita and Gandhian Dialectical Historicism

In Gandhi's opinion, Vyasa, the author of the Mahabharata, was not a mere reporter of events but a poet who recorded in the Gita what, in his experience, was 'the most excellent way to attain self-realization':[89] 'From the bitter experiences of desire for fruit the author of the Gita discovered the path of renunciation of fruit and put it before the world in a most convincing manner.'[90] As has been discussed previously in this chapter, experience is a keyword in Gandhian hermeneutics and the source from which Gandhi claims his authority to interpret the Gita. By asserting that Vyasa, too, drew from his experiences the message he encrypted into the Gita, Gandhi constructs Vyasa into a precedent for his own unconventional interpretive method based on lived experience. Such a construction accords legitimacy to his interpretive authority, which he claims to derive by following the example set by the author of the Gita himself, and glosses over his self-professed lack of other qualities like Sanskrit scholasticism, which were conventionally associated with authoritative commentators on the Gita.

The fact that the Gita was 'a great religious poem' bearing a profound truth did not imply that Vyasa had 'worked out all its great consequences',[91] which, Gandhi states, accounted for his use of war as a setting of the poem at a historical moment when the contradiction between war and non-violence was not apparent. However, Vyasa had, based on his experience with *anasaktiyoga*, opened up a hermeneutic possibility by attributing novel meanings to words in the Gita. He had, in Gandhi's opinion, transformed the semantics of *yajna* (sacrifice), which signified animal sacrifice in prior times, to mean 'concentration on God' and 'bodily labor for service'. *Sannyasa* had similarly been transmuted into 'work in the spirit of no work' instead of 'cessation of all activity' in his usage. As Gandhi saw it, Vyasa had, 'by extending meaning of words, taught [his readers] to imitate him'. From his 40 years of experience to enforcing the message of the Gita in his life following the example of Vyasa, Gandhi had inferred that 'perfect realization is impossible without perfect observance of ahimsa',[92] which made ethical action derived from the Gita in contemporary times incompatible with warfare or violence.

Gandhi invested the concept of *anasaktiyoga*, or selfless action, which he believed to be the central message of the Gita, with a teleological structure of dialectical historicism. He thus states that the *anasaktiyoga* taught by Vyasa in the Gita is a concept which undergoes constant historical development as man progresses from cannibalism to the collective adoption of the doctrine of non-violence:

> If we turn our eye to the time of which history has any record down to our time, we shall find that man has been steadily progressing towards ahimsa. Our remote ancestors were cannibals. Then came a time when they were fed up with cannibalism and they began to live on chase. Next came a stage when man was ashamed of leading the life of a wandering hunter. He therefore took to agriculture and depended principally on mother earth for his food. Thus from being a nomad he settled down to a civilized stable life, founded villages and towns, and from member of a family he became member of a community and a nation. All these signs are signs of progressive ahimsa and diminishing himsa.[93]

Behind this historical progression, Gandhi found the 'operation of the Divine Spirit in history'. Joan V. Bondurant has called this process 'Gandhian dialectics' whereby conflict between opposing ideas, people, and classes is resolved through the means of *satyagraha*, which brings about unity of the opposing sides on a higher plane of truth.[94] Such a historical evolution towards a non-violent and just social order did not come 'fully fashioned out of God's hands but ha[d] to be carved out through repeated experiments and repeated failures by'[95] individuals who are 'incarnations of Divine Spirit'. These 'avatars' secured the advance of mankind by investing 'human history with new meanings',[96] and it was their footsteps Gandhi and his associates sought to follow in generating new meanings of selfless action through their 'experiments with truth'.

Bhave, as a firm believer in Gandhian ideologies, grafts Gandhi's dialectical historicism of man's progress towards a non-violent social order in his reading of the Gita. Like Gandhi, he identifies the battlefield of Gita as the allegorical site of the dialectical interplay of vices and virtues that takes place within the human mind. While discussing the 16th chapter of the Gita titled 'Daivasura Sampada Bibhaga Yoga', which distinguishes the divine qualities (*daivisampad*) from demoniacal (*asuric*) ones, he claims that all the virtues listed in the Gita 'are contained in truth and non-violence', with fearlessness as 'commander' and humility as 'rearguard'. Therefore, an individual ought to 'carry ... out experiments in truth and nonviolence' till '*perfection*'[97] – which he identifies as the 'Purushottam Yoga' mentioned by the Gita, translated by him as 'Supreme Self' – is achieved at social, national, and global levels.[98]

Moreover, he develops Gandhi's idea further, identifying 'four stages in the [historical] development of non-violence' marked by experiments of sages in the past. The first such experiment was made when the 'special class of fighters', the Kshatriyas, whom non-violent Brahmins had invested with the duty of protecting society from violent attacks, themselves turned 'against the people'. Parashuram, a non-violent Brahmin, made a flawed attempt to counteract their violence by resorting to violence himself, which failed to restore non-violence since the 'seed of violence survived'. By the 'age of Rama', the Brahmins had decided to sacrifice their lives, if necessary, but not commit violence, choosing instead to entrust Kshatriyas with the task again. Thus, 'Sage Vishwamitra ... brought Rama and Lakshman to protect his *yagna* (sacrificial worship) from the demons'. Though such a form of non-violence had 'the element of sacrifice in it, [there was an inherent weakness in expecting] protection from others'.[99] 'The third experiment' was carried out by 'saints of the medieval times' and led to the perfection of non-violence and truth at individual planes. The Gandhian *satyagraha* was to constitute the 'fourth experiment' through which 'the whole society [was to be] engaged in resisting violence through non-violent means'.[100]

The Gita as a Blueprint of a Collective Society

Such a conceptualization of historical progress through the evolution of experience and experiments towards the collective adoption of non-violence, as I will show in this final section of the chapter, required Bhave to reconfigure the Gandhian principle of *satyagraha* and transform it from an individual practice of the Gandhian to a collectivist enterprise. Not surprisingly, he derived his vision of a collective order with non-violence as its foundation from the Gita, adapting its contents in light of the changing circumstances of the Cold War as well as the popularity of other contending visions of collective social change.

While Gandhi did envision a society based on collective non-violence, the *anasaktiyoga* of the Gita represented for him a guide to an individual *satyagrahi* on how to act in accordance with truth and non-violence in the midst of social and political conflict. Bhave, however, was faced with the question of merging the individual with the social, of re-conceptualizing *satyagraha* as a tool which could reconcile the pursuit of inner spiritual development with collective progress towards *sarvodaya*, or 'a society in which the good of all is achieved'.[101] *Sarvodaya* (the welfare of all) was the Gujarati concept Gandhi formulated, inspired by John Ruskin's work *Unto This Last*, which advocated for the dignity of all forms of labour and was based on the philosophy that 'the good of the individual is contained in the good of all'.[102] However, it was Bhave who transformed it into a social movement for the establishment of a non-violent egalitarian society.

Bhave had already mapped out a notion of *yajna* as 'free' social action in the course of his *Talks on the Gita* (1932), particularly while discussing the 17th chapter ('Shraddha Traya Vibhaga Yoga'). This chapter of the Gita underscores the difference between social and individual actions undertaken with *sattvic*, *rajasic*, and *tamasic* intentions.[103] Bhave, in his commentary, renamed it as *karyakramyoga* and redefined *yajna* (sacrifice), *dana* (donation), and *tapas* (austerities) with new semantics of social and individual action suitable for the seeker of 'freedom'. *Yajna*, which he defined as 'productive labour', was to be done in the spirit of sacrifice so that it would become a means to reimburse what has been taken from nature. *Dana* and *tapas* are transformed into service rendered to pay off the debt owed to society and austerities undertaken for the purification of the wear and tear of the body, respectively.

Gandhi had endorsed spinning, which he called *sutrayajna* (spinning as sacrifice), alongside celibacy as 'practices in the materiality of action as a characteristic of everyday life' that would help a *satyagrahi* escape the 'idealizing violence' that accompanied any 'instrumental action' undertaken to realize a future-oriented vision.[104] Bhave, who was a distinguished spinner among the Gandhians, also identifies spinning as one among the three moral actions that he clubs together under the umbrella term of *yajna* (others being *dravyayajna*, or 'sacrifice with material gifts', and *tapoyajna*, or 'sacrifice with austerities'). Such *yajna*, in his opinion, are 'free' acts devoid of altruistic instrumentality, 'the secret of [their] freedom being [their] regularity'.[105] Such daily actions were to be undertaken to reimburse the debt every individual owed to the three institutions of nature, society, and the human body since it is only with such a reimbursement that an individual could submerge into the collective and become free. Therefore, the 'thin yarn', Bhave claimed, was to 'link [the Gandhian actor] to the society, to the people, to the Lord. [Just as] Yashoda saw the whole universe in the mouth of child Krishna, [the spinner charged with the mantra of sacrifice and free of instrumentality] will see the universe in the thin yarn.'[106]

However, there is a noticeable shift when the post-Gandhi Bhave explains the meaning of *bhoodanyajna*.[107] He was no longer just a disciple of Gandhi reiterating the course of ethical action for individual Gandhian seekers but the leader of a movement aimed at altering the nature of society through an alternative blueprint for collective action. Action taken to effect such change, by its very own logic, demanded the restoration of instrumentality to individual action. The new model of Gandhian action for those involved in *bhoodanyajna* was therefore *samyayoga*, a term Bhave coined to denote 'spiritually inspired non-violent and scientific effort for the achievement of socio-economic equality in which the emphasis is as much on the inner evolution of man as on changing the outward form of society'. 'In the age of science,' Bhave claims, 'samyayoga [which] was so long the roof, ... has to become the foundation'[108] for a *satyagrahi* who, while pursuing 'a state of spiritual quiescence or *Nivrithi*' could not give up *pravrithi*, or world-affirmation.[109]

It is important to note that Bhave derived the ideological basis for a 'non-violent revolution' with the aim of bringing about a 'Samyayogi social structure' in which 'all land, all property, and all wealth should belong to society' from the concept of '*Atmopamya* (like-Self)' or the precept to 'treat others in the same manner as [they] want to be treated'.[110] The striking similarity of the term *samyayogi* with *samyavad*, or communism, as well as Bhave's conception of an egalitarian social order based on collective ownership, reveals the ideological influence of Marxist discourses on him, besides, of course, the context of communist-led conflict within which the Bhoodan campaign originated as an alternative mode of transformative action. Notwithstanding his commitment to Gandhian principles, the impact of Marxist ideas on Bhave is evident from his remark: 'If the last century were boiled down, the residue would be Marx ... and Gandhi.'[111] Merging and tweaking the ideologies of both, Bhave suggested that change in relations of production and removal of inequality could be brought into reality neither through violence incited by Marxist activism nor by a rejection of modern scientific apparatus as Gandhi envisioned, but through *samyayoga*.

Sarvodaya, which Bhave translated into practical terms as 'collective non-violence', was a product of a dialectical resolution of the conflict between 'the cultures of India and the West', representing the union of 'non-violence [which] was a result of self-knowledge' and 'the social point of view [that was] a product of western science', through which the 'Kingdom of Heaven could be realized on this earth'.[112] In the Atomic Age, when 'Science has brought it within the power of a few to destroy the universe', the spiritual power of *satyagraha* could effectively be wielded to solve international problems only by individuals who 'transcend ... the limits of mind [which is subordinate to the power of science] and attains ... the supramental level of consciousness'.[113] *Satyagraha* therefore could no longer be merely selfless non-violent action of an individual in the pursuit of truth, as Gandhi saw it, but required the foundation of 'an inviolable law of truth', with science as the basis and the transformation of a *satyagrahi* into a *visva-manava*, or universal man.[114] 'Collective non-violence' could only become possible through a *satyagraha* that had the integral transformation of society, or 'collective samadhi', as its goal.[115] This was a realization that dawned on him when he visited the spot where Ramakrishna Paramahamsa, the noted Bengali saint, had attained *samadhi* (a trance-like state which is considered a marker of an exalted yogic state where the human becomes one with the divine), in the course of his *padayatra* (nationwide travel by foot to promote the Sarvodaya movement) in Bengal. Such an experience left him convinced that the aim of the Bhoodan campaign was 'to give shape to the collective form of that Samadhi which Shri Ramakrishna Paramahamsa had experienced [there]'.[116]

Such a concept of *samyayoga*, which marked Bhave's leap from the individual to the collective domain of action that was oriented towards bringing about 'collective samadhi', came quite close to the Integral Yoga doctrine developed by the revolutionary nationalist-turned-spiritual leader Aurobindo Ghose. Aurobindo, who had made the French colony of Pondicherry in southern India his base, also claimed that his yoga was aimed at the spiritual evolution of mankind to 'supramental consciousness'. Bhave's *samyayoga* therefore – as J. N. Mohanty, who edited a series of lectures given by Bhave in the course of the Bhoodan Movement, aptly remarked – represented the 'bridging [of] the gap that had separated Gandhian thought from ... Aurobindonism'.[117] Bhave had read Aurobindo's *The Life Divine* while Gandhi was alive and admitted to having been as impressed by it as he was by Karl Marx's *Das Kapital* (Capital),

while recounting his visit to Aurobindo's ashram in Pondicherry in 1956.
While referring to Aurobindo with admiration in the course of his lectures,
Bhave ambiguously averts claims that he had become his follower, claiming that
thoughts on a novel experiment to bring about a social transcendence from the
individual realizations of saints to a collective consciousness that was suitable to
the post-atomic 'scientific age' were 'not new to' him.[118]

Irrespective of whether Vinoba derived his insights from Aurobindo, the
spiritual evolutionist perspective alongside his emphasis on collectivism marks
a noteworthy shift introduced by Bhave in Gandhian philosophy in a crucial
historical context. With India's attainment of independence from colonial rule,
the goal of the Gandhian struggle under the leadership of Bhave shifted from
swarajya (self-rule) to *sarvodaya* in post-independence India, rife with socio-
economic disparity. Such a change required that techniques of *satyagraha* be
reinvented to suit the needs of the 'non-violent revolution'. This intellectual
drift also coincided with and was somewhat informed by a more global role
Bhave found himself in, as a leading Gandhian philosopher and activist. The
widespread publicity of the Bhoodan Movement in the international press
put Bhave on a global platform. At the same time, the ideological impact of
Gandhian ideology on the struggle of Martin Luther King Jr for civil rights and
racial justice in America from 1955 instilled new aspirations for the application
of Gandhian action against social injustice on a global scale. This is evident from
the conversations Martin Luther King Jr had with Bhave, Jayprakash Narayan,
and other Gandhians during his visit to India in 1959, in the course of which
he accompanied them on a Bhoodan *padayatra* to Kishangarh.[119] All of these
compelled Bhave to re-evaluate the relevance of Gandhian activism in the Cold
War era, charged with a looming nuclear threat in the backdrop. Like Gandhi's
conceptualisation of *satyagraha* while reading the Gita in terms of Leo Tolstoy's
non-violent resistance in South Africa and Desai's search for *karma-yogi*s across
the world, Bhave's *samyayoga* therefore marked another 'global moment' in the
hermeneutic experiments that mediated the ideological interface between the
Gita and Gandhian philosophy.

Conclusion

In this chapter, I have opened the way for an intellectual history of Gandhian
thought, which does not exclusively focus on the figure of Gandhi but also
recognizes the intellectual agency of his associates in working out the global
applicability of Gandhian action. The Gita being the ideological source of

Gandhi's conceptualization of non-violent action in a spirit of selflessness, any attempt to globalize Gandhian thought inevitably involved the intellectual exercise of rethinking the Gita in universal terms and the production of new meanings consistent with Gandhian philosophy. A study of such exercises by the Gandhians, as I have shown, could be situated within the broader entangled history of global exchanges which had come to inform Orientalist and nationalist engagements with the Gita since the nineteenth century.

I have therefore shown that Gandhi translates the Gita as *Anasaktiyoga*, which endorses selfless non-violent action in pursuit of renunciation and truth, in the shadow of the immensely popular *Gita Rahasya*, a rival interpretation by Tilak which draws ideological support from the Gita for a violent struggle waged for the greater good. Tilak's scriptural–intellectual authority being uncontestable by Gandhi, who is self-professedly lacking in it, Gandhi constructs for himself an alternative hermeneutic authority. He claims to derive such authority from his 'experiments' to shape his life in accordance with the message of the Gita, thus launching a claim that would resonate in the writings of his followers.

However, unlike Gandhi, Desai and Bhave could not avoid the seminal presence of Tilak while clarifying pivotal questions on the origins, nature, and doctrinal aspects of the Gita even while addressing two divergent sets of readership and audiences: scholars with Western education and political prisoners in Dhule Jail, respectively. This generates schisms between the writings of Gandhi and Desai, as the latter, in an attempt to construct a global pantheon of exemplary actors who could be shown to have performed 'selfless action' as endorsed by Gandhi, ends up incorporating figures who had resorted to violence, though only reluctantly. The anxiety to globalize the 'interpretive community' that would share Gandhi's approach to the Gita as the 'gospel of selfless action', nevertheless, drives Desai to question Tilak's treatment of the Mahabharata as a historical narrative of war, in order to assert the universal relevance of the Gita as a philosophical discourse of timeless appeal embedded in an ahistorical setting of a metaphorical battlefield.

Gandhi and Bhave, however, proceed to embed the Gita and the Mahabharata into an alternative historicism which unfolds with the dialectical interplay of the soul-force. The Mahabharata becomes the 'real history of mankind' that records this dialectical progress, with the 'Purushottam Yoga' of the Gita redefined as a state of perfect truth and non-violence in which such a progress would culminate. Instruments of such historical change were identified as 'experiments with truth' performed by sages such as Vyasa, who produced new notions of morality and social action at different historical stages. It was this hermeneutic precedent set by the likes of Vyasa that Gandhi and Bhave claimed to emulate by underscoring the indispensability of non-violence in performing selfless action sanctified by the Gita.

As this chapter shows, with the independence of India and the death of Gandhi, ideological shifts appeared in the Gandhian movement and discourse, led mostly by Bhave, Gandhi's spiritual heir. As the goal shifted from *swarajya* to *sarvodaya*, or the removal of social inequality, and Cold War tensions elevated the threat of nuclear war in the Atomic Age, Bhave was compelled to rethink the relevance of the Gandhian mode of struggle at a global level and redefine the relationship between the individual and the collective. Departing from action solely committed in the spirit of self-negation shorn of all instrumentality, Bhave championed *samyayoga*, a pursuit of individual self-realization which could co-exist with non-violent action to bring about collective social transformation. Bhave conceptualized *samyayoga* (launched in India in the form of the Bhoodan Movement) as a global movement with the aim to establish collective non-violence through the realization of 'Purushottam Yoga' of the Gita on a global scale. In such a reconceptualization of Gandhian ethical action operable globally, Bhave derives inspiration from not only the historical collectivism of Marxists but also the spiritual evolutionist discourse of the revolutionary nationalist-turned-yogi Aurobindo Ghose.

To conclude, this chapter has shown that the Gita continued to enjoy significance in the ideological reproduction of Gandhian philosophy and moral action by the 'interpretive community' of Gandhians, both during Gandhi's lifetime and after his death. In doing so, I have problematized the dual tendencies of individual-centricity as well as the over-emphasis on Western influences on Gandhi that have characterized the global intellectual histories of Gandhian thought. By decentring but not deposing Gandhi the individual, the chapter has shown how the hermeneutic encounters between Gandhians and the Gita, along with the Mahabharata, constituted 'global moments' of significance for the intellectual history of Gandhian thought.

Notes

1. M. K. Gandhi, 'Anasaktiyoga', in *The Gospel of Selfless Action: Or The Gita According to Gandhi*, trans. Mahadev Desai (Ahmedabad: Navajivan Mudranalaya, 1946), 132.

2. Richard H. Davis, 'Introduction', in *The Bhagavad Gita: A Biography*, by Richard H. Davis, 1–7 (Princeton [NJ] and Oxford: Princeton University Press, 2015).

3. Shruti Kapila and Faisal Devji, 'Introduction', in *Political Thought in Action: The Bhagavad Gita and Modern India*, ed. Shruti Kapila and Faisal Devji, ix–xv (Delhi: Cambridge University Press, 2013), xii.

4. Notable in this regard is Martin Green's comparative study of the historical backgrounds of Leo Tolstoy and Gandhi, which accounts for their interest and influence on each other in shaping the importance of non-violence in anti-imperial action. Martin Green, *The Origins of Non-Violence: Tolstoy and Gandhi in Their Historical Settings* (University Park, PA: Pennsylvania State University Press, 1986). Recent works like that of Michael Bergunder have pointed out the role of the esotericism, especially the Theosophical Society and some Jain associates, such as Virchand Gandhi and Raychandbhai Mehta, in informing Gandhi's views on Hinduism with Advaita Vedanta as its central philosophy. See Michael Bergunder, 'Experiments with Theosophical Truth: Gandhi, Esotericism, and Global Religious History', *Journal of the American Academy of Religion* 82, no. 2: 398–426.

5. Gandhi, 'Anasaktiyoga'.

6. *Satyagraha*, meaning holding to truth firmly, was a term used by Gandhi to refer to his philosophy of passive resistance.

7. Davis proceeds from the original location of the text within the 'broader devotional cult surrounding the divine character of Krishna' and meanders its way through the different ontological positions derived by medieval commentators, the popularity of the text among colonial enthusiasts, German Romantics, and its subsequent endorsement as the 'national text' meant to provide national cohesiveness and ideological support for anti-colonial action in the works of nationalists. Davis subsequently also explores four adaptations of the Gita since the Second World War, including the historically contextualized version by the Dutch Indologist J. A. B. van Buitenen, the poet Stephen Mitchell who situates the Gita in a perennial philosophy perspective, the philosopher S. Radhakrishnan who saw in the text a drive towards reconciliation, and Swami Prabhupada, the founder of the International Society for Krishna Consciousness (ISKON), whose rendition was the first transnational version to ground the Gita in terms of the Indian Bhakti tradition conceptualizing Krishna unambiguously as supreme reality in order to transform the reader into a Krishna devotee. Davis, *The Bhagavad Gita*. See also the work of Catherine Robinson who traces through the multiple commentaries on the Gita and many interpretations and images of the Hindu tradition. Catherine A. Robinson, *Interpretations of the Bhagavad-Gita and Images of the Hindu Tradition: The Song of the Lord* (London: Routledge, 2006).

8. Bhave defines samyayoga as 'levelling the field' in order to establish 'an equilibrium or an equality in society'. Vinoba Bhave, *The Principles and Philosophy of The Bhoodan Yagna* (Tanjore: Sarvodaya Prachuralaya, 1955), 5.

9. Angelika Malinar, *The Bhagavadgita: Doctrines and Contexts* (Cambridge, UK: Cambridge University Press, 2007).

10. Sibaji Bandyopadhyay, *Three Essays on the Mahabharata: Exercises in Literary Hermeneutics* (Hyderabad: Orient BlackSwan, 2016).

11. Kanad Sinha, *From Dasarajna to Kuruksetra: Making of a Historical Tradition* (New Delhi: Oxford University Press, 2021).

12. Michael Bergunder, 'Hinduism, Theosophy, and the Bhagavad Gita within a Global Religious History of the Nineteenth Century', in *Theosophy across Boundaries: Transcultural and Interdisciplinary Perspectives on a Modern Esoteric Movement*, ed. Hans Martin Krämer and Julian Strube, 65–108 (Albany, NY: State University of New York Press, 2020).

13. For a detailed exposition on Tilak and Gandhi's differing interpretations of the Gita as a treatise of sociopolitical activism, see Robinson, *Interpretations of the Bhagavad-Gita*, 54–64. Davis also discusses the resonances and dissonances between Gandhi's and Tilak's interpretations and points out the specific junctures at which Gandhi diverts from Tilak in Davis, *The Bhagavad Gita*.

14. Bal Gangadhar Tilak, Śrimad Bhagavadgītā-Rahasya, *or Karma-Yoga-Śāstra*, vol. 1, trans. B. S. Sukthankar (Poona: Tilak Brothers, 1935), xxv.

15. Robert W. Stevenson, 'Tilak and the Bhagavadgita's Doctrine of Karmayoga', in *Modern Indian Interpreters of the Bhagavadgita*, ed. Robert N. Minor, 44–60 (Albany, NY: State University of New York Press, 1986), 58.

16. Bal Gangadhar Tilak cited in Dipesh Chakrabarty and Rochona Majumdar, 'Gandhi's Gita and Politics as Such', in *Political Thought in Action: The Bhagavad Gita and Modern India*, ed. Shruti Kapila and Faisal Devji, 66–87 (Delhi: Cambridge University Press, 2013), 71–77.

17. Gandhi, 'Anasaktiyoga', 124.

18. Vinoba Bhave, *Moved by Love: The Memoirs of Vinoba Bhave*, ed. Kalindi, trans. Marjorie Sykes (Wardha: Paramdham Prakashan, 1994), 58.

19. Vinoba Bhave cited in Green, *The Origins of Non-Violence*, 228.

20. M. K. Gandhi, 'Brute Force', in *Hind Swaraj or Indian Home Rule*, by M. K. Gandhi, 62–67 (Ahmedabad: Navajivan Publishing House, 1938), 63.

21. Gandhi, 'Anasaktiyoga', 128.

22. Gandhi, 'Anasaktiyoga', 131.

23. Tridip Suhrud, 'Gandhi's Key Writings: In Search of Unity', in *The Cambridge Companion to Gandhi*, ed. Judith M. Brown and Anthony Parel, 71–92 (New York: Cambridge University Press, 2011), 75.

24. Tilak, Śrimad Bhagavadgītā-Rahasya, xliv.

25. Gandhi, 'Anasaktiyoga', 126.

26. 'Mahadev Desai', Associates and Disciples of Mahatma Gandhi, https://www.mkgandhi.org/associates/Mahadev.htm (accessed on 10 October 2020).

27. For a detailed analysis of the grammatical, lexical, contextual, structural, and comparative frameworks employed by Bhave in his interpretation of the Gita, see Boyd H. Wilson, 'Vinoba Bhave's Talks on the Gita', in *Modern Indian Interpreters of the Bhagavad Gita*, ed. Robert N. Minor, 110–30 (Albany, NY: State University of New York Press, 1986).

28. Wilson, 'Vinoba Bhave's Talks on the Gita', 110–12.

29. Vinoba Bhave, *Talks on the Gita* (Wardha: Paramdham Prakashan, 2019), 10.

30. Bhave, *Talks on the Gita*, 11.

31. The concept of 'interpretive community' is derived from reader response critical theory, especially Stanley Fish's notion of readers constituting a community who share a common meaning about literary texts. I use it here to imply that the Gandhians constituted a group which shared common strategies of interpreting and engaging with the Gita, which relied on lived experience in Gandhian ashrams as well as the ideological commitment to non-violence, truth, and selfless action. See Dan Berkowitz, 'Interpretive Community', in *International Encyclopedia of Journalism Studies*, ed. Tim P. Vos, Folker Hanusch, Dimitra Dimitrakopoulou, Margaretha Geertsema-Sligh, and Annika Sehl (Wiley, 2018), DOI: 10.1002/9781118841570.iejs0024.

32. Karline McLain, 'Living the Bhagavad Gita at Gandhi's Ashrams', *Religions* 10, no. 619 (2019): 1–18, 12, https://www.mdpi.com/2077-1444/10/11/619 (accessed on 21 Ocotber 2019).

33. Bhave, *Moved by Love*, 62.

34. From Davis' account of contemporary rituals at Gandhi's ashram in Wardha and Vinoba's ashram at Paunar, the centrality of the Gita to the Gandhian ascetic community, especially the section concerning the *sthitaprajna* which is recited daily at both the ashrams, becomes apparent. See Davis, *The Bhagavad Gita*.

35. Bergunder, 'Experiments with Theosophical Truth', 414.

36. M. K. Gandhi cited in Bergunder, 'Experiments with Theosophical Truth', 411.

37. Bergunder, 'Experiments with Theosophical Truth', 407.

38. Bergunder, 'Experiments with Theosophical Truth', 406.

39. M. K. Gandhi, 'Acquaintance with Religions', in *An Autobiography or the Story of My Experiments with Truth*, trans. Mahadev Desai, 90–94 (Ahmedabad: Navajivan Publishing House, 1927), 93.

40. Gandhi, 'Anasaktiyoga', 125.

41. Mahadev Desai, 'My Submission', in *The Gospel of Selfless Action or The Gita According to Gandhi*, trans. Mahadev Desai, 3–120 (Ahmedabad: Navajivan Mudranalaya, 1946), 3.
42. Desai, 'My Submission', 3–4.
43. Desai, 'My Submission', 117–18.
44. Bergunder, 'Hinduism, Theosophy, and the Bhagavad Gita', 78 (emphasis original).
45. Desai, 'My Submission', 118.
46. Desai, 'My Submission', 118.
47. Desai, 'My Submission', 118 (emphasis mine).
48. Desai, 'My Submission', 118.
49. Desai, 'My Submission', 114.
50. Bhave, *Talks on the Gita*, 73.
51. Bhave, *Talks on the Gita*, 67–69.
52. Bhave, *Talks on the Gita*, 69.
53. Desai, 'My Submission', 115.
54. Robert Ernest Hume, *The Thirteen Principal Upanishads: Translated from the Sanskrit with an Outline of the Philosophy of the Upanishads and an Annotated Bibliography* (London: Oxford University Press, 1921), 66.
55. Desai, 'My Submission', 105.
56. Desai, 'My Submission', 109.
57. Desai, 'My Submission', 109–110.
58. Desai, 'My Submission', 5.
59. Bergunder, 'Hinduism, Theosophy, and the Bhagavad Gita', 73–74.
60. Bergunder, 'Hinduism, Theosophy, and the Bhagavad Gita', 94.
61. Bal Gangadhar Tilak, 'Part VII: The Gītā and the Christian Bible', in Śrimad Bhagavadgītā-Rahasya, *or Karma-Yoga-Śāstra*, vol. 2, trans. B. S. Sukthankar (Poona: Tilak Brothers, 1935), 831.
62. Bergunder, 'Hinduism, Theosophy, and the Bhagavad Gita', 88–90.
63. Bal Gangadhar Tilak, 'Part IV: The Rise of the Bhāgavata Religion and the Gītā', in Śrimad Bhagavadgītā-Rahasya, *or Karma-Yoga-Śāstra*, vol. 2, trans. B. S. Sukthankar (Poona: Tilak Brothers, 1935), 777–82.
64. Desai, 'My Submission', 5–6.
65. Desai, 'My Submission', 6.
66. Tilak, *Śrimad Bhagavadgītā-Rahasya*, vol. 2, 737–39.
67. Gandhi, 'Anasaktiyoga', 126–27.
68. Gandhi, 'Anasaktiyoga', 126.
69. Gandhi, 'Anasaktiyoga', 127.
70. Desai, 'My Submission', 10.
71. Desai, 'My Submission', 11.

72. 'But as all the acts of the Avatâra are symbolical, we may pass from the outer to the inner planes, and see in the field of Kurukshetra the battlefield of the Soul, and in the sons of Dhritarâshtra enemies it meets in its progress; Arjuna becomes the type of the struggling soul of the disciple, and Shrî Krishna is the Logos of the soul.' See Annie Besant, *The Bhagavad Gîtâ or the Lord's Song (New and Revised Edition)* (London: Theosophical Publishing Society, 1896), 9.

73. Ronald W. Neufeldt, 'A Lesson in Allegory: Theosophical Interpretations of the Bhagavadgita', in *Modern Indian Interpreters of the Bhagavad Gita*, ed. Robert N. Minor, 11–33 (Albany: State University of New York Press, 1986), 25. Bergunder draws the connection further; he argues that Gandhi's allegorical approach was influenced by his contacts with the Theosophists most notably his admiration for Besant, whose translation of the Gita he circulated among the Indian youth in South Africa along with her portrait. See Bergunder, 'Experiments with Theosophical Truth', 398–426.

74. Desai, 'My Submission', 11.

75. Desai, 'My Submission', 7.

76. Desai, 'My Submission', 12–13.

77. Desai, 'My Submission', 10.

78. Gandhi cited in Balkrishna Govind Gokhale, 'Gandhi and History', *History and Theory* 11, no. 2 (1972): 214–225, https://www.jstor.org/stable/2504587 (accessed on 6 February 2024).

79. Gokhale, 'Gandhi and History', 217–18.

80. Gokhale, 'Gandhi and History', 217.

81. Gokhale, 'Gandhi and History', 217.

82. Desai, 'My Submission', 9.

83. Bhave, *Talks on the Gita*, 12.

84. Bhave, *Talks on the Gita*, 12.

85. Bhave, *Talks on the Gita*, 11.

86. Hallam Tennyson, *Saint on the March: The Story of Vinoba* (London: Victor Gollancz Ltd, 1956), 134–35.

87. Vinoba Bhave cited in Satish Kumar, 'Introduction', in *Moved by Love: The Memoirs of Vinoba Bhave*, ed. Kalindi, trans. Marjorie Sykes, 7–10 (Wardha: Paramdham Prakashan, 1994), 9.

88. Vinoba Bhave, 'The Basis of Bhoodan Yagna', in *The Principles and Philosophy of The Bhoodan Yagna*, by Vinoba Bhave, 1–5 (Tanjore: Sarvodaya Prachuralaya, 1955), 3.

89. Gandhi, 'Anasaktiyoga', 127.

90. Gandhi, 'Anasaktiyoga', 130.

91. Gandhi, 'Anasaktiyoga', 132.

92. Gandhi, 'Anasaktiyoga', 132

93. Gandhi, 'Anasaktiyoga', 29.

94. Joan V. Bondurant, *Conquest of Violence: The Gandhian Philosophy of Conflict* (Princeton, NJ: Princeton University Press, 1988 [1958]), 192.

95. Gokhale, 'Gandhi and History', 219.

96. Gokhale, 'Gandhi and History', 222.

97. Bhave, *Talks on the Gita*, 217–21 (emphasis mine).

98. Bhave, *Talks on the Gita*, 217–18.

99. Bhave, *Talks on the Gita*, 219–20.

100. Bhave, *Talks on the Gita*, 221.

101. Jayaprakash Narayan, 'Introduction', *Talks on the Gita*, by Vinoba Bhave, 2–5 (Wardha: Paramdham Prakashan, 2019), 4.

102. M. K. Gandhi, *An Autobiography or the Story of My Experiments with Truth*, trans. Mahadev Desai (Ahmedabad: Navajivan Publishing House, 1927), 336.

103. In Sankhya and Yoga philosophies, creation, or *prakriti*, is constituted through the interrelated operation of three *guna*s, or propensities. These are *sattva* manifested as joy, peace, and harmony; *rajas* represented by drive towards action motivated by desire and attachment; and *tamas* associated with indolence and ignorance.

104. Faisal Devji, 'Morality in the Shadow of Politics', in *Political Thought in Action: The Bhagavad Gita and Modern India*, ed. Shruti Kapila and Faisal Devji, 107–126 (Delhi: Cambridge University Press, 2013), 113.

105. Bhave, *Talks on the Gita*, 228.

106. Bhave, *Talks on the Gita*, 233–34.

107. Bhave calls *bhoodan*, or the gifting of land, a *yajna*, or sacrifice, in discourses he delivered during his nationwide campaign to promote it. Bhave, *The Principles and Philosophy of The Bhoodan Yagna*.

108. Vinoba Bhave, 'Collective Samadhi', in *Science and Self-Knowledge*, trans. and ed. Jitendra Nath Mohanty, 35–38 (Kashi: Akhil Bharat Sarva Seva Sangh Prakashan, 1959), 36.

109. Vinoba Bhave, 'Satyagraha in the Scientific Age', in *Science and Self-Knowledge*, trans. and ed. Jitendra Nath Mohanty, 44–47 (Kashi: Akhil Bharat Sarva Seva Sangh Prakashan, 1959), 47.

110. Bhave, *The Principles and Philosophy of The Bhoodan Yagna*, 1–2.

111. Vinoba Bhave cited in Green, *The Origins of Non-Violence*, 132.

112. Vinoba Bhave, 'The Union of Self-Knowledge and Science', in *Science and Self-Knowledge*, trans. and ed. Jitendra Nath Mohanty (Kashi: Akhil Bharat Sarva Seva Sangh Prakashan, 1959), 9.

113. Vinoba Bhave, *Science and Self-Knowledge*, trans. and ed. Jitendra Nath Mohanty (Kashi: Akhil Bharat Sarva Seva Sangh Prakashan, 1959), 47.

114. Vinoba Bhave,'Creation of the Universal Man', in *Science and Self-Knowledge*, trans. and ed. Jitendra Nath Mohanty, 32–34 (Kashi: Akhil Bharat Sarva Seva Sangh Prakashan, 1959).

115. Bhave, 'Collective Samadhi'.

116. Bhave, *Science and Self-Knowledge*, 36.

117. Jitendra Nath Mohanty, 'Introduction', in Vinoba Bhave, *Science and Self-Knowledge*, trans. and ed. Jitendra Nath Mohanty, 5–6 (Kashi: Akhil Bharat Sarva Seva Sangh Prakashan, 1959), 6.

118. Bhave, 'Satyagraha in the Scientific Age', 46.

119. Martin Luther King Jr, 'My Trip to the Land of Gandhi', *Ebony*, July 1959, 84–92.

4

A Nostalgia for Transcendental Closure

The Relationship between the Mahabharata and Notions
of Nationalism in the Works of Friedrich Schlegel,
Maithilisharan Gupt, and Jawaharlal Nehru

Philipp Sperner

Introduction

The renewed and persistent interest in the Mahabharata in the twentieth century
has most often been linked to the rise of the Indian national(ist) movement in
general and a specific nativist and parochial understanding of nationalism in
particular. Seen from this perspective, the interest in the Mahabharata stands
for an understanding of modern India that is based on the presumption of
an ancient and everlasting homogeneous identity of the Indian people as well
as a forced equation of 'Indian' with 'Hindu'. While this standard account
of the relationship between the Indian epics and right-wing nationalism has
been as influential as it is convincing, it fails to analyse the larger historical and
epistemological changes that provided the background for the renewed interest
in the epic *as form*. In order to address this epistemological aspect, I propose to
look at the larger history of the epic and the construction of a national identity
in a global context in order to ask what prompted the interest in the epics on a
functional level. Why were they read and retold so many times apart from the
certainly true but hardly sufficient reason of them serving as a reminder of and
evidence for the existence of a historical basis for the allegedly homogeneous
identity in question?

In order to engage with the global significance as well as the philosophical
and political implications of the relationship between the epic and nationalism,
I look at three specific actors and at how they drew from, as well as referred and

contributed to, the discourse on the epic form through their specific reading and reception of the Mahabharata: Friedrich Schlegel's analysis of the allegedly shared roots of Indo-European philosophical thought in ancient folk literature (specifically in his book *Über die Sprache und Weisheit der Indier*, 1808), Maithilisharan Gupt's attempt to recount the history of India as the history of the Aryan race from the mythico-historical times of the Mahabharata to the future of an independent India in his long narrative poem *Bharat Bharati* (1912), and Jawaharlal Nehru's seemingly uneasy (as well as rather sporadic) rejection of any form of a potentially political engagement with the Mahabharata as inevitably contributing to a parochial and Hindu supremacist notion of Indian nationalism.

Each one of the three authors can be seen as standing for a distinct approach to the Mahabharata, but they are also more than mere representatives of a specific group. Regarded as the founder of the discipline of philology, Schlegel and his work were pivotal for the proliferation of the idea of the nation in nineteenth-century Europe. While it is often overlooked in the scholarly engagement with his ideas, the Mahabharata had to play a decisive role in it. The centrality of the Mahabharata in the work of Gupt, on the other hand, is simply impossible to overlook. What makes him all the more interesting for my analysis is not only that he was one of the first Hindi authors to be deemed a 'national poet', but also that his work is full of references to the stories and histories of other, mainly European, nations. With Nehru, an entirely new relationship between the Mahabharata and the nation emerges. In his work, the epic (in the broadest sense of the term) is no longer located in the past nor projected into the future, but it becomes a project of the here and now.

My argument is that concepts and ideas such as 'nation', *Volk*, '(the Aryan) race', and 'folk' were not just developed in Europe and then exported to India, but that they have instead already been developed and shaped through a bi-directional (or rather multi-directional) exchange between different cultural regions and literary traditions. The European reception of Indian literary sources is often portrayed as a conscious use, adoption, and analysis on the part of European thinkers, while later influences in the other direction – from European sources to Indian texts and actors – are mostly regarded as resulting from the sheer dominance or universal applicability of European terms and concepts. While the European side is thus always seen as playing the active part, the non-European side is seen as much more passive or as the unconscious adopter of universal(ized) European ideas. In order to go beyond the paradigm of a European 'export' of discourses and non-discursive practices, I will take the shared desire for transcendental closure as the starting point for my analysis.[1] Doing so will allow me to not only focus on the epistemological implications of the various phases of engagement with the Mahabharata but also showcase the fruitful and particular contributions of literary theory to the field of global intellectual history.

As Andrew Sartori has argued, 'the presence of Germany' functioned as a key trope for Indian nationalism and the underlying philosophical and theological structures that sustained and fed the nationalist discourse. By making the emerging Indian nationalism strongly reliant on the Romantic notion of a golden age of Indian antiquity, Indian intellectuals were 'attempting to make ancient India do precisely the work for the modern Indian nation that Greece had been pressed into service to do for nineteenth-century Germans'.[2] They were thus knowingly or unknowingly, Sartori further argues, 'consolidating and substantiating a historical narrative that already structurally implied ... that India was Asia's Germany'.[3] Sartori provides a compelling argument and a useful framework to conceptualize the global exchange of ideas beyond the 'conventional spectrum of analysis of colonial intellectual history'[4] that is based on the notion of a dialogue between continuous traditions, regardless of whether this dialogue is perceived to be fully determined by structural hierarchies ('colonial discourse') or seen as a sequence of 'authentic intercultural encounters' ('culture contact'). What is missing from Sartori's argument, however, is its own prehistory: the fact that German Romanticism was itself already hugely influenced by the encounter with ancient Indian texts and thought. If we want to understand the structural and historico-philosophical reasons that led to the prevalence of German thought in the discourse of Indian nationalism, we thus have to begin with this part of the story: the development of the notion of a national self-consciousness in German Romanticism and the crucial role ancient Indian texts such as the Mahabharata had to play in it.

Friedrich Schlegel and the Indian Renaissance in Germany

In September 1803, the 31-year-old Friedrich Schlegel (1772–1829), who has been living and working in Paris for about a year, writes a letter to his friend Ludwig Tieck, in which he reports on his progress in the study of Sanskrit: 'This [Sanskrit] is the true source of all languages, every thought and poem of human spirit; *everything*, everything came from India without exception.'[5] For Schlegel, the engagement with Indian language(s) and philosophy was closely linked to his search for the origins of the German language and culture as well as for what he considered to be the original true revelation and civilization as such.[6] The two years that he spent in Paris and studied Sanskrit with Alexander Hamilton were also a time in which he was actively working on an edition of the Nibelungenlied and generally preoccupied with questions of origins. His study of Sanskrit led to the publication of *Über die Sprache und Weisheit der Indier* (*On the Language and Wisdom of the Indians*) in 1808. After that he seems to have lost the fascination and enthusiasm for the study of India almost as suddenly as he had developed it in the first place.

As Ernst Behler has observed, however, the time in Paris marked a decisive turning point in Schlegel's work.[7] One of the main aspects of this change in Schlegel's thought was his transition from pantheism to a dualistic notion of theism and a shift from a focus on mythology as direct representation of ancient life to a philosophical understanding of mythology that required an analysis on the basis of the 'truth' of religious revelation. This turn from mythology to religion was accompanied by the re-evaluation of the question of national origins. Far from merely losing its significance, the question instead prompted an even stronger emphasis on the notion that any origin was irretrievably and irrevocably lost and that a return was utterly impossible. Following Paul de Man, the turn from the immanence of mythology to the transcendence of religion can itself be seen as directly resulting from the Romantic search for origins: 'Trying to conceive of the natural object in terms of origin leads to a transcendental concept of the Idea: the quest for the Idea that takes the natural object for its starting-point begins with the incarnated "minute particular" and works its way upwards to a transcendental essence.'[8] In the case of Friedrich Schlegel, this decisive shift can be observed most clearly in his engagement with Indian sources –including parts of the Mahabharata – in *Über die Sprache und Weisheit der Indier*.[9]

As the title of the book indicates, it is first of all concerned with Sanskrit as *the* Indian language. While Schlegel was not the first European to note the similarity between Sanskrit, Persian, and European languages, he was the first to make this the basis of a systematic comparative analysis between languages.[10] Since he was convinced that Sanskrit was the most ancient language and India the cradle of civilization, he saw the study of Sanskrit texts as a way to engage with the prehistory of Europe.[11] This was combined with a strong narrative of pure origins and historical decline. Schlegel asserted that in order to overcome the present state of cultural corruption, Europe had to return to its own origins through the study of ancient Indian sources.[12] Due to its purity, authenticity, and philosophical character, Sanskrit afforded a privileged access to these philosophical and religious origins and thus guaranteed 'the noble simplicity of a primal revelation'.[13]

Schlegel was not merely interested in the spiritual renewal of Europe. He also envisioned this renewal to be led and brought about by a reinvigorated German culture that he believed to be most closely related to its Asian ancestors and therefore uniquely able to counter the corrupting dominance of French culture that symbolized artificiality, imitation, and a one-sided overemphasis of reason, therefore embodying the most depraved aspects of the times.[14] Schlegel thus participated in a strongly political debate in which German Romanticism was pitted against French Enlightenment: a new 'Oriental Renaissance' (as Raymond Schwab would call it) to counter the excessive emphasis on the 'Classical Renaissance' in France. The supposedly close kinship between Germany and India enabled Schlegel to disassociate Germany from contemporary Europe and its civilizational decline and to argue that Germany had an even older claim to leadership than France, which traced its heritage merely to Greece and Rome.[15] This 'romantic counterrevolution' was not meant to be purely 'philosophical', however, since Schlegel's 'thought about cultural hegemony also implied the notion of political supremacy'[16] when he dreamed about the unification of all German(ic) states in order to dominate all other European nations.[17]

The political debate in turn generated its very own philosophical dimension. In this sense, then, Schlegel's turning point – from ancient Rome and Greece to India and Persia and from the immanence of myth to the transcendence of religion – has to be understood as part of a larger epistemological turning point in the history of Europe that can be seen as a consequence of the outcome of the French Revolution and the rise of Napoleon.[18] As Joep Leerssen has argued, most proponents of German Romanticism regarded Napoleon's military and political achievements all over Europe as a threat to the native and organically grown traditions (of monarchic power, Catholicism, German culture, and so on) and thus responded with a '*nostalgic* resistance against a despotically-imposed modernization'.[19] For Schlegel, who had just left Paris and was still busily working with his Indian sources when Napoleon crowned himself in late 1804, this meant a change in his attitude towards the French Revolution and France in general. His ardent republicanism waned and he became the proponent of a 'true' empire and a 'German ... Christian universal monarchy'.[20]

That Romanticism is marked by a nostalgia for 'lost' or 'forgotten' origins has been rehearsed repeatedly. It is important to note, however, that the emphasis is very much on the 'forgotten'.[21] This nostalgia was thus not just a conservative desire for the simplicity and authenticity of the times past, but instead a result of the realization that such simplicity was irrecoverably lost. It is not a restorative reflex against modernity but instead itself a symptom of modernity and, despite seemingly being oriented towards the past, essentially forward-looking.[22] The romantic nostalgia that Schlegel developed in those years was not just a nostalgia for lost origins but, more specifically, a nostalgia for an irrecoverable natural totality and thus a *nostalgia for transcendental closure*. It surfaced most clearly in his engagement with excerpts from the Mahabharata and other Sanskrit sources and was certainly, at least in parts, induced by them.

Jean-Luc Nancy and Philippe Lacoue-Labarthe have argued that the project of (early) Romanticism was driven by the quest for an autopoiesis of the subject in art and particularly literature. Precisely because the subject was no longer just there, could no longer just be *represented*, the question of its production became pertinent. This is one of the main reasons why the epic became important at a time that has been credited with the 'invention' of the novel (and Schlegel has been so in particular). In the epic, Nancy and Lacoue-Labarthe argue, the subject is at once already present and representable (as object and totality) and yet, at the same time, always in the process of its everlasting emergence.[23] While this kind of subject was irretrievably lost in modernity and epics could no longer be written (only as their own mockery or satire[24]), they could still provide the experience of this now-lost totality. A turn to the epic could thus help to recover a kind of blueprint for the (auto)production of a subject through literature. This has been expressed most forcefully by Georg Lukács, who argued that the world of the epic is characterized by a complete totality, a transcendental closure that shelters the subject insofar as it is organically connected with the world. In the modern world of the novel, however, this totality is lost and is replaced by the 'transcendental homelessness' of the subject.[25] As Schlegel was sitting in a library in Paris amidst the tumult of the Napoleonic Wars, learning to read the Sanskrit epics, it must have dawned on him that the world he was living in was no longer a natural, organic, and naive totality but an artificially produced and 'fragmentary totality'.[26] In the epics that he was reading, however, he could still get a glimpse of the older, transcendental totality that was now lost. Such a notion of a transcendental totality is even more pronounced in the Mahabharata than in the Greek epics since its truly universal validity (including its cosmogeny) becomes obvious already from its title.[27]

Schlegel's interest in the Mahabharata was twofold: from the perspective of mythology and the perspective of philosophy and religion. Generally speaking, though, his mythological engagement with Indian texts was much less pronounced, which he attributed to the 'scarcity of our materials'.[28] In regard to the Mahabharata, he thus focused mostly on the Bhagavadgita and a few sections of the 'Sakuntala' episode. What made the Mahabharata and also the Ramayana particularly interesting for Schlegel was their age and philosophical complexity, due to which he believed that they would 'probably prove equally instructive and important' as the Vedas.[29] Despite the fact that he focused only on excerpts and not the politico-philosophical background to the 'great civil wars between two kindred heroes', he was thus definitely keenly aware of the systematic complexity of the epic.

Schlegel argued that because the Indian system was so old, deviations from the truth could be recognized more easily, which made it particularly useful in order to recover or even reconstruct, as it were, the 'divine truth' of Holy Revelation.[30] One of the most important of such corruptions for Schlegel was undoubtedly pantheism. He devotes a whole chapter to it in the section on Indian philosophy, and it forms the defining topic of his engagement with the Gita. He was intent on showing that pantheism did not form the core of Indian philosophy but was instead a later deviation from philosophical dualism, which was in turn an abstraction of the original 'doctrine of the Two Principles', the opposition of the forces of good and evil, which had an 'epic quality' to him, as Bradley Herling puts it.[31] The Gita provided a unique opportunity to strengthen his argument. Through a selective reading and translation, he sought to show that the pantheistic notions present in the Gita were later interpolations and resulted from an increasing philosophical abstraction and a deviation from the primary 'doctrine of the Two Principles'.[32] The Gita and, more broadly, the Mahabharata were thus themselves a liminal text for Schlegel. It still contained the core of the true revelation but also showed signs of its initial degradation. Additionally, it was also liminal for him in the sense that it marked the transition from Indian or Oriental philosophy to European ideas:

> It must not be forgotten that the Pantheistic philosophy is considered the latest of the Oriental systems ... and ... that the profound and vital idea originally entertained of the Eternal and his almighty power, must have been greatly vitiated and enfeebled before it could descend to lose itself in the false and visionary notion of the oneness or unity of all things.... All other Oriental doctrines, however disguised by error and fiction, are founded in, and dependent on, divine and marvellous revelations; but Pantheism is the offspring of unassisted reason ['das System der reinen Vernunft' (the system of pure reason)], and therefore marks the transition from the Oriental to the European philosophy.[33]

The supposed liminality of the Gita, which is so crucial for Schlegel's engagement with it, is also already present in the narrative of the Mahabharata itself (or has at least been part of the earliest comments on the epic), as the war at Kurukshetra is generally thought to mark the transition to the Kali Yuga, the age of discord and moral decline.[34]

In order to properly understand the role of the Mahabharata within German Romanticism as well as the role of German Romanticism within the epistemological history of nationalism, it is necessary to look at the political implications of Schlegel's philosophical interests and vice versa. That the epic in general occupies a very significant role in the history of nationalism does not have to be repeated here. What I do want to briefly mention, however, is the curious transformation in the reception of the epics that happened somewhat around the time that Schlegel was reading and translating excerpts from the Mahabharata. What is today called an 'epic', 'epic poem', or *Epos* in German would, until roughly 1800, have been called a *Heldengedicht* (a poem of a hero, or 'heroic poem').[35] As such, it was not as closely associated with or rather tied to the history of a specific nation of which the later epos was supposed to present an authentic account. While Schlegel did not use the term *Epos* at all in *Über die Sprache und Weisheit der Indier* and called the Mahabharata the 'second great heroic poem [Heldengedicht] of the Indians',[36] he was convinced that the study of Indian myths would reveal much about its oldest history.[37] This discovery of the epic as history coincided with the death of the epic as a genre – they could no longer be actively written but only discovered or rediscovered.[38] What probably contributed more to the developing notion that epics were not just old stories but *Nationale Grundbücher* (national books of origin or first reason), as G. W. F. Hegel would later call them,[39] was not so much their specific content but the fact that with the 'discovery' and first translation of what later would be called Indian epics, Schlegel developed and established a practice of comparison between these mythological texts and their European equivalents and thus also between the nations that they represented.[40]

My argument, then, is not that Schlegel took the notion of nationalism from the Mahabharata, nor that his reading of the Mahabharata was amongst the most important influences for the development of what could be called proto-nationalist ideas. Rather, I want to argue that it was no coincidence that Schlegel turned towards the Sanskrit texts at precisely this time. He certainly read them selectively and in line with his broader interests and arguments, but he did not just read the notion of transcendental closure *into* the epic. Instead, his work must be understood as reacting to some ideas that were already inscribed in it. Acknowledging the imaginative or constructivist aspect of Schlegel's Orientalism does not mean we should assume that he and his contemporaries just made everything up. After all, he *was* studying Sanskrit and *was* reading the Mahabharata and other manuscripts. If these readings are taken seriously – and I think that despite all their shortcomings, they certainly should not be dismissed as *just* Orientalist constructions – it also means that the return to ancient India during the early phase of Indian nationalism was not only partially (albeit indirectly) influenced by a similar renaissance during the early phase of German nationalism, but that this early German nationalism was decisively influenced by the Mahabharata, a text that professes to tell the story of the emergence of the Bharata lineage and the political unification of large parts of northern India. 'The peculiar resonance of German thought'[41] in India was thus not a one-way interaction but itself based on the peculiar resonance of Indian thought in Germany. The transcultural or global exchange of political and social ideas becomes visible not so much even as a back-and-forth, but as a series of cyclical interactions in which every instance of exchange is based on and framed by prior instances of such interactions.

Maithilisharan Gupt and the German Renaissance in India

In this section, I turn to another instance in the history of the engagement with the Mahabharata by looking at the role the epic played in the development of nationalism in India itself. This allows me to shed some light on the reasons or preconditions that lay behind the peculiar resonances of German thought in India. My focus lies on the Hindi author Maithilisharan Gupt (1886–1964) and his contributions to the 'New Awakening'[42] in the Hindi literature of the early twentieth century.[43] Gupt is specifically interesting in this context not only because he was one of the first Hindi poets to be called *rashtra kavi*, or 'national poet', but also because the Mahabharata played a very significant role in his own work. In the three years from 1907 to 1909 alone, Gupt published at least 14 poems on themes from the Mahabharata in *Saraswati*, the leading Hindi literary magazine of the time. Most of these dealt with the role of Draupadi,[44] but he also retold the stories of several other characters from the epic, such as the killing of Jayadratha, to which he devoted a book-length narrative poem in 1910.[45]

According to Pamela Lothspeich, the themes of the attempted assault or rape of Draupadi and the slaying of Jayadratha are among the most often retold episodes from the Mahabharata during the nationalist period. They worked as powerful metaphors for the anti-colonial struggle by emphasizing the need to protect Indian women from evil foreign men and characterizing the successful beheading of the evil other as a major step towards re-establishing just rule. Through such hugely popular retellings of the epics, Draupadi also became the quintessential model of the dutiful wife and Indian woman and thus an important point of reference for the figure of Bharat Mata, or Mother India.[46] Similar allegorical figures were neither limited to Gupt nor to works drawing from the Mahabharata or the *pauranik* (literally, 'old' or 'ancient', referring to the genre of ancient Indian literature known as the Puranas) literature, but were part of a rich tradition of allegories in popular literature throughout the various phases of anti-colonialism.[47] A detailed analysis of the way in which an allegorical reading of the epics played a significant role for a (re)constructed national identity can thus certainly provide interesting insights into the genesis of Indian nationalism. Insofar as such an analysis relies solely on the metaphorical yet relatively overt 'meaning' of the texts and neglects the importance of the formal features of the epic *as genre*, however, it remains limited in its capacity to explain the underlying epistemological reasons for the development of Indian nationalism and the role the Mahabharata had to play in it.[48]

To address this lacuna, a turn to the so-called Bengal Renaissance can be of help. It has since long figured as the pinnacle of the twin narrative of modernity and nationalism in late-nineteenth-century India. According to this narrative, the influence of Western education led to a rapid modernization of the Bengali intelligentsia and a 'western style "Renaissance" in contemporary thought and the liberal arts'.[49] These developments would then have spread from Bengal all over India and thus heralded the national as well as modern 'awakening' of the whole subcontinent in what has accordingly been termed 'Indian Renaissance'. I am not interested here in the merits or problems of this narrative,[50] but in the way in which this narrative was partially appropriated and also thoroughly rejected by some Hindi intellectuals – such as Ramvilas Sharma – who claimed that the 'Hindi Renaissance' ('Nav Jagran', or 'New Awakening', in Hindi) was neither the result of Western influence nor based on the example of the Bengal Renaissance but instead an unequivocal consequence of the Revolt of 1857.[51] For Sharma, the revolt led to an unprecedented unity and a newly found national consciousness that would eventually find its expression in the nationalist Hindi literature of the first decades of the twentieth century.[52] The Hindi Renaissance was thus not primarily a cultural or intellectual development but the result of the first national people's movement in India. This turns the conventional narrative from its head to its feet: rather than Western education and European notions of modernity providing the impetus for a nationalist awakening in India, it was the developing national consciousness, brought about by the unifying spirit of a shared fight against feudal and colonial masters, that led to a turn towards what was seen as the oldest history of this re-founded community.[53]

Sharma's argument in favour of a direct line of influence from 1857 to the Nav Jagran in Hindi literature has repeatedly and convincingly been questioned for its reductionism[54] and its anachronistic construction of a nationalist teleology.[55] It does have some heuristic merit, however, because it offers useful clues for an analysis of the relationship between the structural conditions for the development of nationalist ideas and a renewed interest in a particular representation of community and totality as found in the Mahabharata. In the present case, this means that I propose to read the structural similarity of the historical situations in early nineteenth-century Germany and early twentieth-century India as the philosophical precondition for the turn to the Mahabharata and ancient India in Germany and India, respectively. In order to do so, I first turn to Gupt's treatment of ancient India and the Mahabharata in his most celebrated epic poem, *Bharat Bharati*, first published in 1912. Although *Bharat Bharati* does not retell any specific episode from the Mahabharata, the epic occupies a central place in the poem's narrative structure – a eulogy for and invocation of India's glorious past, described as the golden age of the 'Aryan civilization', which had subsequently experienced a dramatic and mostly self-afflicted spiritual decline that affected all aspects of life and led to the oppression by foreign invaders (first Muslim and then British). These Aryans, or rather their present-day descendants, are also the collective subject of the poem's narration, who are called upon to return to their forgotten virtues in order to ensure the full recovery of India's glory in the future:

> Ham kaun the, kyā ho gaye hai aur kyā homge abhī,
> Āo, vicārem āj milkar ye samasyāem sabhī.
> Yadyapi hamem itihās apnā prāpt pūrā hai nahīm,
> Ham kaun the, is jñān ko, phir bhī adhūrā hai nahīm.[56]

> Who we were, we are and we shall be,
> Come, let's ponder over it together.
> Though we do not have our full history
> we still know fully who we were.[57]

The first line of this stanza relates the structure of the poem, which consists of three sections that deal with India's past, present, and future, respectively. The first section on India's heroic past is by far the longest and develops the defining theme of national unity. While Gupt is not very explicit about who exactly is part of this nation, his focus on an unequivocally *Hindu* past and his portrayal of the Muslim period as 'an interlude, an almost insignificant episode in the longue durée of Indian time'[58] leaves little doubt as to the specific make-up of the national 'we' that the poem invokes.[59] The disunity that the poem laments is thus not portrayed as a consequence of foreign invasion but as the result of an almost inevitable civilizational decline and self-inflicted moral degradation.[60] As with Schlegel's narrative of historical degeneration, the natural decline of the Aryan civilization is not absolutely inevitable or irreversible, however. Since the present-day Indian people are direct descendants of the once heroic Aryans, their future can hold the promise of a return to past glory.[61] The Mahabharata occupies a central position in this narrative of decline and lost unity. A short section entitled 'Mahabharat' directly follows the section on 'the beginning of decadence' (avanati ka aarambh) and thus – just as with Schlegel – marks the beginning of the decline of the 'Aryan nation':

> Is sarvanāśī yuddh kā vah dṛśya kaisā ghora thā,
> Us or thā yadi putra to laṛtā pitā is or thā!
> Santān hī ke rakta meṁ yah mātṛbhūmi sunī yahāṁ,
> Us svarg kī-sī vāṭikā kī hāy! Rākh banī yahāṁ!

> How horrible was the scene of this all-annihilating war,
> If the son was on that side, the fighting father was on the other!
> The motherland drowned in the children's blood,
> That paradise-like garden, alas, turned into ashes then.[62]

The Mahabharata and particularly the Kurukshetra war comes to stand for the quintessential moment of familial and national disunity. When sons fight against their fathers and brothers with each other, the civilizational decline of the Aryans had to be the natural result. 'The Mahabharata was the product of this process and marked the beginning of decadence', as Francesca Orsini puts it. At the same time, the war was not treated as a solely traumatic event but also as the source of inspiration for a moral and political resurgence.[63]

Another very striking similarity between Gupt and Schlegel is their portrayal of India as the cradle of civilization. Gupt goes a step further and claims that the land itself ('Bharatvarsh') is the oldest on the planet and the first to have been created by god. As with other arguments about India's ancient past, the claim is propped up by a range of references. Gupt refers to the Puranas, James Tod's *Annals and Antiquities of Rajasthan* (1829), the Bible, the Koran, and Sir Walter Raleigh's *History of the World* (1614) – all allegedly confirming his claim that god's act of creation started with or 'in' India.[64] Connected with the primacy of India is also Gupt's assertion that the Aryans acted as teachers for all other nations and people.[65] They were the 'progenitors of all the world's literatures, religions and civilizations'[66] and their knowledge – again strikingly in line with Schlegel's argument – spread from India to Greece and from there all over Europe and Arabia.[67] According to Gupt, the Aryans even travelled themselves – a claim for which he quotes several sources again and also refers to the Mahabharata, from which 'it is evident that during the Kurukṣetra war many Hindu clans went west and settled in countries like Greece, Phoenicia, Philistine, Carthago, Rome and Egypt'.[68] In order to highlight the unity and shared descent of contemporary Indians from their Aryan ancestors, Gupt also had to emphasize the superiority of Sanskrit and to show that Hindi was its only true heir.[69] This, once again, strikingly resembles Schlegel's argument about the uniqueness of Sanskrit and his emphasis on the relationship between language and culture more broadly.[70] The most significant similarities between Gupt and Schlegel, however, have to do with an epistemological shift in the treatment of the past and the reception of 'ancient' literary texts, specifically those called 'epics'. This is particularly true for the Mahabharata, which was often regarded as an inauspicious text that centred on 'fratricide and familial disintegration' up until the late nineteenth century, when writers such as Gupt started to treat the text 'more as revered national literature and national history' as Lothspeich points out.[71]

These examples show that there are strong similarities and parallels in the construction of German and Indian nationalism. So far, however, the comparative analysis has remained on the textual surface of *Bharat Bharati*. The similarities between Gupt and Schlegel can thus be seen as somewhat superficial insofar as the underlying structural conditions that enabled them are not taken into consideration. They can also not sufficiently explain *why* the Mahabharata provided such an important reference point and marked the moment of philosophical, spiritual, moral, and political decline for both Gupt and Schlegel. In order to expand the scope of this analysis, it is thus necessary to take a closer look at some of the structural themes of *Bharat Bharati* before briefly returning to Sharma's claim that the Hindi Renaissance grew out of the experience of 1857.

Gupt's call to a return to past glory is underwritten by a cyclical notion of history that structures the whole poem. The return of India's strength, freedom, and greatness does not appear as just a distant possibility but as a promise that needs to be redeemed by the young generation. This can already be sensed in Gupt's description of India's downfall:

Is bhāṁti jab jag meṁ hamārī pūrṇ unnati ho cukī,
Pāyā jahāṁ tak path vahāṁ tak pragati kī gati ho cukī.
Tab aur kyā hotā? hamāre cakra nīce ke phire;
Jaise uṭhe, ant meṁ ham ṭhīk vaise hī gire!

Utthān ke pīche patan sambhav sadā hai sarvathā,
Prauḍhatv ke pīche svayaṁ vṛddhatv hotā hai yathā.
Hā! kintu avanati bhī hamārī hai samunnati-sī baṛhī;
Jaisī baṛhī thī pūrṇimā vaisī amāvāsyā paṛī!

In this way, when we had reached our full development in this world,
We got as far on our path as the motion of progress had taken us.
Then what happened? Our discus turned downwards;
As we had risen, in the end we fell just like that.

A fall after a rise is always natural, after all,
Just as there comes old age after adulthood.
Yes, but the degradation is also ours, [just as] the salvation-like growth;
As the full moon had risen, so the new moon night had fallen.[72]

The two stanzas abound with images of circularity and self-contained totality. The degradation sets in after the 'full' development had been reached, like a discus that falls when its momentum has expired. And behind the darkness of a new moon night, a new dawn, and with it a new moon cycle, is already palpable. The notion of a cyclical time is of course central to several Indian traditions of thought and also an important aspect of the Yuga concept, as discussed previously. That this concept is transposed onto what Gupt calls 'our' (Indian) 'civilization' is remarkable insofar as it presupposes an eternal and clearly defined collective Indian subject and implies its inherent stability and self-contained totality that does not appear *in* time but rather becomes the bearer *of* time. Although such a difference-transcending unity could not have been established through a single event, it seems reasonable to argue that the rebellion of 1857 represented a crucial moment for the formation of a new kind of consciousness that let at least the perception of such a unity emerge. In order to make this point, it is not necessary to determine the exact social make-up of the rebellion nor its various intents and purposes at the time. What seems important instead is that it marks the moment at which it became possible to perceive the distinction between colonizers and colonized as the principal distinction of sociopolitical life in India and thus enabled the emergence or development of a national consciousness.[73] It is in this sense, then, that Sharma seems justified in claiming that the Nav Jagran of Hindi literature was based on the experience or, rather, the collective memory of 1857. Nonetheless, the turn to the Puranas and the Mahabharata was just as much based on the exact opposite of the process of national unification. Precisely because the national unity always remained precarious and threatened – by general processes of individuation in modernity and ferocious political debates that questioned the primacy of nationality as the defining socio-political factor (most strongly through the various radical socialist and anarchist groups that did not necessarily base their rejection of colonial rule on the assumption of a national identity) – the turn towards the epic and its figure of totality and closure proved so important.[74]

As this reading of *Bharat Bharati* shows, nationalism needs to be understood not just as a political but also as a philosophical concept. Pheng Cheah traces the emergence of the very concept of nationality to the historical turn towards 'organismic metaphors' in the thinking of sociability and community when a society was no longer seen as a complex system of distinct groups and classes but as 'a rationally organized totality, or living organic whole'.[75] Cheah further argues that the specific nationalist turn of philosophical thinking was itself pre-configured by far-reaching social transformations or the 'common historical experience of modernity's exhilarating and shocking impact' that led to an instability of hitherto existing narratives of community and belonging. Since these transformations were structural, they were not tied to a specific historic moment and could be encountered in very similar ways in late-eighteenth-century Germany and early-twentieth-century India:

> The fact that these ideas received their first elaborate formalization in German philosophy does not make decolonizing and postcolonial nationalisms derivative of a European model. They are comparable responses to a common experience of intense structural transformation – whether this takes the form of Napoleonic invasion, nineteenth-century territorial imperialism, or uneven globalization.[76]

As a response to a common experience of intense transformation, nationalism becomes itself discernible as a structural formation that serves to retain a notion of totality at a time in which nothing seemed less certain than the possibility of absolute closure. In the context of the global reception of the Mahabharata, the French hegemony under Napoleon, which so troubled Schlegel, and the rebellion of 1857, which inspired Gupt and his colleagues, were structurally equivalent in the sense that both events elicited a strong desire for social totality and thus led to a nostalgia for the kind of transcendental closure that could now only be found in the Mahabharata and other epics.

Gupt's preoccupation with the Mahabharata and its central place in Indian history is not just the result of the gradual adoption of colonial and hegemonic political ideas but must instead be understood as arising from the need to respond to the momentous transformation of society on a philosophical level. At the same time, however, the Indian Renaissance (including what Sartori would call its 'Germanism') did not remain only structurally similar to the Oriental Renaissance of late-eighteenth- and early-nineteenth-century Germany since the salvaging of one's 'own' Indian past was accompanied by an active salvaging of 'foreign' concepts and ideas for the purpose of national liberation. This was made easier insofar as supposedly foreign concepts such as nationality were in turn at least partially based on an engagement with Indian texts.[77] In both cases or at both moments, the Mahabharata represented a kind of liminality. For Gupt and for Schlegel, the text marked the historic moment at which the spiritual force was at its very height and thus guaranteed the inner stability and closure of the Indian social totality. At the same time, they also saw this very moment as the beginning of the spiritual and then political decline of the Indian nation.

Jawaharlal Nehru and the Eschewal of Nostalgia

Let me end my argument with a short discussion of another moment in the history of (Indian) nationalism during which a strikingly different role of the Mahabharata was at play. Once the notion of nationality had become hegemonic, the Mahabharata was no longer needed as an inspiring source for and memorial of the national community as a primordial self-contained totality. With 'the stroke of the midnight hour' on 15 August 1947, as India was 'awakening to life and freedom',[78] the hitherto unsettled question of whether the Indian people were, in fact, a nation was finally settled for good. There was no need to assure oneself of being part of a glorious national community by reading about the long-gone glory of the Aryans and the heroic deeds of the Pandava princes when a simple glance at the Indian flag flowing above the village school was enough proof of the nation's present strength and power. For nationalists, 1947 was clearly not the time for nostalgia.

The very fact of India's independence as nation state paradoxically meant that the nation did not have to appear as having existed from times immemorial but as something that was constantly evolving and had to be actively built by its members. There was thus no need for transcendental closure. What remained central, however, was the notion of the nation as an inherent totality, albeit a totality of a radically different kind that was not transcendental but immanent and had to be constantly recreated and built anew. For such a project of nation-building – the communal construction of a national community whose principal existence was out of doubt – the Mahabharata did not seem to be useful. At least not in the eyes of one of the most important principal architects of the project of constructing the Indian nation: Jawaharlal Nehru (1889–1964).

In his numerous speeches, letters, articles, and books, Nehru only rarely talks about the Mahabharata and almost never in detail or at length. He was primarily interested in the very present and not in the nation's past, as this exemplary quotation from one of his later speeches as India's first prime minister shows so well:

> India is an ancient country. The Ramayana and the Mahabharata contain the stories of the Indian people dating back to thousands of years. People from abroad came and became part of this nation. It is a process like the rivers coming from far-off distances and falling into an ocean. Now we have to see what is our contribution to that story in our times. We won independence under the leadership of Mahatma Gandhi and with it ended a great epic. Now another epic has started, and that is how a newly independent people raise their nation.[79]

Nehru is referring to the Mahabharata and the Ramayana here in order to emphasize the significance as well as the difficulty of the *epic* project of nation-building. While he also seems to historically date the two epics somewhere close to the birth of 'the Indian people', he is quick to add that the present-day Indian nation is very different from this past, that there is not just one source of origin, but many rivers and streams that contributed to the 'ocean' that is India. Rather than reading the epics of old, he seems keen on writing a new epic instead. Although this approach to the Mahabharata and the Ramayana is very different from that of Schlegel and Gupt, the epics do stand for some kind of historic past in Nehru's writing as well. Similarly to Gupt and Schlegel, then, they are not just some old stories but contain some sort of historic truth.

The relationship between history and the epics is fragile, however, and Nehru seems to be troubled by it occasionally – particularly when he is arguing against an overly literal interpretation of the epics. Insofar as he sees the epics as containing a kind of higher and abstract truth, his view is very much in line with Schlegel's understanding of the epics as a direct gateway to the ideas and the mindset of one's oldest ancestors:

> Sometimes the story is pure myth, or else it is a mixture of fact and myth, an exaggerated account of some incident that tradition preserved. Facts and fiction are so interwoven together as to be inseparable, and this amalgam becomes an imagined history, which may not tell us exactly what happened but does tell us something that is equally important – what people believed had taken place, what they thought their heroic ancestors were capable of, and what ideals inspired them.[80]

Despite such acknowledgements of their significance and their continued relevance for 'the unread masses of our people'[81] – particularly in Nehru's pre-independence works, such as *The Discovery of India* (1946) – his formulations at times betray a certain uneasiness with this continuing relevance. It is as if he is arguing against two sides at once when he is underscoring their importance and simultaneously hinting towards a threatening danger that might compel him to take action against the influence of the epics for India today: 'That influence is a good influence both culturally and ethically, and *I would hate to destroy or throw away* all the beauty and imaginative symbolism that these stories and allegories contain.'[82] Nehru does not say why he might feel compelled to 'destroy' them or why the question even comes up for him. In light of several of his other references to the Mahabharata and mythological literature more generally, though, it seems likely that what he is concerned about is precisely a kind of nostalgia for the nation's past that would prevent or hamper the national development in the present.

At first, such a rejection of an engagement with the past might seem surprising since Nehru had demonstrated a keen interest in Indian and world history, expressed particularly in *The Discovery of India* and *Glimpses of World History* (1934). When he talks about India's past, however, Nehru is very careful to emphasize India's cultural diversity and to depict its national unity as a result of India's ability to adapt to historical changes and to absorb foreign newcomers. His narrative of India's history is thus not one of decline and degradation – as found in those of Schlegel and Gupt – but one of an ever-adapting continuity.[83] The only real rupture in this continuing flow of historic time and the constant evolution of the Indian nation comes with the colonization and exploitation of the East India Company and the British Empire.[84] For him, the present state of India – which he occasionally described as an 'ancient country' steeped in a 'morass of ignorance, weakness and fear'[85] – is not the result of an earlier self-inflicted or naturally occurring spiritual decline or degradation – as Gupt and Schlegel had argued – but the consequence of imperialism, which had forcefully interrupted the nation's natural growth and development. From this perspective, an extensive engagement with the Mahabharata was not only unnecessary, but could even be potentially dangerous insofar as it would distract from the 'real' and more immediate political issues at hand. For someone like Nehru, who was so keen on strengthening the integrative function of nationalism and thus promoted the notion of 'diversity' as an integral part of the Indian nation, a strong emphasis on the significance of the Mahabharata posed the threat of jeopardizing a pluralistic vision of India.

Even when Nehru does talk about the Mahabharata in some detail – as in the short section in *The Discovery of India* that is specifically dedicated to it – difference and diversity are absolutely central. He neither presents the epic as a totality or even just a coherent whole nor does he say that it portrays, depicts, or talks about something that could be seen as a totality. Instead, he calls it 'a vast and miscellaneous collection of ancient lore' and argues that it marked 'the period when foreign elements were coming into India', which resulted in 'a curious mixture of opposing ideas and customs'.[86] His emphasis on the diversity and variety of themes and people in the Mahabharata does not mean, however, that Nehru entirely rejects the linkage between the epic and national unity. The moment of pluralization and diversification becomes instead itself intertwined with the process of unification, when Nehru sees in the Mahabharata 'a very definite attempt ... to emphasize the fundamental unity of India' and particularly perceives the Kurukshetra war – the most obvious symbol of conflict and difference – as marking 'the beginning of the conception of India as a whole, of Bhāratvarsha'.[87] It is only apt then that he finishes a selection of exemplary quotes from the Mahabharata with a positive appraisal of the social function of difference and conflict: 'Finally, the injunction so typical of a living and advancing people'; 'Discontent is the spur of progress.'[88] Despite his effort in *The Discovery of India* to promote a different understanding of the Mahabharata, Nehru did not return to this topic in any detail in his later texts, in which he mostly seems to regard an extensive engagement with the Mahabharata as parochial, conservative, and communalist. It is as if he gave up trying to wrest the Mahabharata from the more essentialist nationalist discourse and instead let it stand for a reactionary and backwards-looking approach to history and nationalism simultaneously.[89]

Nehru's view of the Mahabharata, or rather his lack of interest in the epic, could also be explained on an epistemological level that affords a closer look at the relationship between the changing understanding of nationalism and an equally changing notion of literature and its social function – both of which can be explored exceptionally well in Nehru's writing. While *nationalism* has had, from its very beginning, a particularly close relationship to the genre of the *epic*, the development of the *nation* itself has most directly been linked to the emergence of the *novel*. As Cheah reminds us, the connection between nation and novel has not only been drawn explicitly by Benedict Anderson but must also be understood as being heavily indebted to Walter Benjamin's work on historical time and Lukács' theory of the novel.[90] This brings me back to the question of totality. I have already argued that Nehru had no interest in nor use for a concept of transcendental closure. As his deliberate use of river metaphors for India shows, however, he still relied on a notion of totality – albeit a totality that was constantly changing and had to be perpetually rebuilt. This turn from a nostalgia for transcendental closure in Gupt's and Schlegel's writing to the always-changing totality of the Indian nation as a conglomeration of rivers and streams as well as a site of constant construction in Nehru – from Gupt's contribution to the development of *nationalism* in *Bharat Bharati* to Nehru's contribution to the development of *the nation* in his numerous speeches, articles, and letters – this turn conforms to the very same structure as the turn from the epic to the novel that Lukács writes about in his *Theory of the Novel*:

> The epic and the novel, these two major forms of great epic literature, differ from one another not by their authors' fundamental intentions but by the given historico-philosophical realities with which the authors were confronted. The novel is the epic of an age in which the extensive totality of life is no longer directly given, in which the immanence of meaning in life has become a problem, yet which still thinks in terms of totality.[91]

As an author of actual books (and not 'history' as such), Nehru wrote neither epics nor novels. Yet he was still confronted by the same 'historico-philosophical realities' that led to the gradual replacement of the epic by the novel.[92] In two essays[93] published in his last book, *Rajniti Se Dur* (*Far from Politics*)[94] – written in Hindi unlike his other books – Nehru explicitly dealt with the state of Indian literature. After admitting his limited knowledge of the subject,[95] Nehru bemoans the state of Indian literature, particularly in Hindi and other vernacular languages. He specifically criticizes the lack of any literature in India that could help one to understand 'today's world' ('aajakal ki duniya').[96]

While he is primarily talking about non-fiction writing, he also adds that this equally applies to fiction and particularly novels as well, when he declares: 'To my regret, I have not yet found any novel that could be compared to famous foreign novels.'[97] Nehru nonchalantly displays a quite extraordinary ignorance of Hindi literature, which he readily acknowledges but which does not keep him from giving suggestions and advice on what kind of topics authors should work on.[98] He is clearly arguing against what he perceives to be an overly strong engagement with the past at the expense of the present: 'A nation that remains attached only to its old literature, no matter how advanced it will be, will not be fully alive and unable to advance further.'[99] Therefore, he concludes that 'we have to prepare a foundation for *our new culture* in which the ideas of today's world can take roots so that we don't move about haphazardly when we encounter difficult issues'.[100]

In Nehru's eyes, then, the task of literature is not to inspire feelings of national identity and belonging – as Gupt had still argued in his foreword to *Bharat Bharati* – but to provide the tools that would allow the members of the nation to create a new space for them in a modern and global world, in which the individual had to experience the condition of a 'transcendental homelessness' as Lukács famously put it. Where Gupt was concerned with the identity and constitution of the national community as such – and turned to narratives about divine creation and transcendental closure – Nehru was more interested in the means that would allow the community to act and to construct a new – immanent – home within the nation state. In complaining about the continuing attachment to 'old literature', however, Nehru seems to have missed a crucial aspect of the texts he was implicitly criticizing. Gupt and other writers of the Hindi Renaissance were interested in the past not because they wanted to return to it, but because they hoped that it would provide a blueprint for the construction of a better future. And while the potentially parochial and essentialist aspects of texts such as *Bharat Bharati* can certainly not be ignored, it seems important to acknowledge that it did, in fact, contribute to a remarkably different future for the colonized Indian subjects. Conversely, however, it can also be seen as having paved the way for a very narrow and potentially racist understanding of Indian identity. However, because Nehru could not see the former, his view of the Mahabharata kept him from developing a more progressive reading of the epic that could have countered the latter.

Just as Schlegel's and Gupt's interest in the Mahabharata was premised on what Lukács called 'historico-philosophical realities' that in turn resulted from politico-historical events such as the Napoleonic Wars or the Rebellion of 1857, so was Nehru's disinterest in the Mahabharata equally connected to historical events and the historico-philosophical realities shaped by them. With the Indian nation being an established fact, the Mahabharata lost its appeal and most immediate effectivity for a progressive politics and became associated again with the more politically conservative and parochial aspects of Indian nationalism.

Notes

1. The notion of transcendental closure is indebted to Georg Lukács' work on the novel. Georg Lukács, *The Theory of the Novel: A Historico-Philosophical Essay on the Forms of Great Epic Literature* (Cambridge, MA: MIT Press, 1973).
2. Aandrew Sartori, 'Beyond Culture-Contact and Colonial Discourse: "Germanism" in Colonial Bengal', *Modern Intellectual History* 4, no. 1 (2007): 77–93, 82.
3. Sartori, 'Beyond Culture-Contact and Colonial Discourse', 84.
4. Sartori, 'Beyond Culture-Contact and Colonial Discourse', 78.
5. 'Friedrich Schlegel to Ludwig Tieck, 15 September 1803', in *Briefe an Ludwig Tieck*, ed. Karl von Holtei, 328–31 (Breslau: E. Trewendt, 1864), 329 (emphasis original, translation mine).
6. The relationship between the search for origins and an interest in Indian literature and culture in German romanticism and Friedrich Schlegel in particular has most recently been explored by Chen Tzoref-Ashkenazi in his *Der romantische Mythos vom Ursprung der Deutschen* (Göttingen: Wallstein, 2009).
7. Ernst Behler, 'Der Wendepunkt Friedrich Schlegels', *Philosophisches Jahrbuch* 64 (1956): 245–71, 245, 249, 250, and passim.
8. Paul de Man, 'Intentional Structure of the Romantic Image', in *Romanticism and Consciousness*, ed. Harold Bloom 65–77 (New York: Norton, 1970), 68.
9. This point about *Über die Sprache und Weisheit der Indier* 'offering the most clear picture of Schlegels Weltanschauung' at this decisive moment has been made by Behler as early as 1956. Ernst Behler, 'Der Wendepunkt Friedrich Schlegels', 248. Despite this assessment, however, he, like most other Schlegel scholars, did not really engage with the text on a philosophical basis.
10. Henry M. Hoenigswald, 'On the History of the Comparative Method', *Anthropological Linguistics* 35, nos. 1–4 (1993): 54–65; Thomas Lindner, 'Der präkomparatistische Sprachvergleich von Moses über Leibniz bis zum 16. Mai 1816', *Historische Sprachforschung/Historical Linguistics* 129 (2016): 221–32; Jean-Claude Muller, 'Early Stages of Language Comparison from Sassetti to Sir William Jones (1786)', *Kratylos* 31, no. 1 (1986): 1–31.

11. Friedrich Schlegel, 'On the Language and Wisdom of the Indians', in *Aesthetic and Miscellaneous Works of Frederick von Schlegel*, trans. Ellen J. Millington, 425–533 (London: Henry G. Bohn, 1849), 457; For the original German, see Friedrich Schlegel, 'Über die Sprache und Weisheit der Indier', in *Kritische Friedrich-Schlegel-Ausgabe*, Abteilung I, Band 8: *Studien zur Philosophie und Theologie (1796–1824)*, ed. Ernst Behler and Ursula Struc-Oppenberg, 105–433 (München: Ferdinand Schöningh, 1975), 173.

12. Schlegel, 'On the Language and Wisdom of the Indians', 465.

13. Bradley L. Herling, *The German Gītā: Hermeneutics and Discipline in the German Reception of Indian Thought, 1778–1831* (New York: Routledge, 2014), 134.

14. The political dimension of Schlegel's work has often been overlooked. An important early exception was an article by Günter Oesterle, originally published in 1989: 'Friedrich Schlegel in Paris oder die romantische Gegenrevolution', Goethezeitportal, 8 October 2005, http://www.goethezeitportal.de/db/wiss/schlegel_fr/oesterle_revolution.pdf (accessed on 9 January 2024). For an overview of more recent works in a similar vein as well as other new approaches to the study of German Orientalism, see Robert Cowan, 'Introduction: New Models for Indo-German Scholarship within the Critical Reappraisal of Orientalism', *The Comparatist* 34 (2010): 47–62.

15. Nicholas A. Germana, 'Self-Othering in German Orientalism: The Case of Friedrich Schlegel', *The Comparatist* 34, no. 1 (2010): 80–94, 90; Robert Cowan, *The Indo-German Identification: Reconciling South Asian Origins and European Destinies, 1765–1885* (Cambridge, UK: Cambridge University Press, 2013).

16. Oesterle, 'Friedrich Schlegel in Paris oder die romantische Gegenrevolution', 10 (translation mine).

17. For a detailed analysis of the relationship between Schlegel's Orientalism and an emerging nationalism, see Chen Tzoref-Ashkenazi, 'The Nationalist Aspect of Friedrich Schlegel's "On the Language and Wisdom of the Indians"', in *Sanskrit and 'Orientalism': Indology and Comparative Linguistics in Germany, 1750–1958*, ed. Douglas T. McGetchin, Peter K. J. Park, D. R. SarDesai, 107–31 (New Delhi: Manohar, 2004); Michael Dusche, 'German Romantics Imagining India: Friedrich Schlegel in Paris and Roots of Ethnic Nationalism in Europe', Goethezeitportal 21 November 2011, http://www.goethezeitportal.de/fileadmin/PDF/kk/df/postkoloniale_studien/dusche_romantics_imagining_india.pdf (accessed on 9 January 2024).

18. Joep Leerssen calls this time, the time of the Napoleonic Wars between 1801 and 1806, 'a turbulent watershed in European cultural history'. Joep Leerssen, 'From Bökendorf to Berlin: Private Careers, Public Sphere, and How the Past

Changed in Jacob Grimm's Lifetime', in *Free Access to the Past: Romanticism, Cultural Heritage and the Nation*, ed. Lotte Jensen, Joep Leerssen, and Marita Mathijsen-Verkooijen, 55–70 (Boston: Brill, 2010), 55.

19. Leerssen, 'From Bökendorf to Berlin', 58 (emphasis mine).

20. Klaus Peter, *Friedrich Schlegel* (Stuttgart: Metzler, 1978), 61 (translation mine).

21. The locus classicus would again be Paul de Man: 'The [Romantic] image is inspired by a nostalgia for the natural object, expanding to become nostalgia for the origin of this object. Such a nostalgia can only exist when the transcendental presence is forgotten.' de Man, 'Intentional Structure of the Romantic Image', 69.

22. Kevis Goodman, 'Romantic Poetry and the Science of Nostalgia', in *The Cambridge Companion to British Romantic Poetry*, ed. James Chandler, 195–216 (Cambridge, UK: Cambridge University Press, 2008), 196. For how this ties in with Schlegel's philosophy of history, see Herling, *The German Gītā*, 123.

23. Philippe Lacoue-Labarthe and Jean-Luc Nancy, *The Literary Absolute: The Theory of Literature in German Romanticism* (Albany, NY: State University of New York Press, 1988), 96.

24. Lacoue-Labarthe and Nancy, *The Literary Absolute*, 80.

25. Lukács, *The Theory of the Novel*, 33.

26. Lacoue-Labarthe and Nancy, *The Literary Absolute*, 44.

27. Achim Hölter points out that there is a range of epics that claim to represent and include within them the whole universe, or to be of universal applicability. Most of these epics carry this claim already in their titles that often include references to 'the Great ...', 'the Whole ...' , 'World ...', or 'Panto ...'. Achim Hölter, 'Totalität', in *Figuren des Globalen: Weltbezug und Welterzeugung in Literatur, Kunst und Medien*, ed. Christian Moser and Linda Simonis, 85–104 (Göttingen: V&R Unipress, 2014), 93. For the Mahabharata, this claim of a being a representation of totality is not only apparent from its title ('The Great Story of the Bharatas') but also from the famous verse 1.56.33: 'yadihāsti tadanyatra yannehāsti na tatkvachit' (Whatever can be found here is also elsewhere, what is not here is nowhere else).

28. Schlegel, 'On the Language and Wisdom of the Indians', 467.

29. Schlegel, 'On the Language and Wisdom of the Indians', 494.

30. Schlegel, 'On the Language and Wisdom of the Indians', 517–18.

31. Herling, *The German Gītā*, 136.

32. Herling, *The German Gītā*, 147–48.

33. Schlegel, 'On the Language and Wisdom of the Indians', 489. See also Herling, *The German Gītā*, 150.

34. See W. J. Johnson (ed.), *The Sauptikaparvan of the Mahabharata: The Massacre at Night* (Oxford: Oxford University Press, 2008), xxviii–xxxv. Johnson also refers to George Dumezil's analysis in *Mythe et épopée I,* according to which 'the whole Kurukṣetra war ... is an Indo-European eschatological conflict between good and evil, transposed to the battle between the Pandavas and the Kauravas.' Johnson, *The Sauptikaparvan of the Mahabharata,* xxxi.

35. The term *Epopee or Epopöe* from the French 'épopée' was also widely used at that time, but had a slightly broader scope and was usually used to refer to any kind of narrative poetry that was neither 'historical' or 'factual' nor 'dramatic.'

36. '[Das] zweite große Heldengedicht der Indier', whereas the *Ramayana* was presumably regarded as the 'first' of the heroic poems. Schlegel, 'Über die Sprache und Weisheit der Indier', 393 (translation mine).

37. Schlegel, 'On the Language and Wisdom of the Indians', 496–504, also 513.

38. In 1799, Wilhelm von Humboldt explicitly linked this death of the epic to the historic transformation initiated by the French Revolution. Thomas Taterka, 'Die Nation erzählt sich selbst. Zum europäischen Nationalepos des 19. Jahrhunderts', in *Nationalepen zwischen Fakten und Fiktionen,* ed. Detering Heinrich, Pasewalck Silke, Hoffmann Torsten, Pormeister Eve, 20–72 (Tartu: University of Tartu Press, 2011), 23.

39. Hegel uses the term *Nationale Grundbücher* in a section of his *Lectures on Aesthetics* that bears the headline 'Das Epos als einheitsvolle Totalität' (The Epic as Fully Unified Totality). Georg Wilhelm Friedrich Hegel, *Vorlesungen über die Ästhetik,* vol. 3 (Frankfurt am Main: Suhrkamp, 1970), 373. See also Taterka, 'Die Nation erzählt sich selbst', 31.

40. Lukács also suggested that the 'community' of the epic (which is understood as the nation at the moment of its own becoming) presents an organic and concrete totality. Lukács, *The Theory of the Novel,* 67.

41. Sartori, 'Beyond Culture-Contact and Colonial Discourse', 79.

42. 'Nav Jagran', or 'New Awakening', is the Hindi term used for the turn to India's ancient past in search for a new national identity and eventually freedom and independence.

43. Gupt is generally regarded as *the* central figure of the Nav Jagran, or Hindi Renaissance: 'Just as Rabindranāth Tagore is the poet of the Renaissance in Bengali, Maithilīśaraṇa Gupta is considered the poet of the new awakening in Hindi.' Ramdhari Singh Dinkar, 'Maithilīśaraṇa Gupta as a Poet of the Renaissance', in *Maithilīśaraṇa Gupta: An Anthology,* ed. Nagendra, 88–114 (Delhi: Bansal & Co., 1981), 96.

44. Pamela Lothspeich, *Epic Nation: Reimagining the Mahabharata in the Age of the Empire* (New Delhi: Oxford University Press, 2009), 109.

45. Maithilisharan Gupt, *Jayadrath-Vadh* (Jhansi: Sahitya Sadan, 1994 [1910]).

46. Lothspeich, *Epic Nation*, 20.
47. Rakesh H. Solomon, 'Culture, Imperialism, and Nationalist Resistance: Performance in Colonial India', *Theatre Journal* 46, no. 3 (1994): 323–47, 326–28.
48. The strong emphasis on the allegorical aspects can also be seen as falling squarely into Frederic Jameson's paradigm of 'national allegory', despite Lothspeich's own critique of Jameson. Lothspeich, *Epic Nation*, 222. The problem does not so much lie in the allegorical reading per se, but rather in the fact that the analysis of the rhetorics of the texts in question remains limited to their (national) allegories and an all too narrow understanding of the 'tropical' aspects of literature. Curiously, one could argue that even Sartori remains within Jameson's paradigm insofar as the trope of 'Germany' stands in for the very idea of nationality itself (hence the need to identify with Germany in order to become one's own nation).
49. Anindita Ghosh, 'Revisiting the "'Bengal Renaissance'": Literary Bengali and Low-Life Print in Colonial Calcutta', *Economic and Political Weekly* 37, no. 42 (2002): 4329–38, 4329.
50. For this, see Ghosh, 'Revisiting the "'Bengal Renaissance'"' and, more broadly, Sumit Sarkar, 'Orientalism Revisited: Saidian Frameworks in the Writing of Modern Indian History', *Oxford Literary Review* 16, nos. 1–2 (1994): 205–24.
51. Ramesh Rawat, '1857 and the "Renaissance" in Hindi Literature', *Social Scientist* 26, nos. 1–4 (1998): 95–112, 96.
52. I. N. Choudhuri emphasises the particularly important role of *Bharat Bharati* in this process when he calls it the 'barometer of the political consciousness of that era'. I. N. Choudhuri, 'National Trends in Maithilīśaraṇa's Poetry', in *Maithilīśaraṇa Gupta: An Anthology*, ed. Nagendra, 115–21 (Delhi: Bansal & Co., 1981), 119.
53. Rawat, '1857 and the "Renaissance" in Hindi Literature', 96–99.
54. Rawat, '1857 and the "Renaissance" in Hindi Literature', 99.
55. See particularly the introduction as well as the other articles in a special issue on the Revolt of 1857 in *Economic and Political Weekly*. Biswamoy Pati, 'Historians and Historiography: Situating 1857', *Economic and Political Weekly* 42, no. 19 (2007): 1686–91.
56. Maithilisharan Gupt, *Bharat Bharati* (Jhansi: Sahitya Sadan, 1927), 4.
57. Francesca Orsini, *The Hindi Public Sphere 1920–1940: Language and Literature in the Age of Nationalism* (Oxford: Oxford University Press, 2009), 192.
58. Orsini, *The Hindi Public Sphere*, 195.

59. This is all the more striking since the text was largely inspired by 'Musaddas', a poem about the present state and history of the Muslim community in India by Altaf Husain Hali, which had been published in 1869. See Orsini, *The Hindi Public Sphere*, 193; Shamsher Bahadur Singh, '"Musaddas" Aur "Bharat-Bharti" Ki Sanskritik Bhumika', *Naya Sahitya* 5 (1945): 67–74.

60. Gupt, *Bharat Bharati*, 68.

61. Orsini, *The Hindi Public Sphere*, 197.

62. Gupt, *Bharat Bharati*, 69 (translation mine).

63. Orsini, *The Hindi Public Sphere*, 200.

64. Gupt, *Bharat Bharati*, 4.

65. Gupt, *Bharat Bharati*, 5.

66. This is a quote that Gupt seems to have taken from an article by D. O. Brown that was published in the *Daily Tribune* in 1884. Gupt, *Bharat Bharati*, 16.

67. Gupt, *Bharat Bharati*, 22.

68. Gupt does not cite a specific place in the Mahabharata for this claim. Gupt, *Bharat Bharati*, 23. He goes even further, however, and claims that there is ample evidence that would suggest that the Aryans also travelled to South America, settled there, and thus colonized and 'discovered' the land long before Columbus did. Gupt, *Bharat Bharati*, 21. Schlegel raises a similar point in regard to Peru and and refers to unnamed Chinese sources for this claim. Schlegel, 'On the Language and Wisdom of the Indians', 505.

69. Gupt specifically refers to the praise of Kalidasa and his *Abhijñanashakuntalam* by Alexander von Humboldt. He had probably read a translated quotation of Humboldt's praise in Monier Monier-Williams' introduction to his own English translation of *Shakuntala*, published in 1855. Gupt, *Bharat Bharati*, 42; Romila Thapar, *Śakuntalā: Texts, Readings, Histories* (New York: Columbia University Press, 2011), 223.

70. Gesine Lenore Schiewer, 'Übersetzung und Rezeption des "Mahâbhârata": Literarische Interkulturalität bei Friedrich Schlegel, Franz Bopp, Friedrich Rückert und Alfred Döblin', in *Der Gott der Anderen: Interkulturelle Transformationen religiöser Traditionen*, ed. Ernest W. B. Hess-Lüttich and Arupon Natarajan, 225–47 (Frankfurt am Main: Lang, 2009).

71. Lothspeich, *Epic Nation*, 2–3.

72. Gupt, *Bharat Bharati*, 68 (translation mine).

73. Pramod Kumar Srivastava, 'Nationalism Imagined? Hidden Impacts of the Uprising of 1857', *South Asia Research* 38, no. 3 (2018): 229–46.

74. See also Charlton Payne, *The Epic Imaginary, Political Power and Its Legitimations in Eighteenth-Century German Literature* (Berlin: De Gruyter, 2012), 13; Heiko Christians, *Der Traum vom Epos: Romankritik und*

politische Poetik in Deutschland (1750–2000) (Freiburg im Breisgau: Rombach, 2004).

75.   Pheng Cheah, *Spectral Nationality: Passages of Freedom from Kant to Postcolonial Literatures of Liberation* (New York: Columbia University Press, 2003), 32.

76.   Cheah, *Spectral Nationality*, 6.

77.   It should be added here again that the Mahabharata was not the only Indian text that played a role in the construction of the concept of nationality in Schlegel's work. In *Über die Sprache und Weisheit der Indier*, Schlegel showed a keen interest in the *Manusmriti* and used it in order to makes assumptions about the 'racial' make-up of the Indian subcontinent and the global migration of its various peoples, tribes, and races (he uses all these terms). Schlegel, 'On the Language and Wisdom of the Indians', 510. Gupt's *Bharat Bharati* also shows significant influence of the *Manusmriti*, according to Shamsher Bahadur Singh, who argues that 'the base of the poet's social ideals are the caste system of the Ramayana and Mahabharata period'. Singh, '"Musaddas" Aur "Bharat-Bharti"', 68 (translation mine).

78.   This is from the famous speech that Nehru delivered on the eve of India's independence. Jawaharlal Nehru, 'A Tryst with Destiny', in *Selected Works of Jawaharlal Nehru* (Second Series), vol. 3, ed. Sarvepalli Gopal, 135–36 (New Delhi: Jawaharlal Nehru Memorial Fund, 1985).

79.   Jawaharlal Nehru, 'India's March towards Prosperity (Speech at the Concluding Function of the All-India Gram Pracharak Training Camp, Indraprastha Gurukul, Near Delhi, 13 April 1958)', in *Selected Works of Jawaharlal Nehru* (Second Series), vol. 42, ed. Aditya Mukherjee and Mridula Mukherjee, 81–84 (New Delhi: Jawaharlal Nehru Memorial Fund, 2010), 82.

80.   Jawaharlal Nehru, *The Discovery of India* (New Delhi: Oxford University Press, 1989), 101.

81.   Nehru, *The Discovery of India*, 101.

82.   Nehru, *The Discovery of India,* 101 (emphasis mine).

83.   This understanding of history is aptly illustrated by Nehru's frequent use of river metaphors, such as the one cited earlier or this example from *Glimpses of World History*: 'The river of history has run on from age to age, continuously, interminably, with its eddies and whirlpools and backwaters, and still rushes on to an unknown sea.' Jawaharlal Nehru, *Glimpses Of World History* (New York: Asia Publishing House, 1962), 177.

84.   Nalini Bhushan and Jay L. Garfield, *Minds without Fear: Philosophy in the Indian Renaissance* (New York: Oxford University Press, 2017), 106.

85.   This description of India is part of a speech that again uses the Mahabharata to construct an analogy between the heroic stories of the past and the epic task

of Gandhi. Jawaharlal Nehru, 'Gandhian India: Speech at a Public Meeting Organized by the Delhi State Congress Committee to Commemorate the Sixth Death Anniversary of Mahatma Gandhi, New Delhi, 30 January 1954', in *Selected Works of Jawaharlal Nehru* (Second Series), vol. 24, ed. Ravinder Kumar and Sharada Prasad, 103–20 (New Delhi: Jawaharlal Nehru Memorial Fund, 1999), 104.

86. Nehru, *The Discovery of India,* 106.
87. Nehru, *The Discovery of India,* 107.
88. Nehru, *The Discovery of India,* 108.
89. As already mentioned, most of Nehru's later references to the Mahabharata are only in passing and use the epics to draw an analogy to the current political situation. In several instances, however, he seems to criticize a certain tendency to take the epic too literally or to read it as a guideline for contemporary issues. See, for example, Jawaharlal Nehru, 'The Arduous Task Ahead: Speech in Parliament on the Presidents Address, 3 February 1950', in *Selected Works of Jawaharlal Nehru* (Second Series), vol. 14, pt 1, ed. Sarvepalli Gopal, 270–84 (New Delhi: Jawaharlal Nehru Memorial Fund, 1992), 272.
90. Cheah, *Spectral Nationality,* 241. See also Pieter Vermeulen, 'The Novel and the Nation: The Case of David Grossman's See Under: Love', *Neophilologus* 96, no. 1 (2012): 1–15.
91. Lukács, *The Theory of the Novel,* 56. See also Cheah, *Spectral Nationality,* 242.
92. See his discussion of the development of the novel in England. Nehru, *Glimpses Of World History,* 350.
93. The essays are 'Hamara Sahitya' (Our Literature) and 'Sahitya Ki Buniyad' (The Foundation of Literature) in Jawaharlal Nehru, *Rajniti Se Dur* (New Delhi: Sasta Sahitya Mandal, 1957), 121–30, 130–33.
94. For a closer look at this often neglected book, see Swapna Kona Nayudu, 'Swadeshi Ink on Swadeshi Paper: Jawaharlal Nehru's Rajneeti Se Door', *Global Intellectual History* 2, no. 3 (2017): 389–407.
95. A somewhat surprising declaration from the first serving president of the Sahitya Akademi, India's academy of literature. Vinay Lal, 'Nehru as a Writer', *Indian Literature* 33, no. 135 (1990): 20–46, 21.
96. Nehru, *Rajniti Se Dur,* 124.
97. Nehru, *Rajniti Se Dur,* 125 (translation mine).
98. Nehru, *Rajniti Se Dur,* 127.
99. Nehru, *Rajniti Se Dur,* 130.
100. Nehru, *Rajniti Se Dur,* 132 (emphasis mine, translation mine).

5

The Production and Deconstruction of the 'Ideal Indian Woman' on the Basis of the Mahabharata in the Twentieth and Twenty-First Centuries

Melanie J. Müller

Introduction

The Mahabharata and the Ramayana have significantly shaped South Asian norms of gender roles. The ideals transmitted through them are still often considered the proper mode of conduct by many actors and social groups, especially those influenced by Sanskritic *varna–jati* (the Indian caste system) norms. While the most popular female prototype among many actors is Sita from the Ramayana, the Mahabharata offers a number of exemplary characters as well. Not only Draupadi but also characters such as Damayanti and Savitri play an important role in shaping the myth of the ideal woman. The French philosopher Roland Barthes explains in his book *Mythologies* (1957) that myth is born out of history but disconnects from it and evolves into nature. As the content of the myth seems like an eternal truth, its motive appears invisible.[1] The Mahabharata shaped an understanding of women and their role in society, which was accepted for centuries as the natural rule. The gendered basis of this discourse was rarely explicitly questioned until recent times.

This chapter begins by first tracing the origin of how mythological women became the ideal prototype in the nationalist discourse, which will be followed by a focus on M. K. Gandhi's politics regarding women. Traits which most of the epic female characters share are that they suffer silently and resist through loyalty and devotion – characteristics that modern reformers like Gandhi foregrounded in an attempt to mobilize women for the Indian nationalist cause.

While his discourse elevated the status of women to a higher position, it came at a cost, and by fortifying the image of the ideal Indian woman, he put them in a gilded cage. The rest of the chapter will focus on feminist revision of myths, necessary to deconstruct the female prototype born out of the epics, based on the theoretical framework offered by Adrienne Rich's 'When We Dead Awaken: Writing as Re-Vision' (1972) and Alicia Ostriker's 'The Thieves of Language: Women Poets and Revisionist Mythmaking' (1982). For this, I will take into account several literary texts. Pratibha Ray's (b. 1943) Odia novel *Yajnaseni* (1984) and Chitra Banerjee Divakaruni's (b. 1956) novel *The Palace of Illusions* (2008) are two important landmarks in this paradigm shift. However, since they have already been amply discussed and analysed, like in Beena G.'s *Vision and Re-Vision: Revisiting Mythologies, Rethinking Women* (2019) or Pamela Lothspeich's 'Draupadī, Yājñaseni, Pāñcālī, Kṛṣṇā: Representations of an Epic Heroine in Three Novels' (2021),[2] I will summarize them briefly before I focus on Mahasweta Devi's (1926–2016) short story collection *After Kurukshetra* (2005), which focuses on subaltern women who were marginalized in the traditional Mahabharata and suppressed by the privileged elite.

The Birth of the Myth of the 'Ideal Indian Woman'

Myths help humans explain the order of the world and legitimize social hierarchy. According to the German philosopher Hans Blumenberg, the function of myth is to solve existential problems in a way that no further questions arise. Myths came into existence to name things, a means of helping humans cope with the anxieties of the world.[3] This aligns with Stephen Ausband, who equates myth with language because it brings new experiences into a familiar context. Humans need to name things in order to understand them.[4] The ideology born out of myths achieves a status of being 'natural' through being constantly repeated. There is a tight codependency between myth and nationalism. Nationalist discourses fall back on myth and fill the meaning of mythological symbols with the values necessary for their cause. Nationalism gives life to myth through its constant repetition and through elevating it to a universal truth. However, at the same time, nationalism needs myth to legitimize itself.[5]

In her article 'Whatever Happened to the Vedic Dasi?', the Indian historian Uma Chakravarti depicts how the nationalist myth of the ideal Indian woman came to life. In the eighteenth century, European Orientalists took interest in South Asian languages and literatures and reconstructed a golden Vedic age with the intention to approximate it to the Indian people as their historic past.[6]

Their intention was to reveal the true national identity of the Indian people, influenced by Johann Gottfried von Herder's theory that this could be achieved through studying the mythology of the culture in question.[7] Early Indian nationalist writers took up this idealized depiction of a glorious past and contrasted it with the difficulties of the present. The British Sanskrit scholar Henry Thomas Colebrooke was the first to focus on the condition of women in his work *On the Duties of the Faithful Hindu Widow* (1795), where he mainly focused on the practice of sati. From that moment on, the focus went over to the women's condition, and it became the political playground on which the British legitimized the colonisation of India: 'The "higher" morality of the imperial masters could be effectively established by highlighting the low status of women among the subject population as it was an issue by which the moral "inferiority" of the subject population could simultaneously be demonstrated.'[8]

In the 1830s, a new cultural nationalism arose as a response to the criticism of Hindu civilization, the threat through Christian missionaries, and the prohibition of sati, the latter of which was experienced like an intrusion in private family matters. The Scottish historian James Mill's *History of British India* (1817) was the catalyst for Indian proto-nationalists to defend themselves through their glorious past and the high status of women during the golden age. In 1856, Charlotte Speier published her *Life in Ancient India*, where she drew a romantic picture of Indian womanhood in the past. She admired the women from ancient literature, such as Damayanti and Savitri, but criticized the loss of the high status of women in the present.

However, it was not only the condition of women which was criticized by the Orientalists; men too were pictured as weak and lazy. To revoke this feeling of weakness, the nationalists constructed 'a trans-regional unified Hindu identity ... using elements from history and folklore to valorize heroic action.'[9] Aspects of the Kshatriya code and spirituality were the key elements of this new aggressive nationalism. The Orientalist wave of studying the ancient Sanskrit scriptures like the Vedas, Puranas, and the two epics Mahabharata and Ramayana swapped back to the Indian intellectuals. Nationalist propaganda, literature, and school schedules[10] had great influence on the shaping of a text-based Indian identity. They worked with the Orientalist construct of a script-based 'Hinduism' to build a new unified Hindu identity, which was at the same time understood as Indian identity. And as Uma Narayan states: 'Essentialist pictures of "national culture and traditions" ... are used to dismiss a variety of political demands for justice, equality, rights, or democracy as symptoms of the "cultural corruption" wrought by "Western ideas.'"[11] This made it difficult for women to fight for their own rights while fighting colonialism at the same time.

There were various important factors involved in the building of a new Indian identity during the colonial period. On the one hand, the nationalists adopted the material world of the West, which 'had given the European countries the strength to subjugate non-European peoples'.[12] On the other hand, there existed the romantic Orientalist idea of the East's 'spiritual' superiority. Western academics identified the Indian spiritual essence as pure and non-violent. These positive stereotypes were employed by Indian reformers such as Ram Mohan Roy, Swami Vivekananda, and Mohandas Gandhi to develop an anti-colonial nationalist discourse, a procedure Richard Fox calls 'affirmative Orientalism'.[13] There existed the simultaneous need to evolve in the material sphere, while at the same time ensuring that the spiritual sphere remains fortified. This material–spiritual distinction parallels the outer–inner and the world–home dichotomy.[14] This dichotomy played an important role in nationalism. In the outside world, they were humiliated and oppressed by the colonial rulers, but in the home, in their inner self, they found superiority through their spiritual qualities. The spiritual (or inner or home) sphere was associated with the feminine, since women have been honoured for their spiritual potential, while the material (or outer or world) sphere was represented by the masculine, assigning women the important task of protecting the spiritual superiority. This task was elevated to a high status during Gandhian nationalism. The ideology of separate social spheres is defined

> as a belief system that claims that: 1) gender differences in society are innate, rather than culturally or situationally created; 2) these innate differences lead men and women to freely participate in different spheres of society; and 3) gendered differences in participation in public and private spheres are natural, inevitable, and desirable.[15]

This belief system refers to a separate-but-equal logic that separates the different spheres by gender, but sees the female role in the household and the masculine role in the working world as equally important, an idea adopted by many nationalist reformers.

For the construction of the ideal Indian woman of the nineteenth century, the reformists resorted to the Vedic past, and an image of a prototypical woman was constructed, one who was educated and spiritual and who stood in unwavering support of her husband. The Bengali novelist Bankim Chandra

Chattopadhyay pictured the ideal Indian woman as devoted to her husband with her primary aspiration centred around embodying the essence of true wifehood. This commitment was extended to the support of the husband in the nationalist struggle. He also thought that only the Aryan invaders had a sense of nation but lost it when they were separated into smaller groups.[16] This is a frequent claim by nationalists, who say that nations have always existed, but people lost their sense of nationhood and only recently their national identity has been recovered.[17] As in other nationalist movements in the world, myth was used to create the image of a unified nation. It is common for nationalist discourses to depict the unified nation as already present and at the same time as the aim for the future.[18] The unity of 'us' stands in opposition to the hostile 'them', as in 'us, the Indians' and 'them, the Western invaders'. In the Indian nationalist discourse of the nineteenth century, Western and Westernized women were caricatured and ridiculed to such an extent that no South Asian woman wanted to resemble them.[19] There was a clear differentiation between the ideal Indian woman and the image of the women of the enemy.

Women had internalized the female role model of the traditional texts, which became the leading image by the second half of the nineteenth century. The Polish philosopher Kołakowski explains that 'the inheritance of myths is the inheritance of values which myths impose'.[20] This descriptive–prescriptive function of myth works as long as no one questions those values. The image of the female prototype had been passed on through generations, but it became especially fortified through the nationalist discourse. Many reformists such as Vivekananda idealized epic heroines such as Damayanti and Sita. Especially the latter was worthy of his reverence:

> Sita is unique.... She is the very type of the true Indian woman, for all the Indian ideals of a perfected woman have grown out of that one life of Sita ... purer than purity itself, all patience and all suffering. She who suffered that life of suffering without a murmur, she the ever-chaste and ever-pure wife, she the ideal of the people, the ideal of the gods, the great Sita, our national God she must always remain.[21]

Even though Draupadi and Kunti did not form part of his group of ideal women, in his summary of the Mahabharata he describes the heroines as 'the loving mother Kunti, the ever-devoted and all-suffering Draupadi',[22] alluding to the female ideal of the self-sacrificing mother and wife.

Gandhi and the Production of the 'Ideal Indian Woman'

Operating through the gendered binary of separate spheres, the women were relegated to the sphere of the domestic, even if this domestic household space was also extended into the nation. Gandhi rejected violence as a political strategy for women, and even though Draupadi is one of the most important female characters in the Mahabharata, he only praised her faith but condemned her anger. He wanted to improve the female conditions in society but confined this freedom to the ideal Sita–Savitri-like woman. The idea of the British that women's position indicates a society's advancement echoed with Indian nationalists, and one step on the way to independence was to redefine 'femininity' and, by this, also 'Indian tradition'.[23] He thought that women, and India in general, had abandoned the high qualities of chastity, self-control, and sacrifice, and in order to be free and equal, they had to incorporate them again. In the following quote, he explains his goal:

> In my humble opinion, in order to make the attempt we will have to produce women, pure, firm and self-controlled as Sita, Damayanti and Draupadi. If we do produce them, such modern sisters will receive the same homage from Hindu society as is being paid to their prototypes of yore.[24]

He used the term 'produce'. He did not say that 'we have to educate', 'we have to support', or 'we have to build up'; he said 'we will have to produce', and by this he reduced the ideal woman to a product, a tradeable good in the nationalist movement.

Gandhi proclaimed that women and men were equal and that there were certain qualities inherent to women, which were just the right qualities for a non-violent struggle. It was not his intention to create full gender equality. His ideology relied on the separate-but-equal logic described earlier. He declared that wife and husband are equal, saying 'it is the duty of the husband to consider his wife a true companion, helper and his better half. A wife is never to be considered her husband's slave, nor merely meant to be the object of his lust.'[25] This understanding of gender roles resulted in the early women's movements having a *difference feminist* trait, one that is still very strong in modern feminist movements. Difference feminism proclaims that there are biological and social differences between men and women but that they are equal in their worth. The problem of difference feminism is that while it might be empowering for some, the essentialist gender binary through which it operates punishes everyone who does not or does not want to fit in their socially predetermined role.[26]

Narayan explains that the problem with gender essentialism is that what is presented as 'women's issues' are in fact the issues of privileged women.[27]

At first, Gandhi did not encourage women to step into the public sphere. He wanted them to support the independence movement through the spinning of *khadi*, which they could do from their homes. Later it was the higher-caste women who urged him to let them participate more actively in the struggle, and slowly he started to see the advantages of women's participation. He knew that the image of thousands of women protesting peacefully would have a huge impact in international media. He wanted to convince the Indians and the world that Indian women were strong and equal to men, and he empowered women by relating their household chores to their duties towards their country. Geraldine Forbes points out that 'women could "come out" because the house was on fire. The expectation was that once the fire was out, women would go back inside the house.'[28] The women who participated in the freedom struggle usually did this under male patronage. They marched in separate groups from the men or with their families. The exception were the women of the revolutionary movement, who worked alongside men, but they were not considered 'real' women. The kind of pride that elite Hindu women got through invoking the epic women also made them look down on women who were not as 'pure'. Most lower-caste women had to work outside the private sphere in order to provide for their families, while the women of the higher castes were supposed to stay at home in order to conserve their purity.[29] In the public sphere they and their sexuality could not be monitored, and thus they were seen as '"impure" or "lacking in virtue"'.[30] While upper-caste women are controlled and experience violence within the family, lower caste women are vulnerable to rape and sexual harassment because of their exposure to the public sphere, which makes their sexuality seem available to everyone at all times.[31] They refused to work and march with 'unworthy' women because they were afraid to be confused with sex workers.[32] Ironically, it was the 'fallen sisters',[33] as Gandhi called them, who took the first steps into the public sphere to fight for independence. 'Fallen from where?' asks Mridula Garg. 'Not a position of influence or power but from the image of Sati Savitri or the purity of the body.'[34] Gandhi suggested that the sex workers give up prostitution and earn their living through spinning, but they did not earn enough money by that, so he was not really able to find a realistic alternative for them.[35] When a group of sex workers from Barishal in present-day Bangladesh was trying to reform themselves through education and spinning and wanted to join 'all other institutions, which have satyagraha and non-violence as their creed',[36] Gandhi appealed for a boycott of their organization, calling them thieves of virtue.[37] He was not able to find a solution for either the sex workers or the women who wanted to participate in the movement without risking their reputations. This was because he did not question the basic economic and social condition of women. He wanted the women of the higher class and respectable families to be the leaders of the movement, not the 'wrong' kind of women. Women's organizations such as the Desh Sevika Sangha were worried about the unrespectable or lower-caste women who wanted to join their movement, and they made it clear that they only wanted class- and caste-privileged women, because they were dependent on the respect from the public for their picketing practices.[38] Therefore, even though in theory their membership was open to all women, they restricted it to the 'pure women'. By this, the invoking of the female prototype from the epics turned out to be harmful, pushing the 'undesirable' women even more into the social periphery, even though they were the most vulnerable ones.

But even if women started to participate in politics, Gandhi stressed that a woman's place was in the household as a mother and wife, using essentialist arguments like the female innate capacity to suffer or to care, as pictured in epic women such as Sita, Savitri, Damayanti, and even Draupadi. The recurring image of the self-sacrificing mother and wife is strongly linked to the heroines of the epics. Draupadi, for instance, is known for her unconditional devotion to her husbands. This self-sacrifice happened under the disguise of *stri dharma*. *Stri dharma* is a set of the duties regarding marriage, sexuality, and motherhood of the ideal wife, although it is aimed at high-caste elite women. One important part of matrimony is reproduction, so women must 'consider childbearing, sexual duties aimed toward the birth of sons and heirs, and domestic duties as their prime responsibility'.[39] A woman who follows *stri dharma* becomes a *pativrata* (a devoted and virtuous wife), such as Sita, Savitri, or Draupadi, and will be honoured and socially respected. *Stri dharma* claims that loyalty and devotion to their husbands is the only way by which women will get the highest spiritual merit. It is a guide for women to help them with their flawed female characters, and 'men can indirectly control women by "allowing" women to control themselves; and to control themselves in a way that promotes the interests of a patriarchal social structure'.[40] In order to uphold endogamy and the separation of castes, women's bodies are controlled since they are seen 'as gateways ... into the caste system'.[41] *Stri dharma* makes women believe that if they control their own sexuality they would gain 'power and respect through the codes they adopted'.[42] Thus, women who support the caste system, thinking it would benefit them, have to subordinate themselves to Brahmanical patriarchy and thereby play an important role in sustaining gender inequality. It is a code that directly benefits men and patriarchy and makes women believe that it benefits them too. As the renowned feminist Simone de Beauvoir said: 'History has shown that men have always held all the concrete powers; from patriarchy's earliest times they have deemed it useful to keep woman in a state of dependence; their codes were set up against her; she was thus concretely established as the Other.'[43] Epic heroines such as Draupadi and Damayanti show infinite loyalty to their husbands – by following their husbands into exile, in the case of these two women. Even though Gandhi never used the term *stri dharma*, he spoke about women's duties, paralleling the rules of *stri dharma*, and whenever doing so, he invoked the heroines of the epics. However, there is one important distinction, which is that Gandhi did not want women to devote themselves entirely to their husbands but to the freedom struggle. He often pictured the ideal woman as sister instead of wife because the latter only serves one, while the sister serves the whole nation.

Gandhi's construction of the ideal woman was empowering because it gave women a high status in society, but he did not analyse the origins and nature of women's oppression. Since he did not prioritize emancipation, he was primarily concerned with the moral condition of women rather than their material circumstances. Gandhi gave women the chance to participate in the freedom movement, but he prioritized India's independence over women's necessities, such as safety and education: 'the way to women's freedom is not through education but through the change of attitude on the part of men and corresponding action. Education is necessary, but it must follow the freedom.'[44] He also was not particularly fond of the feminist movement, as we can see in the following example:

> If the women do not remind themselves of the examples of Draupadi and Sita and display the same strength of virtue, they will never be able to serve the country well no matter how many of them get educated.... I know that today women have taken the downward path. In their craze for equality with men, they have forgotten their duty.[45]

Stri dharma is loyalty to not only the husband but the whole clan, which in this case is the Indian nation. Thereby, women were expected to do what was best for the nation, even if this meant sacrificing their own independence. He failed to realize that oppression is also related to historical and economic factors, such as the difficulties women were presented with when entering the working world. The extension of the household for the nationalist movement into the public sphere shows similarity with the understanding of women's work in the nineteenth and early twentieth centuries.

The traditional occupations for women were in superior crafts for extended markets, caste-specific occupations, or in subsistence crafts. All these occupations were linked to the household, and traditionally women would work as part of the family team.[46] With the rise of industrialization, there was a notable decline in these occupations, and even though new jobs were created, they did not provide the possibility to work inside the private sphere. Still, in times of need, women sought out work in factories or jute mills to provide for their families.[47] Similarly, when the 'motherland' was in need, women were urged to participate in the freedom struggle. This was also possible because of the non-violent form of the freedom struggle that allowed women to enter the public sphere without losing their 'purity'.

When asked how a woman can contradict her husband without risking losing everything when she is totally economically dependent on him, Gandhi replied: 'If you study statistics, you will find that what you say about the economic condition of a Hindu woman holds good only in the case of a microscopic minority. Do you not know that in Indian houses it is the woman that is generally the master?'[48] This proves that he had no idea as to what women's economic reality actually looked like.

In one instance, Gandhi wished for women to achieve equality with men, but at the same time he stressed the different places in society for them.[49] This is a statement he repeated on several occasions:

> Equality of the sexes does not mean equality of occupations. There may be no legal bar against a woman hunting or wielding a lance. But she instinctively recoils from a function that belongs to man. Nature has created sexes as complements of each other. Their functions are defined as are their forms.[50]

> The duty of motherhood, which the vast majority of women will always undertake, requires qualities which man need not possess.... He is the bread-winner, she is the keeper and distributor of the bread. She is caretaker in every sense of the term. The art of bringing up the infants of the race is her special and sole prerogative.[51]

The images of mother and householder are combined in the image of *annapurna*, the 'provider of food and comfort in the family'.[52] Even in misery women are supposed to provide food, water, and other basic needs for their families. Woman as the provider of food is an image we also find in the Mahabharata.

When Draupadi follows her husbands into exile, it is her task to provide them with food. She receives a magic pot that fills up with food once she puts the cooking spoon in it and repeats filling itself until she eats from it. This underlines that Draupadi is responsible for providing the family with food, but also that she would eat last, in concordance with the right conduct for women.[53]

Gandhi went as far as to say that the separation of the spheres should start with education: '[I]t is my confirmed opinion that women should get a distinct kind of education. The two [referring to men and women] have separate spheres of activity and their training, therefore, should also be different.'[54] This manner of confining the private sphere of the home as the main place for women is still a major obstacle for them in order to achieve leading positions in the working world. Nowadays women are allowed to go out into the public sphere to reach for a career, but at the same time society expects them to keep their role as homemakers. Women take on the dual role of employee and wife–mother in the household.[55] For women to be entirely free and equal, they must be independent from men. They must lose their sole definition as wife or mother and gain the definition of human being. For this, it is imperative that their economic condition betters and not just their moral standing in society.

Gandhi's use of Draupadi as an example is quite interesting since she actually possesses qualities that are contrary to what he was praising as ideal. Draupadi is often described as aggressive and proud, even though she just points out the injustices she is suffering. However, these very qualities make her an attractive candidate for the radical feminist movement. For example, the socialist politician Ram Manohar Lohia explained in his essay 'Draupadi or Savitri' (1962) why Draupadi is a better example to follow than Savitri, even though he recognized the patriarchal structure of myths. In his opinion, the Sita–Savitri ideal is mostly superficial given that it is based on physical purity, while Draupadi comes across as more multifaceted since she is intelligent and determined.[56] She does not act in an erratic way; she was humiliated repeatedly and sexually assaulted while none of her five husbands defended her. She turned the tables around when she resisted the men who were about to humiliate her and shamed them for doing so. Nevertheless, Gandhi praises her devotion and her purity, as seen in the following examples, and not her outspokenness: 'When as if to mock man, her natural protectors became helpless to prevent Draupadi from being denuded of her last piece of cloth, the power of her own virtue preserved her honour';[57] 'Draupadi has shown what a women's true dharma is. Even if the husband falls the wife must not.'[58]

Gandhi propagated Sita's and Damayanti's purity, humbleness, and gentleness, but he used Draupadi as an example of strength and faith. They all have in common their capacity to suffer, and his message to women is that suffering is purifying. His image of women was out of touch with reality. Not all women had the possibility of sacrificing themselves for the nationalist cause. Not all women had the possibility of remaining pure. However, he put all the responsibility of purity on women:

> If we take count of cases of rape in the world, we shall discover that such incidents are very rare. A woman's virtue is violated through both the man and the woman acting voluntarily, and if a woman is self-controlled and pure in mind, violation of her virtue is impossible.[59]

After this he goes on explaining his statement by the example of Sita. The problem with these statements is that women who were sexually assaulted are blamed and condemned as 'not pure enough'. His was an idealistic construct that was completely out of touch with reality. Rape does not happen because of women's behaviour but because of rapists.

In a letter to the freedom fighter Nirmala Desai, Gandhi wrote that women should rather kill themselves than the attacker: 'Moreover, a woman [who believes] in ahimsa will protect herself by killing herself rather than the evil-doer. A woman should have faith, like Sita and Draupadi, that God will protect her honour.'[60] This is but another example of the harmfulness coming from the patriarchal image of the ideal woman.

Rewriting the Image of the 'Ideal Indian Woman'

Epic-based nationalist discourses still constitute a dominant trope in modern Indian literature. However, the old epic ideals have also been radically transformed by feminist interventions. To understand this reworking, I take a cue from feminist theory. In her speech 'When We Dead Awaken: Writing as Re-Vision', the American feminist Adrienne Rich states: 'Re-vision – the act of looking back, of seeing with fresh eyes, of entering an old text from a new critical direction – is for us more than a chapter in cultural history: it is an act of survival.'[61] Many feminists have stressed the need for revising myths and fairy tales. As stated earlier, myths originally came into existence to help with the anxieties of life, and the most powerful of them were passed on through generations as social inheritance. They are institutions in the canonical centre that classify and encode reality, pushing all other stories to the periphery.

They work through classical universalism: they are based on a dualistic logic that combines the masculine with the universal and puts the feminine in a secondary position. Simone de Beauvoir explained: 'In addition to their [men's] concrete power, they are invested with a prestige whose tradition is reinforced by the child's whole education: the present incorporates the past, and in the past all history was made by males.'[62] Myths name things but are made by men, so women are misrepresented or not represented at all. Since myths establish a system of beliefs that is passed on through generations, the patriarchal image of women became natural. The problem with the term 'natural' is that it usually represents a masculine reality. What we believe to be reality is the product of language. We are born into a phallocentric language, in which the masculine is the rule, while the feminine is condemned to be 'the other' and women are deprived of their own language and stories.[63] The patriarchy paints a surreal image of women, claiming it to be natural, and by depriving women of their voice, it prevents them from discovering their true selves.

This does not mean that myths cannot be reworked. Vida Pavesich sees gender as a myth itself. This perspective is based on the shared characteristics of apparent self-evidence and timelessness associated with gender. Using gender as an analytical tool is a way to deconstruct myths that misrepresent women and helps them find their own voice and language.[64] Blumenberg does not see 'myth' as an irrevocable text, but rather as an eternal process, one in which the narrative adjusts to its social surroundings.[65] Alicia Ostriker makes an influential argument regarding feminist revisionist mythmaking in her article 'The Thieves of Language: Women Poets and Revisionist Mythmaking':

> The old stories are changed, changed utterly, by female knowledge of female experience, so that they can no longer stand as foundations of collective male fantasy or as the pillars sustaining phallocentric 'high' culture. Instead, they are corrections; they are representations of what women find divine and demonic in themselves.[66]

This means that by adjusting the oppressor's 'language' – the myths – female authors can deconstruct the stereotypes forced upon women and give them a voice of their own. To emphasize this latter point, the rest of the chapter will examine various retellings of the Mahabharata that have shifted the focus of the story to female agency.

An important landmark in this shift is Pratibha Ray's novel *Yajnaseni*, which gained great popularity. It is a retelling of the traditional Mahabharata, told from Draupadi's perspective. Even though Ray focused on this female character, she failed to deconstruct the traditional female ideal. Ray presents herself as a humanist who believes in separate roles for men and women.[67] In this novel she exposes the hardships and inequality women suffer in conjugal life but fails to offer an alternative. Beena G. states: 'She [Draupadi] is not "cheerful" in accepting the directions of domination. She sees through the game of power that enables patriarchy to realize for themselves particular possibilities which it denies to others.'[68] Still, she does not speak up for herself. One example is the scene after the *svayamvara* (self-choice, the election of a husband by a princess). Draupadi is supposed to leave with her new husband, Arjuna, walking on foot, but her brother protests. She tells him: 'Brother, now permit me to follow my dharma. This is what is proper for every woman. I, too, should do the same.'[69] This is a direct allusion to *stri dharma*, which is a patriarchal construct suppressing women's autonomy, as discussed earlier. Nevertheless, its importance of being one of the earliest modern retellings of the Mahabharata told from Draupadi's point of view should not be dismissed.

Draupadi assumes an even more central role in the novel *The Palace of Illusions* by Indian American author Chitra Banerjee Divakaruni. The novel remains loyal to the traditional story but is written from the perspective of the female hero Draupadi. Draupadi's subjective thoughts were omitted in the traditional Mahabharata but are necessary to deconstruct the ideal gender roles propagated through the epics and later on through the nationalist discourse. Divakaruni successfully humanizes Draupadi and manages to deconstruct the patriarchal idealization of womanhood. Draupadi criticizes patriarchal structures; indeed, throughout the novel, we are given an insight into her mind, which enables us to understand her anger and thirst for revenge. While it breaks her to realize that her husbands prioritized their honour and loyalty towards each other over her safety, this realization ends up making her strong and independent. After the battle of Kurukshetra, the focus shifts to the widows who are about to commit a mass sati. Draupadi prioritizes sisterhood over her own interests and steps forward to convince the women to build a new community, 'a place where women could speak their sorrows to other women'.[70] This understanding of sisterhood is crucial in the evolution of feminism. Draupadi, Kunti, Gandhari, Subhadra, and Uttara put their forces together to build a new city. Draupadi narrates:

> All this allowed us to set up the destitute in homes of their own and buy merchandise to start businesses for them.... We trained those who showed interest in learning to become tutors for girls and young boys. And even in the later years of Pariksit's reign ... Hastinapur remained one of the few cities where women could go about their daily lives without harassment.[71]

Divakaruni complements the story of the Mahabharata with feminist suggestions for an improvement of women's situation through economic independence and education. Although this is a contemporary topic, she does this through the parameters of the Mahabharata.

Even though telling Draupadi's story is a helpful tool in the dismantling of patriarchal structures, there are also some works that focus on the subaltern women who are relegated to the margins in the mainstream Mahabharata. The term 'subaltern' was criticized by the Indian literary theorist and feminist critic Gayatri Chakravorty Spivak as being essentialist since the different subaltern groups do not necessarily share the same kind of subordination and discrimination. The history of subalterns is as important as that of the elite, but it is often left out in the official historical tradition. Spivak explains that the elite discourse controls not only the way the subaltern are represented but also how they are understood.[72] Focusing on epic heroines like Draupadi means maintaining the discourse on an eliterian level, which results in gender essentialism. Narayan explains that 'the generalizations are hegemonic in that they represent the problems of privileged women ... as paradigmatic "women's issues"'.[73] Even though Draupadi is humanized through the retellings, she still represents a privileged, high-caste minority.

The short story collection *After Kurukshetra* by the Bengali writer and socio-political activist Mahasweta Devi includes three translated stories focusing on marginalized women, such as widows, servants, and low-caste women. All three stories deal with the aftermath of the war and offer criticisms of caste- and class-related oppression through the marginalized women. In Devi's stories, the subaltern women question the justifications of history, for example, by the greater good or dharma, and Devi points to the parts in the Mahabharata where alternative discourses to the dominant one were omitted. It is not enough to reverse the myth of the ideal Indian woman based on the elite heroines of the Mahabharata, because this myth is still dominant and suppresses all the other stories, namely those of the subaltern women, who do not suffer discrimination only through their gender but also through their caste.

The first story, 'The Five Women' (1999, original: 'Panchakanya'), revolves around five recently widowed villagers who come to Kurukshetra in search for their husbands' bodies. They are asked to keep company and distract the also widowed and pregnant Uttara, but 'refuse to serve as dasis [female servants or slaves]'.[74] Still, the *rajavritta* (royal people) women view them as mere servants: 'They will stay with you. Do whatever you ask them to.'[75] Devi uses this episode to underline the difference between the *rajavritta* and the *janavritta* (common folk). During various conversations between the five women and the women living in the palace, the differences between these two worlds become visible. While the *rajavritta* widows have to live as 'shadowy ghosts',[76] the *janavritta* women follow the laws of nature and remarry in order to create new life. They explain: 'We need husbands, we need children. The village needs to hear the sound of chatter and laughter. We will ... create life. That's what Nature teaches us.'[77] The women question to what end this *dharmayuddha* (righteous war) was held, seeing as it caused the deaths of thousands of innocent people.

> These women are not of the rajavritta, women of royalty, nor are they servants or attendants. These women are from the families of the hundreds of foot soldiers – padatiks – from various other little kingdoms. They had been slaughtered every day, in their thousands, their function being to protect the chariot-mounted heroes. They were issued no armour. So they died in large numbers.[78]

Ultimately this evolves into a broader critique of the notion of *dharma* itself: 'This was not our dharmayuddha. Brother kills brother, uncle kills nephew, shishya [disciple] kills guru. It may be your idea of dharma, it's not ours.'[79] The dominant groups paint an essentialist image of the greater good as if it were best for all, but this is only true for the elite, and it is achieved at the expense of marginalized people.

I do not believe the original title 'Panchakanya' to be coincidental. The *panchakanya* are five epic heroines part of the following hymn that has the power to demolish one's greatest sins:

> Ahalya draupadi kunti tara mandodari tatha
> Pancakanyah smaren nityam maha-pataka-nashinim[80]

> Ahalya, Draupadi, Kunti, Tara, and Mandodari,
> The five virgins, destroyers of the greatest sins, may be remembered constantly.

The question arises as to how these heroines, who had extramarital affairs or unconventional marriages, can be considered *kanya,* which, among several meanings, also translates as 'virgin' (besides 'girl' or 'daughter'). Ralla Guha Niyogi explains:

> Being a *Kanya [sic]* has nothing to do with the physical status of 'virgo intacta' or sexual experience.... The boon of virginity is not just a physical condition but refers to an inner state of the psyche that remains untrammeled by any

slavish dependence on another, on a particular man. She is 'one-in-herself', an integrated personality.[81]

This resembles the five *janavritta* women from the short story, who do not depend on anyone. In a conversation with Uttara, they tell her that in their village women work in the fields along with their husbands, and that they are able to protect themselves: 'When the men go off to war, we women protect our homes.'[82] They do not depend on anyone but themselves, and thus these women are real *panchakanya*.

In the next story, 'Kunti and the Nishadin' (2000, original: 'Kunti O Nishadi'), Kunti is confronted by the daughter-in-law of the woman who died alongside her five sons in the fire that was supposed to kill Kunti and the Pandavas in the lac-house episode. The story begins at the forest hermitage, where Kunti, Gandhari, and Dhritarashtra would spend their final days. One night Kunti roams around the forest, and reflecting on her life, she begins to confess her laments. When she suddenly sees a Nishadin[83] watching her, she runs away. The next night she sees a group of Nishadins fleeing, and the woman from the night before approaches her. This woman is the daughter-in-law of the Nishadin who was killed with her sons in the lac house, but Kunti does not even seem to remember them. The Nishadin tells her: 'Causing six innocent forest tribals to be burnt to death to serve your own interests. That was not even a crime in your book. In our eyes, by the laws of Mother Nature, you, your sons, your allies, are all held guilty.'[84] Similar to the first story, it is criticized how the *rajavritta*, the elite, see no value in the lives of the common people. Kunti saw more value in the lives of her royal sons than in the lives of the Nishada family. In the traditional Mahabharata, this scene is not criticized; just the ingenious escape of the Pandavas is celebrated. The story ends with the forest fire that kills Kunti and her companions, closing with the question of whether she is going to beg the Nishadin mother who died in the lac house for forgiveness for her greatest sin.

The final story, 'Souvali' (2000, original: 'Saubali'), is about Souvali, a servant who bore a child named Yuyutsu to Dhritarashtra. Souvali does not accept this name, since it was given to him by his father, and calls him Souvalya, defying patriarchal tradition. Although her son was never accepted by the Kauravas as a legitimate child, he was the only son of Dhritarashtra who survived the war and was thus the only one who could complete the funeral rituals. Souvali criticizes her former status as a *dasi* even as she celebrates her present status as a free woman among the common people. She states: 'I was nothing but a dasi in

the royal household but here, amongst the common people, I'm a free woman.'[85]
When Souvali and her son meet, she questions the way he was marginalized all
these years. By refusing to mourn for her son's father, she defies him and the
royal customs. In this story, Souvali's freedom, caused by her leaving the palace
voluntarily, is contrasted with the way in which Souvalya, who always tried to
be accepted by his paternal relatives, was suppressed by them. He was allowed
to live in the palace, but only as a servant to his half-brothers, who bullied him
on several occasions. When the war was about to start, he allied himself with the
Pandavas to get revenge for the ill-treatment he suffered all his life and hoped to
be accepted at least by them. However, Souvali knows that they will not. She tries
to show him how by defying the *rajavritta* and not letting them subject her, she
attained freedom.

In all three stories, the suppression of the marginalized women through
the elite is the central theme. When close to the *rajavritta*, they are suppressed:
'No matter how fond they are of you, with you they can never be totally free',[86]
as Subhadra tells Uttara in the first story. However, Devi also shows how the
dharma of the *rajavritta* suppresses the elite women due to its strict code of
behaviour. The Nishadin tells Kunti, who is filled with regret and guilt towards
her illegitimate son, Karna: 'The rajavritta folk and the lokavritta folk have
different values, different ideas of right and wrong. If a young nishad girl makes
love to the boy of her choice and gets pregnant, we celebrate it with a wedding.'[87]
The five women question the *rajavritta*'s customs revolving around death:
'There, the world is full of bustle and activity. Here, you white-clad widows
float around like shadowy ghosts. We wonder, won't you ever laugh, talk loudly,
run outside on restless feet?'[88] Souvali, being the mother of Dhritarashtra's only
surviving son, is expected to follow the rituals of his death, but she rejects being
put into this position, since to this point her son was never fully accepted by the
Kauravas. Complacently, she says: 'I'm just a dasi. Was I his wedded wife that
I should undergo the death rites?... Do tarpan? Wear white cloth, fast? Why?...
I'll feast on sweet laddoos, ghee-rich jowar pitas, golden honey. And after I'm
full, I'll sleep peacefully holding my son in my arms.'[89] The subaltern women
invoke their own *dharma*, which gives them freedom and independence,
elevating their subalternity to a status of power.

Conclusion

Feminist retellings such as Divakaruni's and Ray's are of great importance
regarding female representation and voice since they demonstrate that women

are not one-dimensional monoliths of virtue. However, they fail to show the different realities of Indian women. Most women are oppressed and oppressors at the same time since upper-caste and middle-caste women benefit from the caste system itself, even though they are being limited by the rules of Brahmanical patriarchy.[90] This is the reason why they cannot serve as generalized role models.

The image of the ideal Indian woman originated in epics like the Mahabharata and was propagated by Indian nationalists such as Gandhi in order to mobilize and instrumentalize women for their cause. This helped many women to step out of their homes and gain respect, but at the same time it set limitations and pushed 'non-ideal' women further into the social periphery. He praised Indian women and elevated their status because the treatment of women had been deeply criticized by the British, but he did not try to truly liberate them. Women were told that if they were pure and virtuous, they would have power and honour, but he did not see that there were many women whose social or economic conditions did not allow them to follow *stri dharma*. He did not see class- or caste-related feminist issues and, in fact, fortified the differences between women through the propagation of the ideal Indian woman. The caste system is being sustained through the limitation of women and female sexuality. Caste-privileged women are accomplices in sustaining the caste system because they are made to believe that they benefit from it if they are pure and virtuous: 'From the brahmanical texts and mythologies it is apparent that ultimate social control is achieved when the subordinated women not only accept their condition but actually regard it as a mark of distinction.'[91]

Class- and caste-related feminist issues have been ignored for too long, as the Indian sociologist Sharmila Rege points out in her essay 'Dalit Women Talk Differently: A Critique of "Difference" and towards a Dalit Feminist Standpoint Position'. Caste-oppressed women's movements have been seen as a subsection of feminism, but their issues have not been adopted by most women's movements. At the same time, the Dalit movements have not focused on female-specific oppression. Rege points out 'the subject of Dalit feminist liberatory knowledge must also be the subject of every other liberatory project and this requires a sharp focus on the processes by which gender, race, class, caste, sexuality – all construct each other'.[92] Since the twentieth century, the voices of Dalit women have become louder, and there are many important recently published works on Dalit feminist theory, such as Sunaina Arya and Aakash Singh Rathore's *Dalit Feminist Theory: A Reader* (2019) and Uma Chakravarti's *Gendering Caste through a Feminist Lens* (2002), but there is still a long way to go, as recent published reports show. From 2017 to 2019, there was an increase of

22.14 per cent in rape cases against women from lower castes, while the pendency in crimes against lower-caste women and children is at 84.09 per cent. As renowned feminist author bell hooks postulated: 'As long as women are using class or race power to dominate other women, feminist sisterhood cannot be fully realized.'[93]

Devi's short story collection is of great importance because we tend to look for role models in elite women. Even though it is important to revise and retell the dominant myths through a gendered lens in order to deconstruct the patriarchal image of the ideal woman, these women are not representative of the women who suffer from patriarchal as well as class–caste oppression. Works like Devi's remind us that feminism cannot complete its goal until it is inclusive and intersectional.

Notes

1. Roland Barthes, *Mythologies* (London: Vintage Books, 2009 [1957]), 140–41.
2. Pamela Lothspeich, 'Draupadī, Yājñasenī, Pāñcālī, Kṛṣṇā: Representations of an Epic Heroine in Three Novels', in *Many Mahābhāratas*, ed. Nell Hawley and Sohini Pillai, 325–42 (Albany: SUNY Press, 2021).
3. Hans Blumenberg, *Arbeit am Mythos* (Frankfurt am Main: Suhrkamp, 1979).
4. Stephen C. Ausband, *Myth and Meaning, Myth and Order* (Macon, GA: Mercer University Press, 2003).
5. Andrew Lohrey, 'Nationalism as Myth', *ETC: A Review of General Semantics* 3, no. 1 (1986): 15–26.
6. Uma Chakravarti, 'Whatever Happened to the Vedic Dasi?' in *Recasting Women: Essays in Indian Colonial History*, ed. Kumkum Sangari and Sudesh Vaid, 27–87 (New Brunswick: Rutgers University Press, 1999), 31.
7. Tok Thompson and Gregory Schrempp, *The Truth of Myth: World Mythology in Theory and Everyday Life* (New York: Oxford University Press, 2020), 46–49.
8. Chakravarti, 'Whatever Happened to the Vedic *Dasi*?' 34.
9. Chakravarti, 'Whatever Happened to the Vedic *Dasi*?' 47.
10. Annie Besant stressed the importance of moral education for Indian women, and her school schedules included the study of the epics. She said: '[W]e teach religion through the lives of Hindu heroes and Hindu heroines of the past. In short, we are trying to give Hindu girls an education which shall help and not hinder, an education which shall elevate and not degrade.' Besant (1942), cited in Chandra Lekha Singh, 'Making "Ideal" Indian Women: Annie Besant's Engagement with the Issue of Female Education in Early

Twentieth-Century India', *Paedagogica Historica: International Journal of the History of Education* 54, no. 5 (2018): 606–25.

11. Uma Narayan, 'Essence of Culture and a Sense of History: A Feminist Critique of Cultural Essentialism', *Hypatia* 13, no. 2 (1998): 86–106, 91.

12. Partha Chatterjee, 'The Nationalist Resolution of the Women's Question', in *Recasting Women: Essays in Indian Colonial History*, ed. Kumkum Sangari and Sudesh Vaid, 233–53 (New Brunswick: Rutgers University Press, 1999), 237.

13. Richard Fox, *Gandhian Utopia: Experiments with Culture* (Boston, MA: Beacon Press, 1989), 95–109.

14. Chatterjee, 'The Nationalist Resolution', 237–38.

15. Andrea L. Miller and Eugene Borgida, 'The Separate Spheres Model of Gendered Inequality', *PLoS ONE* 11, no. 41 (2016), https://doi.org/10.1371/journal.pone.0147315 (accessed on 14 June 2020), 3.

16. Chakravarti, 'Whatever Happened to the Vedic Dasi?', 49.

17. Anthony D. Smith, 'The Myth of the "Modern Nation" and the Myths of Nations', *Ethnic and Racial Studies* 11, no. 1 (1988): 1–26.

18. Lohrey, 'Nationalism as Myth', 21.

19. Partha Chatterjee, *The Nation and Its Fragments: Colonial and Postcolonial Histories* (Princeton, NJ: Princeton University Press, 1993), 121–26.

20. Leszek Kolakowski, *The Presence of Myth* (Chicago, IL: University of Chicago Press, 2001), 7.

21. Swami Vivekananda, *The Complete Works of Swami Vivekananda* (Calcutta: Advaita Ashrama, 1989), 662.

22. Vivekananda, *The Complete Works*, 842.

23. Benu Verma, 'Plenitude of the Singular: Draupadi in Literature and Life', *Society and Culture in South Asia* 1, no. 1 (2015): 56–74.

24. M. K. Gandhi, *The Collected Works of Mahatma Gandhi*, vol. 14, https://www.gandhiheritageportal.org/the-collected-works-of-mahatma-gandhi (accessed on 14 June 2020), 204.

25. Gandhi, *The Collected Works*, vol. 41, 268.

26. Judith Butler, *Gender Trouble* (New York: Routledge, 1990).

27. Narayan, 'Essence of Culture', 86.

28. Geraldine Forbes, *Women in Modern India* (Cambridge, UK: Cambridge University Press, 2007), 156.

29. Sharmila Rege, 'Dalit Women Talk Differently: A Critique of "Difference" and towards a Dalit Feminist Standpoint Position', *Economic and Political Weekly* 33, no. 44 (1998): 39–46, 44.

30. Sunaina Arya and Aakash Singh Rathore, *Dalit Feminist Theory: A Reader* (Abingdon: Routledge, 2020), 111.

31. Rege, 'Dalit Women Talk Differently', 44.

32. Forbes, *Women in Modern India*, 134.

33. Gandhi, *The Collected Works*, vol. 21, 92.

34. Mridula Garg, 'Metaphors of Womanhood in Indian Literature', *Alternatives* 16 (1991): 407–24, 412.

35. Gandhi, *The Collected Works*, vol. 21, 92–95.

36. Gandhi, *The Collected Works*, vol. 27, 290.

37. Gandhi, *The Collected Works*, vol. 27, 291.

38. Forbes, *Women in Modern India*, 133.

39. Deepra Dandekar, 'Ideals of Womanhood', in *Encyclopedia of Women in World Religions: Faith and Culture across History*, vol. 1: *African Religions to Hinduism*, ed. Susan de-Gaia, 345–48 (Santa Barbara: ABC-CLIO, 2019), 346.

40. Anne Mackenzie Pearson, *'Because It Gives Me Peace of Mind': Ritual Fasts in the Religious Lives of Hindu Women* (Albany, NY: SUNY Press, 1996), 84.

41. Uma Chakravarti, *Gendering Caste through a Feminist Lens* (New Delhi: Sage Publications, 2018), 34.

42. Chakravarti, *Gendering Caste*, 70.

43. Simone de Beauvoir, *The Second Sex* (New York: Vintage Books, 2010), 193.

44. Gandhi, *The Collected Works*, vol. 14, 127.

45. Gandhi, *The Collected Works*, vol. 88, 105.

46. Nirmala Banerjee, 'Working Women in Colonial Bengal: Modernization and Marginalization', in *Recasting Women: Essays in Indian Colonial History*, ed. Kumkum Sangari and Sudesh Vaid, 269–301 (New Brunswick: Rutgers University Press, 1999).

47. Samita Sen, *Women and Labour in Late Colonial India: The Bengal Jute Industry* (Cambridge, UK: Cambridge University Press, 2004).

48. Gandhi, *The Collected Works*, vol. 60, 69.

49. Gandhi, *The Collected Works*, vol. 48, 80–81.

50. Gandhi, *The Collected Works*, vol. 70, 381.

51. Gandhi, *The Collected Works*, vol. 71, 207–08.

52. Garg, 'Metaphors of Womanhood', 409.

53. Garg, 'Metaphors of Womanhood', 409–10.

54. Gandhi, *The Collected Works*, vol. 61, 125.

55. Sanghamitra Chaudhura, Ashutosh Muduli, and Ridhi Arora, 'Family Roles Posing Challenges for Women Leaders in India', in *Indian Women in Leadership*, ed. Rajashi Ghosh and Gary N. McLean, 13–30 (Cham: Springer, Publishing 2018).

56. Kumkum Yadav, 'Draupadi or Savitri: Lohia's Feminist Reading of Mythology', *Economic and Political Weekly* 45, no. 48 (2010): 107–12.

57. Gandhi, *The Collected Works*, vol. 22, 22.

58. Gandhi, *The Collected Works*, vol. 62, 233.

59. Gandhi, *The Collected Works*, vol. 33, 434–35.

60. Gandhi, *The Collected Works*, vol. 50, 317.

61. Adrienne Rich, 'When We Dead Awaken: Writing as Re-Vision', *College English* 34, no. 1 (1972): 18–30, 18.

62. De Beauvoir, *The Second Sex*, 30.

63. A. Marie Josephine Aruna, 'Patriarchal Myths in Postmodern Feminist Fiction: A Select Study', PhD dissertation, Department of English, Pondicherry University, 2010, 46–48.

64. Vida Pavesich, 'Gender and Hans Blumenberg's Theory of Myth', *International Studies in Philosophy* 32, no. 4 (2000): 83–105, 96.

65. Blumenberg, *Arbeit am Mythos*, 40.

66. Alicia Ostriker, 'The Thieves of Language: Women Poets and Revisionist Mythmaking', *Journal of Women in Culture and Society* 8, no. 1 (1982): 68–90, 73.

67. Pratibha Ray's personal website, http://www.pratibharay.org (accessed on 15 June 2020).

68. Beena G., *Vision and Re-Vision: Revisiting Mythologies, Rethinking Women* (Chennai: Notion Press, 2019) (e-book), ch. 6, para. 63.

69. Pratibha Ray, *Yajnaseni* (New Delhi: Rupa Publications, 1995), 48.

70. Chitra Banerjee Divakaruni, *The Palace of Illusions* (New York: Anchor Books, 2009), 323.

71. Divakaruni, *The Palace of Illusions*, 325.

72. Gayatri Chakravorty Spivak, *Can the Subaltern Speak?* (Vienna: Turia + Kant, 2008).

73. Narayan, 'Essence of Culture', 86.

74. Mahasweta Devi, *After Kurukshetra* (Calcutta: Seagull Books, 2014), 4.

75. Devi, *After Kurukshetra*, 4.

76. Devi, *After Kurukshetra*, 19.

77. Devi, *After Kurukshetra*, 25.

78. Devi, *After Kurukshetra*, 1.

79. Devi, *After Kurukshetra*, 26.

80. Pradip Bhattacharya, 'The Riddle of the "Pancha Kanyā" (Five Maidens)', *South Asia: Journal of South Asian Studies* 32, no. 1 (2009): 3–45, 3.

81. Ralla Guha Niyogi, 'The "Magic Suggestiveness" of Pancha Kanya', (2010), https://www.boloji.com/articles/7381/the-magic-suggestiveness (accessed on 14 June 2020).

82. Devi, *After Kurukshetra*, 14.

83. Nishadin refers to a a female member of the Nishada, a non-Aryan tribe
    consisting of fishermen and hunters.
84. Devi, *After Kurukshetra*, 43.
85. Devi, *After Kurukshetra*, 54.
86. Devi, *After Kurukshetra*, 7.
87. Devi, *After Kurukshetra*, 40.
88. Devi, *After Kurukshetra*, 19.
89. Devi, *After Kurukshetra*, 53.
90. Chakravarti, *Gendering Caste*, 136.
91. Chakravarti, *Gendering Caste*, 71.
92. Rege, 'Dalit Women Talk Differently', 45.
93. bell hooks, *Feminism Is for Everyone* (New York: Routledge, 2015), 16.

6

Rethinking Transnational Intellectual History and Epic Nationalisms through Lithographic Labour

Persian and Urdu Mahabharatas in India and Iran

Amanda Lanzillo

When Perso-Arabic script renditions of the Mahabharata receive popular or academic attention, it is often in defence of elite Indo-Islamic cosmopolitanism. Mughal engagement with the Mahabharata is held up as evidence of interest in Hinduism or pre-Islamic Indic traditions among Muslim South Asian dynasties. Because the Mughal Persian translation of the Mahabharata, known as the *Razmnamah* (Book of War), was a courtly project, it is easy to overlook the fact that Mahabharatas in Perso-Arabic script reached broader, and increasingly transregional, publics, especially in the age of lithographic print. Focusing on the preparation and circulation of Persian and Urdu print editions of the Mahabharata, this chapter aims to reorient discussions of Persianate understandings of Sanskrit epics, emphasizing middle-class, popular readerships in both Iran and India.

Following a brief overview of the translation and circulation of the *Razmnamah* in Mughal India, the chapter analyses lithographic publications of Persian and Urdu Mahabharatas. In the second half of the nineteenth century, the rapid growth of lithographic print in South Asia allowed for the relatively inexpensive publication and circulation of Mahabharatas in Perso-Arabic script. The chapter argues for a reconsideration of the intellectual work of cadres of printers, translators, scribes, and other workers employed by Indian presses. Late nineteenth-century Persian and Urdu Mahabharatas reflected norms of production within a negotiated system of capitalist print labour, distinguishing them from their courtly manuscript predecessors.

The chapter subsequently turns to the transregional consumption and reception of these Mahabharatas in Perso-Arabic script. In the late nineteenth century in both India and Iran, readers within a Persianate cultural–intellectual milieu understood the Mahabharata in a comparative frame, often with reference to the Persian epic poem, the Shahnamah. Popular audiences in Iran often read the two works through an emerging 'national' lens that associated epic literature with discrete peoples and nations. In India, on the other hand, middle-class Persian and Urdu readers often used both the Mahabharata–*Razmnamah* and the Shahnamah to claim an elite Persianate and cosmopolitan past.

Ultimately, the chapter reorients narratives of shared Indo-Iranian intellectual history by critiquing portrayals of Persianate transregional exchange as exclusively elite or courtly projects. Centring lithographic printers and popular reading publics, the chapter interrogates the reinterpretation of the Mahabharata within transregional communities of Persian and Urdu readers in the late nineteenth and early twentieth centuries.

Background: The Persian Mahabharata–*Razmnamah* in Mughal India

The efforts of the Mughal court to engage with Sanskrit have attracted significant academic attention and debate over the previous two decades. The *Razmnamah*, the Persian translation of the Mahabharata, was among the signature literary and cultural projects of the Mughal emperor Jalaluddin Akbar (r. 1556–1605 CE).[1] Coinciding with efforts to translate the Ramayana and the Sanskrit chronicle of Kashmir, the *Rajatarangini*, into Persian, the development of the *Razmnamah* was part of a broader effort to adapt bodies of Indic literature into the court's official language. Translation at the Mughal court was a collaborative process involving both Sanskrit readers and Persian compilers.[2] While multiple Mughal sources identify Naqib Khan as the primary translator of the *Razmnamah*, the project drew on the talents of an intellectually diverse cohort of courtly writers. At various points, the prominent historian Abdul Qadir Badayuni, the court poet Abdul Faiz "Faizi", and his brother, the court historian Abul Fazl, were all involved in the translation, introduction, or compilation of the *Razmnamah*.[3]

The involvement of ideologically diverse luminaries of Mughal writing in the translation of the Mahabharata suggests the importance that Akbar's court placed on translation between languages, cultures, and religions. Persian was the primary language of literature and administration among the religiously plural members of the Mughal court. Translating the Mahabharata into Persian ensured broad courtly access to the text. At the same time, as Audrey Truschke has argued, the Mughals 'emphasized their cross-cultural partnership' in the production of translations, and the *Razmnamah* explicitly noted the work of Brahman scholars in the translation process.[4] Abul Fazl, who authored the introduction to the 1598–99 *Razmnamah*, characterized the project as focused on religious commonalities between Muslims and Hindus.[5] He wrote that the 'the books of the two communities [Hindus and Muslims] were translated into the common language' to benefit the mutual pursuit of knowledge. For Abul Fazl, translation was central to Mughal courtly ideals of cosmopolitanism and ecumenicism.[6]

Mughal courtly translation projects focused not only on building shared literary knowledge, but also on claiming regional authority within a transregional literary milieu. Rajeev Kinra has argued that Persian created a shared 'cultural playing field' for Indian, Iranian, and other writers by the sixteenth century.[7] Across large swaths of India, Iran, Central Asia, and the Ottoman Empire, shared norms and practices of Persian meant that writers 'balanced their rootedness in particular localities' with participation in a 'larger cosmopolitan ecumene'.[8]

While engaging with transregional Persian literary norms, the translators of the Mahabharata at Akbar's court do not seem to have intended for the work to circulate beyond the subcontinent.[9] Instead, Akbar's translation bureau focused on creating a corpus of localized, Persian literature for a Mughal and Indian context, translated from languages as diverse as Sanskrit, Chagatai Turkic, and Arabic.[10] These works were tied together by their adaptation into a shared Persian literary culture as well as by their circulation within the court, royal households, and bureaucratic cadres. The translation office contributed to the consolidation of Persian as the primary shared language of Mughal culture and bureaucracy while also rooting 'local' or 'Indic' texts within the transregional norms of Persian. As recent scholarship on the Mughal-era Persian translations of the Mahabharata has noted, translation was a collaborative – though hierarchical – project that relied on vernacular intermediary translation and contributed to a courtly culture of literary, linguistic, and religious exchange.[11]

Given the typically limited circulation of ornate, illustrated Mughal manuscripts, scholarly analyses have focused on the elite production and consumption of the *Razmnamah*. Yael Rice has noted that while the first copy of the *Razmnamah* (1584–86) was intended for the emperor's personal use, the second copy (1598–99) seemed to be 'a more modest endeavour', likely intended for a member of the royal family.[12] In both cases, the production and consumption of the manuscript were confined primarily to royal workshops and palaces. Ultimately, four illustrated copies of the text were completed for the Mughal court, all between 1584 and 1617.[13] Outside of these, however, hundreds of copies were produced, with the text circulating at the sub-imperial level among Mughal appointees, regional princes, and bureaucrats.

Scholarship on the production of the *Razmnamah* has primarily focused on the role of translators. However, labour in Mughal-era manuscript workshops extended to the design, illustration, layout, and physical construction of books. Aside from illustrators, many book workers had limited direct influence on the books' contents, but their labour was nonetheless central to the production of the *Razmnamah*. Workers in state and royal workshops – manuscript or otherwise – were among the most financially secure artists and artisans in Mughal India.[14] The most accomplished were provided salaries, while others lived off of high-paid commissions or wages. Their livelihoods were predicated on continued courtly interest, but those employed in the development of royal manuscripts remained well remunerated.[15]

The production of royal illustrated manuscripts of the *Razmnamah* reflected the working cultures of relatively financially secure state-employed artists and artisans. However, as the text spread and was recopied, its production also reached calligraphers, bookbinders, and illustrators who depended on popular demand. The *Razmnamah*'s popularity among the lower echelons of the Mughal bureaucracy meant that a wider array of book workers engaged in its production. The reproduction of the text in the two centuries following Akbar's initial commission of the translation and the courtly commission of the illustrated manuscripts thus predicted book labour practices within lithographic printing houses in the nineteenth century. Exceeding the bounds of state and palace workshops, the reproduction of the text became the purview of a cohort of calligraphers, scribes, binders, and others reliant on market demand. By the seventeenth and eighteenth centuries, members of these cadres in Mughal successor states also likely began partial Urdu translations of the texts. Today, some north Indian families boast 300-year-old Urdu-language Mahabharatas that appear to be partial adaptions of the *Razmnamah*.[16]

Ultimately, the reproduction of the *Razmnamah* through sub-imperial workshops, and its circulation among cadres of regional bureaucrats and administrators laid the ground for broadened spaces of textual consumption after the rise of lithographic print. As we shall see, lithographic publishers printed the Mahabharata–*Razmnamah* in both Persian and Urdu rapidly and frequently. They often employed their most prestigious and well-paid translators, calligraphers, scribes, and illustrators in the production of these texts. These facts suggest that by the mid-nineteenth century, there was widespread demand for Mahabharatas in Perso-Arabic script among the literate classes and that the *Razmnamah* was popularly considered a prestigious text, in part due to its associations with the Mughal court. At the same time, even as publishers sought to benefit from popular awareness of the Mughal *Razmnamah*, their interventions in textual production sparked changes in the contents and circulation of Mahabharatas in Perso-Arabic script.

Lithographic Print and the Production of Mahabharatas in Perso-Arabic Script

Projects to translate and circulate the Mahabharata in languages that used Perso-Arabic script did not cease with the end of Akbar's reign or, indeed, with the end of the Mughal dynasty. To the contrary, in colonial-era India, the rise of lithographic print made it possible for wider publics to engage with the Mahabharata in Persian and Urdu. Moreover, the prominent and prolific Indian lithographic presses never published exclusively for an Indian audience. By the mid-nineteenth century, Urdu increasingly displaced Persian as a literary language among many Indian readers. Nonetheless, Indian lithographic presses founded in the second half of the nineteenth century published extensively in Persian. In part, this was because Persian retained cultural prestige in India, but it was also because Iran, Afghanistan, and the wider Persian-reading world were major markets for Indian presses.[17] In both Urdu and Persian, the rise of popularly accessible Mahabharatas was rooted in a lithographic print revolution that swept the subcontinent in the mid-nineteenth century and reshaped the work of textual production.

What Kinra termed the 'larger cosmopolitan ecumene' of Persian readership was disrupted in the nineteenth century by both imperial formations and new articulations of national identity. However, this disruption of historical connections across the Persianate world did not render the 'cosmopolitan ecumene' suddenly meaningless for Persian readers, nor for readers of languages like Urdu that engaged heavily with the Persian cannon. To the contrary, because the same period saw the rise of print, the Persianate literary ecumene became legible and meaningful to members of classes previously excluded from it. The elite cosmopolitanism of the preceding centuries gave way to popular and middle-class readerships. Members of the emerging capitalist class of textual producers – particularly north Indian publishers in cities such as Lucknow, Kanpur, and

Agra – saw the transregional market of Persian readers as a site for growth.[18] They designed new Persian Mahabharatas to attract a new transregional audience, particularly in Iran.[19]

Urdu and Persian renditions published in the second half of the nineteenth century enable us to analyse the impact of print capitalism on the reception of the Mahabharata in India and the broader Persianate world, especially Iran. This analysis demands first a reconsideration of the intellectual work of book workers, including printers, translators, lithographic scribes, and calligraphers. At prominent lithographic presses, these workers prepared inexpensive Urdu and Persian Mahabharatas, which saw multiple print runs. These employees included members of traditional scribal castes and Muslim clerks and writers, as well as an emerging class trained in the technical processes of lithography. As Ulrike Stark has argued, Indian lithographic presses were sites of new technological hierarchies led by members of emerging capitalist classes.[20] Within the presses, printers, scribes, illustrators, and new groups of lithographic workers leveraged these new forms of technical authority to assert agency in producing translations of the Mahabharata for both Indian and transregional audiences.

Lithography and Shifting Practices of Work on Printed Mahabharatas in Perso–Arabic Script

Experiments in printing in Perso-Arabic script took place in Europe, Iran, and India from the mid-seventeenth century; but before the invention of lithography in 1796, publications of Mahabharatas in Perso-Arabic script remained curiosities in India.[21] Movable type printing was unpopular because of the expense and complexity of the typographic press and because Perso-Arabic typography could not capture calligraphic aesthetics and was popularly seen as ugly.[22] Lithographic print required less initial investment on the part of publishers and preserved stylistic elements of handwritten texts familiar to manuscript readers.[23]

Lithographic book publishing rapidly gained popularity in India following its introduction in 1824. In the subsequent decades, publishing houses emerged as central sites of intellectual, literary, and artistic production. Presses provided employment for members of scribal families who had been displaced by the British annexation of regional dynasties and states.[24] While presses enabled members of these families to secure work focused on textual production, they also brought them into contact with new cadres of lithographic labourers. These new book workers included litho-correctors, copyists, pressmen, and stone-wipers. Trained within the presses in the technical work of lithography, they supplied a technological expertise that writers trained in scribal lineages lacked.

Editors and publishers within these lithographic presses evolved new forms of social authority. They exerted this authority not only using what Dipesh Chakrabarty termed 'the social control of the workforce' based on community, religion, or kinship but also through new technological hierarchies.[25] While those workers rooted in kinship groups with long scribal traditions retained prestige, they were also reliant on those with the technological education to run to presses.

The production of Mahabharatas in Perso-Arabic script in the late nineteenth century was predicated on this system of capitalist print labour and negotiated authority. The structures of employment and authority within lithographic production distinguished these new Mahabharatas from their pre-colonial Persian-language predecessors. Compilers of mid-nineteenth-century Mahabharatas in Perso-Arabic script continued to use older models of attributing intellectual work, modelling versified attributions on manuscript practices. Still, through close readings of their attributions, it is possible to identify shifts in the work of intellectual and textual production.

Translation and Publication: *The* Mahabharat-i Manzum *and the* Mahabharat-i Farsi

Two Mahabharatas published in north India in the late nineteenth century reflect these changes in spaces and practices of textual production. The *Mahabharat-i Manzum* was a versified Urdu edition published from Lucknow by the Naval Kishore Press first in 1862 and repeatedly re-released by the press over the subsequent decades. The *Mahabharat-i Farsi* was a massive 18-volume Persian edition published by the same press beginning in 1880. Both texts reflect the ways in which the labour of lithographic print and intended circulation to popular transregional audiences shaped the translation and contents of Mahabharatas in Perso-Arabic script.

The Urdu-language *Mahabharat-i Manzum* was among the earliest Mahabharatas, in any language, released by the prominent Naval Kishore Press, arriving on the market in 1862, only four years after the press' foundation in 1858.[26] The text was presented as a translation of a translation: its introduction explained that Munshi Tota Ram Shayan translated, abridged, and versified 'Abul Fazl's *Razmnamah*' in Urdu in order to make it more broadly accessible to Indian readers. A member of a Kayastha scribal family from Ayodhya, whose ancestors were employed by the Awadhi nawabs, Tota Ram Shayan was among the most prodigious and prestigious translators employed by the Naval Kishore Press in this period.[27] His *Mahabharat-i Manzum* was a commercial success and was reprinted repeatedly, and in 1874 the press also commissioned him to author an Urdu compilation of popular tales from the Mahabharata and the Ramayana titled *Naiyirain-i Hind* (The Two Luminaries of India).[28]

The publication of the *Mahabharat-i Manzum* reflected the work of the Naval Kishore Press and other major north Indian lithographic presses to build a popularly accessible canon of South Asian literature through Urdu. To that end, the translations released by the press in the decade immediately following its foundation in 1858 mirrored the translations developed by Akbar's court. Akbar's court had sought to enable access to a shared body of literature through Persian. Likewise, nineteenth-century presses translated Persian, Arabic, Sanskrit, and a variety of vernacular texts into Urdu to create a new popularly accessible regional canon. The Naval Kishore Press also published extensively in other languages, but its early releases point to the centrality of Urdu in creating a shared popular canon for the print age. As Robert Lowell Phillips has noted, 1862 also saw the release of the Naval Kishore Press' first Urdu Ramayana, the *Ramayan-i Khushtar*, based on a translation completed at the Awadhi court a decade earlier. Like many translations into Urdu, the *Ramayan-i Khushtar* was wildly popular, reissued by the press at least 16 times over the subsequent six decades.[29]

Like many of the press' early publications, the introduction and colophon of the *Mahabharat-i Manzum* (Figure 6.1) explicitly referenced the work of lithographic textual production. These materials were modelled off of manuscripts, rendering the labour of press workers marginal.

Nonetheless, choices of terminology, language, and organization suggest the intellectual role of print workers in developing new Mahabharatas in Perso-Arabic script. Reflecting the centrality of the publisher himself to the process, the introductions included a section titled 'Reasons for the Publication of this Book, Containing Praise for Naval Kishore Sahib':

> The motivation for completing this masnavi
> Is to use poetry to elevate the great and small
> Everyone has longed to hear these verses
> So the publication was ordered by this man of taste
> Here, where publishing is so reliable
> And here, where most books are now printed ...
> So extreme is his appreciation of poetry
> That he gives words fresh and new life
> Here dignity and honour for the people of the arts
> Is kept in mind in all situations
> If his attributes were written down upon the pages

They would take up every scratch and image ...
For ordering the publication of this historic book of the religion of the nation
May he receive every just reward
It is certain that when these words are set to print
His name will be remembered until judgement day ...[30]

Figure 6.1 The cover page of the 1862 edition of the *Mahabharat-i Manzum* published by the Naval Kishore Press in Lucknow

These verses mirrored the panegyric praise of royal and elite patrons of manuscripts in the pre-print era. Despite this mirroring, Naval Kishore was not a royal patron but a member of the subcontinent's ascendant capitalist class. The author of the verses – Tota Ram – was not a Mughal poet eager to ensure continued patronage, but a salaried employee of a press. By adapting the language of literary patronage to a context of print capitalism, the translator not only connected his own work with an earlier tradition but made the economic structures of publishing accessible to audiences familiar with manuscript patronage.

In the context of an Urdu Mahabharata, these references to earlier traditions of textual production are particularly relevant because they established a connection with the broader popular awareness of the *Razmnamah*. It communicated to middle-class consumers that in purchasing this Urdu Mahabharata, they had engaged with a literary tradition that connected them to the elites of Akbar's court. The attribution of the earlier Persian text to Abul Fazl, among the most famous of the *Razmnamah*'s contributors, but not its primary author or translator, likewise reflected the efforts of the author and the publisher to connect a growing body of middle-class readers to a perceived elite Mughal past.

At the same time, the author's praise of Naval Kishore suggests new forms of textual production within nineteenth-century Indian print capitalism. For instance, he used the word *hazz*, literally meaning scratch or incision, to describe the work of writing the text, evoking the work of etching on lithographic stones.[31] Likewise, the verses claimed that the press and its founder provided honour for the *ahl-i hunar* – artists or skilled people of the arts. Tota Ram thus noted the role of presses in providing a source of income for calligraphers, illustrators, and others in a period of economic and social upheaval.

The introductory verses also explicitly tied the labour of textual production to the contents of the text. Tota Ram's claim that the text had emerged from the 'religion of the nation' (*millat ki mazhab*) was in part an example of the nationalization of the Mahabharata, which we will explore in greater detail soon. Even beyond this, however, Tota Ram seemed to consider the work of producing a Mahabharata and making it broadly accessible a religious boon. Despite referencing Hindu traditions as the 'religion of the nation', the language of the poem was ecumenical, in recognition of the presumed religious diversity of Urdu readers. The following verse switched to an Islamic dialectic, asking for the remembrance of Naval Kishore's name until *qiamat ka din* (judgement day).[32]

Just as Abul Fazl had evoked 'the two communities' in his *Razmnamah* introduction, Tota Ram used language evocative of both Hindu and Muslim traditions in his introduction to assert that producing an Urdu Mahabharata was relevant and good work across any religious divide.[33]

The verses that followed the praise of the publisher, which explained 'the reasons for compiling this versified Mahabharata', likewise evoked the labour of textual production, praised presses for providing employment, and asserted that involvement in translating the Mahabharata was a religious boon across traditions. For instance, Tota Ram explained that the work of the book was done 'by the work of the pen', which 'cleared the way' for the text as if 'flashes of lightening from a sword'.[34] This language suggested both the occasionally physically challenging world of lithographic production, with its stone presses requiring etching, pressing, and clearing, as well as the battles to come in the contents of the *Razmnamah*.

The blending of religious imagery from a plurality of South Asian traditions likewise continued throughout the text's opening and concluding sections, with the work of publishing and textual reproduction itself praised in both 'Hindu' and 'Muslim' idioms. A series of introductory verses on 'the avatars of god (*baghvan*)' described knowledge of god as the 'imprinting (*tab*) of joy'.[35] In doing so, they made an explicit connection between the 'Hindu' content of the text and its printing in a language accessible to a religiously diverse array of Indian readers. At the same time, in the 'conclusion to the publication (*khatmat al-tab*')', Tota Ram praised the history of Muslim interest in the text, claiming a longer history for the Mahabharata in Perso-Arabic script and rooting it in Mughal religious magnanimity.[36]

As in the *Mahabharat-i Manzum*, the printers and compilers of the *Mahabharat-i Farsi* (Figure 6.2) connected the labour of publishing to the contents of the text. Published beginning in 1880, the *Mahabharat-i Farsi* claimed to reflect the entirety of the *Razmnamah* produced at Akbar's court. Because the publisher sought to benefit from the prestige associated with the Mughal *Razmnamah*, the work of lithographic workers became more liminal and less explicit within the text. Published in 18 volumes, following the organization of the Sanskrit *parvas* (books or volumes), the *Mahabharat-i Farsi* was among the signature Persian-language undertakings of the Naval Kishore Press in the late nineteenth century. Like most of its Persian-language publications, the work was designed for audiences not only in India, but also for readers abroad, particularly in Iran, and in Afghanistan and Central Asia.[37]

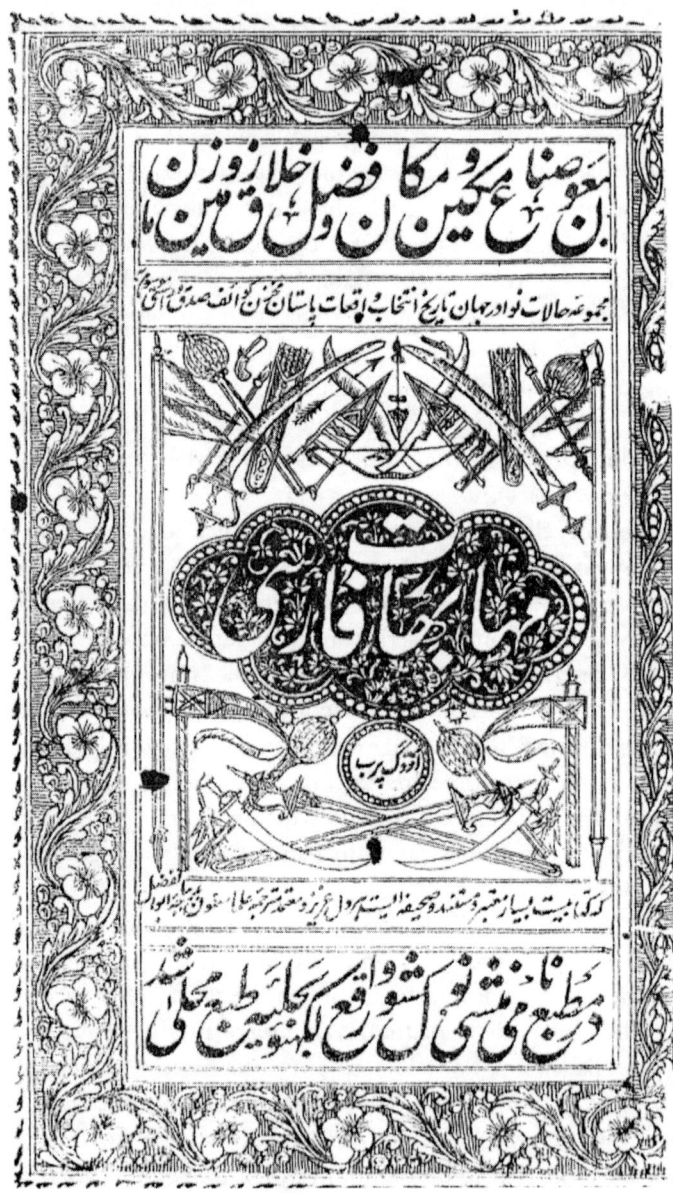

Figure 6.2 The cover page of the *Mahabharat-i Farsi*'s *fan-i panchum* (fifth volume), titled *Udyug Parb* (Udyoga Parva), published by the Naval Kishore Press in Lucknow in the late nineteenth century

Note: Both the Persian and Urdu translations featured cover pages that adhered to the design norms of the Naval Kishore Press.

The design of the text reflected the publisher's attempts to claim historical authenticity in ways that would attract both Indian Persian readers familiar with the *Razmnamah* and Iranian readers who viewed the Mahabharata through an emerging comparativist frame. Descriptive text on the cover of each volume described the work as

[a] compendium of the rare conditions of the world, with selected histories and a repository of past events, all truthful and honest, adorned with excellence, in which the authentic and truthful writings are found for every dear hearted one, compiled by the trustworthy translator and intellectual, Abul Fazl.[38]

By explicitly claiming the text as the printed edition of the manuscripts that circulated first at Akbar's court and later through South Asian courtly society, the publishers promised the middle-class reading public – whether in India or Iran – entry into an elite literary space. The emphasis on the 'truthful' (*durusti mausum*) nature of the text suggests that the publisher hoped to capitalize on the perception that texts produced by the Mughal court were bearers of literary authority. As with the *Mahabharat-i Manzum*, the publisher centred the role of Abul Fazl, who was the most well-remembered contributor to the *Razmnamah* by the late nineteenth century, in order to remind readers of the prestige and heritage of the translation.

Reflecting the centrality of the text's Mughal origins to the publisher's claim that it was an authoritative translation of the Mahabharata, the publication also included Abul Fazl's preface. As in the manuscript copies, the preface explained Akbar's motivations for the translation project and the court's interest in promoting knowledge of Indian literary and religious traditions across religious communities. It also emphasized the challenges of translating between Sanskrit and Persian and the collaboration of scholars learned in each language in the translation process.[39] Beyond a desire to reproduce the *Razmnamah* in its entirety, the inclusion of Abul Fazl's preface in the printed edition suggests that the publisher aimed to inform a new potential audience about the history of the text and the process of translation. The role of the Mughal court in translating the Mahabharata was well known among Persian-literate Indians of the period, but as Indian presses set their eyes on transregional audiences, Abul Fazl's preface gained new relevance as an explanatory note.

The printers of the *Mahabharat-i Farsi* likewise claimed a more explicit rooting in the Sanskrit tradition for the Persian text than they had for the *Mahabharat-i Manzum*. While the Urdu *Mahabharat-i Manzum* focused on summarizing and versifying well-known tales from the Mahabharata for an Urdu-literate audience, the *Mahabharat-i Farsi* claimed to be a nearly unabridged translation of the entire Sanskrit epic. Each volume was labelled with the transliterated title of the *parva*, which was also referenced throughout.[40] Each of the volumes also typically opened with a reference back to the 'the narrators of the events of this book' or 'the narrators of the events of India', who had 'passed on this tradition' before returning to the narrative.[41] A reference to the scholars of Sanskrit involved in the translation of the work at Akbar's court, these brief mentions served to remind readers of the act of linguistic and cultural translation necessary to produce the *Razmnamah*.

In transliterating volume titles directly from Sanskrit and noting the role of 'narrators', the published Persian edition emphasized Akbar's courtly projects of translation rather than the role of the press and lithographic workers. This focus makes sense in the context of an intended transregional Persian-literate audience. By the 1880s, Iranian readers were increasingly familiar with prominent Indian presses, particularly the Naval Kishore Press, because these presses often produced Persian texts more cheaply than their local counterparts.[42] However, they lacked the familiarity of Urdu- and Persian-literate Indians with the history of the *Razmnamah* and Mughal translation projects more broadly. Although a few manuscripts of the Mughal *Razmnamah* were brought to Iran by merchants and collectors earlier in the nineteenth century, the text does not appear to have been in wide circulation there prior to its publication. By foregrounding the Mughal history of the production and translation of the text, the publishers made Iranian readers familiar with their claims of authenticity and authority.

Ultimately, although nineteenth-century lithographic production did share some labour practices with earlier South Asian manuscript production, lithographic labourers were rooted more explicitly in an emerging print economy directed by local Indian capitalists. The intellectual agency of the lithographic labourers who adapted the Mahabharata for Persian- and Urdu-reading audiences of the late nineteenth century was predicated on their ability to negotiate both the private capitalist oversight of their work and its popular reception. In the case of the *Mahabharat-i Manzum*, this meant that they emphasized the 'patronage' of the press and its owners in their description of the production of the text. Conversely, in the case of the *Mahabharat-i Farsi*, it meant building up an argument for the legitimacy and authenticity of the text for a partially foreign audience by emphasizing and centring its pre-print history.

Reading Perso-Arabic Script Mahabharatas in India and Iran

The printers who translated, edited, and published Mahabharatas in Perso-Arabic script in the late nineteenth century sought to capture two distinct, broad markets. The first was the large Urdu- and Persian-reading public across the Indian subcontinent, members of which were increasingly able to afford to invest in personal libraries because of the relative cheapness of lithographic print. The second was the transregional audience, especially in Iran but also in Afghanistan, Central Asia, and elsewhere. Demand from this audience was primarily for Persian texts, but, as Nile Green has argued, there was also a notable transregional audience of Urdu readers.[43]

Readers in Iran and India engaged with Mahabharatas in Perso-Arabic script as material objects reflective of the shifts of the print revolution. They also engaged with these texts as intellectual products of the time, reflective of emerging nationalist claims and comparativist understandings of epic literature. We will turn now to these claims, asking how new popular literary comparativist discourses situated the Mahabharata within understandings of the relationships between nations and epics.

Reading the Persian Mahabharata in Comparative Literary Context in Iran

As we saw in the case of Akbar's court, in earlier Indo-Islamic dynastic contexts, interest in the Mahabharata was sometimes based on religious comparison and exchange. However, the popular late-nineteenth-century reading of Persian and Urdu Mahabharatas in both Iran and India was increasingly rooted in a comparative understanding, not of Islam and Hinduism but of 'national' epics. Particularly but not exclusively among readers of Persian, the Mahabharata–Razmnamah was understood through comparison with the Shahnamah, an epic poem that traced mythical heroes and reclaimed a pre-Islamic history for Persia. Written by Abul Qasim Ferdowsi at the turn of the eleventh century CE, the Shahnamah was based on Sassanid (r. 224–651 CE) and other pre-Islamic Persian narratives. Despite its more recent provenance, the Shahnamah was endlessly compared with the Mahabharata in the late nineteenth century because both offered epic narratives of regions home to emerging nationalist movements and projects.

In mid- and late-nineteenth-century Qajar (r. 1789–1925) Iran, the release of the printed Persian Mahabharata coincided with the emergence of both state and popular nationalist narratives that positioned the Shahnamah as the 'national' epic of Iran.[44] In these narratives, the Shahnamah was not only a foundational epic of Persian literature but also *the* foundational epic of Iranian identity and culture.[45] Scholars of Persian, including Franklin Lewis and Hamid Dabashi, have analysed the tensions between expressions of the Shahnamah as a national epic and as 'world literature'. The nationalization of epic narratives – whether the Shahnamah, the Mahabharata, or others – created new sites for comparative projects but also ruptured earlier models of the transregional circulation of epic literature.[46] Lewis noted the wide-reaching circulation and reproduction of the Shahnamah across the post-Mongol Persianate world –including the Delhi Sultanate – beginning in the fourteenth century, with European interest in the text beginning in the seventeenth century.[47] Likewise, Dabashi argued that the Shahnamah spread through 'the triumphant rise of Persianate empires with the Persian language as the lingua franca' across portions of the Middle East, Central Asia, and the Indian subcontinent. As a result, the Shahnamah itself became 'a defining force field' of Persianate literary, political, and historical writing.[48] This 'global' circulation and positionality meant that the epic was frequently included in the attempts of both Europeans and intellectuals from the Persianate world to identify and define a shared 'world literature' in the nineteenth century.

Attempts to situate the Mahabharata and Shahnamah within 'world literature' and identify a global literary canon beyond Europe occurred roughly contemporaneously with Qajar attempts to use the Shahnamah to articulate Iranian identity. As they positioned the Shahnamah within artistic, literary, and political claims on an Iranian past, comparisons with other 'national' traditions allowed Qajar intellectuals both to assert difference and to demonstrate international exchange.[49] Persian readers in Iran encountered the printed Mahabharata–*Razmnamah* in this new comparative frame.

The thematic parallels between the Mahabharata and Shahnamah, particularly regarding justifications of war, relationships between enemy combatants, qualities of warriors, and consequences of individual choices, would have been readily apparent to Iranian readers. In both epics, for instance, vengeful wars are broadly condemned, even as the responsibility of the warrior to fight and lead in battle is broadly embraced.[50] Indeed, the strong thematic overlap between the two epics prompted European scholarly speculation, particularly in the early twentieth century, about the influence of a shared Indo-European 'Aryan' mythic tradition.[51]

Iranian interest in the Mahabharata often focused on the Bhagavadgita, and the 'Bhishma Parva' was the one book of the Mahabharata that circulated, to a limited degree, in Iran in manuscript form.[52] Moreover, as Finbarr Barry Flood has noted, the 'sections of the Mahabharata involving' the 'exploits' of the five Pandava brothers "has been translated into Persian" – via Arabic – since the eleventh century CE'. In these tellings, figures from the Mahabharata were portrayed as model warriors and kings alongside Alexander the Great and figures from the Shahnamah, although, as Flood notes, the 'Indianness' of narratives was emphasized less than their models of kingliness.[53]

For Iranian readers, the vocabulary of the printed Persian Gita was likely particularly evocative of that found in well-known stories of the Shahnamah. For instance, in one of the most famous tales of the Shahnamah, the hero Rustam considers flight away from a challenging battle with Esfandiar, a warrior prince rendered nearly invincible. When the Simurgh, a mythical bird that raised Rustam's father, dresses Rustam's wounds, the two discuss the consequences of continuing the battle and killing Esfandiar. Although the discussion is far more focused on individual outcomes than on the debate over the efficacy of war between Krishna and Arjuna in the Gita, the Persian vocabulary in the two discussions is similar. Both reference the connection between a warrior (*lashkar*) and sword (*shamshir*) or arrow (*tir*).[54] Both highlight a hero's (Rustam's and Arjuna's) justified fear (*tars*) of the impact of a battle.[55] In the Persian Gita, and more broadly throughout the *Mahabharat-i Farsi*, the translators use *khudawand* (god, lord) when characters spoke of 'God', a term that was also preferred by Ferdowsi, likely in part because it was derived from pre-Islamic Persian rather than Arabic.[56] Indeed, Ferdowsi famously eschewed some Arabic-derived terms. The *Mahabharat-i Farsi* did not hold to this tradition, but key terms for heroes and gods, weapons and battles were almost always rendered in vocabulary that did not borrow from Arabic, a practice which may have drawn attention to thematic parallels with the Shahnamah.

Terminology in the *Mahabharat-i Farsi* was likely not chosen for the specific purpose of evoking comparisons with the Shahnamah among Iranian readers, particularly since the printed edition hewed closely to the language of Mughal *Razmnamah* manuscripts. Nonetheless, it played into the emerging Iranian discourse that the Mahabharata was the Indian parallel to the Shahnamah.[57] The printers of the *Mahabharat-i Farsi* also took specific steps to mark the 'Indianness' of the text, suggesting that they were aware of the 'nationalization' of epic literature among Iranian readers of Persian. Orthographic choices were among the strongest reminders of the Indian origin of both the epic and the publication. The press used Urdu orthographic markers to indicate retroflex letters in names and places – for example, the retroflex 'ḍ' in Pandava – even though neither these sounds nor their markers exist traditionally in modern Persian.[58] Using Urdu orthography for Indic terms in Persian texts was relatively common practice among north Indian lithographic publishers, but for an Iranian readership, it likely served to 'other' the printed Mahabharata and remind readers of its foreign origins.

Ultimately, for Iranian readers, situating the printed Mahabharata–*Razmnamah* in a comparative, nationalized context contributed to what Kevin Schwartz termed the 'forgetting of the Persianate' in the face of 'literary nationalism'.[59] If the Mahabharata was the 'Indian' epic, published in Persian to allow Iranians to understand Indian literary heritage, then the Shahnamah was equally the 'Iranian' epic, divorced from its transregional context and non-Iranian uses. In this narrative, terminology and themes reflected the shared status of the two works as 'national epics', and perhaps historical links between Iran and India, but these links and parallels were understood through the modern frame of 'national' identity.

Comparative Readings of the Mahabharata and the Shahnamah in India

Because the *Razmnamah* had not circulated widely outside of India prior to the nineteenth century, many Iranian readers encountered most sections of the Mahabharata for the first time through print and placed it in a 'new' comparative dialectic with the Shahnamah. However, the Shahnamah itself had seen extensive transregional circulation in what Lewis termed the 'post-Mongol Persianate world' and retained expansive popularity in India in the nineteenth century.[60] As Ulrich Marzolph has noted, approximately 25 lithographed editions of the Shahnamah were published in India sometime between 1850 and 1920, compared with only five in Iran.[61] In part, this suggests the aforementioned export of books from India to Iran, but it also reflects the continued widespread popularity of the Shahnamah among Indian readers. Indian readers brought a longer tradition of comparison to their readings of the two epics.[62]

Indeed, one of the few explicit references to the Shahnamah within a Mahabharata in Perso-Arabic script came not in a Persian-language edition but in Tota Ram's Urdu *Mahabharat-i Manzum*. In his introductory verse on 'the reasons for compiling this versified Mahabharata', Tota Ram compared his work as a writer and translator to the battles of legendary warriors of the Shahnamah. Assuming his readers' familiarity with the Shahnamah, he noted the skill of both the conqueror Zal and Suhrab, his grandson, by his son Rustam, who ultimately killed Suhrab without knowing his identity. He asked that the tip of his pen hold the same power as the 'swords and daggers' (*tigh o khanjar*) of these warriors and create the same drumbeat or tumult (*damdamah*) of war. By referencing the heroes of the Shahnamah, however briefly, and comparing his pen to their swords, Tota Ram drew his readers' attention to the thematic parallels between the two epics.

Tota Ram assumed an awareness of the significant narratives of the Shahnamah among Indian readers of Persian. The text was widely circulated, in both Persian and Urdu, by Indian presses of the period. Its heroes and stories remained common reference points in Indian poetry in both languages. Thus, even as the Shahnamah and the Mahabharata were slotted into new 'literary nationalisms' in the age of print, these claims were complicated by popular awareness of longer Persianate literary geographies and genealogies in India.

Among Indian readers, engagement with Persian epic traditions and efforts to draw parallels between the Shahnamah and the Mahabharata beyond nationalist discourses also cut across religious divides through at least the late nineteenth century. As noted earlier, Tota Ram characterized engagement with the Urdu Mahabharata as a religious boon regardless of one's background, and the Naval Kishore Press anticipated both Muslim and Hindu readership for the Urdu text. Tota Ram also clearly considered popular Indian awareness of the Shahnamah to lack religious boundaries. Instead, a rootedness in the narratives of the Shahnamah marked Urdu literacy and an awareness of the region's Persianate literary heritage. Ultimately, the continued engagement of Indian readers of diverse religious backgrounds with both texts reflects the degree to which emerging national claims on epic literature did not, at least in the nineteenth century, fully erase the earlier, transregional, and transcultural circulation of ideas through Persian.

Towards a Transnational Intellectual History of Printed Mahabharatas in Perso-Arabic script

This chapter has interrogated the ways in which Indian and Iranian understandings of Persian and Urdu Mahabharatas changed as a result of the spread of lithographic print technology. Through an analysis of the labour of lithographic production, it has worked to complicate our understandings of the transregional intellectual history of the Mahabharata, providing a new site for the study of Indo-Iranian exchange that incorporates print capitalism. By analysing the reception of printed Persian and Urdu Mahabharatas, it has argued that late-nineteenth-century literary nationalism disrupted understandings of a shared

Persianate literary past. At the same time, the circulation and consumption of these texts relied, to a large degree, on the continued relevance of an earlier transregional Persianate literary ecumene.

The work of new textual producers at Indian printing presses shaped the consumption and reception of the text among both Indian and Iranian audiences. Roger Chartier has argued that there is an innate connection between the material construction of a text and its reception among readers, maintaining that 'readers never confront abstract, idealized texts detached from any materiality' and instead engage with books as physical objects.[63] When Iranian readers purchased the *Mahabharat-i Farsi*, they encountered a physical object that both evoked the foreignness of the 'Indian' epic and paralleled the Shahnamah epic tradition that they increasingly conceptualized as 'Iranian'.

The *Mahabharat-i Farsi* was published by a press – the Naval Kishore Press – that also released editions of the Shahnamah and other Persian classics intended for transregional audiences. The design of its *Mahabharat-i Farsi* and the Shahnamah both adhered to the press' internal norms. Iranian readers of the *Mahabharat-i Farsi* and Shahnamahs printed in India thus encountered parallels in both form and content. Parallels in form suggested the continued shared space of Persianate intellectual exchange with India. But late-nineteenth-century Iranian readers increasingly framed parallels in content as reflective of the fact that the Mahabharata and the Shahnamah were each 'national epics' that could be claimed by a specific region and people.

On the other hand, for Persian and Urdu readers in India, this narrative was complicated by the fact that they retained a literary rootedness in the transregional Persianate canon, which included the Shahnamah. Continued popular engagement with an earlier cosmopolitan literary ecumene made it more difficult to slot the Mahabharata and the Shahnamah into 'national' categories. Even as translators such as Tota Ram gestured towards a 'national' heritage for the Mahabharata, they equally assumed that Urdu readers in India of diverse religious and social backgrounds retained a cultural awareness of the heroes and tales of the Shahnamah. In India, popular engagement with the parallels in form and content between Mahabharatas in Perso-Arabic script and Shahnamahs did not diverge in the same way they did in Iran. Both the form and the content of the texts instead reflected the popularization of a formerly courtly tradition of translation that, through the intervention of lithographic book workers and publishers, circulated among a new middle-class readership.

These differences in engagement with Mahabharatas in Perso-Arabic script between India and Iran suggest that lithographic publishers sought to make the Mahabharata accessible to wider transregional audiences that approached the text through divergent comparativist practices. These publishers produced translations that claimed the Persianate, Indo-Islamic courtly past of the Mahabharata–*Razmnamah* as a way of asserting the authority and prestige of the text. They consciously developed texts-as-objects that could be used within both Indian and Iranian late-nineteenth-century understandings of of Persianate pasts and literary cultures. Printed Mahabharatas in Perso-Arabic script were used to further a middle-class Indian narrative of the expansion of an earlier, cosmopolitan Persianate interest in Sanskrit epics. At the same time, the printers ensured that Persian Mahabharatas could also be used to further an emerging Iranian narrative of epics as reflective of distinct 'national' cultures. Ultimately, the intellectual contributions of lithographic book workers and publishers allowed popular Persian and Urdu readerships in India and Iran to develop new, divergent narratives of the social positionality of the Mahabharata.

Notes

1. Ruby Lal, 'Settled, Sacred and All-Powerful: Making of New Genealogies and Traditions of Empire under Akbar', *Economic and Political Weekly* 36, no. 11 (2001): 941–943, 945–958.
2. Audrey Truschke, 'The Mughal Book of War: A Persian Translation of the Sanskrit Mahabharata', *Comparative Studies of South Asia, Africa and the Middle East* 31, no. 2 (2011): 506–20, 507–08.
3. M. Athar Ali, 'Translations of Sanskrit Works at Akbar's Court', *Social Scientist* 20, nos. 9–10 (1992): 38–45, 40–41.
4. Truschke, 'The Mughal Book of War', 507.
5. Yael Rice, 'A Persian Mahabharata: 1598–99 Razmnama', *Mānoa* 22, no. 1 (2010): 125–31, 126.
6. Rice, 'A Persian Mahabharata', 126.
7. Rajeev Kinra, *Writing Self, Writing Empire: Chandar Bhan Brahman and the Cultural World of the Indo-Persian State Secretary* (Oakland, CA: University of California Press, 2015), 226–227.
8. Kinra, *Writing Self, Writing Empire*, 227.
9. A few portions of the *Razmnamah* manuscripts do seem to have been acquired by Iranian collectors by the nineteenth century; see, for instance, National Library of Iran, 'Mahābhārāt', Online Catalogue, no. 30129, for a copy of the 'Bhishma Parva' copied in 1837 CE.
10. Rice, 'A Persian Mahabharata', 125.

11. Razieh B. Koshtely, Saarthak Singh, Vafa Movahedian, Muntazir Ali, and Michael Willis, 'Translation and State', in *Translation and State: The Mahabharata at the Mughal Court*, ed. Michael Willis, 1–66 (Berlin: De Gruyter, 2002), 12–17.

12. Rice, 'A Persian Mahabharata', 126.

13. John Seyller, 'Model and Copy: The Illustration of Three Razmnama Manuscripts', *Archives of Asian Art* 38 (1985): 37–66, 37.

14. Shireen Moosvi, 'The World of Labour in Mughal India (c. 1500–1750)', *International Review of Social History* 56, no. 19 (2011): 245–261, 247.

15. For a detailed breakdown of some of the workers employed in Mughal manuscript workshops, see Najaf Haidar, 'Manuscript Production and Preservation in Medieval India', *Journal of the Asiatic Society* 52, no. 1 (2010): 23–52, 34–43.

16. Shailvee Sharda, '300-Year-Old Urdu Mahabharat in Lucknow Home', *Times of India*, 2 October 2015, https://timesofindia.indiatimes.com/city/lucknow/300-yr-old-urdu-mahabharat-in-lucknow-home/articleshow/49189118.cms (accessed on 19 April 2023).

17. M. Tavakoli Targhi, 'Rediscovering Munshi Newal Kishore (1836–1895)', *South Asia Library Notes and Queries* 29 (1993): 14–22, 19.

18. I focus here on these north Indian cities because they were the site of publication of Persian and Urdu Mahabharatas. It should be noted, however, the publishers in Bombay likewise engaged closely with the Iranian market. See Nile Green, *Bombay Islam: The Religious Economy of the West Indian Ocean, 1840–1915* (Cambridge, UK: Cambridge University Press, 2011), 148–52.

19. For references to Indian lithographic production for Iranian audiences, see Ulrich Marzolph, 'The Shahnama in Print: Lithographed Editions of the Persian National Epic', in *Heroic Times: A Thousand Years of the Persian Book of Kings*, ed. Julia Gonnella and Christoph Rauch, 64–71 (Munich: Edition Minerva, 2012), 66; Abbas Amanat, 'Remembering the Persianate', in *The Persianate World: Rethinking a Shared Sphere*, ed. Abbas Amanat and Assef Ashraf, 15–62 (Leiden: Brill, 2014), 57.

20. Ulrike Stark, *An Empire of Books: The Naval Kishore Press and the Diffusion of the Printed Word in Colonial India, 1858–1895* (Delhi: Permanent Black, 2007).

21. Olimpiada Shcheglova, "Lithography ii. In India', Encyclopædia Iranica (online edition), 2012, http://www.iranicaonline.org/articles/lithography-ii-in-india (accessed on 19 April 2023).

22. Shcheglova, "Lithography ii. In India'.

23. Stark, *An Empire of Books*, 46–47.

24. For examples from Benares, see Francesca Orsini, 'Pandits, Printers and Others: Publishing in Nineteenth-Century Benares', in *Print Areas: Book History in India*, ed. Abhijit Gupta and Swapan Chakravorty, 103–38 (New Delhi: Permanent Black, 2004).

25. Dipesh Chakrabarty, *Rethinking World Class Histories: Bengal 1890–1940* (Princeton, NJ: Princeton University Press, 1989), 112–13.

26. Munshi Tota Ram Shayan, *Mahabharat-i Manzum* (Lucknow: Naval Kishore Press, 1862), 216.

27. Stark, *An Empire of Books*, 308–09.

28. J. F. Blumhardt, *Catalogue of the Library of the India Office: Hindustani Books* (London: Eyre & Spottiswoode, 1900), 145.

29. Robert Lowell Phillips, 'Garden of Endless Blossoms: Urdu Ramayans of the 19th and early 20th Century', PhD dissertation, University of Wisconsin–Madison, 2010, 93.

30. Shayan, *Mahabharat-i Manzum*, 4 (translation mine).

31. Shayan, *Mahabharat-i Manzum*, 4.

32. Shayan, *Mahabharat-i Manzum*, 4.

33. Rice, 'A Persian Mahabharata', 126.

34. Shayan, *Mahabharat-i Manzum*, 4.

35. Shayan, *Mahabharat-i Manzum*, 3.

36. Shayan, *Mahabharat-i Manzum*, 214.

37. On the transregional and global circulation of printed Persian texts, see Nile Green, 'Stones from Bavaria: Iranian Lithography in Its Global Contexts', *Iranian Studies* 43, no. 3 (2010): 305–31; Hamid Dabashi, *The World of Persian Literary Humanism* (Cambridge, MA: Harvard University Press, 2012), 252–57.

38. Cover page of *Mahabharat-i Farsi*'s *fan-i shishum* (vol. 6), titled *Bhishm Parb* (Lucknow: Naval Kishore Press).

39. S. A. A. Rizvi, 'Abdul Fazl's Preface to the Persian Translation of the Mahabharat', *Proceedings of the Indian History Conference* 13 (1950): 197–201, 198–99.

40. *Mahabharat-i Farsi, fan-i shishum* (vol. 6), 1 and 76; *Mahabharat-i Farsi, fan-i sizdahum* (vol. 13): *Anusasan Parb* (Lucknow: Naval Kishore Press), 1.

41. *Mahabharat-i Farsi, fan-i shishum*, 1.

42. Marzolph, 'The Shahnama in Print', 66.

43. Nile Green, 'The Trans-Border Traffic of Afghan Modernism: Afghanistan and the Indian Urdusphere', *Comparative Studies in History and Society* 53, no. 3 (2011): 479–508, 481, 500.

44. This trend became more pronounced in the twentieth century but originated in nineteenth-century Qajar articulations of nation and homeland

through literature. See Juan R. I. Cole, 'Marking Boundaries, Marking Time: The Iranian Past and the Construction of the Self by Qajar Thinkers', *Iranian Studies* 29, nos. 1–2 (1996): 35–56.

45. Mohammad Tavakoli-Targhi, 'Refashioning Iran: Language and Culture during the Constitutional Revolution', *Iranian Studies* 23, nos. 1–4 (1990): 77–101, 80; Afsaneh Najmabadi, *Women with Mustaches and Men without Beards: Gender and Sexual Anxieties of Iranian Modernity* (Berkeley,CA: University of California Press, 2005), 109.

46. Franklin Lewis, 'The Shahnameh of Ferdowsi as World Literature', *Iranian Studies* 48, no. 3 (2015): 313–36; Hamid Dabashi, *The Shahnameh: The Persian Epic as World Literature* (New York: Columbia University Press, 2019).

47. Lewis, 'The Shahnameh of Ferdowsi', 319.

48. Dabashi, *The Shahnameh*, 153–54.

49. For examples of Qajar comparative projects with European literature, see Iraj Afshar, 'Book Translations as a Cultural Activity in Iran 1806–1896', *Iran* 41 (2013): 279–89.

50. See Mohammad Jafar Amir Mahallati, 'Ethics of War and Peace in the Shahnameh of Ferdowsi', *Iranian Studies* 48, no. 6 (2015): 905–31, 911–13.

51. C. Scott Littleton, *A New Comparative Mythology: An Anthropological Assessment of the Theories of Georges Dumezil* (Berkeley, CA: University of California Press, 1973), 157–61.

52. See National Library of Iran, 'Mahābhārāt', Online Catalogue, no. 30129, https://scripts.nlai.ir/result/MyG85S1V/%D9%85%D9%87%D8%A7%D8%A8%D8%A7%D8%B1%D8%A7%D8%AA%D8%A7-%D9%86%D8%B3%D8%AE%D9%87-%D8%AE%D8%B7%DB%8C (accessed on 10 April 2023).

53. Finbarr Barry Flood, *Objects of Translation: Material Culture and Medieval 'Hindu–Muslim' Encounter* (Princeton, NJ: Princeton University Press, 2009), 251.

54. *Mahabharat-i Farsi, fan-i shishum*, 8–9.

55. *Mahabharat-i Farsi, fan-i shishum*, 8.

56. *Mahabharat-i Farsi, fan-i shishum*, 7–10. See also *Mahabharat-i Farsi, fan-i panchum* (fifth volume): *Udyug Parb* (Lucknow: Naval Kishore Press), 7.

57. For attempts at asserting Iranian nationalism through the Shahnamah from the Qajar period through the present, see Dabashi, *The Shahnameh*, 164–69.

58. See, for instance, *Mahabharat-i Farsi, fan-i shishum*, 2; *Mahabharat-i Farsi, fan-i panchum*, 1.

59. Kevin Shwartz, *Remapping Persian Literary History, 1700–1900* (Edinburgh: Edinburgh University Press, 2020), 59.

60. Lewis, 'The Shahnameh of Ferdowsi', 319.

61. Marzolph, 'The Shahnama in Print', 66.

62. On Indian interpretations and uses of the Shahnamah, see Pasha Khan, 'Marvellous Histories: Reading the Shahnamah in India', *Indian Economic and Social History Review* 49, no. 4 (2012): 527–56.

63. Roger Chartier, 'Laborers and Voyagers: From the Text to the Reader', *Diacritics* 22, no. 2 (1992): 49–61.

7

'Philosophical Poetry' or a 'Failed Beginning'?

A Metaphilosophical Enquiry into Wilhelm von Humboldt's and G. W. F. Hegel's Perspectives on the Bhagavadgita

Paulus Kaufmann

Introduction

German philosophers of the eighteenth and nineteenth centuries reacted with much interest and even enthusiasm to the growth of knowledge about Indian intellectual history at that time. Johann Gottfried Herder[1] and Friedrich Schlegel[2] praised India as the cradle of human culture, and Indian thinkers were dealt with in contemporary histories of philosophy. Philosopher and philologist Wilhelm von Humboldt participated in this intellectual development. He was proficient in Sanskrit, knowledgeable about Indian culture, and keen to share his knowledge with his contemporaries. His publication of two commendatory articles about the Bhagavadgita can be seen as the apex of the positive reception of Indian philosophy in Germany.

The positive attitude towards Indian thought changed at some point in history. It seems to be the influence of G. W. F. Hegel, in particular, that led to a negative evaluation or, more often, to a disinterest in Indian literature and thought that is typical for German philosophers since the second half of the nineteenth century. Hegel expressed his position concisely in his critical review of Humboldt's two positive articles about the Gita. Basically, he denies that the Gita – or any other ancient Indian text – deserves to be included in the scope of philosophy. The dispute between Humboldt and Hegel was a crucial turning point for the evaluation of Indian thought in Germany and, thereby, for the future development of philosophy as a discipline. It is thus no exaggeration when

Aakash Singh Rathore and Rimina Mohapatra state that 'the reception of the Gita was critical to philosophical developments taking place in Germany'.[3]

In the globalized world of the twenty-first century, the question of whether there are philosophical texts and debates that are *not* 'footnotes to Plato' – as Alfred North Whitehead poignantly defined Western philosophy[4] – is of eminent concern. Although the question still does not receive the attention it deserves,[5] there is nowadays an ongoing debate about non-Western philosophy.[6] The controversy between Humboldt and Hegel is an important contribution to this debate for two reasons. First, it is a very *early* dispute that defined the contours of later discussions. Second, in contrast to many contemporary debates about non-Western thought, Humboldt and Hegel argue *explicitly* and *elaborately* about the question of whether such thought should be understood as philosophy. They focus on a specific text and discuss its philosophical properties. It is thus worthwhile to analyse their arguments about the philosophic character of the Gita in detail.

It has been claimed that Hegel's negative evaluation of Indian philosophy was driven by personal ambitions and ethnocentric biases.[7] Other commentators point to Hegel's insufficient knowledge of Indian culture and philosophy.[8] These biographical and historical objections seem justified. However, they should not have us neglect the concrete arguments of Humboldt and Hegel. Both authors carefully analyse the text and weigh the factors that speak in favour of and against the philosophic character of the Gita. By analysing their considerations, we arrive at thoughtful arguments concerning the existence of philosophy in India and Asia. These arguments contribute, in turn, to the larger question of what philosophy is. We should therefore read the dispute between Humboldt and Hegel as a debate in metaphilosophy. With this systematic, rather than biographical or historical, focus, Humboldt's and Hegel's positions can be made fruitful for contemporary debates about the existence and character of philosophy in the non-Western world.

In this chapter, I argue that Hegel offers two arguments for excluding a text from the scope of philosophy: the *argument from lack of freedom* and the *argument from lack of systematicity*. I try to show that these arguments propose reasonable criteria and can – if properly reconstructed – be integrated into an attractive account of philosophy. However, against Hegel's own conclusion, I argue that his arguments do not exclude the Gita, let alone all other Indian texts from the scope of philosophy.

Notably, Humboldt and Hegel do not only offer formal arguments. Both writers also exemplify attitudes towards philosophical texts from different cultures. We could label Hegel's attitude 'critical' and Humboldt's attitude 'enthusiastic'. I will argue that both attitudes are equally valuable. Although Hegel is right in rejecting a naive enthusiasm about foreign cultures, an enthusiasm as exemplified by Humboldt is necessary to be inspired by thoughts that are foreign to us.

A Short History of the German Reception of Indian Thought

The discussion between Humboldt and Hegel takes place within a specific historical context. India's thought and literature were largely unknown in Europe until the eighteenth century. Except for a few missionary reports of the seventeenth century, no texts from and about India reached early modern Europe.[9] This situation began to change in the eighteenth century when more and more reports about India and Asia began to appear. First translations of Indian texts were published; grammars and vocabularies of Sanskrit were composed in Western languages. In European philosophy, Gottfried Wilhelm Leibniz (1646–1716), Christian Wolff (1679–1754), and Voltaire (1694–1778) reacted positively to this new knowledge about India and welcomed the alternative cultural models they learnt to know.[10] This positive attitude towards Indian and Asian thought can also be detected in early histories of philosophy. The first German historiographer of philosophy, Johann Jacob Brucker (1696–1770), integrated chapters on Egyptian, Persian, Arab, and Indian philosophy into his seven-volume work *Short Question from the History of Philosophy*, published in 1731–36.[11]

An interest in Indian and Asian thought cannot be presumed for German philosophy in general. Immanuel Kant and Johann Gottlieb Fichte, for example, showed little interest in Indian philosophy.[12] Historians such as Dietrich Tiedemann and Wilhelm Gottlieb Tennemann did not include any non-Western philosophers in their histories of philosophy that appeared between 1791 and 1819. However, the first direct translations of Indian texts, such as Charles Wilkins' translation of the Gita from 1785, aroused a renewed interest of numerous German philosophers. By the turn of the nineteenth century, Johann Gottfried Herder (1744–1803), Friedrich Schlegel (1772–1829), and Friedrich Wilhelm Josef Schelling (1775–1854) celebrated India as the cradle of humanity.[13] In their eyes, Indian thought contained a unity that has been lost in the West. Therefore, they propagated a reorientation following Indian models. Romantic authors such as Novalis (1772–1801), Friedrich Majer (1772–1818), and Joseph Görres (1776–1848) adopted this positive image of India and used it as a critique of contemporary society. Indian thought was also included in contemporary histories of philosophy such as Thaddäus Anselm Rixner's (1766–1838) *Handbuch der Geschichte der Philosophie* (Handbook on the History of Philosophy) from 1823[14] and Karl Josef Hieronymous Windischmann's (1775–1839) *Die Philosophie im Fortgang der Weltgeschichte* (Philosophy in the Course of World History) from 1829.[15]

In spite of their positive reception, we cannot say that Romantic thinkers were uncritical towards the ideas they found in Indian texts. Herder, for example, harshly criticized the caste system and the idea of rebirth.[16] Schlegel rejected Indian pantheism and criticized the emptiness of Indian religious practices.[17] We should notice, moreover, that in contrast to earlier aficionados such as Leibniz and Voltaire, nineteenth-century thinkers had much more information at hand and sometimes actively produced such knowledge. Herder followed all new publications on India, and Schlegel studied Sanskrit. His older brother, August Wilhelm Schlegel (1767–1845), even became the first Indologist in Germany with a newly established chair of Indology at the University of Bonn.

It was in this dynamic atmosphere that Prussian statesman and philologist Wilhelm von Humboldt (1767–1835) started to engage in Indian thought. He studied Sanskrit and commented in detail upon A. W. Schlegel's Latin translation of the Gita. In his comments, he praises the Gita as 'the most beautiful, maybe the only true philosophical poem that all literatures known to us have to offer'.[18] In 1825, Humboldt gave a lecture on the Gita with the aim of presenting concisely the 'philosophical system'[19] contained in this unique example of 'philosophical poetry'[20]. Curiously, it was this discussion of the Gita that Georg Wilhelm Friedrich Hegel (1770–1831) chose for his most elaborate and extensive critique of Indian thought. Although Hegel expresses great respect for Humboldt's scholarship, he rejects his enthusiasm about the Gita. He uses his discussion of the text for a thorough critique of Indian thought in general. This critique is meant to justify Hegel's claim that 'Oriental thought' should not be considered part of the history of philosophy.[21] Even if we concede that the history of Indian thought contains philosophical elements and forms part of our historical consciousness, it has been, in Hegel's eyes, a 'failed beginning'.[22]

Hegel's negative verdict about Indian and Asian philosophy strongly influenced the future course of Western philosophy. Except for Hegel's archenemy, Arthur Schopenhauer (1788–1860), few German philosophers after Hegel showed any interest in Indian or Asian philosophy. Friedrich Nietzsche (1844–1900) is an interesting case because he was a classmate and friend of

Paul Deussen (1845–1919), one of the most proliferous German translators of Sanskrit philosophical literature. Nietzsche thus knew about current research on India, but he did not highly estimate Indian thought and did not engage with it.[23] Twentieth-century philosophers such as Husserl, Heidegger, and Gadamer excluded oriental thought from the realm of philosophy.[24] They renewed Hegel's negative verdict about Oriental thought – sometimes repeating his arguments – without taking the pains of studying them in detail.

Hegel's Defence of Philosophy

Due to his infamous role in coining the reception of Indian thought in Germany, Hegel has been criticized by numerous modern authors. He has been accused of Eurocentrism and racism.[25] Rathore and Mohapatra choose another line of interpretation. They suggest that Hegel despised Indian thought and the Gita in particular because the position defended therein was too close to his own. They write:

> And yet that which was most impressive to Hegel about Indian philosophy also posed a grave threat to him. At times it might have struck him that all his thankless, laborious cultivation and development of a cutting-edge, end-all philosophy, to which indeed he had devoted his entire life, culminated in no more than those precious insights already enjoyed by distant Indian philosophers centuries before.[26]

All these critiques contain some truth in them. On the other hand, we should not forget that very few Western philosophers studied Indian thought as intensely as Hegel did. Robert Bernasconi therefore demurs that 'Hegel was more open to the possibility of Indian philosophy ... than many of us ... even today.'[27] Rathore and Mohapatra add that 'it is arguable that given the changed global environment and proliferation of accurate source material, Hegel showed *less* prejudice and arbitrary cultural preference than contemporary philosophers and philosophy department curricula continue to do today'.[28] Therefore, we would not do justice to Hegel if we were to conclude that he has nothing substantial to say about the Gita and Indian philosophy. It is certainly worthwhile to carefully consider his ideas and arguments.

We can sum up the results of Hegel's analysis of the Gita in three steps. First, Hegel criticizes *specific ideas* of the Gita, especially its adherence to the caste system and its conception of God. Second, he concludes that the Gita is not a philosophical text. Third, he argues that the Gita is characteristic of Indian thought as a whole. This leads him to the further conclusion that Indian thought in general should not be considered philosophy. These three steps of Hegel's argument will be evaluated separately in the following discussion. However, Hegel's concatenation of these three steps proves, on the other hand, that his analysis of the Gita is part of a larger project. He aims to defend a specific conception of philosophy.

In Hegel's times, Indian philosophy found its most fervent followers among literary scholars and critics, novelists and poets, cultural historians, and philologists. Academic philosophers such as Kant and Fichte were much more reserved about non-Western philosophy. Hegel associates with these authors. He defends a specifically *philosophical* approach to texts when he characterizes the adherents of Indian thought as daydreamers:

> For should we approach the charm of this Flower-life – a charm rich in imagination and genius – in which its whole environment and all its relations are permeated by the rose-breath of the Soul, and the World is transformed into a Garden of Love – should we look at it more closely, and examine it in the light of Human Dignity and Freedom – the more attractive the first sight of it had been, so much the more unworthy shall we ultimately find it in every respect.[29]

In Hegel's eyes, Indian thought is only apparently attractive. He assumes that his contemporaries are blinded by the exotic charm of Indian texts and do not critically examine the ideas they find in them. This critical examination, however, would be the task of philosophy.[30] In his analysis of the Gita, Hegel thus wishes to demonstrate how a philosopher should approach a text from a foreign intellectual tradition. When Hegel chooses Humboldt as the main target of his critical review of the Gita, he does not pick out a weak opponent. Humboldt was a distinguished philologist and an expert on Indian thought. Nevertheless, Hegel found the uncritical stance he deemed unphilosophical even in his work. Humboldt, in turn, felt this depreciation very clearly. He describes his reaction to Hegel's review in a letter: 'I cannot in the least appreciate it ... the entire review is also directed, though, concealed, against me personally and clearly reveals his firm opinion that I am anything but a philosopher.'[31]

Humboldt himself considered Hegel's arguments to be ad hominem. However, we also see that he detects in Hegel's reaction a hidden question of general concern. Humboldt feels depreciated *as a philosopher* by Hegel's review. He feels that Hegel wants to draw a line between critical philosophers on the one hand and naive philologists on the other. Humboldt does not agree with Hegel's conception of a philosopher. In order to understand the debate between

Humboldt and Hegel, we should thus take it seriously as a debate about the questions of what philosophy is and how philosophy should deal with texts from intellectual traditions that are not directly connected to the Greco-European discourse. Their disagreement on these questions is not only asserted in the texts but also manifests practically in the way Humboldt and Hegel deal with the Gita. Therefore, we have to carefully analyse how Humboldt and Hegel handle the text.

Humboldt's Reading of the Gita

In a letter to philologist Friedrich Gottlieb Welcker (1784–1868) in 1823, Humboldt congratulated himself for having had the chance to read the Gita. Humboldt admitted in this letter that his enthusiasm about the Gita might be disconcerting to his friend. For this reason, he went on to explain what had fascinated him so much about that text. Humboldt pointed, first, to deep and sublime philosophical passages that can be enjoyed even in translation. He then mentioned the unique scene of two armies opposing each other, ready to attack, but being frozen by the narrator for a moment of philosophical reflection. Finally, Humboldt explained that the fascination of the text is tied to its language and therefore untranslatable:

> The essential core [of the text] that cannot be emulated by any translation, lies in the tone, in the condensing and unfolding of thoughts in single expressions, in the sequence of thoughts and images, in the kind of metaphors, and in the incomprehensible that, because it is inseparably glued to language, cannot be analysed and stated, but can neither be denied.[32]

Because of the difficulties of transmitting all the fascinating features of the Gita, Humboldt speaks of the peculiar *experience* of reading the text. He does not content himself with these esoteric remarks, however. A few years after the writing of the letter, he presented the Gita in two lectures to an audience that was not able to enjoy it in its original language. In a footnote to the publication of the lectures that appeared in 1828, he justified the focus on a single text by declaring that the Gita is so 'rich in philosophical ideas' that it seems methodologically advisable to fully work out the text's 'philosophical system' before comparing it with other texts.[33] Humboldt left no doubt that the Gita was, in his eyes, a philosophical text.

Humboldt had already mentioned in his letter that the Gita offers a unique setting for a philosophical discussion. The great Indian epic Mahabharata tells us in its first five books of the rivalry between two clans of cousins, the Kauravas and the Pandavas. The conflict about the rule of their homeland finally leads to war, and the two armies line up at the battlefield of Kurukshetra. All await the generals' command to begin the battle, but Arjuna, the commander of the Pandava army, is suddenly plagued by doubts as to whether it is right to kill his enemies who are at the same time his teachers, friends, and family members. He begins to discuss the question with his charioteer, the disguised god Krishna. Krishna tries to relieve Arjuna of his moral scruples and, to this aim, unfolds a complex theory about duty, self, mind, and God. It is this persuasive discourse of Krishna, a philosophical insertion into the great narrative, that we refer to by the name of Bhagavadgita – that is, the 'Song of God'.

For Humboldt, the specific appeal of the Gita does not only lie in its unique narrative embedding.[34] It can also be found in the fact that the text uses a moral dilemma to unfold a 'complete philosophical system'.[35] That system contains a philosophy of mind, a theology, and a theory of religious practice. The moral dilemma that the Gita starts with is a dilemma between the duties of a warrior to fight for a just cause and the social duty towards family members, teachers, and friends. According to Humboldt, Krishna reacts to this dilemma by declaring two propositions: first, that mind is simple and imperishable, and therefore distinct from the composite and mortal body, and, second, that holy men perform acts without regard for consequences, but simply for their own sake.[36] These thoughts resolve the dilemma because they suppose that we cannot really kill a person. In the worldview defended by Krishna, the mind is eternal and cannot be killed. Krishna also argues that guilt – the feeling that haunts Arjuna – can only be brought upon oneself by pursuing specific consequences for selfish reasons. Krishna therefore advises Arjuna not to worry about the apparent killing of his kin and to fight not for glory or any other gain, but simply because it is his duty.

Humboldt anticipates that a modern Western reader would have difficulties in comprehending these arguments. He therefore explains that we can only grasp Krishna's argument if we understand it within a system of thought that believes in reincarnation.[37] With the death of a body, the mind stays alive and is reborn in just another receptacle. Death is therefore no permanent death but only the passage into another form of existence. It follows that there is no act of killing as an absolute annihilation, as Arjuna presupposes.

Although the mind cannot die in Krishna's system of thought, the mind is also never free from the bounds of the body as long as it remains in the cycle of reincarnation. However, human beings can leave this cycle, if they stop to act, because it is the actions (*karman*) that tie the mind to the body. Now, human beings cannot refrain from all sorts of deeds altogether, as Humboldt explains in his first text on the Gita, his critical notes to Alexandre Langlois' (1788–1854) review of Schlegel's translation.[38] However, human beings can avoid desiring specific outcomes of actions; they can perform acts simply for their own sake. Because acting with a view to consequences ties the mind to the body, a wise man does not care about the fruits of action. His acting thereby becomes a form of 'necessary fatalism':[39] the wise man performs acts as if another person or nature itself would commit these deeds. He becomes more of an observer than an agent and stays uninvolved. Humboldt points out that this ideal of action is sometimes expressed in the Gita by the seemingly contradictory statement that wise action is non-action.[40] Krishna thus proposes a new conception of action in order to avoid the moral dilemma that Arjuna faces.

Humboldt goes on to explain that to act in this way means to 'lie down one's acts into the deity'.[41] Refraining from the pursuit of personal goals through action is thus understood as the ultimate proof of one's trust in God. This trust liberates the mind from the fetters of the body and prevents any further reincarnation. The right form of action thereby becomes a service to the deity or even a mystical union with it. This is possible because the mind that is freed by disregarding the fruits of action is not an individual mind but a mind that is common to all beings.[42] This cosmic mind is, finally, the deity itself:

> All the mental is related to each other and one and the same; and man can detect in himself, i.e., in his mental self, all other creatures and God in them.[43]

We clearly sense in Humboldt's texts that he struggles with working out the theology that lies behind this conception of mind and of liberation through non-action. He mentions that the Gita characterizes God as follows:

> He is an eternal, invisible, impartible, and therefore simple principle that is different from everything that is perishable and visible, but that is at the same time distributed to individuals.[44]

This conception of God may sound like a peculiar form of pantheism, and Humboldt indeed sometimes speaks of a 'pantheistic system'.[45] On the other hand, God is said to be the creator of everything and to dwell outside everything created.[46] Although Humboldt does not use this term, we might thus speak of 'panentheism', a combination of theism and pantheism for the Gita.

Humboldt furthermore points out that the God of the Gita is not only the mind but also the body and that 'the whole material world is the body of the Infinite'.[47] The text thus contains a further apparent contradiction between, first, opposing mind and body and, then, ascribing a body to the deity. Humboldt attempts to explain this discrepancy by introducing the idea that God does not only contain positive but also the negative features of existence, the non-being.[48]

In general, Humboldt expends great effort explaining the theological position of the text: he points to a peculiar understanding of causality that lies behind it;[49] he tries to clarify the possible relation between a ubiquitous divine substance and a personalized divine being;[50] he suggests a peculiar form of abstraction behind conception formation;[51] and he proposes to understand the Gita's conception of God as a gradual one that starts with a relatively simple idea of God and ends in an abstract and sophisticated system.[52]

In the next step, Humboldt explains the way in which a human being can interact with God understood in this way. According to the Gita, there are two ways to do so. The first is by rationally understanding the theological system explained so far. This approach is associated with the philosophical system of Samkhya. Even more effective is a form of meditative absorption called 'yoga' in the Gita. This form of meditation aims at a state where all desires and wishes, but also all thoughts and perceptions, come to rest. Humboldt argues that in Krishna's teaching, the pure truth cannot be reached by discursive and rational reasoning alone but only through such states of complete absorption.[53] In the Gita, 'insight has to give way to religion or is a preliminary stage to it'.[54] Rational analysis is a necessary stage, however, without which a complete rest of mind cannot be reached.[55] Meditative absorption thus presupposes rational capacities as well as strength of will.[56] This has an interesting consequence for the moral core of Krishna's teaching:

> The Yoga-Teaching is from its inner essence, and more than any other philosophy, built on the necessity of moral freedom, because the firmness and persistence of the will, which is its final aim, can only spring from absolute freedom that opposes all finite impulses.[57]

In the two preceding quotations, Humboldt broaches the issue of the irrationality of the Gita's teaching. He confirms that the text is finally sceptic regarding purely rational means of salvation. However, Humboldt points out that in the Gita rational understanding and means of transcending rationality complement each other.

These observations allow for the conclusion that Humboldt is a charitable but not uncritical reader. He clearly points to statements and arguments in the text that are difficult to understand for a modern Western reader. Some of these difficulties result from the text's peculiar form of presenting its ideas. The text contains numerous repetitions,[58] related ideas are scattered over the whole text, and important ideas are only treated briefly.[59] In Humboldt's eyes, these shortcomings result from the character and education of the author:

> [The author of the Gita] is a wise man, who speaks from the richness and enthusiasm of his insights and feelings. He is not a philosopher trained in a particular school who divides his content according to some method and reaches the final propositions of his teaching following a thread artfully connecting his ideas.[60]

Humboldt attempts to countervail the deficiencies of the text by reconstructing its system of thoughts. Such a reconstruction presupposes empathy with the text. As the Gita was written in a completely different cultural environment, one has to completely immerse in the contemporary Indian way of thinking in order to understand its philosophical position.[61]

In sum, Humboldt's enthusiasm for the Gita does not blind him regarding the inconsistencies and problems in the text. Instead, it motivates him to search for ideas and arguments that resolve apparent contradictions. Moreover, he consciously rearranges the ideas of the text to render it comprehensible for a modern European audience. In the letter to Welcker, quoted at the beginning of this section, Humboldt tries to convince his friend of the value of the Gita. Humboldt's later lectures and texts about the Gita can also be read as attempts to transmit his own fascination and enthusiasm to his listeners and readers.

Hegel's Review

It appears to be this enthusiasm that provoked Hegel to choose Humboldt's publication as the target of his most elaborate critique of the Gita and Indian philosophy. When reading Hegel's review, one cannot but feel that he wishes to make an example of Humboldt and of his positive approach to a text from a non-Western intellectual tradition.

Hegel begins his review of Humboldt's text with a general remark about Indian wisdom as a time-honoured topos in Western intellectual history. He mentions the traditional story of Pythagoras visiting India. However, he also stresses that most of this tradition is legendary at best and that only recently

Europeans achieved reliable information about India's literature, science, and arts. Hegel also includes Humboldt in the list of scientists who promoted European knowledge of India and praises his qualifications:

> Real information can only derive from what has been achieved in the essay under consideration: the rare combination of a profound knowledge of the original language, intimate acquaintance with the philosophy and the wise reservation not to transcend the strict meaning of the original, to see nothing more than what is precisely expressed in it.[62]

Hegel also agrees with Humboldt's method of concentrating on a single text and working out its philosophical content before comparing it to other texts and systems of thought. Although Hegel hides his evaluation of the Gita in a positive remark about Humboldt, he leaves no doubt that, in spite of its distinguished role, the text is not likely to arouse admiration:

> Yet even in this poem it is necessary to cope with many things and to abstract much in order to emphasize what is interesting.... Von Humboldt, through his laborious and diligent compilation of the main ideas that are contained in the eighteen hymns of the work without distinct order, has eased or spared us the labor of such abstractions; and such an extract also spares us especially from the exhaustion caused by tedious repetitions of Indian poetry.[63]

In Hegel's eyes the Gita is without order and full of tedious repetitions. However, he seems to admit that it contains some interesting thoughts, which have been usefully highlighted in Humboldt's essay. A few pages later, Hegel clarifies that he is even sceptical regarding this concession, however. In his eyes, many statements that we find in Indian texts 'sound generally very well for our European understanding',[64] but they lose their initial plausibility when we put them into their concrete context. As an example, Hegel points to the moral dilemma at the beginning of the Gita.[65] It might seem plausible 'to the moral sense of a European' that Arjuna is moved by a feeling of love for his family members and therefore hesitates to start a war against them.[66] A closer look at the text reveals, however, that what is really at stake for Arjuna is not compassion for his cousins but what would happen after their deaths. Their women would be without adequate husbands, and they would inevitably mix with men from lower castes. These impure relations would spoil all sacrifices for their ancestors, who would then lose their place in heaven. In consequence, the whole tribe would be ruined. We thus see that instead of a right and universal moral principle of compassion and love for family members, the Gita actually promotes religious superstition and an immoral system of castes:

> One should consider it rather important to show that this poem, which is in such a high repute as to Indian wisdom and morality, rests upon the well-known caste distinction, without indication of any elevation to moral freedom.[67]

In Hegel's perception, modern European readers of Indian texts pick out ideas that appear familiar to them and then praise the texts for their insights. These readers ignore, however, that the ideas in question are taken out of context.

Hegel believes that the positive reception of Indian *theology* is also due to this uncritical attitude. He severely criticizes the theology of the Gita in his review of Humboldt. Having first denounced the subjective aspect of Indian religion – that is, the individual practice of immersion – as an empty abstraction, Hegel turns to the objective conception of God:

> The thus inevitable inconsistency appears as the unsteady reeling, the subjective aspect of which we have mentioned above and which is equally inevitable with regard to its objective aspect – as the flow from the One into the manifold of gods and the falling back from this abundance and splendor of fanciful imagination into the veil, dull oneness.[68]

In his lectures, Hegel similarly points to several inconsistencies in the Indian conception of God. He remarks, for example, that according to Indian theology 'out of Brahman issues everything – gods, the world, mankind'. At the same time, people believe that Brahman 'is inactive'.[69] He goes on to explain that, in Indian thought, 'outside of this One existed nothing, and this brooded in solitude with itself'. This, however, contradicts the further claim that 'through the energy of contemplation it brought forth a world out of itself'.[70] Hegel summarizes his critique of Indian theology by saying that one is left with 'only a monstrous inconsistency', a strange monotheistic account, as also 'the maddest of polytheism'.[71]

In his review of Humboldt, Hegel negatively evaluates Indian religious practice in a similar vein. He criticizes offerings and acts of worship as ruled by 'absurd regulations of a crude superstition'.[72] In passing, Hegel mentions ritual forms of reading[73] and religious suicide.[74] However, he concentrates on meditative practices called 'yoga'. While incautious readers – Humboldt is explicitly excluded – might interpret these religious practices as sources of profound insight, careful analysis reveals that 'yoga' practices are characterized as mental states without thoughts and feelings. Hegel concludes:

The Indian isolation of the soul into emptiness is rather a stupefaction which perhaps does not at all deserve the name mysticism and which cannot lead to the discovery of true insights, because it is void of any content.[75]

Hegel's Critique of the Gita

Hegel's approach to the Gita is certainly very different from Humboldt's. Hegel does not attempt to resolve the contradictions of the text.[76] He is not a charitable interpreter.[77] Nevertheless, Hegel's article presents an example of solid scholarship and fair philosophical critique. He diligently references the original text, employs the available background knowledge, and points to relevant contexts.[78] Moreover, he offers *arguments* to explain why he considers the Gita's positions unconvincing. He criticizes, in particular, the text's theology and its adherence to the unjust and discriminatory caste system. These critical evaluations will appear plausible to most modern readers.

However, Hegel does not stop at a critique of the ideas presented in the Gita. He not only argues that the text's position is unconvincing, but he also proceeds to the conclusion that the text is not a philosophical text. This conclusion requires further arguments. The fact that a text defends a disagreeable position does not provide sufficient reason to exclude this text from philosophy. However, Hegel argues that the Gita is not a philosophical text – and ridicules Humboldt's remark that it offers a whole 'philosophical system'.[79] In order to draw this conclusion, Hegel would have to name criteria that a text must fulfil to count as philosophic or not. But Hegel does not mention any such criteria in his review of Humboldt. This neglect is due to Hegel's general approach: he does not focus on the philosophical evaluation of individual texts, but on the question of whether philosophy can be found in entire cultures and periods of history.[80] Hegel thus proceeds from the question of whether the Gita is a philosophical text to the problem of the existence of philosophy in India.

For Hegel, the Gita represents Indian thought and expresses the 'the most general and highest of Indian religion'.[81] He thus states at various points of his text that he considers the Gita to be an expression of Indian mentality as a whole. His arguments against the positions of the text are thus meant to work at the same time as arguments against the Gita and as arguments against Indian philosophy in toto. The fact that the Gita supposedly promotes an abstract but empty conception of God serves Hegel as an argument to say that Indian culture has not developed intellectual systems that can be deemed philosophical.[82] As the Gita can represent the whole of Indian thought in Hegel's eyes, we can conclude therefore that Indian intellectual history as such does not offer much of philosophy.

For Hegel, the question of 'what merited inclusion in the history of philosophy and what did not' is an important philosophical project.[83] For him, it is a merit to be included in the scope of philosophy. In this respect, philosophy differs from religion in Hegel's eyes. Whereas every culture has to offer religious thoughts – and some of these thoughts may be interesting for philosophers – only a few cultures developed intellectual discourses that can claim the rank of philosophy. He deals with philosophy and its relation to religion in many places in his work. He also argues against the existence of Asian philosophy in the context of a larger discussion about philosophy, especially in his *Lectures on the History of Philosophy*. Although Hegel does not offer explicit arguments for the exclusion of Indian thought from philosophy in the review on Humboldt, his work certainly contains such arguments.[84]

Hegel's Metaphilosophical Arguments

One of Hegel's most influential[85] arguments for the position that there is no philosophy in India is the position that philosophy needs freedom, and there has been no freedom in India or Asia.[86] He says:

> The state of the Asian people is that of despotism. It lacks the stage of self-consciousness that man knows to be absolutely free. This is the starting point of philosophy. General thoughts do not make for philosophy. The thought in the Orient is only of the sort of religion.[87]

Here, as well as in his remarks about the supposed freedom of Western philosophy, Hegel moves back and forth between a political and an intellectual conception of freedom. The first *political* version of the argument claims that European societies since ancient Greece are characterized by civil freedom, but that 'despotism is the state of the Asian people'.[88] Second, Hegel claims that Asian thought is *intellectually* unfree because 'thought in the Orient is only the sort of religion'. It is correct to say that numerous philosophical traditions developed inside of the religious traditions in India or in other Asian countries. Hegel is well aware, however, that a strict separation between philosophy and religion is rather difficult for much of European philosophy as well as for his own thought. Hegel is thus not arguing in general against a possible reconciliation of philosophy and religion.[89] His reference to freedom points to a more specific critique, and I propose to understand his argument as an argument against what has been called 'traditionalism'. A traditionalist system of thought accepts some person or text as authoritative in the sense that it is held to express *only* truths and *all* the truths that humans should know about.[90]

In this vein, Hegel criticizes the Christian thought of scholasticism. This thought is not free because it builds on immovable presuppositions.[91] In his *Lectures on the History of Philosophy*, Hegel explicitly compares India's intellectual tradition to such scholastic thought:

> Indian philosophy stands within religion just as scholastic philosophy stands within Christian dogmatism, having at its basis and presupposing the doctrines of the church.[92]

For Hegel, these presuppositions are against the spirit of philosophy. And in India, it was such traditionalism that precluded the emergence of a genuine philosophy.[93]

Hegel's second argument for the exclusion of Oriental thought from the scope of philosophy is its supposed lack of systematicity. For Hegel, the systematic arrangement of thoughts is an important criterion of philosophy. He mentions this criterion already in the preface to his *Phenomenology of Spirit*:

> The true form in which truth exists can only be the scientific system of it. To contribute to this end, that philosophy might come closer to the form of science – the goal being that it might be able to relinquish the name of love of knowledge and be actual knowledge – that is what I have resolved to try.[94]

Philosophical systems stand in contrast to mere ideas. In Oriental texts, one might find interesting philosophical ideas – so called *philosopheme*s – but there are no systems of philosophy like they have been developed in the West, according to Hegel.[95]

We have seen that Humboldt also considered the Gita to be unsystematic. He believed, however, that this is a mere superficial aspect of the text that can be remedied by a thoughtful edition of the text's ideas. Hegel, in contrast, believes that the lack of clarity of thought is irremediable. It is just a symptom that shows an inherent lack of thoughtfulness:

> In this very unsystematic form we see only the first beginnings of reflection, which seem to be put together as a universal. But this arrangement is, to say nothing of being unsystematic, not even intelligent.[96]

Evaluation of Hegel's Arguments

Hegel pursues a metaphilosophical project. He argues against a conception of philosophy according to which any interesting thought found in the mythology or literature of some culture is already an expression of philosophy. Hegel belongs to a tradition that considers philosophy a particularly valuable human activity. In order to explain the value of this activity and to delimit the activity from other – possibly less valuable – activities, we need criteria for what philosophy is. Hegel proposes such criteria. He applies them to Asian thought and arrives at a negative result; for Hegel, philosophy does not exist in 'Oriental thought'.

Hegel's metaphilosophical project, the criteria he proposes, and the conclusion he draws in his application of these criteria to Indian or Asian thought can be evaluated separately. In this chapter, I assume that Hegel's general metaphilosophical project is worthwhile. If we consider philosophy an important concept, we need to reflect on what its content is. However, we can welcome this project without accepting Hegel's conclusion. There is philosophy in India – and in many other non-Western cultures. We do not have to conclude that Hegel's errors in evaluating Indian thought are due to the criteria he proposes. The error may lie in the way he applies them. His criteria must be reconsidered, but we can use them in a more positive way, namely to state more clearly what philosophy is.[97]

Lack of Freedom

Hegel uses the term 'freedom' in a political as well as in an intellectual sense. In his eyes, India lacks both the political and the intellectual freedom to develop philosophy. The political argument claims that, in contrast to ancient Europe, there was no political freedom in India. This empirical argument is much too general for both sides of the description and will not convince modern readers.[98] Hegel knew that the ancient societies of Greece and Rome did not provide freedom for everybody. Therefore, he argues that their cultures at least began to develop liberal institutions.[99] However, Hegel does not show the same charitable evaluation towards Asian societies. Moreover, Hegel lacked the knowledge to judge the political situation in the history of India and other Asian countries. He was ignorant, for example, of the existence of ancient Indian republics.[100]

With regard to intellectual freedom, it is clear that many religions such as Christianity, Judaism, Islam, and Confucianism are traditionalist, and the same is true for Indian religions such as Hinduism, Buddhism, Jainism, and so on. The same is true, however, for late antique pagan thought in the Mediterranean world – that is, for Stoic, Epicurean, or Platonist schools of philosophy, for example. Although traditionalism is rejected by most modern philosophers, it would thus significantly reduce the historical scope of philosophy to use the idea of traditionalism as an argument to exclude certain schools or thinkers from the scope of philosophy.[101] More importantly, a closer look at these traditions shows that a traditionalist paradigm actually allows for much freedom of thought. First, there are intriguing debates *between different* traditionalist schools, such as those between Stoics and Epicureans or between Buddhist and Brahmanic thinkers, for example. Second, intense discussions about the right interpretation of the authority also take place *within* one and the same tradition, among different Buddhist thinkers, for example. Relying on these examples, I think that we have no general reason to exclude Indian thought from philosophy because of its traditionalism. Hegel's argument nevertheless contains an idea that can serve as a criterion to distinguish philosophy from traditionalist forms of religion. I take Hegel to embrace a normative conception of philosophy according to which what is valuable about philosophy is its willingness to reconsider given opinions. Traditionalism is compatible with this kind of intellectual freedom as long as it leaves room for *discussion with other traditions* and for *interpretation of its own traditional authority*. Where this room is lacking, however, we should indeed refrain from calling a system of thought 'philosophical'.

Lack of Systematicity

Hegel certainly argues from insufficient knowledge concerning the detailed thought systems of many Indian schools of philosophy.[102] Later in his life, knowledge about classical schools such as Nyaya, Vaisheshika, Samkhya, and Buddhism convinced Hegel that 'genuine philosophical systems' did indeed exist in India. He also admits in his review of Humboldt that these schools produced 'truly philosophical works'.[103] Hegel still insists, however, that these were only philosophical systems 'of the poorest kind'.[104] Leaving aside this inconsistency in Hegel's evaluation, there is some truth in his statements. If we do not use Hegel's argument as an argument against the existence of philosophy in India but as a criterion of philosophy, it appears more plausible. Most modern readers will agree with Hegel that singular, philosophically interesting statements, as they can be found in myths, novels, or law texts, do not already make for philosophy.

To capture this Hegelian intuition, I will propose that a text can only be seen as philosophical if it systematically deals with a philosophical problem. This does not necessarily mean that the text constructs a philosophical system, as was fashionable in German philosophy in the nineteenth century. Very few modern philosophical texts would fulfil this criterion. However, a text can only be seen as a philosophical text if it tries to solve a dialectical problem – that is, if it at least implicitly deals with a problem that arises because we feel inclined to endorse two or more statements that contradict each other. There is thus a contradiction in our system of thought, and we try to solve this systematic conflict. In the case of philosophical problems, such contradictions cannot simply be removed by observation or by gathering further information, but they make it necessary to weigh reasons and reconsider our understanding of the concepts involved.[105] It is this activity that renders a text or discourse philosophical. According to this proposal, philosophy is systematic in the sense that it tries to solve contradictions within individual or collective systems of thought.

A Revaluation of the Gita?

Once we have reworked Hegel's two arguments into more applicable criteria of philosophy, we can judge the philosophical character of the Mahabharata and the Gita in a new way.

The Gita is actually a remarkably clear case with regard to the second criterion: the idea that a philosophical text must be systematic in the sense that it deals with a contradiction in the system of thought of some person. The Gita passage just starts with such a problem when it has Arjuna confess his inner conflict. He is torn between his duties as a warrior, on the one hand, and as a member of the Kuru clan, on the other. This conflict is present even if it is based on an acceptance of a clan culture that we nowadays reject. Moreover, the Gita tackles the problem systematically by trying to elucidate the different concepts that are involved in its solution.

We can now proceed to the question of whether the text approaches the philosophical problem with intellectual openness and freedom. The question of Arjuna is clearly dealt with in a dialogical manner, with Krishna responding to Arjuna's questions and troubles. At least in some parts of the Gita, this dialogue can be understood as a real exchange of arguments and thus as a free and systematic treatment of a philosophical problem. We might still have some doubts about the philosophical character of this dialogue if we emphasize that the dialogue is hardly a dialogue among equals. Arjuna talks to a god in the end, and Krishna has by far the larger role in the dialogue. However, if we look at the Gita in the context of the whole Mahabharata, we see that Krishna's position in the dialogue is not that of an undeniable divine revelation.

In the end, Krishna is cursed for his role in the war by Gandhari, and the war is again philosophically discussed in the 'Shanti Parva' chapter with results that seem to differ from the position defended by Krishna. It thus seems hard to deny that there is a philosophical struggle that drives the Gita and that runs through the Mahabharata as a whole.[106]

In their reworked form, Hegel's arguments do not exclude the Gita, let alone all Indian texts, from the scope of philosophy. Nonetheless, the arguments allow us to draw a line between philosophical and non-philosophical texts. They thus help to pursue Hegel's heartfelt intention and defend philosophy as an independent discipline and a particularly worthwhile human activity.

Handling the Other

Hegel's review of Humboldt's articles on the Gita was motivated by the impression that his contemporaries showed a naive enthusiasm for India without critical reflection. He wishes to criticize a particular handling of texts from a foreign culture. At the very end of his review, Hegel praises the improved knowledge about India gained through the efforts of scholars such as Henry Thomas Colebrooke and Humboldt because this knowledge improves our understanding of Indian thought:

> But the more those riches present themselves to us in their original color, the more we must abandon the superficial ideas of Indian religiosity and its contents, that originated partly from an application of first best categories of our culture, partly from a European philosophy which itself was often in a state of disorder.[107]

Hegel here is arguing against an appropriation of Indian thought. We still know this phenomenon from our own times: people adore Indian religiosity, Buddhist meditation, or samurai spirit, ignoring those aspects of the practices and worldviews that are incompatible with the standards and ideals that most people share nowadays. Hegel's critique of this naive acceptance of foreign cultures, often wedded to a rash devaluation of modernity, is plausible. Hegel's critique of the Gita can thus serve as a reminder for a careful, sober reading of philosophical texts, especially those from foreign cultures or from the distant past.

It is creditable that Hegel chose a strong opponent like Humboldt as the target of his critique. However, finally, he does not do justice to Humboldt's approach. Humboldt does not appropriate the Gita as a relic from a past that was better than our own times. For Humboldt, it is our duty as historians of philosophy to read a text with charity. Readers from later eras and different cultural backgrounds should take an ancient text for what it is and try to make as much sense of it as possible. Humboldt, moreover, shows enthusiasm for the Gita but certainly no naive adoration.

At some moments, Hegel is willing to ascribe a positive role to texts from Asia. He points out that 'bathing' in such texts can be used as a remedy against exaltations of our own times.[108] Engagement with foreign texts can widen our intellectual horizon by offering cultural alternatives. Hegel sometimes engages with Asian texts in this way and comes closer than he thought himself to an ideal that Humboldt describes as an 'immersion into a different way of thinking'.[109]

Notes

1. Johann Gottfried Herder, *Ideen zur Philosophie der Geschichte der Menschheit*, Sämtliche Werke, vol. 13 (Hildesheim: Georg Olms Verlag, 1887), 406–11.
2. Schlegel writes to Ludwick Tieck: 'Here is the actual source of all languages, all the thoughts and poems of the human spirit; everything, everything without exception comes from India.' See H. Lüdeke (ed.), *L. Tieck und die Brüder Schlegel* (Frankfurt: Joseph Baer & Co.), 140, quoted in Wilhelm Halbfass, *India and Europe: An Essay in Understanding* (Albany, NY: SUNY Press, 1988), 75.
3. Aakash Singh Rathore and Rimina Mohapatra, *Hegel's India: A Reinterpretation, with Texts* (New Delhi: Oxford University Press, 2017), 15.
4. Alfred North Whitehead, *Process and Reality: An Essay in Cosmology* (New York: Free Press, 1978), 39.
5. Even more startling than the marginality of the discourse on non-Western philosophy are the prevailing institutional practices; cf. Robert Bernasconi, 'Philosophy's Paradoxical Parochialism: The Reinvention of Philosophy as Greek', in *Cultural Readings of Imperialism: Edward Said and the Gravity of History*, ed. Keith Ansell-Pearson, Benita Parry, and Judith Squires, 212–26 (New York: St. Martin's Press, 1997), 213.
6. There is a large amount of literature on non-Western philosophy, and I have to limit myself to some representative titles with regard to India, China, and Japan: Hajime Nakamura, 'The Meaning of the Terms "Philosophy" and "Religion" in various Traditions', in *Interpreting across Boundaries: New Essays in Comparative Philosophy*, ed. Eliot Deutsch and Gerald James Larson, 137–51 (Princeton, NJ: Princeton University Press, 1988); Frits Staal, 'Is There Philosophy in Asia?' in *Interpreting across Boundaries: New Essays in Comparative Philosophy*, ed. Eliot Deutsch and Gerald James

Larson, 203–29 (Princeton, NJ: Princeton University Press, 1988); Robert Solomon, '"What Is Philosophy?" The Status of World Philosophy in the Profession', *Philosophy East and West* 51, no. 1 (2001): 100–04; Bimal K. Matilal, 'On the Concept of Philosophy in India', in *Philosophical Essays: Anantalal Thakur Felicitation Volume*, 358–69 (Calcutta: Sanskrit Pustak Bhandar, 1987); Jonardon Ganeri, *Philosophy in Classical India: The Proper Work of Reason* (London: Routledge Press, 2001); Mark Siderits, *Buddhism as Philosophy: An Introduction* (Indianapolis [IN] and Cambridge: Hackett Publishing Company, 2007); Carine Defoort, 'Is There Such a Thing as Chinese Philosophy? Arguments of an Implicit Debate', *Philosophy East and West* 51, no. 3, (2001): 393–413; Carine Defoort, 'Is "Chinese Philosophy" a Proper Name? A Response to Rein Raud', *Philosophy East and West* 56, no. 4 (2006): 625–60; Rein Raud, 'Philosophies versus Philosophy: In Defense of a Flexible Definition', *Philosophy East and West* 56, no. 4 (2006): 618–25; Heiner Roetz, 'Philosophy in China? Notes on a Debate', *Extrême-Orient, Extrême-Occident* 27 (2005): 49–65; John Maraldo, 'Japanese Philosophy as a Lens on Greco-European Thought', *Journal of Japanese Philosophy* 1, no. 1 (2013): 21–56.

7. Bernasconi points out that this critique was already proffered by Hegel's contemporaries. See H.E.G. Paulus, 'Rezension von Dr. G.W.Fr. Hegel: Grundlinien der Philosophie des Rechts', *Heidelberger Jahrbücher der Literatur* 14, no. 1 (1821): 392–405, 402–03; Robert Bernasconi, 'With What Must the Philosophy of World History Begin? On the Racial Basis of Hegel's Eurocentrism', *Nineteenth Century Contexts* 22, no. 2 (2000): 171–201, 172. See also Joseph McCarney, *Hegel on History* (London: Routledge, 2000), 142. Bradley L. Herling calls Hegel the 'arch-Orientalist'. See Bradley L. Herling, *The German Gita: Hermeneutics and Discipline in the German Reception of Indian Thought* (New York and London: Routledge, 2006), 205.

8. Cf. Walter Leifer, *India and the Germans: 500 Years of Indo-German Contacts* (Bombay: Shakuntala Publishing House, 1971), 94; Helmuth von Glasenapp, *Das Indienbild deutscher Denker* (Stuttgart: K. F. Koehler Verlag, 1960), 39.

9. Cf. Ernst Windisch, *Geschichte der Sanskrit-Philologie und indischen Altertumskunde* (Strassburg: K. J. Trübner, 1917), 1–22; Halbfass, *India and Europe: An Essay in Understanding*, 36–68.

10. See, for example, Roetz, 'Philosophy in China?' 50; Bernasconi, 'Philosophy's Paradoxical Parochialism', 214–15. We should be aware, however, that Leibniz, Wolff, and Voltaire still had only little concrete information about Asian thought. They did not, moreover, always use the little information they had cautiously, but instrumentalized it against their European opponents. See Jean W. Sedlar, *India in the Mind of Germany: Schelling, Schopenhauer,*

and Their Times (Washington, DC: University Press of America, 1982), 16. Regarding Voltaire, see Urs App, *The Birth of Orientalism* (Philadelphia, PA: University of Pennsylvania Press, 2010), 15–76.

11. Cf. Kurt Flasch, 'Jacob Brucker und die Philosophie des Mittelalters', in *Jacob Brucker (1696–1770)*, ed. Wilhelm Schmidt-Biggemann and Theo Stammen, 187–97 (Berlin: De Gruyter, 1998).

12. Sedlar, *India in the Mind of Germany*, 41; but see Glasenapp, *Das Indienbild deutscher Denker*, 5–13.

13. See notes 1 and 2 for Schelling; see especially his early work 'Ueber Mythen, historische Sagen und Philosopheme der ältesten Welt', in *Historisch-kritische Ausgabe*, vol. 1, ed. Hans Michael Baumgartner, Wilhelm G. Jacobs, Hermann Krings, and Hermann Zeltner (Stuttgart-Bad Cannstatt: frommann-holzboog, 1976 [1903]).

14. Rixner had also published an article on Indian philosophy in 1808, 'Versuch einer neuen Darstellung der uralten indischen Alleinslehre', and translated the *Chandogya Upanishad* from Sanskrit into German.

15. Cf. Halbfass, *India and Europe: An Essay in Understanding*, ch. 5.

16. Johann Gottfried Herder, *Ideen zur Philosophie der Geschichte der Menschheit*, Sämtliche Werke, vol. 14 (Hildesheim: Georg Olms Verlag, 1887), 25.

17. Friedrich Schlegel, *Über die Sprache und Weisheit der Indier* (Heidelberg: Mohr und Zimmer, 1808), 107.

18. Humboldt published two articles on the Gita. The first is a review of A. W. Schlegel's Latin translation. It is simply entitled '*Über* die Bhagavad-Gita' (On the Bhagavad-Gita). The second text is the written version of a lecture given at the Prussian Academy of Science with the title '*Über* die unter dem Namen Bhagavad-Gita bekannte Episode des Maha-Bharata' (On the Episode of the Maha-Bharata Known by the Name Bhagavad-Gita). Both texts are published in *Wilhelm von Humboldts Gesammelte Schriften*, vol. 5, ed. Albert Leitzmann and Königlich Preussische Akademie der Wissenschaften (Berlin: B. Behr's Verlag, 1906). All page numbers refer to this edition and volume; the translations are mine. For the quotation, see Humboldt, *Gesammelte Schriften*, 159.

19. Humboldt, *Gesammelte Schriften*, 191.

20. Humboldt, *Gesammelte Schriften*, 159.

21. G. W. F. Hegel, *Vorlesungen über die Geschichte der Philosophie: Einleitung, Orientalische Philosophie* (Hamburg: Felix Meiner Verlag, 1993), 103, 193, 269.

22. Hegel, *Vorlesungen über die Geschichte der Philosophie*, 365.

23. Careful speculations about a possible influence of Indian or Asian philosophy on Nietzsche can be found in Halbfass, *India and Europe*, ch. 8.

24. Roetz, 'Philosophy in China?' 51; Robert Bernasconi, 'On Heidegger's Other Sins of Omission: His Exclusion of Asian Thought from the Origins of Accidental Metaphysics and His Denial of the Possibility of Christian Philosophy', *American Catholic Philosophical Quarterly* 69, no. 2 (1995): 333–50.

25. See note 7.

26. Rathore and Mohapatra, *Hegel's India*, 31; cf. Herling, *The German Gita*, 237.

27. Bernasconi, 'With What Must the Philosophy of World History Begin?' 46; also quoted by Rathore and Mohapatra, *Hegel's India*, 19.

28. Rathore and Mohapatra, *Hegel's India*, 19 (emphasis original); cf. Halbfass, *India and Europe*, 85.

29. G. W. F. Hegel, 'Vorlesungen über die Philosophie der Weltgeschichte I', in *Gesammelte Werke*, vol. 27.1, ed. Nordrhein-Westfälische Akademie der Wissenschaften (Hamburg: Felix Meiner Verlag, 2015), 143–44; G. W. F. Hegel, *The Philosophy of History*, trans. J. Sibree (New York: Colonial Press, 1900), 140. Hegel at many places argued against the somewhat naive India enthusiasts of his time. He therefore also described India in the following way: 'It has always been the land for which people long, and still it appears to us as a realm of wonder, as an enchanted world,' quoted in Terry P. Pinkard, *Does History Make Sense? Hegel on the Historical Shapes of Justice* (Cambridge [MA] and London: Harvard University Press, 2017), 61. See also G. W. F. Hegel, *Vorlesungen über die Ästhetik III* (Frankfurt: Suhrkamp, 1970), 396–97; cf. G. W. F. Hegel, *Lectures on Fine Arts*, trans. T. M. Knox (Oxford: Clarendon Press, 1975), 1095. Hegel wanted to stress that the disenchantment that took place in the West was actually a positive development.

30. Cf. Halbfass, *India and Europe*, 84–85: 'Hegel deals with India as a European philosopher *whose philosophy commits him to not being neutral*' (emphasis mine). A few pages later, Halbfass writes: 'Hegel was not a neutral scholar and expert. He was a philosopher par excellence, representing like few others the glory and greatness … and arrogance of philosophy'. Halbfass, *India and Europe*, 98.

31. Johannes Hoffmeister (ed.), *Briefe von und an Hegel*, vol. 3 (Berlin: Akademie Verlag, 1970), 406. For the translation, see Rathore and Mohapatra, *Hegel's India*, 16.

32. Wilhelm von Humboldt, 'Wilhelm von Humboldt an Friedrich Gottlieb Welcker, 25.09.1823', Online Edition der Sprachwissenschaftlichen Korrespondenz, published 18 October 2021, https://wvh-briefe.bbaw.de/Brief?id=1114 (accessed on 14 September 2022).

33. Humboldt, *Gesammelte Schriften*, 190.

34. Humboldt, *Gesammelte Schriften*, 159.
35. Humboldt, *Gesammelte Schriften*, 191.
36. Humboldt, *Gesammelte Schriften*, 192.
37. Humboldt, *Gesammelte Schriften*, 192–93.
38. Humboldt, *Gesammelte Schriften*, 161–62.
39. Humboldt, *Gesammelte Schriften*, 194.
40. Humboldt, *Gesammelte Schriften*, 166, 185.
41. Humboldt, *Gesammelte Schriften*, 195.
42. Humboldt, *Gesammelte Schriften*, 199.
43. Humboldt, *Gesammelte Schriften*, 199.
44. Humboldt, *Gesammelte Schriften*, 198.
45. Notably, these remarks appear only in Humboldt's handwritten notes to his earlier text on the Gita. See Humboldt, *Gesammelte Schriften*, 162, 177.
46. Humboldt, *Gesammelte Schriften*, 199.
47. Humboldt, *Gesammelte Schriften*, 201.
48. Humboldt, *Gesammelte Schriften*, 203.
49. Humboldt, *Gesammelte Schriften*, 199.
50. Humboldt, *Gesammelte Schriften*, 210.
51. Humboldt, *Gesammelte Schriften*, 211.
52. Humboldt, *Gesammelte Schriften*, 216.
53. Humboldt, *Gesammelte Schriften*, 225.
54. Humboldt, *Gesammelte Schriften*, 180.
55. Humboldt, *Gesammelte Schriften*, 226.
56. Humboldt, *Gesammelte Schriften*, 164.
57. Humboldt, *Gesammelte Schriften*, 232.
58. Humboldt, *Gesammelte Schriften*, 326.
59. Humboldt, *Gesammelte Schriften*, 327.
60. Humboldt, *Gesammelte Schriften*, 325.
61. Humboldt, *Gesammelte Schriften*, 203.
62. G. W. F. Hegel, 'Humboldt-Rezension: Über die unter dem Namen Bhagavad-Gita bekannte Episode des Mahabharata', in *Gesammelte Werke*, vol. 16, ed. Nordrhein-Westfälische Akademie der Wissenschaften, 119–75 (Hamburg: Felix Meiner Verlag, 2001), 20. The translation of Hegel's review has been undertaken by Herbert Herring. It was originally published by the Indian Council of Philosophical Research in 1995. The translation was reproduced in Rathore and Mohapatra's *Hegel's India*. All page numbers refer to this reproduction. For the present quotation, see page 89.
63. Hegel, 'Humboldt-Rezension', 21–22; Rathore and Mohapatra, *Hegel's India*, 89–90.

64. Hegel, 'Humboldt-Rezension', 26; Rathore and Mohapatra, *Hegel's India*, 93.

65. As Humboldt and Hegel did not know the Mahabharata as a whole, they were not aware that there are more dilemmas in the text and that Krishna also appears in other places to solve dilemmas for Arjuna. See Bimal K. Matilal, 'Moral Dilemmas: Insights from Indian Epics', in *Moral Dilemmas in the Mahabharata*, 1–19 (Delhi: Motilal Banardisass, 1989).

66. Humboldt, however, was clearly aware, that Krishna's arguments aimed primarily at the preservation of the caste system. See Humboldt, *Gesammelte Schriften*, 160–61.

67. Hegel, 'Humboldt-Rezension', 37; Rathore and Mohapatra, *Hegel's India*, 103. Peter della Santina agrees with Hegel that Arjuna is basically worried about the destruction of the caste system. He also argues, however, that Arjuna's inner conflict reflects a larger social conflict within the Brahmanical system. See Peter della Santina, 'Conceptions of Dharma in the Sramanical and Brahmanical Traditions: Buddhism and the Mahābhārata', in *Moral Dilemmas in the Mahābhārata*, ed. Bimal K. Matilal, 97–115 (Delhi: Motilal Banardisass, 1989), especially 105–06.

68. Hegel, 'Humboldt-Rezension', 67; Rathore and Mohapatra, *Hegel's India*, 131–32.

69. G. W. F. Hegel, *Lectures on the Philosophy of Religion*, vol. 2, trans. E. B. Speirs and J. B. Sanderson (London: Routledge and Kegan Paul, 1895), 16.

70. Hegel, *Lectures on the Philosophy of Religion*, vol. 2, 18.

71. Rathore and Mohapatra, *Hegel's India*, 53.

72. Hegel, 'Humboldt-Rezension', 38; Rathore and Mohapatra, *Hegel's India*, 105.

73. Hegel, 'Humboldt-Rezension', 52; Rathore and Mohapatra, *Hegel's India*, 117.

74. Hegel, 'Humboldt-Rezension', 53; Rathore and Mohapatra, *Hegel's India*, 118. See also G. W. F Hegel, *Philosophy of Fine Art*, vol. 2, trans. F. P. B. Osmaston (London: G. Bell & Sons, 1920), 72; Rathore and Mohapatra, *Hegel's India*, 40.

75. Hegel, 'Humboldt-Rezension', 42; Rathore and Mohapatra, *Hegel's India*, 108–09. See also G. W. F. Hegel, *Lectures on the History of Philosophy*, vol. 1, trans. E. S. Haldane (London: Routledge & Kegan Paul, 1892), 119: 'The superficial and "dry" understanding also reflects in "worship", which is complete immersion in devotion and then an endless number of ceremonials and of religious actions; and this on the other side is the exaltitude of that illimitable in which everything disappears.' According to Hegel, the union of a practitioner and Brahman takes place unconsciously: 'The highest point

212   Paulus Kaufmann

which is thus attained to in worship is that union with God which consists in the annihilation and stupefaction of self-consciousness'. see Hegel, *Lectures on the Philosophy of Religion*, vol. 2, 33. See also Rathore and Mohapatra, *Hegel's India*, 36, 46. Although Hegel's depreciatory tone is unjustified, the content of his reading is confirmed by contemporary Indologists. See, for example, Lambert Schmithausen, 'Ich und Erlösung im Buddhismus', *Zeitschrift für Missionswissenschaft und Religionswissenschaft* 53, no. 2 (1969): 161–64. See also Angelika Malinar's comment that Hegel's criticism of his Romantic predecessors 'is often appropriate'. Angelika Malinar, *Bhagavadgita: Doctrines and Contexts* (Cambridge, UK: Cambridge University Press, 2007), 20.

76. Compare, for example, Humboldt's exegetical attempt to explain the apparently contradictory statement that wise action is non-action (see Humboldt, *Gesammelte Schriften*, 166, 185) with Hegel's snarky treatment of this textual tension: 'It is one of the tedious aspects of the poem to see how this contradiction between the instruction to act and the instruction to refrain from action and to firmly and solely concentrate on Krishna always comes to the fore, without finding a solution of this contradiction.' See Hegel, 'Humboldt-Rezension', 14; Rathore and Mohapatra, *Hegel's India*, 106.

77. Cf. Helmuth von Glasenapp's harsh verdict on Hegel: 'He was not an open-minded person, unable to empathise with loving understanding with an unfamiliar train of thought.' See Glasenapp, *Das Indienbild deutscher Denker*, 39.

78. His interpretations are often deemed correct by contemporary Indologists. See, for example, Sanjay Palshikar, *Evil and the Philosophy of Retribution* (New Delhi: Routledge, 2014), 42; cf. also fns. 67 and 76.

79. Hegel, 'Humboldt-Rezension', 28; Rathore and Mohapatra, *Hegel's India*, 95.

80. Hegel argues for this approach in his *Lectures on the History of Philosophy*, vol. 1, 53.

81. Hegel, 'Humboldt-Rezension', 21; Rathore and Mohapatra, *Hegel's India*, 89.

82. See also Terry P. Pinkard's remarks regarding Hegel's attitude towards Africa: 'Hegel, like many people even today, seemed to have been blind to the variety of cultures alive there, such that he interpreted them as one homogeneous mass living in a geographically homogeneous area.' Pinkard, *Does History Make Sense?* 51.

83. Cf. Robert Bernasconi, 'Krimskrams: Hegel and the Current Controversy about the Beginnings of Philosophy', in *Interrogating the Tradition: Hermeneutics and the History of Philosophy*, ed. C.E. Scott and J. Sallis, 191–208 (Albany: SUNY Press, 2000), 194.

84. Rathore and Mohapatra work out twelve characterizations for Indian thought that repeatedly appear in Hegel's works. They summarize these into these three rubrics: absence of individuality or particularity; conflation of religion and philosophy; and lack of freedom. See Rathore and Mohapatra, *Hegel's India*, 55–56. For Hegel, to be sure, the three arguments are internally connected – for example, the emptiness of God and the freedom argument:

> The Freedom of man just consists in being with himself – not in emptiness, but in willing, knowing, acting. To the Hindu, on the contrary, complete the submergence and stupefaction of the consciousness is what is highest, and he who maintains himself in this abstraction and has died to the world is called yogi. (Hegel, *Lectures on the Philosophy of Religion*, vol. 2, 34)

85. This argument was later repeated by Martin Heidegger, for example. See Martin Heidegger, *Was ist das - die Philosophie?* (Pfullingen: G. Neske, 1956), 13; Martin Heidegger, *Was heißt Denken?* (Frankfurt a. Main: Vittorio Klostermann, 1954), 228.

86. We should recall that for Hegel freedom is not an arbitrary value. For Hegel history is the 'development of spirit in time' (see his *The Philosophy of History*, 72) and the spirit aims at knowing itself as free (*The Philosophy of History*, 17). Freedom is thus necessarily self-conscious. With regard to such self-conscious freedom, Hegel says: 'The Orientals have not attained the knowledge that Spirit – Man as such – is free; and because they do not know this, they are not free.' Hegel, *The Philosophy of History*, 18. See Rathore and Mohapatra, *Hegel's India*, 10. Hegel also mentions the lack of freedom in the Mahabharata in his *Lectures on Fine Arts*. See Hegel, *Vorlesungen über die Ästhetik III*, 397; Hegel, *Lectures on Fine Arts*, 1095.

87. Hegel, *Vorlesungen über die Geschichte der Philosophie*, 94.

88. Hegel was influenced, as Pinkard has argued, by ancient Greek historians: 'He also took up Herodotus' basic theme of Greek freedom triumphing over eastern (and therefore Asiatic) despotism and made that into one of the key themes of his own account'. See Pinkard, *Does History Make Sense?* 52.

89. Hegel, *Vorlesungen über die Geschichte der Philosophie*, 254; cf. Hegel, *Lectures on the History of Philosophy*, vol. 1, 50, 76.

90. Cf. A. H. Armstrong, 'Pagan and Christian Traditionalism in the First Three Centuries A.D. ', in *Studia Patristica* 15, no. 1 (1975): 414–31.

91. Hegel, *Vorlesungen über die Geschichte der Philosophie*, 264; cf. Hegel *Lectures on the History of Philosophy*, vol. 1, 91.

92. Hegel, *Vorlesungen über die Geschichte der Philosophie*, 375; cf. Hegel, *Lectures on the History of Philosophy*, vol. 1, 126–27; Rathore and Mohapatra, *Hegel's India*, 58.

93. Cf. Pinkard, *Does History Make Sense?*

> Hegel's view is not that such people are irrational. It is that they are completely or almost completely absorbed in their natural and social worlds and have not yet worked their way out of that immersion …; their own ethical life lacks the proper critical distance…. They thus typically form themselves into traditional societies, where everything is to be done exactly as it has supposedly been done in the past. Even if this is in fact false, and they actually shift their existing norms for behaviour over time, such a shift has to go unnoticed by them or to be regarded as merely contingent change (p. 53).

My interpretation also fits with Hegel's critique of the lack of historiography in India or his idea that 'they contribute nothing to progress in history since they themselves can have no conception of progress' (p. 54).

94. Rathore and Mohapatra, *Hegel's India*, 79. For the importance of systematicity, see also Hegel, *Lectures on the History of Philosophy*, vol. 1, 29.

95. Hegel, *Vorlesungen über die Geschichte der Philosophie*, 26.

96. Hegel, *Lectures on the History of Philosophy*, vol. 1, 131; cf. Rathore and Mohapatra, *Hegel's India*, 63. A similar evaluation can be found in Hegel, *Vorlesungen über die Ästhetik III*, 397; cf. Hegel, *Lectures on Fine Arts*, 1095–96.

97. I thus also 'reinterpret Hegel by means of Hegel', as Pinkard has called his own attempt to interpret Hegel's writings on India in a more fruitful way. See Pinkard, *Does History Make Sense?* 50.

98. See, for example, Glasenapp, *Das Indienbild deutscher Denker*, 43.

99. Hegel writes:

> The consciousness of freedom first arose among the Greeks, and therefore they were free; but they, and the Romans likewise, knew only that some are free – not man as such. Even Plato and Aristotle did not know this. The Greeks, therefore, had slaves. … The German nation, under the influence of Christianity, were the first to attain the consciousness, that man, as man, is free: that it is the freedom of Spirit which constitutes its essence. (Glasenapp, *Das Indienbild deutscher Denker*, 18; Rathore and Mohapatra, *Hegel's India*, 10–11)

100. Romila Thapar, *Early India: From the Origins to AD 1300* (Berkeley, CA: University of California Press, 2003), 146–50.

101. Hegel seems to be particularly sceptical towards Indian philosophy because of its ultimate spiritual aims, because all Indian philosophical systems seek 'the means whereby eternal happiness can be attained before, as well as after, death'. Hegel, *Lectures on the History of Philosophy*, vol. 1, 129. This seems to be true, but this feature is characteristic of European philosophical schools as well, as Pierre Hadot has convincingly argued. See Pierre Hadot, *Philosophy as a Way of Life: Spiritual Exercises from Socrates to Foucault*, ed. Arnold I. Davidson (Oxford: Blackwell Publishing, 1995).

102. Hegel knew the Vedic schools through the summaries of Henry Thomas Colebrooke. See Rathore and Mohapatra, *Hegel's India*, 58–59. He is particularly positive regarding Samkhya which he considers 'scientific'. He is also quite positive about Nyaya: 'Nyaya is the most developed; it more particularly gives the rules for reasoning, and may be compared to the Logic of Aristotle.' Hegel, *Lectures on the History of Philosophy*, vol.1, 128; Rathore and Rimina Mohapatra, *Hegel's India*, 70.

103. Hegel, 'Humboldt-Rezension', 28; Rathore and Mohapatra, *Hegel's India*, 95.

104. See also Pinkard, *Does History Make Sense?* 62: 'The Indians (on Hegel's mature account of them) had indeed worked out a version of reflective thought that can be properly called "philosophical", even though the only philosophical results they could reach were essentially empty.'

105. According to Pinkard, Hegel asks for something similar:

> In effect, Hegel charges that the Chinese shape of life has not allowed 'negativity' to be at work there. That is, it has not promoted the way in which a given set of problems often requires the drawing of distinctions and separation of spheres if the problems are to be solved or tamed. In theory, that requires positing new concepts and constellations of concepts, but in practice, it means carving out new spheres of authority in social life. (Pinkard, *Does History Make Sense?* 58)

106. Cf. Prabal Kumar Sen, 'Moral Doubts, Moral Dilemmas and Situational Ethics in the Mahābhārata', in *Mahabharata Now*, ed. Arindam Chakrabarti and Sibaji Bandyopadhyay, 153–202 (London: Routledge, 2014). See also Angelika Malinar's careful analysis of the text's doctrines in *Bhagavadgita: Doctrines and Contexts*, 54–225. For me, there are still remaining doubts about the Gita's philosophical character for different reasons: Can we surely suppose that the philosophical standpoint that is expressed in the text is the standpoint of some real person? Or is it possible that the author only inserted the position to make the story run more smoothly? The Gita would then

narrate a philosophical position rather than argue for it. Arguably, a text that only narrates a philosophical position is not itself a philosophical text.

107. Hegel, 'Humboldt-Rezension', 35; Rathore and Mohapatra, *Hegel's India*, 138.
108. Hegel, *Vorlesungen über die Geschichte der Philosophie*, 396–97; also quoted in Halbfass, *India and Europe*, 94.
109. Hegel, *Lectures on the History of Philosophy*, vol. 1, 145.

8

East Asian Uses of Indian Epic Literature

Refractions of the Mahabharata in Japan and China, Late Nineteenth–Early Twentieth Century[*]

Egas Moniz Bandeira

Introduction

In 1909, the Sino-Japanese poet Su Manshu painted an image of Cai Yan (Lady Wenji), a poetess of the late second century who had spent 12 years in captivity abroad before returning to the Han Empire, and sent it to his friend, the art collector Liu Jiping (also known as Liu San). Liu wrote a series of poems to appreciate Su's gift, including the following verses:

> 'China' is not a transformed pronunciation of Qin;
> It was first seen in the poem *Bharata*.
> It were monks who determined it as the country's name,
> but within the country no one knows this.[1]

Why would a Chinese literatus at the turn of the twentieth century write a poem mentioning the Indian epic Mahabharata to match a seemingly unrelated painting?

Until well into the twentieth century, the name of the Mahabharata had been mostly unknown in East Asia, except for a few isolated references in

[*] I am grateful to Milinda Banerjee, Peilin Chiu, Viren Murthy, Christopher Atwood, Simon Cubelic, Lisa Zhang, Orion Klautau, Stanley Ong Gieshen Setiawan, Pei-Chih Chou, Asanuma Chie, Emily Mae Graf, Barbara Witt, Suzuki Minami, Marc Matten, Ying-Kit Chan, Geoff Wade, and Maren Wicher for their helpful comments and suggestions.

Buddhist texts. Against the sheer preponderance of Buddhist thought in the intellectual flows between India and China, it might even have seemed futile to look for an East Asian reception of the Mahabharata. Yet, over the centuries, various elements related to the Mahabharata circulated between South Asia and East Asia and played significant roles within East Asian culture itself.

By the late nineteenth and early twentieth centuries, Indian thought continued to play a major role in East Asia amidst intense contact between China, Japan, Europe, and India itself. In close interdependence with the notion of the 'West', the category of 'Asia' emerged in the Japanese and Chinese imaginary by the turn of the twentieth century, when intellectuals developed a globalized sense of their position in the world.[2] India became a renewed object of study but, at the same time, also a 'method'[3] to deal with the challenges posed by modernity. Interest in India and its role within 'Asia' was a significant element not only in understanding the geopolitical realities and 'catching up' with the 'West,' but also in the quest for a 'world beyond the material and epistemological constraints' posed by Western modernity.[4] While Buddhism still played a crucial role as the connecting bond between the two macroregions of East Asia and South Asia, some intellectuals came to understand it in a wider framework that also encompassed other traditions such as that of the Mahabharata.

In the past decade, scholarship begun to explore this entangled relationship, which had previously often been overlooked, producing a considerable output.[5] This chapter illuminates an aspect of the creation of a new regional imaginary in East Asia by reconstructing how, against this background, the Mahabharata emerged as one of the symbols of India among East Asian intellectuals. On the one hand, by retracing 'what is connected to what',[6] it seeks to reconstruct the connections between Japanese, Chinese, Indian, and European intellectual actors which underpinned this process. On the other hand, it shows how this process also entailed and was informed by a search for common traditions. Some intellectuals saw it as a symbol of Hindu backwardness, denouncing alleged Brahmin corruptions of the sacred texts, condemning Hinduism for allegedly being cruel, and blaming religion for India's decay. For others, however, India was a fellow victim of imperialist pressures. Such intellectuals strove not only to build cross-border political alliances but also to recover their own Asian intellectual traditions from their Indian origins. As a product of this effort, the chapter shows that literature such as the Mahabharata became a significant element of a broader pan-Asian civilization.

The Mahabharata in Pre-Modern China

Not belonging to the canon of Buddhist literature, the Mahabharata is barely mentioned directly in pre-modern East Asian sources. A table of contents of an early version of the Mahabharata, dated to the third century CE, has been found among a number of Sanskrit manuscripts related to the Sarvastivada school of Buddhism unearthed in the Kizil caves in the Tarim Basin.[7] Ramnath Subbaraman suggests that the presence of this list in Kizil 'strongly suggests that the Mahabharata may have been known in other parts of China as well',[8] but there is little hard evidence to corroborate this hypothesis. However, direct mentions of the Mahabharata and its legendary author, Vyasa, can be found in Chinese-language texts of both the Sarvastivada and the Yogacara schools of Buddhism. Sarvastivada sutras mention the Mahabharata a few times, always in conjunction with the Ramayana, which is referred to a few more times alone. These were polemic comments against the Indian epic tradition, showing a vision of the epics being the product of a violent religion.[9]

More detailed discussions of Brahminic philosophy can be found in the writings of the Yogacara school – for example, in a partial commentary to the prominent *Lankavatara Sutra* (*Lengqie jing*). The commentary attributes the belief that 'Nirvana is recognising that Ishvara engendered the creatures' to the school of 'preceptor Mathara', a name which refers to none other than Vyasa.[10] Furthermore, its commentary explains the teachings of the devotees of Vishnu/Narayana with a long string of sometimes literal quotations from one of their central texts, the Bhagavadgita.[11]

The disparaging comments against the Mahabharata and the Ramayana in the writings of the Sarvastivada school, as well as the explanations about the teachings of Mathara (Vyasa) in the writings of the Yogacara school, are indications of a larger phenomenon. The original sutras were written in an environment in which the epics were of supreme importance and stood in dialogue with them. In this regard, perhaps the single most influential Indian oeuvre was the Ramayana. Scholarship has been long fascinated by the striking similarities between Rama's simian companion, Hanuman – who also plays an important role in the Mahabharata traditions – and the Chinese Monkey King, Sun Wukong, who is the central figure of the novel *Journey to the West*, attributed to Wu Cheng'en (1506?–1582?). The hypothesis that Hanuman was an inspiration for Sun Wukong was first brought forward in 1923 by Alexander von Staël-Holstein (1877–1937) and Hu Shi (1891–1962).[12] Meanwhile, research has shown that the Monkey King is an amalgamation of indigenous elements with features imported from the Ramayana, mainly through the Southeast Asian sea route.[13]

At first, von Staël-Holstein's and Hu Shi's suggestion provoked heated discussions and strong criticisms, for many were reluctant to accept that the cherished Sun Wukong had origins outside of China.[14] However, sensibilities have calmed down, and it is now widely accepted that the Indian ascendent of Sun Wukong was just the top of the iceberg. In the words of Ramnath Subbaraman, there are also numerous 'connections between other characters (Sita, for instance), other texts (the *Mahabharata*), and literary elements other than character traits and plot events (such as themes)'.[15] Hence, although scholarship was initially slow in acknowledging the importance of the Mahabharata for pre-modern China, scholars in recent decades have enthusiastically proposed a large number of refractions of the Mahabharata in China.[16] Certainly, not all proposed relations can be conclusively proven, remain either speculative or sometimes even seem quite far-fetched. Some of the equivalences found refer to the Ramayana; others refer to general similarities found in many literatures which need not be specifically from the Mahabharata. As Steven Collins writes of the *Vessantara Jataka*, the 'complex mixture and overlap of orality and literacy makes the search for origins quixotic at best'.[17]

There are, however, cases in which specific connections to the Mahabharata in East Asian literature can be seen with reasonable clarity. For example, the story about King Shibi cutting off a piece of his own flesh to save a pigeon is narrated several times in the Mahabharata.[18] According to Moriz Winternitz, this tale of self-sacrifice is an example of Brahmanical ascetic poetry, but it has gained strong traction in various other traditions as well.[19] As a popular Buddhist parable, it is collected, among others, in the *Sutra of the Wise and the Foolish* (*Xianyu jing*).[20]

Of the stories found in the Mahabharata which are also present in East Asia, the most striking example is perhaps the story of the 'man in the well'.[21] This story of a man who flees wild beasts in a gloomy wood, falls into a well, and gets to taste a few drops of honey falling down from above is found in myriad versions in world literature as well as in world art.[22] Whereas the Mahabharata version is the only one to be found in 'orthodox' Hindu literature, it is recounted at least 15 times in the Sinophone Buddhist canon written between the later Qin (384–414 CE) and the Ming (1368–1644 CE) periods.[23]

Scholarship has long debated whether the parable is of Buddhist origin or whether it is a piece of early Indian ascetic poetry and the Mahabharata version is the oldest extant one.[24] As Monica Zin argues, the version in the Mahabharata was only incorporated into the epic quite late.[25] Rather, the original text was probably a non-surviving Buddhist one, the closest textual version having been preserved in the Jain scriptures.[26] Nonetheless, all these versions are surface manifestations of a travelling story which has been so successful throughout Eurasia because of its vivid depiction of the *conditio humana* (human condition) transcending time, space, and religion.[27] Although the relationship between the Mahabharata version and the extant East Asian ones is not one of direct descendence, the story shows that Chinese imagination shared significant, albeit mostly unacknowledged, elements with the world of the Mahabharata.

The Mahabharata in Japanese Indology

The political and social upheavals of the second half of the nineteenth century, coupled with the dramatic acceleration of transport and communication, also created a new, globalized, geographic consciousness within the intellectual elites of East Asia. Given the roots of Buddhism in India as well as the geopolitical realities of the modern world, India commanded particular interest among a section of both Japanese and Chinese intellectuals. After having mostly lived an undercover life in pre-modern East Asia, the Mahabharata thus resurfaced as an element of East Asian Indological knowledge and, at times, even as a symbol of Brahmanism and of Indian civilization itself.

In Japan, the renewed study of India was conducted in close cooperation with European Indologists, who in turn built on the Buddhological expertise of their Japanese colleagues.[28] In addition to knowledge exchange with Europe, a sizeable number of Japanese intellectuals personally visited India, and Japan's newly founded universities also began to attract Indian students.[29] In 1876, a group of Buddhist monks set out to study Sanskrit at the University of Oxford with the Sanskritist Friedrich Max Müller. One of them was Nanjo Bun'yu, who was made the first lecturer of Sanskrit studies at the Imperial University in Tokyo in 1885. Making use of English- and German-language Indological literature by Müller, Romesh Chunder Dutt, Monier Monier-Williams, Albrecht Weber, and others, they participated in global discourses about India. At the same time, they analysed India through Japanese and Buddhist lenses.

Both premises – the global debate and the local perspective – led to mostly, although not exclusively, negative assessments of the Brahmanic religions. In the words of the scholar Anezaki Masaharu, Hinduism, as it existed in contemporary India, was an 'utterly depraved religion'.[30] The prolific writer and translator Takahashi Goro, too, gave damning verdicts on Indian religion in his books on Indian history and comparative religious studies. In his 1881 *History of India*, for example, he wrote that the Aryans had been a 'civilized people' who had developed an elaborate philosophy.[31] However, the development of the caste system caused the exquisite and profound principles found in ancient philosophy to be corrupted over time, and the Mahabharata was full of such elements inserted by Brahmins over time to secure the privileges of their caste.[32] In his *Practical Overview over All Religions*, published in the same year of 1881, Takahashi used even harsher words to describe Brahmanism (which he equated with Hinduism) and its scriptures, essentially describing them as dull works of little interest:[33]

> [Its] doctrines are not profound in meaning like in Buddhism…. Brahmanism, as its name says, has been produced by India's Brahmin caste, and its basis are the ancient writings, the four *Vedas*. Its religious principles can be seen in the *Classic of Manu* as well as other ancient poems[34] and are mediocre. The things that could be seen in these *Veda* writings are largely about festivals and ceremonies and did not have profound reasonings. In later generations, the Brahmin caste arbitrarily added fantasies and delusions to it, finally producing Brahmanism…. In this religion, there were not that many serious aberrations at first, but the fallacies gradually increased. Eventually, from ridiculous behaviours to cruel and despicable customs much came to be mixed into it.[35]

Mentioning the Mahabharata and the Gita, Takahashi uses the English bishop Reginald Heber's meeting with the Hindu religious leader Swaminarayan in 1825 to explain the centrality of Krishna (and of his avatar Brahma) in Hinduism.[36] While Swaminarayan's theological explanation was positively received by Heber as a cautious 'advance towards the truth' for its apparent closeness to monotheism, it did not put an end to negative outside views of Hinduism.[37] In general, Takahashi saves the reputation of early Indian philosophy while it repudiates contemporary Brahmanism as the result of Brahminic manipulations. Such a stance resonated with a global discursive trope, present even inside India,[38] which condemned Hinduism for allegedly being cruel and for being the result of later corruptions by the Brahmin caste.

Yet not all descriptions of the Indian classics were as polemically negative as Takahashi's. Tokiwa Daijo, for example, concurs that classical Indian literature had 'serious deficiencies', the main one being that the Indians were allegedly an 'ahistoric nation'.[39] However, his comments on the various genres of Indian literature are full of praise. When describing dramatic literature, he acclaims Kalidasa as 'India's Shakespeare' and mentions his influence on Johann Gottfried von Herder and Johann Wolfgang von Goethe, translating Goethe's Kalidasa- (and indirectly Mahabharata-) inspired poem 'Shakontala' into Japanese.[40]

Tokiwa's description of the epics is a long enumeration of ancient India's great pieces of literature:

> If we turn our eyes again to have a look at other literature, among the epics there is the Story of the Great War of the Bharata People, the *Mahabharata*, which is called the world's longest, and the also very long Story of the Bravery of Prince Rama, the *Ramayana*. In the structure of memories of a real war, the former brings into activity the Heavenly Emperor Indra, who is at the centre of popular veneration, and Prince Arjuna, who is the main protagonist of the whole text.... Thereby, they sing praise for the circumstances under which agriculture was brought to the whole of India. It shouldn't be surprising for someone to be amazed by the rich thoughts of people in ancient India![41]

Most Japanese introductions to Indian religion and philosophy placed the Mahabharata in more global literary contexts. Inoue Tetsujiro, basing himself on Anezaki's notes, compared Adi Shankaracharya, the Gita's great commentator, to Zhu Xi, thus indirectly also comparing the significance of the Gita to that of the Confucian classics.[42] The most obvious and frequent comparison was that of Indian with Greek epic literature – that is, the Greek Iliad and Odyssey.[43] This was also the comparison utilized by Tsuchiya Senkyo in his *History of Indian Philosophy*.[44] Following Dutt's periodization of Indian civilization into five eras,[45] Tsuchiya classified the Mahabharata into the second period, 'epic', and the Gita into the fifth period, 'puranic'.[46] Although he deems the third, 'rationalistic', period as the one most worthy of research, his description of the Mahabharata was rather neutral. To illustrate what the Mahabharata is about, he ended up translating an excerpt of the story of Nala and Damayanti, which he described as being the most interesting one of the epic.[47]

Pan-Asianism and Different Attitudes towards India

The search for the origins of Buddhism was not the only moving factor in the renewed East Asian interest in India. In the face of the international political scenario, intellectuals across Asia also used Indian history to interpret contemporary international politics. As Japan had managed to catch up to the imperialist powers after a process of thorough political reforms, Japanese observers urged Indians to engage in their own far-reaching societal reforms and overcome the corruptions of their own culture. Since around 1900, similar narratives about a decadent India which had perished out of its own faults were also common in China, as reformist intellectuals sought to avert the repetition of India's fate and to instead emulate the Japanese experience of rapid modernization.[48]

Yet a sizeable number of intellectuals across Asia held a different position. The imperialist pressures exerted by the Western powers, which had led to the colonization of India, with which China was still struggling, and which Japan had only recently overcome, engendered a pan-Asian sense of solidarity. 'Asia is one,' proclaimed the Japanese art historian Okakura Kakuzo in his 1903 book *Ideals of the East*.[49] Although his book, not unexpectedly, focused on Buddhism as an element uniting Asia, he also praised the pre-Buddhist traditions of India, where he had travelled extensively, and emphasized the connections between them. To Okakura, the Gita, as contained in the Mahabharata, was essentially an embodiment of Northern Buddhism itself.[50] More generally, he maintained that the Mahabharata was the nurturing soil which had morally prepared the people for the Buddha's teachings, thus possibilitating the emergence of Buddhism:

> Essentially ... the message of Buddha was a message of the Freedom of the Soul, and those who heard were the emancipated children of the Ganges, already drinking to their full of the purity of the Absolute, in their Mahabharata and Upanishads.[51]

Although Okakura is often taken as a representative of Japanese pan-Asian thought, his influence in Japan itself was rather marginal. In 1885, a seminal essay attributed to the paramount intellectual Fukuzawa Yukichi called for Japan to 'leave Asia' and join 'Western civilization' instead. Just a year before Okakura published his book, in January 1902, Japan forged an alliance with Great Britain. Forming an alliance with other Asian nations against the West was not a mainstream position in the Japanese political discourse at that time.[52] Okakura wrote in English, aiming neither at a Japanese nor at a Western audience.[53] Rather, he was communicating with Indian intellectuals, many of whom looked to Japan as an example of non-Western modernity.[54]

For pan-Asianists from China as well as from other parts of the continent, Asia had to rediscover its own strengths and stand in solidarity in order to face the challenges of modernity. Pan-Asianism took both the form of resistance against Western imperialism as well as against the feeling that their own culture was being too Europeanized.[55] In this context, the Mahabharata emerged as one of the representatives of Indian literature and as its equivalent to both the great works of Chinese as well as of European antiquity. The comparison made in order to contextualize the epics for East Asian readerships naturally developed into a value judgement about the quality of the work. When writing about chronicles compiled in a religious context, Anezaki had referred to the Jewish *Book of Numbers* and *Book of Kings*, the Japanese *Kojiki*, and the Indian Puranas, among others.[56] Citing Anezaki in the 1900 edition of his *Book of Urgency* (*Qiushu*),[57] the prominent Chinese revolutionary and philologist Zhang Taiyan extended the comparison to Chinese classics in his highly recondite style:

> The *Book of Songs* [*Shi*] is like the *Bhagavad-Gita*; the *Book of Documents* [*Shu*] is like the myths of the *Puranas*. On the lower [level], they derive from popular righteousness, and above they communicate with the Ninth Heaven. The *Book of Music* [*Yue*] is like the *Sama* (Vedic poems) and the *Black Yajur* (Vedic mantras and secret formulas; there is both a *Black* and a *White Yajur*). Seeing them, all beasts and birds assemble to perform their dances, observing their calls to duty. It is obvious that they impress dwarfs and giants alike.[58]

Sino-Indian-Japanese Intellectual Networks

Zhang Taiyan wrote these lines in Japan, having fled there after a botched attempt at radical political reforms in the Qing Empire in 1898. Tokyo was becoming a highly cosmopolitan city to which students and intellectuals from all over Asia flocked. While many strove to help their places of origin develop within the established political and bureaucratic structures, many Chinese, Koreans, Annamese, Filipinos, and Indians fostered revolutionary views, hoping to overthrow the respective colonial regimes or, in the case of China, the Imperial court's government.

Within this context, Zhang was a member of a network of Chinese intellectuals who grew an intense interest in India's traditions and interacted directly with Indian intellectuals present in Tokyo. In 1907, Zhang was one of the founders and the first president of the 'Asiatic Humanitarian Brotherhood' society.[59] Among the Chinese members of the society were the anarchist Liu Shipei, the future first secretary-general of the Communist Party of China Chen Duxiu, and Su Manshu.[60] Several Indians were also present in the association, including Surendramohan Bose, Taraknath Das, and a certain N. E. Prabhan.[61]

In the preamble to the group's charter, Zhang stressed the influence exerted by Sanskrit culture in South-East Asia and hoped to 'unite India and China' by forming 'a fraternal alliance that will revive the fortunes of our Brahmanism, Confucianism and Daoism'. Accordingly, Zhang wrote that he would like to travel to India to study Sanskrit, a dream which he did not fulfil.[62] Rather, he and around 10 other Chinese friends hired an Indian teacher named

Mishra – the only one of 30 Indians in their circle who mastered Sanskrit – to form a Sanskrit study group in Tokyo.[63] However, as Mishra taught in English, the group had communication difficulties from the start and seems to have made little learning progress.[64]

The member of this network who arguably engaged with Sanskrit and the Mahabharata the most vigorously was Su Manshu. At the same time as he strove to gain direct access to the sources, Su engaged with the European–Japanese Indological scholarship, which had been unfolding since the late nineteenth century. Having studied Sanskrit with a Buddhist master in Bangkok in 1904,[65] he is reported to have received his English-language material on the Sanskrit language from Chen Duxiu.[66] In Su's poetry, prose, and private correspondence, India became a constant element, including several references to the Mahabharata.

Su was particularly fascinated by Kalidasa's works. He planned to translate the poem 'Cloud Messenger' (Meghaduta) together with Mishra, the Sanskrit teacher, although they did not finish it.[67] Liu Yazi, Su's fellow poet and editor of his complete works, claims that Su translated the whole of *Shakuntala* from Sanskrit, but if he ever did, no such translation has survived.[68] *Shakuntala*, however, survived in various forms within Su's oeuvre. He translated Edward Backhouse Eastwick's translation of Goethe's poem into Chinese and embedded translated verses from Monier-William's translation of the play itself into his novella *The Story of Entering into Seclusion on the Beach of Sala* (*Suoluo Haibin Dunji Ji*).[69] As Jane Qian Liu writes, this 'juxtaposition of a Chinese poem with a Chinese translation of an English poem' is a prime example of Su's 'transcultural lyricism'.[70]

Although Su mentioned that Western scholars saw the Mahabharata and the Ramayana as equivalents to the Iliad and the Odyssey,[71] Su himself held the opinion that 'not even Homer is a match for them'.[72] In his chef-d'oeuvre, the novella *The Lone Swan*, Su explicitly mentions the Mahabharata among the books that the protagonist, Saburo, finds among the things of his aunt's adopted daughter and his prospective fiancée, Shizuko:

> If my heart grew heavy with memories, I would lean against a tree and watch the water running at my feet, or read books to while away the time, for the cabinet contained several volumes by the Sung philosophers. Aside from these, there were several kinds of works in Sanskrit and Lü script, which had been so badly worm-eaten that it was impossible to make out the text. All of these books belonged to the Tang period. Again there were Chinese translations of the two

books, the *Mahabharata* and the *Ramayana*, long epic poems, which are no longer extant in China. In the Buddhist canon, the *Huayan jing*[73] there are casual references to these works; and it has been said that the work was that of the god Vyasa. The present English translation of the Bharata tribe's great battles by Dutt, the Indian scholar, is a part of the same work previously mentioned.[74]

While the novella has strong autobiographical elements, the description of Shizuko's library is fictional. Although the scene is set in Japan, the library does not contain Japanese literature.[75] Rather, as Makiko Mori argues, Japan is the embodiment of a 'Chinese utopia' in which China is rejuvenated through a connection to her glorious past.[76] As the references to Indian literature and the conviction that these are superior to the Greek epics demonstrate, Su's hope is for a broader 'return to the East' rather than for 'future-forward move to the West'.[77] India's glorious history, embodied among others by the Mahabharata, thus becomes part of a pan-Asian identity juxtaposed with the encroachment of Western modernity.

Among the books contained in Shizuko's fictional library is also one of Su's own works – an eight-volume primer titled *Sanskrit Classics* (*Fanwen Dian*). Although Su 'undoubtedly completed' the first of the eight volumes, it is no longer extant, and it seems that he never published his manuscript.[78] However, an advertisement containing the table of contents of the first volume, as well as a number of prefaces and accompanying poems, were published in 1907 and 1908 in several important Tokyo- and Shanghai-based journals connected to the members of the Asiatic Humanitarian Brotherhood, the Revolutionary Alliance (Tongmenghui – the predecessor of the Chinese National Party, Kuomintang), and the Chinese 'national essence' (*guocui*) movement.[79]

The advertisement was overwritten with the eye-catching title *Samskritaprathamamargopadeshika* (A First Sanskrit Primer) in Nagari script (Figure 8.1). It was based on the works of Monier-Williams and Müller, to which Su added Chinese sources from the Tang and Song eras.[80] According to the extant table of contents, the book not only contained introductions to Sanskrit grammar and phonology but also carried two texts in Sanskrit. The first one was the original of the *Diamond Sutra*. The second text was the story of Nala and Damayanti from the third *parva* (book) of the Mahabharata. While the *Diamond Sutra* was well known to the readership, the choice of the second text had to be explained and justified. Here, again, Su's views echo those of Tsuchiya: the story of Nala and Damayanti was the Mahabharata's most 'beautiful and exquisite.'

Figure 8.1 Advertisement for Su Manshu's lost first Sanskrit primer, *Samskritaprathamamargopadeshika*, including the story of Nala and Damayanti from the Mahabharata

Source: *Tien Yee*, no. 6, 1 September 1907, https://uni-heidelberg.de/ecpo/publications. php?magid=172&isid=42699&ispage=43 (accessed on 5 January 2024).

The Mahabharata as the Origin of the Name 'China'

Su's efforts to translate parts of the Mahabharata into Chinese remained singular at his time. Yet his efforts and those of his circle to recover the origins of Chinese civilization in India played a role in a wider debate with far-reaching political implications, namely the question of how the prospective Chinese nation state should be named. At the turn of the twentieth century, Chinese intellectuals frequently deplored that, as Liang Qichao put it, 'of all the big shames for our kin, none is bigger than the fact that our country does not have a name'.[81] The successive polities of imperial China were mostly known by a specific name given by each new dynasty. The term 'central country' (Chinese: Zhongguo; Manchu: Dulimbai Gurun) had become a synonym for the empire, but remained closely connected to the old political order and was thus unsatisfactory for reformers and particularly revolutionaries.

Until the nineteenth century, there was no dominant generic name for China in Japan either. One of the various terms used for it, Shina (that is, 'Zhina' in Chinese), was originally derived from the Sanskrit 'Cina' as found in Indian sources like the *Arthashastra* and the Mahabharata. It had appeared in medieval Chinese sources, whence it found its way to Japan.[82] By the last quarter of the nineteenth century, the term became entrenched in Japanese.

Chinese intellectuals noticed the various exonyms for China, including the term 'Shina', now popular in Japan, and, bearing in mind the historical uses of the name both in China and in India, came to debate various possible etymologies for it.

Internationally, the most common explanation was that the Indian term 'Cina' derived from the ancient Chinese Qin state, which had existed since the first half of the first millennium BCE and created a unified Chinese empire in 221 BCE. This etymology had occasionally been espoused in Asia – including by the monk Xuanzang, who had famously visited India in the seventh century to gather Buddhist scriptures, and in at least one Tibetan text – but had not become mainstream.[83] First proposed in the West by the Jesuit Matteo Ricci in 1584, it turned dominant in the following centuries.[84] Variously disputed since the turn of the twentieth century,[85] it continues to be maintained to this day, although it tends to be regarded as unlikely by newer scholarship.[86]

The Sanskritophile circle around Zhang Taiyan and Su Manshu vehemently opposed the derivation of China from Qin, adding the medieval Chinese understanding of the term and their own Sanskrit studies to their arguments. Both Su and Zhang located the origin of the term 'Zhina' in the Mahabharata, but strictly denied a relationship with Qin, arguing that the Mahabharata was much older than the Qin Empire. Zhang Taiyan, for example, wrote a text in which he added the Nagari letters to the possible Sanskrit etymologies he discussed:

> The name *Zhina* was first coined by the Indians. Even before the Buddha was born, its name had the appellation *Zhina* (*Cina*) in the ancient history of those lands, the *Mahabharata* (a book from 1400 BC).... Some say that it has a derogatory connotation, but that has even less basis. Some say it means astute and quick-witted, for as far as I know in those lands one says *sina* (*jnana*) for 'intelligence,' but although the sound is close, one should simply call its original name when one designates another land, and there's no space for expressing virtues through the name. [T]his theory is also false. The theory according to which *Zhina* is Qin is the most reasonable one. However, India called China like this more than a thousand years before unification; hence one knows that it is not the word Qin either. Furthermore, their ancient historian Kalidasa calls China *Zhuinija* (*Cainika* [?]), which is also a variation of the sound of *Zhina*.[87] I say that the *Erya* (chapter 'Explaining earth') and the *Liezi* (chapter 'Questions of Tang') both call China *Qizhou*, with *Qi* meaning 'central.' Before the Shang and Zhou the self-designation to the outside must have been *Qi*, and hence it is

possible that in their country they translated it as *Zhina*, and later variated it to *Zhuinijia*. All other theories are not reliable.[88]

Zhang's reference to a possible pejorative meaning of the word 'Zhina' did not necessarily refer to contemporary Japanese usage. It might rather have been a rebuttal of beliefs about the etymology of the word as found in medieval Chinese literature. The 1143 *Collection of Terms and Meanings in Translation* (*Fanyi Mingyi Ji*) noted that 'Zhina' had a laudatory variant praising a land of culture and education as well as a pejorative one denoting a remote backwater.[89] Su imprecisely referenced the 1143 dictionary, writing that it translated the term 'Zhina' as meaning 'cunning' (*qiaozha*).[90] Nonetheless, similar to what Zhang Taiyan contended, one common explanation in medieval Chinese literature was that the word 'China' was related to the Sanskrit word for 'thought' (*cinta*).[91] Even more than Zhang, Su uses this explanation to, again, recover the lost glory of Chinese civilization in its pan-Asian origins:

> Only now reading the original text of the old Indian poem Mahabharata I have learned that at that time the term 'Zhina' already existed. Now, the Mahabharata is an epic poem of the Indian Bharata reign. Before that, there had been a king named Bharat, in whose time there was a big war. It was only after it that he unified India, and eventually this work was created. The King said that he had single-handedly led a large army and marched to the north, that the cultural accomplishments were particularly splendid there, that their people were very astute [*qiaozhi*] and probably part of the China tribe, and so on. It happens that the Bharata dynasty was in the year −1400 of the Western calendar, right at the time of China's [Zhendan] Shang [dynasty]. At that time, the Indians were jealous of our culture and called it 'dexterous and intelligent'[*zhiqiao*]. Also, everything which the king said about the customs of Persia has been proven in our times.... [T]he research done by the Westerners is full of mistakes. Nowadays, the new intellectuals all say that 'Zhina' is a phonetic transformation of the word 'Qin', but that is actually false.[92]

At the turn of the twentieth century, Chinese intellectuals and politicians debated the term 'Zhina' not only as an academic question. A large number of intellectuals and politicians actively used it to designate their own country, including Sun Yat-Sen and Liang Qichao himself, who used it before settling for 'Zhongguo' and pioneering the reformed usage of the term for the new nation state.[93] A decade later, the demise of the Qing Empire and the establishment of the Republic of China finally settled the case – in the opposite direction of Japan.

Lydia Liu claims that, on the Japanese side, the adoption of 'Shina' was an imperialist act of 'colonial mimicry' and glosses over the fact that some Qing students 'even adopted it for self-identification' both during their stay in Japan and after their return to China.[94] The preference for 'Shina' reflected a reluctance to adopt Sinocentric designations such as 'central country', and in the first half of the twentieth century, the term became increasingly associated with Japanese aggression until it largely fell out of use after Japan's defeat in the Second World War.[95] However, scholarship has conclusively shown that the term was neither coined for the sake of colonial conquest nor intrinsically pejorative.[96] On the Chinese side, the quick waning of 'Zhina' as an endonym following Liang Qichao's endorsement of 'Zhongguo' and the proclamation of the Republic of China conceal that, for a few years around 1900, 'Zhina' was a serious option for how to name the emerging Chinese nation state. It certainly had a fresh and even foreign ring to it,[97] showing China as a 'nation among nations'.[98] Yet Zhang Taiyan's and Su Manshu's readings of the Mahabharata show that it was also part of an effort to rescue the true origins of China within a pan-Asianist anti-imperial framework. Albeit small and fleeting, the Mahabharata thus played an unexpected role in the construction of the modern Chinese nation state.

Conclusion

Reporting about Sanskrit classes conducted in Hangzhou in 2015 'amid a national campaign to rejuvenate traditional culture', a Xinhua reporter saw the large number of attendants as a sign of a 'growing fever with Indology' in China.[99] The reporter's enthusiastic declaration probably overstates contemporary Chinese academic interest in India. However, notwithstanding the drastically changed geopolitical situation in which this 'rejuvenation' takes place, these classes held at the Hangzhou Buddhism Institute are, in a way, a continuation of the Sanskrit classes taught by the teacher Mishra to Chinese students resident in Tokyo more than a century earlier. Based on centuries of historical entanglements, East Asian intellectuals from the late nineteenth and the early twentieth centuries sought to understand India and its literary and religious traditions, including the Mahabharata, as one of its most important literary artefacts. Personal contacts between Japan, China, and India increased, as did the number of writings discussing India in both China and Japan. The exact motivations for the interest in India, as well as the assessments of it, varied greatly. Many writers opined that the Mahabharata was a primitive work of little profoundness or an instrument of depraved Brahmin domination.

Such positions reflected global tropes about India but also local concerns at the same time. At the same time, in the burgeoning Japan at the end of the twentieth century, intellectuals saw traditional culture as the reason for the economic and social woes on the Asian continent and vowed to 'leave Asia' instead. This was just one part of the story, however. Many intellectuals and revolutionaries also felt a strong sense of identification with India. Although some compared the Mahabharata negatively to Buddhism, other Buddhists were looking for the 'true Dharma' in India. More generally, intellectuals were searching for the origins of China's and Japan's own beliefs, thought to have been lost or distorted.

The intellectual most enthusiastic about Sanskrit literature was the poet Su Manshu, who was fascinated by Kalidasa's plays as well as by the Mahabharata itself, which he deemed to be superior to the Homeric epics. His Sanskrit textbook and translations from the Sanskrit originals either have not been completed or have not survived, but they are indicative of significant intellectual trends. At the same time as the new knowledge was partially mediated by European scholarship and literature, the episode also shows direct intellectual exchanges, which co-created a sense of common identity in which India was an ally against the expansion of Europe. Liu Jiping's poem, referring to the debate about the etymology of the very name 'China', shows how the recourse to traditional Indian literature was used in the debates surrounding the creation of nation states in modern East Asia. At the same time, being one of the fundamental texts of Indian culture, the Mahabharata also came to be a marker of a common Asian identity.

Notes

1. Liu Jiping (Liu San), 'Shixuan: Ti Manshu suo hui Wenji tu', *Huaqiao zazhi* 2 (1913), *wenyuan* 10. All translations are by me if not otherwise stated.
2. See Rebecca E. Karl, *Staging the World: Chinese Nationalism at the Turn of the Twentieth Century* (Durham, NC: Duke University Press, 2007), 11.
3. Viren Murthy, 'Rethinking Pan-Asianism through Zhang Taiyan: India as Method', in *Beyond Pan-Asianism: Connecting China and India, 1840s–1960s*, ed. Tansen Sen and Brian Tsui, 94–128 (New Delhi: Oxford University Press, 2021).
4. Murthy, 'Rethinking Pan-Asianism', 95.
5. Tansen Sen (ed.), *Buddhism, Diplomacy, and Trade: The Realignment of Sino-Indian Relations, 600–1400* (Honolulu: University of Hawai'i Press, 2011); Viren Murthy, *The Political Philosophy of Zhang Taiyan: The Resistance of Consciousness* (Leiden and Boston [MA]: Brill, 2011); Tansen Sen, *India,*

China and the World: A Connected History (Lanham, MD: Rowman & Littlefield, 2017); Anne Cheng and Sanchit Kumar (eds.), *India–China: Intersecting Universalities* (Paris: Collège de France, 2020); Kanti Bajpai, Selina Ho, and Manjari Chatterjee Miller, *Routledge Handbook of China–India Relations* (London: Routledge, 2020); Tansen Sen and Brian Tsui (eds.), *Beyond Pan-Asianism* (New Delhi: Oxford University Press, 2021). See also, for China, John Makeham, 'Introduction', in *Transforming Consciousness: Yogacara Thought in Modern China*, ed. John Makeham (Oxford and New York: Oxford University Press, 2014), 1. For an attempt to create a dialogue between Chinese and Indian philosophy, including the Mahabharata, with a normative orientation towards international relations, see Amitav Acharya, Daniel A. Bell, Rajeev Bhargava, and Yan Xuetong (eds.), *Bridging Two Worlds: Comparing Classical Political Thought and Statecraft in India and China* (Oakland, CA: University of California Press, 2023).

6. Pablo Blitstein, 'Sinology: Chinese Intellectual History and Transcultural Studies', *Transcultural Studies* 7, no. 2 (2016): 136–67, 153.

7. Dieter Schlingloff, 'The Oldest Extant Parvan-List of the Mahabharata', *Journal of the American Oriental Society* 89, no. 2 (1969): 334–38.

8. Ramnath Subbaraman, 'Beyond the Question of the Monkey Imposter: Indian Influences on the Chinese Novel *The Journey to the West*', *Sino-Platonic Papers* 114 (2002): 11–12.

9. Giuliana Martini, 'Transmission of the Dharma and Reception of the Text: Oral and Aural Features in the Fifth Chapter of the Book of Zambasta', in *Buddhism, Diplomacy, and Trade: The Realignment of Sino-Indian Relations, 600–1400*, ed. Tansen Sen, 141–42 (Honolulu: University of Hawai'i Press, 2011).

10. Takakusu Junjiro and Watanabe Kaikyoku (eds.), *Taisho Shinshu Daizokyo* (henceforth 'Taisho Tripitaka'), 55 vols. (Tokyo: Taisho Shinshu Daizokyo Kanko Kai, 1924–29), 1640: 157b23–157c04. See Nakamura Hajime, *A History of Early Vedanta Philosophy*, trans. Trevor Leggett, Sengakul Mayeda, Taitetz Unno et al. (Delhi, Varanasi, and Patna: Motilal Banarsidass, 1993), 173–74.

11. *Taisho Tripitaka*, 1640:1.157b2. For the equivalences in the Bhagavadgita, see Vyasa, *The Mahabharata of Krishna-Dwaipayana Vyasa Translated into English Prose*, trans. Kisari Mohan Ganguli, ed. Pratapa Chandra Roy, 11 vols. (Calcutta: Bharata Press, 1883–96), 6:33–34 (108–14). The Mahabharata is cited by the numbers of the *parva* (book) and section and the page in Ganguli's translation (paginated within every *parva*). See Nakamura Hajime, 'Upanisadic Tradition and the Early School of Vedanta as Noticed in Buddhist Scripture', *Harvard Journal of Asiatic Studies* 18, nos. 1–2 (1955): 74–104;

Giuseppe Tucci, 'Un traité d'Aryadeva sur le "Nirvaṇa" des hérétiques', *T'oung-Pao*, Second Series 24, no. 1 (1925): 16–31, 26.

12. Hu Shi, 'Xiyou Ji kaozheng' (a textual study of *Journey to the West*), *Dushu Zazhi*, no. 6 (1923): 1–4, 3.

13. Zhao Guohua, 'Lun Sun Wukong Shenhou Xingxiang de Laili: Xiyou Ji yu Yindu Wenxue Bijiao Yanjiu zhi Yi' (On the Origin of the Monkey King's Image: A Comparative Study of *Journey to the West* with Indian Literature, part 1], *Nanya Yanjiu*, no. 1 (1986): 39–48 and no. 2 (1986): 44–54; Hera Walker, 'Indigenous or Foreign? A Look at the Origins of the Monkey Hero Sun Wukong', *Sino-Platonic Papers* 81 (1998): 53.

14. On the topic, see also Glen Dudbridge, *The Hsi-Yu Chi: A Study of Antecedents to the Sixteenth-Century Chinese Novel* (Cambridge, UK: Cambridge University Press, 1970), 160–64; Victor Mair, 'Suen Wu-Kung = Hanumat? The Progress of a Scholarly Debate', in *Zhongyang Yanjiujuan Di-Er jie Guoji Hanxue Huiyi Lunwenji* (Proceedings of the Second International Conference on Sinology of the Academia Sinica), 2 vols. (Taipei: Academia Sinica, 1989), 2:659–752; Walker, 'Indigenous or Foreign?'

15. Subbaraman, 'Beyond the Question of the Monkey Imposter', 31.

16. See most recently in monographic form, Yan Huizhong, *Zhongguo Gudai de Poluomen Jiao han Poluomen Wenhua Yingxiang* (The Influence of Brahmanism and Brahmanic Culture on Ancient China) (Beijing: Zhonghua Shuju, 2019).

17. Steven Collins, 'Introduction, *Dramatis Personae*, and Chapters in the *Vessantara Jataka*', in *Readings of the Vessantara Jataka*, ed. Steven Collins, 1–35 (New York: Columbia University Press, 2016), 5.

18. Mahabharata, 3:130–31 (391–96), 197 (596–99); Mahabharata, 12:143–49 (481–91); Mahabharata, 13:32 (215–18).

19. Moriz Winternitz, *Geschichte Der Indischen Litteratur* (A History of Indian Literature), 3 vols. (Leipzig: C. F. Amelang, 1909), 352–54.

20. *Taisho Tripitaka*, 202:351c–52b.

21. Mahabharata, 11:5–6 (10–12).

22. See Monika Zin, 'The Parable of "The Man in the Well": Its Travels and Its Pictorial Tradition from Amaravati to Today', in *Art, Myths and Visual Culture of South Asia* (Warsaw Indological Studies, vol. 4), ed. Piotr Balcerowicz and Jerzy Malinowski, 33–93 (Delhi: Mahohar, 2011), 39–40, with further references.

23. *Taisho Tripitaka*, 208:533a27, 217, 1690:787a19, 1775:342b02, 1781:924a09, 2121:233c28, 2122:626b07, 2131:1141c11; Kawamura Kosho (ed.), *Manji Shinsan Dainihon Zokuzokyo* (Manji Tripitaka), 88 vols. (Tokyo: Kokusho

Kankokai, 1975–89), 338:534a10, 348:628c04, 614:729c24, 1240:236a06, 1270:776b12-23, 1304:350b14, 1456:732c01–02.

24. Arguing for the latter Winternitz, *Geschichte der Indischen Litteratur*, 1:351–52.

25. Zin, 'The Parable of "The Man in the Well"', 45–46.

26. Zin, 'The Parable of "The Man in the Well"', 83.

27. Zin, 'The Parable of "The Man in the Well"', 71.

28. See Hans-Martin Krämer, 'Orientalism and the Study of Lived Religions: The Japanese Contribution to European Models of Scholarship on Japan around 1900', in *Scholarly Personae in the History of Orientalism, 1870–1930*, ed. Christiaan Engberts and Herman J. Paul, 143–71 (Leiden: Brill, 2019).

29. See Richard M. Jaffe, *Seeking Śākyamuni: South Asia in the Formation of Modern Japanese Buddhism* (Chicago [IL] and London: Chicago University Press, 2019).

30. Anezaki Masaharu, *Indo Shukyoshi* (A History of Religion in India) (Tokyo: Kinkodo, 1897), 326.

31. Takahashi Goro, *Indoshi* (A History of India) (Tokyo: Jujiya, 1881), 35.

32. Takahashi, *Indoshi*, 22–23, 35–44.

33. Takahashi Goro, *Shokyo Benran* (A Practical Overview over All Religions) (Tokyo: Jujiya, 1881), 59–64. The chapter is titled 'Brahmanism (Also Called Hinduism), Plus the Jain and Lingaya Sects'.

34. Takahashi later expressly refers to the Mahabharata as such.

35. Takahashi, *Shokyo Benran*, 60–61.

36. On Heber's encounter with Swaminarayan, see Raymond Brady Williams, *An Introduction to Swaminarayan Hinduism* (3rd ed.) (Cambridge: Cambridge University Press, 2019 [2001]), 75–106.

37. See Reginald Heber, *Narrative of a Journey through the Upper Provinces of India, from Calcutta to Bombay, 1824–1825 (with Notes upon Ceylon): An Account of a Journey to Madras and the Southern Provinces, 1826, and Letters Written in India*, 2 vols. (Philadelphia, PA: Carey, Lea & Carey, 1828–29), 2:118.

38. Gajendran Ayyathurai, 'Foundations of Anti-Caste Consciousness: Pandit Iyothee Thass, Tamil Buddhism, and the Marginalized in South Asia', PhD thesis, Columbia University, 2011, 29, 37–41.

39. Tokiwa Daijo, *Indo Bunmeishi* (A History of Indian Civilisation) (Tokyo: Hakubunkan, 1906), 7.

40. Tokiwa, *Indo Bunmeishi*, 5.

41. Tokiwa, *Indo Bunmeishi*, 5.

42. Isomae Jun'ichi and Takahashi Hara, 'Inoue Tetsujiro no "Hikaku Shukyo oyobi Toyo Tetsugaku" Kogi: Kaisetsu to Honkoku' (Inoue Tetsujiro's

'Comparative Religion and Oriental Philosophy' Lectures: Commentary and Reprint), *Tokyo Daigaku Shi Kiyo*, no. 21 (2003): 1–55, 22–23.

43. For example, Anezaki Masaharu, *Shukyogaku Gairon* (An Outline of Religious Studies) (Tokyo: Tokyo Senmon Gakko Shuppanbu, 1900), 331.

44. Tsuchiya Senkyo, *Indo Tetsugakushi* (A History of Indian Philosophy) (Tokyo: Waseda Daigaku Shuppanbu, n.d.), 45.

45. Romesh Chunder Dutt, *A History of Civilisation in Ancient India Based on Sanscrit Literature*, 2 vols. (London: Kegan Paul, Trench, Trubner, & Co., 1993).

46. Tsuchiya, *Indo Tetsugakushi*, 45–48.

47. Tsuchiya, *Indo Tetsugakushi*, 45–48; Mahabharata, 3:52–79 (157–234).

48. Rudolf G. Wagner, 'China and India Pre-1939', in *Routledge Handbook of China–India Relations*, ed. Kanti Bajpai, Selina Ho, and Manjari Chatterjee Miller (London: Routledge, 2020), 35.

49. Okakura Kakuzo (Kakasu), *The Ideals of the East with Special Reference to the Arts of Japan* (New York: E. P. Dutton, 1903), 1.

50. Okakura, *The Ideals of the East*, 81.

51. Okakura, *The Ideals of the East*, 67.

52. Sven Saaler, 'Pan-Asianism in Modern Japanese History: Overcoming the Nation, Creating a Region, Forging an Empire', in *Pan-Asianism in Modern Japanese History: Colonialism, Regionalism and Borders*, ed. Sven Saaler and J. Victor Koschmann (Abingdon: Routledge, 2007), 5.

53. Saaler, 'Pan-Asianism in Modern Japanese History', 5.

54. See Milinda Banerjee, 'The Royal Nation and Global Intellectual History: Monarchic Routes to Conceptualizing National Unity', in *Transnational Histories of the 'Royal Nation'*, ed. Milinda Banerjee, Charlotte Backerra, and Cathleen Sarti, 21–44 (Cham: Palgrave MacMillan, 2017).

55. On Pan-Asianism, see Sven Saaler, 'Pan-Asianismus im Japan der Meiji- und der Taisho-Zeit: Wurzeln, Entstehung und Anwendung einer Ideologie' (Pan-Asianism in Meiji- and Taisho-era Japan: Origins, Emergence, and Application of an Ideology), in *Selbsbehauptungsdiskurse in Asien: China–Japan–Korea* (Discourses of Self-Assertion in Asia: China–Japan–Korea], ed. Iwo Amelung, Matthias Koch, Joachim Kurtz, Eun-Jeung Lee, and Sven Saaler, 127–57 (Munich: Ludicium, 2003).

56. Anezaki, *Shukyogaku Gairon*, 212–13.

57. Zhang Taiyan, *Qiushu Chongdingben* (Book of Urgency [revised edition]), in *Zhang Taiyan Quanji* (Complete Works of Zhang Taiyan), ed. Zhu Weizheng, 20 vols. (Shanghai: Shanghai Renmin Chubanshe, 2014), 3:152.

58. Zhang, *Qiushu Chongdingben*, 3:153.

59. For the charter of the Asiatic Humanitarian Brotherhood, see Zhang Taiyan, 'Yazhou Heqinhui Yuezhang (1907 Nian 4 Yue)' (Charter of the Asiatic Humanitarian Brotherhood [April 1907]), in *Zhang Taiyan Quanji* (Complete Works of Zhang Taiyan), ed. Zhu Weizheng, 20 vols. (Shanghai: Shanghai Renmin Chubanshe, 2014), 18:279–81, tanslated in Yuan P. Cai, 'Zhang Taiyan and the Asiatic Humanitarian Brotherhood, 1907', in *Pan-Asianism: A Documentary History*, ed. Sven Saaler and Christopher W. A. Szpilman, vol.1, 177–84 (Lanham, MD: Rowman & Littlefield, 2011).

60. Cai, 'Zhang Taiyan and the Asiatic Humanitarian Brotherhood, 1907', 180.

61. The identification of the Indians connected to the Asiatic Humanitarian Brotherhood, mentioned by their surnames transcribed into Chinese characters, is difficult. The sources mention (*a*) Baoshi (usually transcribed as 'Baoshen', which, while not entirely incorrect, would be a highly unusual reading for the Chinese character representing the second syllable as frequently used in transcriptions), who has been identified as Surendramohan Bose; (*b*) Mr Dai or Daishi, who seems to be Taraknath Das; and (*c*) Boluohan, who had hitherto never been correctly identified. Based on a report found in the English-language Japanese press, I have found that Boluohan was a certain N. E. Prabhan, on whose biography more research is needed. The report additionally mentions a certain G. N. Potdar, who does not seem to appear in the Chinese sources. See 'Sivaji Anniversary', *Japan Times*, 21 April 1907, 6. On previous scholarship about these Indian men, see Rebecca E. Karl, 'Creating Asia: China in the World at the Beginning of the Twentieth Century', *American Historical Review* 103, no. 4 (1998): 1096–1118, 1111–12, with further references; Murthy, 'Rethinking Pan-Asianism through Zhang Taiyan', 125n13, with further references.

62. Cai, 'Zhang Taiyan and the Asiatic Humanitarian Brotherhood, 1907', 181.

63. The information is from a letter by Yang Wenhui (1837–1911), apud Zhou Zuoren, 'Ji Taiyan Xiansheng Xue Fanwen Shi' (A Note about Mr. Taiyan's Study of Sanskrit), *Yuefeng* 2, no. 1 (1937): 20–21, 21. The teacher's (who is rendered as Mishiluo in Chinese) exact identity has not been ascertained yet.

64. Zhou, 'Ji Taiyan Xiansheng Xue Fanwen Shi', 20–21.

65. Liu Wu-Chi (Liu Wuji), *Su Man-Shu* (New York: Twayne Publishers, 1972), 39.

66. See Ma Yijun, 'Su Manshu Nianpu' (Annalistic Biography of Su Manshu), in *Su Manshu Wenji* (Collected Works of Su Manshu), ed. Ma Yijun and Liu Wuji, vol. 2, 781–825 (Guangzhou: Huacheng chubanshe, 1991), 801.

67. Su Manshu, 'Zhi Liu San Shu (Jiyou Si Yue Riben)' (Letter to Liu San [Japan, Fourth Month of the *Jiyou* Year: 1909]), in *Su Manshu Quanji* (Complete

Works of Su Manshu), ed. Liu Yazi, vol. 1, 221–22 (Beijing: Beijing Shi Zhongguo Shudian, 1985), 221.

68. Liu Yazi, 'Su Manshu zhi Wo Guan' (My Opinion of Su Manshu], in *Su Manshu Yanjiu* (Studies on Su Manshu), ed. Liu Wu-Chi (Liu Wuji), 342–51 (Shanghai: Shanghai Renmin Chubanshe, 1987), 345–46.

69. Jane Qian Liu, 'The Making of Transcultural Lyricism in Su Manshu's Fiction', *Modern Chinese Literature and Culture* 28, no. 2 (2016): 55–64.

70. Liu, 'The Making of Transcultural Lyricism in Su Manshu's Fiction', 62.

71. Su Manshu, 'Yanzikan Suibi' (Notes from the Swallow's Shrine), in *Su Manshu Quanji*, ed. Liu Yazi, 5 vols. (Beijing: Beijing Shi Zhongguo Shudian, 1985), 2:58.

72. Su Manshu, 'Da Madeli Zhuangxiang Chushi Shu (Xinhai Qi Yue Zhuawa)' (Letter Answering Mr. Zhuangxiang from Madrid [Java, Seventh Month of the Xinhai Year: 1911]), in *Su Manshu Quanji*, ed. Liu Yazi, 5 vols. (Beijing: Beijing Shi Zhongguo Shudian, 1985), 1:236.

73. This is a reference to the *Flower Garland Sutra* (*Avatamsaka Sutra*). Su Manshu wrote on several occasions that the only explicit reference to the Mahabharata in Chinese literature was to be found in the *Flower Garland Sutra* (*Taisho Tripitaka*, 278) or in Chengguan's (738–839) *Commentary* and *Sub-Commentary to the Flower Garland Sutra* (*Huayan Jing Shuchao*: *Taisho Tripitaka*, 1735 and *Taisho Tripitaka*, 1736). This assertion is false.

74. Su Manshu, 'Duanhong Lingyan Ji', in *Su Manshu Quanji*, ed. Liu Yazi, 5 vols. (Beijing: Beijing Shi Zhongguo Shudian, 1985), 3:65. The translation is adapted from Su Manshu (the Reverend Mandju), *The Lone Swan*, trans. George Kin Leung (Shanghai: Commercial Press, 1924), 53–54.

75. Natal'ia Vladimirovna Zakharova, 'Literaturnyi Protsess v Kitae v Pervoi Chetverti XX Veka: Evolutsiia Prozaicheskikh Zhanrov' (The Literary Process in China in the First Quarter of the 20th Century: The Evolution of the Prose Genres), PhD thesis, Russian Academy of Sciences, 2021, 189–91.

76. Makiko Mori, 'Unfinished Revolution: A Paradox of Mourning Subjectivity in Su Manshu's *The Lone Swan*', *Frontiers of Literary Studies in China* 9, no. 1 (2015): 104–30, 118–19.

77. Mori, 'Unfinished Revolution', 119.

78. Liu, *Su Man-Shu*, 46–48.

79. For the advertisement, see 'Samskritaprathamamargopadeshika', *Tianyi* 6 (1907), 161; *Minbao* 15. For the three prefaces (by Zhang Taiyan, Liu Shipei, and Su Manshu himself), see He Zhen, 'Fanwen Dian Xu' (Preface to Sanskrit Classics), *Tianyi* 6 (1907), 163–70; Zhang Taiyan, 'Fanwen Dian Xu', *Guocui Xuebao* 4, no. 6 (1908), *wenpian* 9–10; Liu Shipei, 'Fanwen Dian Xu', *Guocui Xuebao* 4, no. 7 (1908), *wenpian* 7–8.

80. Liu, *Su Man-Shu*, 46.

81. Liang Qichao (pseudonym Ren Gong), 'Zhongguoshi Xulun' (Introduction to the History of China), in *Qing Yi Bao* (China Discussion) (reprint), vol. 6, 5621–5629 and 5679–5686. (Beijing: Zhonghua Shuju, 2006), 5623.

82. See Joshua Fogel, 'New Thoughts on an Old Controversy: Shina as a Toponym for China', *Sino-Platonic Papers* 229 (2012): 12–17, with further references. On the usage of the term in medieval China, see also Christoph Kleine, 'Anmerkungen zu Herkunft, Gebrauch und Bedeutung des Toponyms "Shina" 支那 und verwandter Bezeichnungen für China' (Notes on the Origin, Use, and Meaning of the Toponym 'Shina' 支那 and Related Designations for China), *Bochumer Jahrbücher zur Ostasienforschung* 32 (2008), 115–36.

83. For Xuanzang's text, see *Taisho Tripitaka*, 2087:894c26–895a12; a translation and commentary can be found in Kleine, 'Anmerkungen zu Herkunft', 127. For the Tibetan text, see Berthold Laufer, 'The Name China', *T'oung Pao* (Second Series) 13, no. 5 (1912): 719–26, 720–23.

84. Apud Paul Pelliot, *Notes on Marco Polo*, 3 vols. (Paris: Imprimerie Nationale, 1963–73), 1:268.

85. For a detailed account of the contemporary debate, see Paul Pelliot, 'Deux itinéraires de Chine en Inde à la fin du VIIIe siècle' (Two Itineraries of China in India at the End of the 8th Century), *Bulletin de l'École Française d'Extrême-Orient* 4, nos. 1–2 (1904): 131–413, 143–49.

86. Geoff Wade, 'The Polity of Yelang (夜郎) and the Origins of the Name "China"', *Sino-Platonic Papers* 188 (2009): 1–26; cf. Kleine, 'Anmerkungen zu Herkunft', 125–27.

87. This passage is somewhat obscure. Zhang's rendering of the Nagari letters is maladroit and leaves room for various interpretations. To the best of my knowledge, the transcription 'Zhuinijia' is not otherwise attested in Chinese. It could refer to the Sanskrit 'Cinaka', a derivation of 'Cina' attested in the Mahabharata. The term 'Cinaka' has left its traces in other languages (albeit not in Chinese), namely in Khotanese, where the forms 'Činga', 'Cimgga' (Chinese), and 'Caiga' (Chinese) can be found. However, neither Zhang's transcription into Chinese nor his record of the original quite match the Sanskrit form. A modern Bengali form, 'Cainika' (with a short vowel on the second syllable rather than a long *i* as recorded by Zhang) would come much closer to Zhang's text. It is tempting to see in the vowel of the first Chinese syllable, 'zhui' (rather than 'zhi' or 'zhai'), a reflex of the colloquial Bengali pronunciation of the first syllable of 'Cainika' as /tʃoi̯/). *Helidashe* is not otherwise attested in Chinese either; its equivalence with Kalidasa is problematic, in particular because of the mismatch in the first consonant (/kaː /; it is otherwise consistently transcribed with syllables pronounced

as *jia* in modern standard Mandarin). Furthermore, Kalidasa is not usually described as a 'historian', and although the Chinese term *shi* could refer to a court scribe or historian in ancient times, the term *gushi* in Zhang's text would more naturally be understood as an 'ancient work of history' rather than as an 'ancient historian'. For the Khotanese words referring to China, see Pelliot, *Notes on Marco Polo*, 1:272.

88. Zhang Taiyan, 'Yu Ren Lun Zhina De Ming Shu' (Letter to Someone Discussing How China Got Her Name), in *Zhang Taiyan Quanji*, ed. Zhu Weizheng, 20 vols. (Shanghai: Shanghai Renmin Chubanshe, 2014), 15:379.

89. *Taisho Tripitaka*, 2131:3.1098b18.

90. Su Manshu, 'Zhi Liu San Shu (Jiyou Si Yue Riben)' (Letter to Liu San [Japan, Fourth Month of the *Jiyou* Year: 1909]), in *Su Manshu Quanji* (Complete Works of Su Manshu), ed. Liu Yazi, vol. 1, 216–17 (Beijing: Beijing Shi Zhongguo Shudian, 1985).

91. The Nagari added to Zhang's text is close to the word *jnana* (knowledge); but to my knowledge, there is no etymology connecting China to *jnana*. Rather, since the medieval ages China is sometimes said to be etymologically related to *cinta* (thought). Endymion Wilkinson, *Chinese History: A Manual* (revised and enlarged edition) (Cambridge [MA] and London: Harvard University Asia Center, 2000), 753, adopts this view, but drops it in later versions of the manual.

92. Su, 'Zhi Liu San Shu', 1:216–17.

93. Liang Qichao (pseudonym Ren Gong), 'Shaonian Zhongguo Shuo' (Fu Zhongguo Shaonian Lun) (Treatise on Young China [Appendix: On China's Youth]), in *Qing Yi Bao* (China Discussion) (reprint), vol. 3, 2249–56 (Beijing: Zhonghua Shuju, 2006).

94. Lydia H. Liu, *The Clash of Empires: The Invention of China in Modern World Making* (Cambridge [MA] and London: Harvard University Press, 2004), 79.

95. See Fogel, 'New Thoughts on an Old Controversy'.

96. Fogel, 'New Thoughts on an Old Controversy'; Kleine, 'Anmerkungen zu Herkunft'.

97. Kleine, 'Anmerkungen zu Herkunft', 5–6.

98. Gotelind Müller, *China, Kropotkin und der Anarchismus: Eine Kulturbewegung im China des frühen 20: Jahrhunderts unter dem Einfluß des Westens und Japanischer Vorbilder* (China, Kropotkin, and Anarchism: A Cultural Movement in Early 20th Century China under the Influence of the West and Japanese Models) (Wiesbaden: Harrassowitz Verlag, 2001), 146.

99. Cheng Yunjie, 'Sanskrit Class Reveals China's Growing Fever with Indology, Buddhism', *People's Daily Online*, 15 May 2015, http://en.people. cn/n/2015/0515/c90882-8893115.html (accessed on 18 April 2022).

9

The Reception of the Mahabharata in Siam

Evolving Conceptions of Kingship*

David M. Malitz

Introduction

In the Kingdom of Thailand, known as Siam until 1939, the great Sanskrit epic of the Ramayana, or rather the Thai-language Ramakien, composed under King Phra Phutthayotfa Chulalok (King Rama I, 1737–1809, r. 1782–1809), is omnipresent. It is the national epic of the Southeast Asian kingdom, taught not only in schools but encountered also in picture books and manga. The epic is deeply embedded in the kingdom's history and culture of everyday life. King Ramkamhaeng ('Rama, the Bold', r. 1279–98) of Sukhothai, named after the epic's hero, is today remembered in official historiography not simply as a great king but also as a founding figure of the Thai nation as a cultural community through his invention of the Thai script. He is depicted on banknotes, and major public works are named after him, such as a university and a major thoroughfare in Bangkok. And according to a late seventeenth-century chronicle, the former capital was founded in 1350 as Phra Nakhon Si Ayutthaya. Its founder took the title Ramathibodi ('Rama, the Mighty', 1315–69, r. 1351–69) upon ascending to his throne and founded the Phra Ram temple in the capital in 1369, the year of his death.[1]

Ayutthaya was destroyed in 1767 by an invading army from Burma. After a short intermezzo under the charismatic King Taksin (1734–82, r. 1767–82)

* I am indebted to comments from Chris Baker and Maria Packman. Mistakes, if any, remain my own.

ruling from Thonburi, the current capital and dynasty were founded by Taksin's former general, King Phra Phutthayotfa Chulalok. He added Ayutthaya to the city's full name and included Ramathibodi to his full royal title.[2] In addition to having had a new version of the Ramakien written, he also had murals with scenes from the epic added to the Temple of the Emerald Buddha, where the kingdom's palladium of the same name is enshrined. The national dance drama of Khon is also based on the epic and can be found recounted in children's literature today. The epic is furthermore the source of proverbs and placenames far from royal palaces, such as Huai Sukhrip, or Sukhrip's Brook, a stream located near the city of Chonburi, close to Bangkok.

While the Ramayana is clearly deeply embedded in Thai history and culture, the second and older great Sanskrit epic, the Mahabharata, seems almost absent from the Southeast Asian kingdom. Indeed, the oldest extant Thai version is from 1920 and was composed following the introduction of European Indology.[3] This is in stark contrast to Indonesia, where one encounters the Bharatayudha, a Javanese rendering of the Mahabharata, with the story of the battle at Kurukshetra set in Java. The epic is recounted through various media, from Wayang shadow plays to comic books and television series; a 2013 Indonesian-dubbed version of an Indian television adaption of the Mahabharata reached a wide audience.[4] Moreover, the epic often even makes its way into political speeches in Indonesia. At the south-west corner of Jakarta's Independence Square, one can find a monumental statue of Arjuna and Krishna in their chariot – a project initiated and overseen by the long-term strongman Suharto and completed in 1987.[5]

As this chapter will demonstrate, however, the Mahabharata's history in Thailand is at least as old as that of the Ramayana, and for roughly a millennium, the epics were cherished equally. The Mahabharata's main storyline began to lose its appeal only around 1600, when Siamese royal culture began to shift in response to socio-economic changes brought on by the transition from an age of warfare to an age of commerce.

Warfare and an Age of Prominence for the Mahabharata in Siam

By at least the early seventh century, the Mahabharata was well known in continental Southeast Asia. Around this time, according to an inscription, a princess donated the 'Ramayana, the Purana, the whole Bharata' to a sanctuary in Veal Kantel, located on the western bank of the Mekong River in northern Cambodia.[6] From Cambodia, the Mahabharata travelled westward to the area of present-day Thailand. The oldest named cultural community and (likely) political entity on the territory of the Thai kingdom is that of Thawarawadi, from the Sanskrit 'Dvaravati' or 'Dvaraka', which was founded by the Mon people and lasted from the seventh to the eleventh centuries. The name Thawarawadi derives from Krishna's capital in the Mahabharata. Knowledge of the name first came from a Chinese text, but the discovery of coins stamped with 'Thawarawadi' proved that the name was used by rulers themselves.[7] From the ninth century onwards, Khmer-Brahmin political and cultural influence radiated westward, extending over what is today eastern Thailand. A number of sanctuaries dating to this period can still be seen, such as Prasat Phimai in Nakhon Ratchasima and Prasat Phnom Rung in Buriram, as can reliefs showing characters from the Mahabharata, especially Krishna.[8]

From the early thirteenth century onwards, the city of Sukhothai asserted itself in northern central Thailand, pushing back Khmer influence. In official historiography, the early kings of Sukhothai (and especially the aforementioned Ramkamhaeng) are credited with introducing the Thai script used today and emphasizing Theravada Buddhism through royal patronage. Brahmanism and Buddhism were not seen as separate religions; rather, Brahmin gods were integrated into the Buddhist cosmos.[9]

The Mahabharata remained widely known during what is officially regarded as the first political incarnation of the Thai nation. Inscription no. 45, discovered at Wat Mahathat in Sukhothai in 1956, commemorates the 1393 alliance between Sukhothai and the northern city of Nan. What remains readable of the inscription includes an elaborate oath invoking the Pandava brothers, namely Bhima, Arjuna, and Yudhishthira, notably doing so before referring to Rama.[10]

Roughly a century later, at the end of the fifteenth century, the epic poem 'Lilit Yuan Phai' (The Defeat of Lanna) was composed. It is a eulogy of King Boromma Trailokanat of Ayutthaya (r. 1448–88), centred on a battle in 1474–75 with his cousin Prince Yudhishthira of Sukhothai, who was named after the oldest of the Pandava brothers. According to the *Chiang Mai Chronicle*, the king of Ayutthaya had not honoured his promise to make his cousin vice-king and let him rule over half the realm after the king's ascension to the throne.[11] Thus, the conflict, just as the one decided at Kurukshetra, was a war of succession. Older histories of Thailand have detailed the absorption of Sukhothai and its realm through conquest into the rising empire of Ayutthaya, located further south at the Chao Phraya River, during the early fifteenth century. More recent scholarship, however, writes of a long, winding process of political and cultural merging of the two royal capitals through marriage ties. Regardless, clearly Ayutthaya had become the dominant city by the early fifteenth century.[12]

The eulogy of the victorious King Boromma Trailokanat likens the ruler of Ayutthaya to many of the heroic characters of the Mahabharata, demonstrating the epic's cultural influence in Siam at the time. The king's 'might is like the Pandava whose fame made Kaurava shake fever-like with fear'. He is described as 'open-hearted like Lord Karna'. The king's actions are 'on par with Bhishma's feats'. As a fighter, he is 'like Bhima [is] outstanding with a club', and as a general, 'in strategy and tactics, [he is] bold and strong, he outperforms Arjuna, gem of yore'. 'On strategy' he even 'rivals lordly Krishna', and 'like Krishna', he 'thwarts them [his enemies], every evil one like Krishna crushing Duryodhana's troops'.[13] While the king is thus compared to heroes from both sides of the conflict, he could, of course, not be likened to the oldest of the Pandava brothers, for his opponent bore his name. The poem's author thus compared the ruler to Yudhishthira's father: '[T]he king upholds the teachings like Lord Yama.'[14] That Rama, the 'Ravanna-killer', in contrast, is only mentioned once in the eulogy of the king of Ayutthaya is at first surprising. However, according to the aristocrat and historian Prince Dhani Nivat (1885–1974), the former 'capital was given the full name of Thawarawadi (Dvaravati) Sri Ayudhya from the time of its foundation', thus combining the names of the capitals of the kings Krishna from the Mahabharata and Rama from the Ramayana, pointing to the equal importance of both epics at the time.[15]

The Fading of the Mahabharata in Late Ayutthaya

There are two further famous eulogies of Ayutthayan kings. The first was written for King Prasat Thong, who reigned from 1629 to 1656, approximately a century and a half after King Boromma Trailokanat.[16] The second is the eulogy of his son, King Narai, who reigned from 1656 to 1688.[17] Strikingly, both eulogies omit references to the Mahabharata and its heroes. This does not mean, however, that Brahmanism was replaced entirely, nor was the epic's whole cast forgotten. In the eulogy of King Prasat Thong, Rama is still mentioned twice, and King Narai's name is derived from the Sanskrit 'Narayana', one of the names of the god Vishnu, because it was said that he appeared to have four arms at birth.

This declining presence of the Mahabharata in Ayutthaya must be understood against the far-reaching socio-economic transformation taking place at that time. The year 1600 has been identified as a threshold between an 'age of warfare' and an 'age of commerce' in the history of Ayutthaya.[18] From the late 1300s to approximately 1600, Ayutthayan kings had expanded their influence over much of mainland Southeast Asia, bringing them into conflict with the rulers of Bago in Burma, who brought Ayutthaya under their sway from 1564 to 1584.

After the turn of the seventeenth century, large-scale warfare in mainland Southeast Asia abated. The construction of fortifications by rulers, as well as large-scale resistance against conscription, made the raising of large armies more difficult and the success of sieges less likely. Meanwhile, in East Asia, the Japanese invasion of Korea ceased, and the Ming court lifted a previous ban on private trade.[19] The beginning of the seventeenth century also saw the unification of the Japanese islands under the Tokugawa shoguns, who issued licenses to rekindle but also control the profitable trade with Southeast Asia.[20]

Located at the crossroads of the trade routes connecting South, East, and Southeast Asia, Ayutthaya was perfectly placed to benefit from these developments as a regional entrepot. Its location, upstream at a considerable distance from the coast, meanwhile protected the city from conquest by the European interlopers.[21] The Portuguese had traded with Siam since their conquest of Malacca in 1511; in the early seventeenth century, the Dutch and the English followed suit.[22] The kings of Ayutthaya carved out for themselves a major share of the profits derived from these developments through royal monopolies and personal trade.[23]

During the first span of Ayutthaya's history, martial prowess and victory on the battlefield, as demonstrated by the heroes of the Mahabharata, proved the merit of kings. Martial skills were also the 'most important way to rise in wealth and status' for all members of Ayutthayan society – from common foot soldiers all the way up to kings. The resulting culture of a 'warrior court' is expressed in the eulogy of Yuan Phai and in royal ceremonies; in the early sixteenth century, it was also found in the Thai version of the story of Aniruddha discussed in the following section.[24]

During this period of peace, the centring of the court's economic relations on overseas trade made access to trade opportunities through royal patronage, rather than the demonstration of martial skills, the premier pathway to status and wealth. Within this new social and economic context, court culture changed. Kings attempted to centralize power to control the flourishing overseas commerce by elevating and mystifying the monarch through court ceremonies and by hiding the royal body from the people. Their ability to do so, however, depended directly on their capacity to generate revenue through said trade.[25]

The band of Pandava brothers as warrior princes visible to their supporters and foes on the battlefield thus ceased to offer role models in this new era.

Moreover, one must also remember that the Kurukshetra War was caused by a succession struggle caused by King Dhritarashtra's ambition and his commitment to his oldest son, which prevented him from acting according to his conscience. At a time when successions in Ayutthaya were becoming increasingly contested and bloody – royal patronage having become the primary conduit to economic and political success – the dominant storyline of the Mahabharata might also have become an uncomfortable one.[26] The Ramayana/Ramakien, with its focus on the one legitimate and righteous king and his loyal servants, did not pose these issues.

The Story of Anirut (Aniruddha) and the Buddhification of Legitimate Kingship

While the story of the Kurukshetra War then vanished from Thai cultural history until its rediscovery in the early twentieth century, characters related to the epic remained popular. This was in particular the case for Krishna's grandson, Aniruddha (Anirut), whose exploits are recounted in the *Harivamsa* (The Genealogy of Hari), which can be considered an appendix to the Mahabharata. The story of his defeat of the Asura king Banasura and his romance with the king's daughter, Usa, has seen several recountings in Thai literature.[27]

Of the Thai texts, the three best-known shall be discussed here.[28] The *Anirut Kham Chan* (The Epic Poem of Anirut [Aniruddha]) has been dated to the early sixteenth century and was therefore written around the time of Yuan Phai. It is based on the Sanskrit *Harivamsa*.[29] The second text, the *Narai Sip Pang* (Ten Incarnations of Vishnu), is difficult to date. Prince Dhani Nivat was of the opinion that the text must have been well known in the early Bangkok period, but it could not have been much older due to its prose style.[30] That it was considered important is evidenced by King Chulalongkorn (1853–1910, r. 1868–1910) having had poems about the 10 incarnations inscribed in the Temple of the Emerald Buddha.[31] The text includes Krishna as Vishnu's eighth incarnation; yet the incarnation's description is essentially the story of Aniruddha.[32] The stories of Krishna as a boy or as a cowherd are not included. This is in line with the incorporation of Brahmin deities into the Buddhist cosmos, where they come into existence without having parents and without experiencing childhood.[33] The omission clearly also served to elevate and mystify monarchs compared with Brahmin deities.

The third version of the story is the *Bot Lakhon Rueang Unarut* (The Drama of Unarut [Aniruddha]), wherein the hero changes his name. King Rama I himself, who also oversaw the re-editing of the Ramakien, directed the writing of this new version – clear evidence of the importance of the story. There are other versions as well, which recount the story of Aniruddha, similar to a Jataka (stories about the past lives of the Buddha) or as local history.[34]

The *Bot Lakhon Rueang Unarut* differs considerably from the older *Anirut Kham Chan*. For one, it is much longer, as scenes were added to the main storyline. However, there are also differences in content between the two epic poems, signifying a further shift in the conceptualization of kingship. As an overseas trade-focused, proto-capitalist economy developed in the late Ayutthaya period, a more rational and philosophical Buddhism emerged, which began to de-emphasize Brahmanism.[35]

The trend towards a Buddhification of kingship intensified during the reign of King Rama I. The identification of the king with Brahmin deities was de-emphasized, while the king continued to claim to be a Bodhisattva.[36] Accordingly, while Anirut is described in keeping with the Indian source as akin to a god, Unarut is a human hero.[37] As it is the case with the Ramakien, the last stanza of the *Bot Lakhon Rueang Unarut* pointed out that the text was written 'in accordance with an old tale', was of no 'abiding importance', and simply served to glorify the capital and offer enjoyment to its people.[38]

Differences between the works also demonstrate a change in values corresponding with the evolving conceptualization of legitimate kingship. This is discernible in the story's key scene, where Anirut/Unarut is spirited away to meet and fall in love with King Banasura's daughter, Usa. In the older *Anirut Kham Chan*, composed around the time of Lilit Yuan Phai, this occurs after a hunting excursion to the forest. In King Rama I's *Bot Lakhon Rueang Unarut*, Anirut/Unarut is lured away from his entourage, which had included his wife, who had come to the forest to enjoy its beauty, by a golden deer. The similarity to the story of the Ramayana is made explicit by the hero himself, but his wife asks him to catch the animal nevertheless.[39] The demonstration of martial prowess through a great slaughter of animals, from snakes and porcupines to tigers and elephants, which is described in great detail and length in the older text, is omitted in the newer one.[40] In this later version, Krishna fights and vanquishes a giant who had attempted to kill the avatar of Vishnu to capture his wife.[41] King Rama ends the poem with Unarut, having vanquished the Asura king and being crowned a king himself, corralling elephants and capturing a white one – the white elephant being an explicit reference to the status of a *chakravartin*, or universal and ideal emperor.[42]

For the warrior kings of early Ayutthaya, hunting offered a pastime through which they could demonstrate their prowess on the battlefield, just as Anirut does in the older poem. However, with the shift towards Buddhist kingship, killing animals for leisure came to be seen as inappropriate for kings. King Narai was said to have gone hunting frequently, according to King Louis XIV's ambassador to his court.[43] His eulogy, however, refers only to the corralling of elephants, a favourite pastime of the monarch; the text allots considerable space to the practice, as it does in the *Bot Lakhon Rueang Unarut*, related as it is to *chakravartin*-ship and thus to righteous Buddhist kingship.[44] The changing perception of hunting is also evident from the chronicles compiled after the destruction of Ayutthaya, which attributed the capital's fall to the moral failings of its last kings.[45] The royal chronicles use the hunting and fishing expeditions of the late Ayutthayan kings more than once to exemplify the sinfulness of the royals.[46] Righteous kings like King Narai in contrast only corral elephants, especially white ones.[47] This shift is also evident in the description of King Suriyenthrathibodi (1661–1709, r. 1703–09), who was known as the Tiger King (Phrachao Suea) for his violent and sinful nature. The chronicles include an episode in which the monarch competes incognito in boxing competitions. His victories are not attributed to skill, however, as they had been in the eulogy of King Boromma Trailokanat, who was compared to characters in the Mahabharata, but rather to his storage of merit acquired in previous lifetimes.[48]

When visiting England, King Rama I's great-grandson, King Chulalongkorn, wrote a letter in which he discussed the hunting of rabbits, a demerit, the meat of which was then donated to a hospital as an act of charity. For the king, this was like 'donating unwanted things to a temple'.[49] In 1931, newspapers falsely reported, however, that his son, King Prajadhipok, or Rama VII, had gone fishing while visiting Japan. This prompted a lay Buddhist reformer to send letters to the supreme patriarch and all members of the Buddhist council of elders, criticizing this as unbecoming of a Buddhist king.[50]

Reminiscences of the Mahabharata in the Built Environment of Bangkok

That not all elements of the Mahabharata disappeared from Siamese cultural memory is also visible in Bangkok's built environment. King Nangklao (Rama III, 1788–1851, r. 1824–51), King Rama I's grandson, had the Phra Chetuphon monastery near the Grand Palace extensively restored, incorporating significant inscriptions.[51] These included sculptures demonstrating yogic postures with some of the depicted ascetics named after characters from the Mahabharata, as well as an inscription of the *Kritsana Son Nong* (Krishna [Draupadi] Teaches Her Younger Sister), an instruction manual for women, composed by the prince-patriarch Paramanuchitchinorot (1790–1853), the king's uncle, based on a dialogue between Draupadi and Satyabhama in the Mahabharata.[52]

The Rediscovery of the Mahabharata: European Indology and Siamese Royal Nationalism

The Kingdom of Siam was never formally colonized in the nineteenth or the early twentieth century. Yet its kings had to sign unequal treaties that limited their sovereignty and were forced to make territorial concessions. The resulting integration into capitalist modernity necessitated ideological and intellectual changes to reconcile Buddhism and its legitimization of the social hierarchy of the kingdom with the modern sciences and institutions that were being adopted from the West. Through their interactions with European visitors as well as their own sojourns in Europe, and particularly in Britain, Siamese royalty became acquainted with modern Indology during this time period, most evident in their relationship with Friedrich Max Müller at the University of Oxford.[53] King Chulalongkorn himself sponsored the translation and publication of important texts of the Theravada tradition in the German scholar's series of the *Sacred Books of the Buddhists*.[54] Crown Prince Vajiravudh (1881–1925, r. 1910–25), who studied at Oxford, attended the German scholar's funeral in 1900 and supported his memorial.[55]

Closely related to these processes and exchanges was the differentiation of Buddhism and Brahmanism as distinct religions.[56] Domestically, this allowed for the understanding of Buddhism as the basis of a paternal monarchy, whereas practices such as slavery and despotic kingship, criticized by European observers, were explained away as Khmer-Brahmin, and thus foreign, influences.[57] The monarchy could then be constructed as the cultural and political centre of the nation, and a royal nationalism was developed around it.[58] This did not mean, however, that the heritage of Sanskrit literature was forgotten and disowned.

Early in his reign, King Vajiravudh was confronted with an attempted coup d'état to overthrow the absolute monarchy. In response, he promoted an official nationalism centred on the monarchy. For this, he could draw on his earlier attempts to promote national pride through history and literature among the Siamese. In a travelogue to historic sites in northern Siam from 1908, he famously pointed out that 'our Thai nation is not a new nation. And it is not one of a jungle people, or as it is said in English an "uncivilized" one.'[59] Literature, in particular, was central to the king's understanding of what it meant to be a cultured and civilized nation. Consequently, the corpus of works derived from Sanskrit literature was embraced as a national cultural heritage of the Siamese. The king's knowledge of the European scholarly interest in Sanskrit texts, including the Mahabharata, might have very well contributed to this development, as did the fact that these texts were centred on royalty. It was also at this junction, in 1916, that Rama was introduced as a dynastic name by King Vajiravudh.[60]

The king's interest in literature was not limited to the preservation of extant works. He also advocated for the composition of new works based on the South Asian and Siamese classics to promote pride in one's nation and its traditions.[61] This point was made by King Vajiravudh explicitly in his introduction to *Phra Non Kham Luang*, his Thai-language poetic retelling of the story of King Nala from the Mahabharata.[62] The flipside to the royal promotion of culturally appropriate literary forms was the criticism of the 'imitationists' for mindlessly copying European pulp literature for newspapers and magazines, which the king famously expressed in an essay published in 1915 under a thinly veiled pen name. For him, a slippery slope led from the adoption of inappropriate literary styles to revolutionary thought and action.[63]

The royal wish was heeded. The aforementioned Prince Dhani Nivat penned his own version of a story about King Nala.[64] The first Thai abbreviated version of the Mahabharata was then published in 1920 by the minor noble and editor of the first Sanskrit–Thai–English dictionary, Luang Bowonbannarak. It was based on a version by Thakur Rajendra Singh, but written with knowledge of the two existing English translations of the time.[65]

Having embraced the modern notion of Buddhism and Brahmanism as distinct religions and having realized that the Thai stories of the ten incarnations of Vishnu were at odds with the Sanskrit ones discussed by Indologists, and not finding an explanation for these differences, King Vajiravudh composed his own version of the text in 1922.[66] The monarch later also produced an academic work about other Brahmin deities.[67]

Strikingly, when the king justified his decision to declare war on the Central Powers in the First World War, the Mahabharata was not invoked as a text providing moral guidance. Rather, with *Thamma Thamma Songkhram* officially translated as 'The War between Right and Might', King Vajiravudh published a poem based on the 'Dhamma Jataka' (no. 457).[68] Likewise, when Siam's supreme patriarch argued that Buddhism was not a pacifist religion and the Siamese could therefore be conscripted into a modern army for the purpose of national defence, he reasoned only on the basis of Buddhist scripture.[69]

King Vajiravudh was succeeded by his brother, King Prajadhipok (1893–1941, r. 1925–35). While likewise educated in Britain, King Prajadhipok did not share his brother's enthusiasm for Indology or literature. Unlike his brother, he did not pen episodes of the Ramakien, and he let lapse the patronage for dance troupes performing the epic. He also rejected the name of 'Rama' for himself. Instead, he concentrated on the administration of the realm, the finances of which had been exhausted by his predecessor's prolific spending.[70]

Against this background, the newly translated Mahabharata never regained the appeal that it once held hundreds of years before, and the epic, as well as related texts, while not forgotten, were largely relegated to the scholarly realm.

Conclusion

In contrast to the national epic of the Ramakien – the Thai version of the Ramayana – the Mahabharata is much less visible in Siam, or Thailand. As this chapter has shown, this has not always been the case. From the early history of the current Kingdom of Thailand to at least the sixteenth century, the Mahabharata was awarded equal importance as the Ramayana. These were the times of warrior kings vying for dominance in the territory of present-day Thailand. Historical evidence such as the coins of Thawarawadi, inscription no. 45 in Sukhothai, or the epic poem 'Lilit Yuan Phai' shows that the heroes of the Kurukshetra War were well known, cherished, and embraced as princely role models during that time period. This changed around the year 1600, when the age of commerce began in Ayutthaya. Kings transformed from commanders-in-chief to chief traders, resulting in a significant change in court culture and in the conceptualization of kingship. The heroes of the Mahabharata lost their appeal, and the epic's main storyline seemingly disappeared from the cultural memory. This was not the case, however, for other characters of the Mahabharata, especially Aniruddha, known as Anirut and later Unarut in Thai. But against the backdrop of a cultural change emphasizing Buddhism and its values, the hero had to change as well, as seen in the Bot Lakhon Rueang Unarut, written during the reign of King Rama I.

In the late nineteenth and early twentieth centuries, European Indology was embraced as a new source of knowledge, and Brahmanism was understood as distinct from Buddhism. This led in the reign of King Vajiravudh to the embracing of Thai-language works based on Sanskrit literature as Siamese classics and as models for the composition of literary works to demonstrate the nation's high culture. Against this backdrop, for the first time, a Thai translation of the Mahabharata was published, which, however, failed to gain mass appeal.

Notes

1.   *Luang Prasoet Chronicle of Ayutthaya, Phraratcha Phongsawadan Krung Kao Chabap Luang Prasoet Akson Niti* (Bangkok: Cremation Volume for Mr. Nat Krataithong, Chapanasathan Khuru Sapha, Wat Sake, 1971), 3.

2.   Chris Baker and Pasuk Phongpaichit, *History of Ayutthaya: Siam in the Early Modern World* (Chiang Mai: Silkworm Books, 2017), 268.

3.   This publication is Luang Bowonbannarak (Niyom Rakthai), *Mahabharata Yut Khong Rajendra Singh* (Bangkok: Rongphim Thai, 1920).

4.   Pallavi Aiyar, 'Love of God: Indonesia Falls for an Indian Television Remake of the Mahabharata', *The Caravan*, 1 December 2014, https://caravanmagazine. in/lede/love-god (accessed on 6 November 2022).

5.   Detha Arya Tifada, 'Suharto Builds Arjuna Wijaya's "Horse" Statue', *VOI*, 2 December 2021, https://voi.id/en/memori/110172/suharto-builds-arjuna-wijayas-horse-statue (accessed on 6 November 2022).

6.   Jean Filliozat, 'The Rāmāyana in South-East Asian Sanskrit Epigraphy and Iconography', in *Asian Variations in Ramayana*, ed. K. R. Iyengar, 192–205 (Madras: Sahitya Akademi, 1963), 194; Auguste Barth, *Inscriptions Sanscrites du Cambodge* (Paris: Imprimerie Nationale, 1885), 28–31.

7.   Jan Jetso Boeles, 'The King of Sri Dvaravati and His Regalia', *Journal of the Siam Society* 52, no. 1 (1964): 99–114, 100.

8.   Vittorio Roveda, *Images of the Gods: Khmer Mythology in Cambodia, Laos & Thailand* (Bangkok: River Books, 2005), 61, 79–80, 89, 91, 99, 104, 111.

9.   Baker and Phongpaichit, *History of Ayutthaya*, 19.

10. Alexander B. Griswold and Prasert na Nagara, 'The Pact between Sukhodaya and Nan: Epigraphic and Historical Studies, No. 3', *Journal of the Siam Society* 57, no. 1 (1969): 57–107, 67, 78, 87.

11. Chris Baker and Pasuk Phongpaichit, *Yuan Phai: The Defeat of Lanna, A Fifteenth-Century Thai Epic Poem* (Chiang Mai: Silkworm Books, 2017), 1, 2, 34.

12. Baker and Phongpaichit, *History of Ayutthaya*, 59–64.

13. Baker and Phongpaichit, *Yuan Phai*, 27–29, 40–42.

14. Baker and Phongpaichit, *Yuan Phai*, 28.

15. Prince Dhani Nivat, 'The City of Thawarawadi Sri Ayudhya', *Journal of the Siam Society* 31, no. 2 (1939): 147–53, 151.

16. Chris Baker and Pasuk Phongpaichit, 'The Eulogy of King Prasat Thong', *Journal of the Siam Society* 108, no. 2 (2020): 167–212.

17. Dhiravat na Pombejra, 'The Eulogy of King Narai', *Journal of the Siam Society* 107, no. 2 (2019): 1–16.

18. Baker and Phongpaichit, *History of Ayutthaya*, 85, 119, 171.

19. Baker and Phongpaichit, *History of Thailand*, 11–13, 120.

20. Arano Yasunori, *'Sakoku' wo Minaosu* (Tokyo: Iwanami, 2019), 146–70.

21. Kennon Breazeale, 'Thai Maritime Trade and the Ministry Responsible', in *From Japan to Arabia: Ayutthaya's Maritime Relations with Asia*, ed. K. Breazeale, 1–52 (Bangkok: Foundation for the Promotion of Social Sciences and Humanities Textbook Project, 1999), 1–4; Sarasin Viraphol, *Tribute and Profit: Sino-Siamese Trade, 1652–1853* (Chiang Mai: Silkworm Books, 2014), 7–22.

22. Bhawan Ruangsilp, *Dutch East India Company Merchants at the Court of Ayutthaya: Dutch Perceptions of the Thai Kingdom, Ca. 16041–765* (Leiden: Brill, 2007), 19–25; Baker and Phongpaichit, *History of Ayutthaya*, 92, 121.

23. Baker and Phongpaichit, *History of Ayutthaya*, 139–140; Dhiravat na Pombejra, 'Crown Trade and Court Politics in Ayutthaya during the Reign of King Narai (1656–88)', in *The Southeast Asian Port and Polity: Rise and Demise*, ed. J. Kathirithamby-Wells and J. Villiers, 126–42 (Singapore: Singapore University Press, 1990), 130–31.

24. Baker and Phongpaichit, *History of Ayutthaya*, 99.

25. Baker and Phongpaichit, *History of Ayutthaya*, 119; Jeyamalar Kathirithamby-Wells, 'Introduction: An Overview', in *The Southeast Asian Port and Polity: Rise and Demise*, ed. J. Kathirithamby-Wells and J. Villiers, 1–16 (Singapore: Singapore University Press, 1990), 4–5.

26. Baker and Phongpaichit, *History of Ayutthaya*, 158.

27. Cholada Ruengruglikit, 'Wannakhadi Thai Rueang Anirut: Kan Sueksa Wikhro', PhD thesis, Chulalongkorn University, Bangkok, 1992; Maneepin Phromsuthirak, 'Hindu Myths in Thai Literature with Special Reference to the Nārāi Sip Pāng', PhD thesis, School of Oriental and African Studies, University of London, 1980; Maneepin Phromsuthirak, 'Thai Interpolations in the Story of Aniruddha', *Journal of the Siam Society* 67, no. 1 (1979): 46–53.

28. Phromsuthirak, 'Hindu Myths in Thai Literature', 181, 198, 213.

29. Phromsuthirak, 'Thai Interpolations in the Story of Aniruddha', 46.

30. Prince Dhani Nivat, 'Narai Sibpang the "Ten Incarnations of Narayana"', *Journal of the Siam Society* 55, no. 2 (1967): 305–07.

31. Phromsuthirak, 'Hindu Myths in Thai Literature', 31.

32. *Narai Sip Pang: Chabap Rongphim Luang* (Thonburi: Cremation Volume for Mr. Kim Kaeosamao, Wat Rangbua, 1935), 43–48.

33. Phromsuthirak, 'Hindu Myths in Thai Literature', 182, 212.

34. Cholada, 'Wannakhadi Thai Rueang Anirut', 19.

35. Baker and Phongpaichit, *History of Ayutthaya*, 246–48.

36. Baker and Phongpaichit, *History of Thailand* (Cambridge, UK: University of Cambridge, 2014), 30; Peter Skilling, 'King Rāma I and Wat Phra Chetuphon: The Buddha-Śāsanā in Early Bangkok', in *How Theravāda Is Theravāda? Exploring Buddhist Identities*, ed. Peter Skilling, Jason A. Carbine, Claudio Cicuzza, and Santi Pakdeekham, 2973–54 (Chiang Mai: Silkworm Books, 2012), 300–01, 329.

37. Cholada, 'Wannakhadi Thai Rueang Anirut', 19.

38. King Rama I, Phra Phutthayotfa Chulalok, *Bot Lakhon Rueang Unarut* (Thonburi: Cremation Volume for Mr. Suwan Wichaidit, Wat Makutkasatriyaram, 1971), 490; Frank E. Reynolds, 'Ramayana, Rama Jataka, and Ramakien: A Comparative Study of Hindu and Buddhist Traditions', in *Many Ramayanas: The Diversity of a Narrative Tradition in South Asia*, ed. Paula Richman, 50–59 (Berkeley, CA: University of California Press, 1991), 505–09.

39. King Rama I, Phra Phutthayotfa Chulalok, *Bot Lakhon Rueang Unarut*, 157–68.

40. Krom Sinlapakon, *Tonchabap Chak Nangsue Anirut Kham Chan, Phrom Duai Banthuek Sop Than Lae Maihet* (Bangkok: Krom Sinlapakon, 1980), 19–25. Klaus Rosenberg, *Die Epischen Chan-Dichtungen in der Literatur Thailands mit einer vollständigen Übersetzung des Anirut Kham Chan* (Hamburg: Gesellschaft für Natur- und Völkerkunde Ostasiens, 1976), 346–50.

41. King Rama I, Phra Phutthayotfa Chulalok, *Bot Lakhon Rueang Unarut*, 22–34.

42. King Rama I, Phra Phutthayotfa Chulalok, *Bot Lakhon Rueang Unarut*, 489–90.

43. Simon de la Loubère, *Du Royaume de Siam, Tome Premier* (Amsterdam: Abraham Wolfgang, 1691), 9.

44. Pombejra, 'The Eulogy of King Narai', 11–13.

45. Nidhi Eoseewong, *Prawatisat Rattanakosin Nai Phraratcha Phongsawadan Ayutthaya* (Bangkok: Matichon, 1980).

46. Richard D. Cushman, *The Royal Chronicles of Ayutthaya: A Synoptic Translation*, ed. D. K. Wyatt (Bangkok: Siam Society, 2000), 373, 384, 392, 399, 405.

47. Richard D. Cushman, *The Royal Chronicles of Ayutthaya*, 246, 290, 324–25, 341–42, 355–58, 369, 423, 425–26, 430–31, 436–37, 443, 436, 453–57.
48. Cushman, *The Royal Chronicles of Ayutthaya*, 385–86.
49. King Chulalongkorn, *Far from Home*, ed. Ampha Otrakul, Pensiri Vongvipanond, Varunee Padmasankh, Sirivan Churakorn, and Sujinda Siriswatwattana (Bangkok: Chulalongkorn University, European Studies Programme, 1997), 126.
50. Peter Koret, *The Man Who Accused the King of Killing a Fish: The Biography of Narin Phasit of Siam (18741–950)* (Chiang Mai: Silkworm Books, 2012), 228–29.
51. Prince Dhani Nivat, 'The Inscriptions of Wat Phra Jetubon', *Journal of the Siam Society* 26, no. 2 (1933): 143–170, 146.
52. Amara Srisuchat, 'Mahabharata in Art and Literature in Thailand', *Indian Literature* 49, no. 1 (2005): 105–114, 110–11, 113.
53. Friedrich Max Müller, 'The King of Siam as a Patron of Buddhist Literature', *The Times*, 28 November 1893, 3.
54. The 'patronage of His Majesty the King of Siam' is, for example, mentioned in Thomas W. Rhys Davids (ed.), *Sacred Books of the Buddhists*, vol. 4: *Dialogues of the Buddha, Part III* (Oxford: Oxford University Press, 1921).
55. *The Times*, 'Funeral of Professor Max Müller', 2 November 1900, 9; *The Times*, 'Max Müller Memorial', 2 November 1900, 7.
56. For a history of comparative religion in Siam, see Thongchai Winichakul, 'Buddhist Apologetics and a Genealogy of Comparative Religion in Siam', *Numen* 62, no. 1 (2015): 76–99. In his work on the annual royal ceremonies, King Chulalongkorn explicitly differentiates between Buddhist and Brahmin ceremonies. See King Chulalongkorn, *Phraratchaphithi Sip Song Duean* (Bangkok: Cremation Volume for General Prince of Chanthaburi Suranath, Prince Nakkhatra Mangala Kitiyakara Wat Benjamaborphit, 1953).
57. See Prince Damrong Rajanubhab, *Laksana Kan Pokkhrong Prathet Sayam Tae Boran* (Bangkok: Rongphim Mahatthai, 1959), 5–9.
58. Eiji Murashima, 'The Origin of Modern Official State Ideology in Thailand', *Journal of Southeast Asian Studies* 19, no. 1 (1988): 80–96. Such 'royal nationalism' was of course not a unique feature of modern Thailand. See Milinda Banerjee, 'The Royal Nation and Global Intellectual History: Monarchic Routes to Conceptualizing National Unity', in *Transnational Histories of the 'Royal Nation'*, ed. Milinda Banerjee, Charlotte Backerra, Cathleen Sarti, 21–43 (Cham: Palgrave Macmillan, 2017).
59. King Vajiravudh, *Rueang Thiao Mueang Phraruang* (Bangkok: Bamrung Nukunkit, 1908), 3.

60. Walter F. Vella, *Chaiyo! King Vajiravudh and the Development of Thai Nationalism* (Honolulu, HI: University of Hawaii Press, 1978), 143.
61. Vella, *Chaiyo! King Vajiravudh*, 186–87, 212, 246–54.
62. King Vajiravudh, *Phra Non Khamluang* (Bangkok: Rongphim Thai, 1916).
63. Asvabahu, 'The Cult of Imitation', *Siam Observer*, 3 April 1915, 4–5. Similarly, see Maecenas, 'Siamese Literature: Necessity for a Complete Catalogue', *Siam Observer*, 11 June 1914, 5–7. See also Vella, *Chaiyo! King Vajiravudh*, 5.
64. Srisuchat, 'Mahabharata in Art and Literature in Thailand', 114.
65. Bowonbannarak, *Mahapharata Yut Khong Rajendra Singh*, 8–12.
66. King Vajiravudh, 'Introduction', in *Lilit Narai Sip Pang* (Bangkok: Cremation Volume for Princess Indrasakdi Sachi, Wat Thepsirintrawat Ratchaworawihan, 1976).
67. King Vajiravudh, *Phrapenchao Khong Phram* (Bangkok: Cremation Volume for Mrs. Supha Sirikanchon, Wat Thepsirintrawat Ratchaworawihan, 1960).
68. King Vajiravudh, *Thamma Thamma Songkhram: Tam Khaorueang Nai Thamma Chadok Ekathotnibat* (Bangkok: Rongphim Thai, 1920).
69. Prince Wachirayanawarōrot, *The Buddhist Attitude towards National Defense and Administration: A Special Allocution by His Holiness Prince Vajirañāna, Surpreme Patriarch of the Kingdom of Siam* (Bangkok: n.p., 1916). See also Vella, *Chaiyo! King Vajiravudh*, 231–37.
70. Benjamin A. Batson, *Siam's Political Future: Documents from the End of the Absolute Monarchy* (Ithaca, NY: Southeast Asia Program, Department of Asian Studies, Cornell Universty), 2–3; Vella, *Chaiyo! King Vajiravudh*, 246.

10

Understanding Global Intellectual Exchanges through Paratexts

Wadiʿ al-Bustani's Introduction to His Arabic Translation of the Mahabharata*

Christopher D. Bahl and Abdallah Soufan

Introduction

In 1953, the Arabic litterateur Wadiʿ al-Bustani received the Golden Medal of Merit for his Arabic versification of the Indian Mahabharata in the United Nations Educational, Scientific, and Cultural Organization (UNESCO) building in central Beirut.[1] Camille Chamoun, then president of Lebanon, awarded the honour to this member of the famous literary and scholarly al-Bustani family. Wadiʿ's life encapsulates the high degree of global mobility of intellectuals in the first half of the twentieth century. His hometown, Dibbieh, now lay in the newly independent state of Lebanon.[2] He was born in 1888 in what was then still the Ottoman Empire, studied at the prestigious Syrian Protestant College (later the American University of Beirut), worked as an interpreter at the British Consulate of Hodeida in Yemen in 1909, translated

* After a request from Milinda Banerjee to contribute a chapter on the Mahabharata in Arabic intellectual histories to this volume, the idea for the chapter formed in 2019 during a research associateship at the Orient-Institut Beirut (OIB), Lebanon, where Christopher Bahl discovered a copy of Wadiʿ al-Bustani's edition of the Arabic translation of the Mahabharata in the institute's library. Abdallah Soufan, also a research associate at the OIB at the time, joined the project shortly afterwards. Due to the Covid-19 pandemic, economic crisis, and political instability in Lebanon, much of the intended archival research in Beirut could not be carried out, unfortunately. We would like to thank Banerjee for his valuable input and the three reviewers for their comments and suggestions. We hope that this chapter offers some additional ideas for further research which can complement Esmat Elhalaby's in-depth study of Wadiʿ al-Bustani and his work (Esmat Elhalaby, 'Empire and Arab Indology', *Modern Intellectual History* 19, no. 4 [2022]: 1081–1105).

Umar al-Khayyam's Persian poems into Arabic in London in 1911, and set sail
to India in 1912 to dedicate himself to Indian literary works. While in India, he
met Rabindranath Tagore. The following years brought him to Johannesburg
in South Africa and through political appointments to Cairo and the British
mandate in Palestine. He became a vocal critic of Zionist politics and a founding
member of several Muslim–Christian societies, taking part in the countrywide
general strike of 1936. Later in life, he turned away from politics and dedicated
most of his time to versifying Arabic translations of Indian literary works.
In 1953, he finally returned to Lebanon, where he died in 1954.

While scholarship has shed light on translation movements from Sanskrit
into Arabic during the early Abbasid period (eighth–tenth centuries), such
as the Arabic 'telling' of *Kalila wa-Dimna*,[3] there is a huge gap in academic
research in terms of studying such translation itineraries between the Arabic
and the Indian literary-intellectual spheres, when it comes to the nineteenth
and twentieth centuries. However, there are several recent advances which aim
to remedy this by approaching those intellectual exchanges and itineraries from
an Indian Ocean perspective. Esmat Elhalaby studied Wadiʿ al-Bustani's life and
work through the notion of an 'Arabic rediscovery of India in the 20th century'.[4]
Elhalaby writes an intellectual history across the modern Indian Ocean region
and thereby globalizes the Nahda, often framed as the 'cultural and literary re-
awakening', beyond the Middle East.[5] He places Wadiʿ within the conceptual
framework of 'a history of global philology and an enabling colonial frame'.[6]
He thereby makes clear to what extent Wadiʿ was entangled in the European
Orientalist discourses of the period and how his engagement with Indian epics,
and in particular the Mahabharata, allowed him to forge an intellectual trajectory
that defied dominant cultural exchanges between metropole and colony to
pursue a south–south dialogue.[7] Elhalaby suggests that Wadiʿ considered that
'the Mahabhārata both is an instructive text for his contemporary political
context on the one hand and parallels Arabo-Islamic principles on the other'.[8]
He deems Wadiʿ's introduction to the edition of the Mahabharata as highly
political and traces how Wadiʿ constructed and construed 'his own' India 'tied
inexorably to his particular place in an unequal colonial geography'.[9] Ultimately,
he highlights that Wadiʿ's 'life and work reflect a history of imperial connections
beyond those of administration and exploitation'.[10]

Yet this 'rediscovery' came after centuries of scholarly and cultural exchanges
between local and mobile communities of the western Indian Ocean world.[11]
Over the early modern period, trade, pilgrimage, and scholarly encounters
sustained an intellectual traffic between the Red Sea region, West Asia,

and South Asia. Scholarship by Nile Green and Sugata Bose has shown that the movement of people and the flow of ideas across the Indian Ocean, in this era, interconnected the Arab world and South Asia.[12] Seema Alavi was able to trace movements of 'Muslim cosmopolitans' finding refuge in Istanbul, Mecca, and Cairo after the unsuccessful uprising of 1857, and thereby moving along the 'fringes' of the British and Ottoman empires.[13] Connectivities and exchanges between these regions were significantly reconfigured through mobilities and networks created through British imperial interventions that took shape from the mid-nineteenth century onwards. By the interwar years, as Milinda Banerjee has recently shown, Indian nationalists were not only drawing inspiration from Arab nationalism but actively dialoguing with them. The Indian Nobel laureate and poet Rabindranath Tagore's visit to Iraq in 1932, at the invitation of King Faisal I, was a landmark moment in the emergence of these anti-colonial solidarities.[14] However, we as yet have only a limited understanding of the intellectual dialogues between the Arab world and South Asia, especially as carried out through Arabic language thinking. This chapter aims at uncovering one facet of these rich exchanges and thereby elaborates on Elhalaby's pioneering work by adding some additional perspectives on Wadiʿ al-Bustani as an Arabic translator of the Mahabharata and how this work was presented in published form to a reading audience.

In doing so, we take inspiration from recent debates in global intellectual history.[15] In methodological terms, we place particular focus on 'paratexts'.[16] Paratexts – such as prefaces, reading notes, and dedications – offer a crucial basis for studying intellectual circulations because they are located at the co-constitutive site of production and reception of the written word. The editors of this volume approach the epic of the Mahabharata conceptually as a narrative of 'sovereignty' which emerges in a dialogue between the narrator and the listener.[17] We consider the preface and paratexts of Wadiʿ's published Mahabharata as a crucial element that can tell us something about the *intended* reception and audience of the translation. The preface shows us how this dialogue was opened by the translator to an Arabic audience, but the analysis of the audience has to remain incomplete for the time being until more copies of the publication are discovered to paint a fuller picture of Wadiʿ's readership.

This chapter provides a case study of paratextual practices regarding the transnational production, circulation, and reception of an Arabic translation of the Mahabharata across the space of British political and cultural dominance during the mid-twentieth century. Given the lacuna in the study of Arabic translations of this epic work, the chapter will situate the 1952 edition produced by Wadiʿ al-Bustani (d. 1954) in its intellectual and publication context. Building on Gerard Genette's work on *paratexts* as 'thresholds of interpretation', the main issue here is the use of title pages, prefaces, and introductory discussions through which the 'translators' of the work envisioned the presentation of their translation to an Arabophone audience and how this presentation was shaped in the publication process.[18]

We shall study how the extensive introduction manages to situate the Mahabharata in a literary discourse about Indian epics. We shall also examine how the literary work was rendered presentable to new audiences outside of the subcontinent and to what extent it remained culturally commensurable across a larger cultural formation of circulation that connected the Middle East and South Asia increasingly shaped by British imperialism. Yet the translation was also supposed to contribute something new to a transnational field of cultural production. We shall see how translation work helped to place the Mahabharata within a canon of world literature.

Creating an Arabic Canon of Epic Literature: From Homer to the Mahabharata

In the introduction, Wadiʿ al-Bustani writes about his scholarly approach to translating the Mahabharata and indicates some of his intellectual aspirations. Accordingly, this was not Wadiʿ's only engagement with the Mahabharata. Throughout his career, he translated several parts separately. These include *Nala and Damayanti*, the Bhagavadgita, and two sections of the Mahabharata that have counterparts in Ibn al-Muqaffaʿ's *Kalila wa-Dimna*. In fact, the first ancient Indian text that Wadiʿ translated was *Shakuntala*, although not from the Mahabharata directly but rather from its dramatized version by Kalidasa. Moreover, his engagement with ancient Indian literature was not confined to the Mahabharata and its derived works. He also translated an abridged version of the Ramayana. His interest in ancient Indian literature left marks on some of his other works too. For example, when he decided to translate selections from al-Maʿarri's poetry into English, his choices portrayed Maʿarri as a poet who was deeply influenced by Indian culture and literature.[19] Similarly, when Wadiʿ wanted to choose a modern Indian author to translate, he chose Tagore, who, despite his modernist tendencies, was, arguably, among the most faithful to the ancient roots of Indian culture among modern Indian authors.

One could argue that no other Arabic translator has in his record this number of translations of ancient Indian literature. Despite that, Wadiʿ was humble enough to consider himself an amateur. His translations were always made through English as a mediating language, indicating that by the twentieth century English could offer an intermediary platform for intellectual exchanges between West Asia and South Asia. One could easily forget these facts when one reads some of his linguistic discussions in his 'endnotes', where elements of Sanskrit grammar or metrics are discussed. But these were always done through carefully reading commentaries by different translators of the same text, rather than by firsthand knowledge of the original texts. But it is precisely this amateurishness that fascinates the reader of his translations and manifests Wadiʿ's fascination with Indian literature.

Wadiʿ al-Bustani's career was shaped to a large extent by the career of his older cousin, Sulayman al-Bustani, the first Arabic translator of Homer's Iliad into verse. According to Fuʾad al-Bustani, Wadiʿ's son, when his father showed some literary inclination, Sulayman was not satisfied with his cousin's eloquence. He advised him to memorize the Quran, an advice that Wadiʿ seems to have followed. However, the cousin's influence was far beyond that. It seems that Wadiʿ took him as a mentor. At least this is what one can infer from a note that Wadiʿ wrote: 'I am a disciple of my cousin, the translator of the Iliad; I learnt from him, and I imitated him.'[20]

A literary inclination coupled with a descendance from an elite literati family must have created a sense of obligation and duty in the young Wadiʿ. This sense of obligation would have been reinforced when his cousin published his celebrated translation of the Iliad. Wadiʿ was only 16 years old back then. Six years later, he started his translation and literary career. One can see from the five titles published between 1910 and 1912, the most notable among them being the Arabic verse translation of Khayyam's Rubaʿiyyat, that Wadiʿ was still searching for his calling. However, his cousin had raised the bar high. In 1912, he read the Gita upon his visit to India. Since that year, he dedicated most of his life and energy to translating ancient Indian literature into Arabic, with the notable exception of several works dictated by developments in Palestine. We would argue that it was not a mere fascination with Indian literature; it was also the discovery of a body of works of comparable value to those of Homer.

Wadiʿ wrote in his introduction: 'The [genuine] epics are precisely four: the Greek Iliad and Odyssey, and the Hindu Mahabharata and Ramayana';[21] other epics are merely 'imitations' of these four. Sulayman, on the other hand, acknowledges the importance of the two Indian epics, but he mentions them among a long list that does not attempt to give preferences,[22] though he prioritizes the Iliad over all other epics.[23] By distinguishing between 'genuine' epics and their 'imitations' and by including the two Indian epics in the shortlist of 'genuine' epics, Wadiʿ seems to indicate that his work 'completes' his cousin's. Further, Wadiʿ suggests that true wisdom should be sought in India, and not in the West.[24] This necessarily prioritizes the Indian epics over the two Greek ones that had acquired canonical value as the origins of Western literature.[25]

Nonetheless, to understand the Arab preoccupation with epics as such, we must first investigate Sulayman's intellectual objectives. In his introduction, Sulayman identified similarities and differences between Homeric poetry and Arabic classical poetry, especially pre-Islamic Arabic poetry. Similarities between the two bodies of texts made the translation possible; differences rendered translation work desirable, as it would enrich the Arabic literary tradition.

Long before modern scholars began to theorize about the oral origins of epic poetry, Sulayman emphasized the oral nature of Arabic poetry and pointed to the great capacity of memorization among early poets and narrators. He also stressed the oral roots of the Iliad.[26] He dismissed references to writing within the Iliad itself as referring to fragmentary types of writing that should not be compared to modern (or even classical) modes of writing. To this end, he compared passages from the Iliad with references to writing in some stories and verses of pre-Islamic poets (such as Tarafah ibn al- ʿAbd), where it is clear that what is meant by writing is merely drawing certain symbols on patches that would indicate certain required actions rather than being the mundane recording of events.[27]

Another similarity between the Iliad and classical Arabic poetry that Sulayman noted was the metrical system. While in many European languages, poetry is not metrical, both the Iliad and classical Arabic poetry have metre.[28] He deemed the fact that classical Greek poetry does not rhyme and Arabic poetry does as not too significant, for rhyme in Arabic comes naturally as the result of the derivation and root system.[29] He decided to put his translation in rhyme. This led him to use 10 (of the 16) classical Arabic metres for his translation as opposed to the only one that the original uses, because otherwise he would have been too restricted by the metre.[30]

Perhaps even more important to him was the supposed similarity between the classical Greek and Arab ways of life as depicted in the two bodies of texts. Sulayman observed: 'When you look at individuals [of the two peoples], you will be astonished by the apparent similarities in their conditions and ways of speech.'[31] He added: 'If you turn your eyes to the clothing, furniture, equipment, and ways of life, you will see ... a bewildering resemblance in their natural [*fitrī*] ways of life, in their moral naivete, and in their unbounded [*jahili*] freedom.'[32]

He offered extensive footnotes to further stress the apparent similarities between these societies.

Sulayman suggested that these social similarities resulted in comparable linguistic registers in the classical Greek and Arabic languages. This, in his view, gives the translator into Arabic an advantage over his European counterparts, who often cannot find close equivalents to the words and expressions they are translating and have to deviate from the original meanings. His experience is the opposite: 'I saw a resemblance between the two languages in the precision of vocabulary that would astonish any poet and writer.'[33] He furthermore gives examples of how words are created similarly and how both Greek and Arabic words are extremely precise in their depictions of the world. Moreover, this correspondence goes beyond vocabulary to similarities in the use of rhetorical devices, such as metaphor and metonymy.[34] At the same time, Sulayman does not ignore the differences between the two languages, nor does he 'equate' them. Rather, he gives Classical Greek a privilege over Arabic in some respects and Arabic over Greek in others.[35] He further highlights the reliance of the two languages on the senses rather than on abstractions.[36] In his view, these similarities make classical Arabic a more suitable vehicle for translating the Greek epics in comparison with modern European languages.

However, in Sulayman's view, Arabic differed from Greek in lacking a surviving tradition of epic poetry. He pondered if there were some lost Arabic epics and named the Biblical story of Job as a possible candidate.[37] He also wondered if *ayyam al-'Arab* (the stories and poetry associated with pre-Islamic and early Islamic fights and wars) originally formed collections of whole epics that were lost later.[38] Whatever the case, he concludes on this subject, what matters is that no Arabic epic has been preserved. In any case, not all nations of the world necessarily had epics, and Arabs might have been one such nation.[39] Sulayman concludes:

> How worthy it is for our Arabic language to possess a version of this unique pearl; for, compared to [the languages] of all the nations who have dealt with it, [Arabic] is the most deserving. Nothing in the poetry and languages of the Westerners (Franks) could provide better conditions for the [*Iliad*] to appear in the most beautiful dress than the apparatus that our language offers. Greek poetry is in a language close to the nature [*fitra*] like our language and the framework is an antiquity [*jahiliyya*] of a people similar to our antiquity. There are no poets among the nations of the world whose themes and motifs correspond to those of the *Iliad* … like our ancient poets.[40]

Thus, according to Sulayman, his translation should be seen as a service to both Arabic and Greek literary traditions. As for being a service to the Greek literary tradition, it is because Arabic is the most suitable language to preserve the literary features of the Iliad. As for being a service to the Arabic literary tradition, it is because it makes the latter more complete and perfect. The underlying assumption here is that the Arabic literary tradition is perfect except for lacking epic poetry. Sulayman wanted his translation to have its place next to the great collections of pre-Islamic poetry, which illuminates many of his choices in his footnote apparatus, where he constantly draws comparisons between verses from the Iliad and verses from pre-Islamic poetry.

Wadiʿ's treatment of the Mahabharata was directly inspired by Sulayman's project, but it took a different turn. Although Wadiʿ also looked for similarities that would make the translation possible and for differences that would make it desirable, he found these elsewhere. While the reference point for Sulayman was pre-Islamic poetry, for Wadiʿ it was the Abrahamic monotheistic tradition. According to him, important similarities existed between this and the Indian tradition. Although, as he admits, it may seem strange to the reader, the ancient Indian tradition was monotheistic in its essence, while paganism and/or polytheism was more of 'an appearance rather than a doctrine'.[41] He supported this claim with quotes from the Mahabharata that resembled the Abrahamic monotheistic tradition.[42]

He found in the ancient Indian tradition the same type of tension that was present in the Abrahamic religions, especially between trinitarian ideas and absolute monotheism.[43] But while in the Abrahamic tradition this tension resulted in the divergence between Christian Trinitarianism and Judaic or Islamic monotheism, Indian tradition had supposedly resolved the tension, harmonizing these seemingly contradictory theological positions. Wadiʿ moved then to the idea of incarnation. In his view, Indian concepts of incarnation corresponded in some ways to the Christian idea of incarnation; ultimately, the two traditions complemented and illuminated each other.[44] Wadiʿ did not shy away from engaging verses from the Quran in the discussion. When the Quranic text was read next to the Indian verses, the Christian idea of incarnation appeared to be Quranically plausible. This seems to be a hermeneutical principle on Wadiʿ's part. The Indian, Christian, and Islamic traditions were to be read in dialogue with each other. This led to a broader argument about the manifestation of divinity in poetry: 'Thus spoke Poetry. It humanized the Creator God and deified the created human being.'[45] In that sense, while Sulayman's project was a literary one, Wadiʿ's project was more of a religious or theological nature. This is ironic, for the latter was far more interested in style and in abiding by poetic norms than the former, as far as his endnotes indicate.

Differences were to be found, of course, in the ways the patterns of divinity materialized in literary texts: YHWH (Yahweh), Jesus, and Allah in Abrahamic traditions versus Brahma, Krishna, Vishnu (or Narayana), and Shiva in Indian traditions. However, recognition of differences also provided pathways for negotiating them. The fact that Abrahamic religions share the same narrative can cause unnecessary disputes for details become the focus of attention. These disputes can cause sectarianism, the greatest vice according to Wadiʿ. He quotes Shibl Faris: '[T]here is no sectarianism in [genuine] culture.'[46] He also prays to God to provide Arabs with a 'culture without sectarianism'.[47] By bringing the Abrahamic traditions into dialogue with India, Wadiʿ sought to emphasize underlying patterns that transcended historical cultural differences. Engaging with India would help Arab readers to identify and historicize common patterns of thought.[48] In that sense, engagement with ancient Indian epic tradition could be intellectually liberating for the modern Arab reader. Ultimately, Wadiʿ's engagement with an Indian literary tradition also had a political dimension in the context of his personal situation in living in British-mandate Palestine.

The Mahabharata as Arabic Text: Production and Reception

The paratextual elements of Wadiʿ's published translation of the Arabic Mahabharata give several clues about how its circulation was intended. The title page introduces the reader to the different parties involved in this project. He entitled the work 'The Mahabharata – the Hindu/Indian Epic – the Largest of the Epics of the World' (al-Mahabarata – al-Malhama al-Hindawiyya – Kubra al-malahim al-ʿalamiyya).[49] Wadiʿ relied on the Indian civil servant, litterateur, and nationalist politician Romesh Chunder Dutt's nineteenth-century translation and versification (more about this later) from Sanskrit into English. It was this selective translation that Wadiʿ 'retold' in Arabic verse. The American University Press published the work in 1952 in two different sets of editions – 50 exemplars in an elaborate version and 500 in a less elaborate one – with the main difference being the quality of the paper.[50]

The title page of Wadiʿ's edition works as a form of 'paratextual' intermediation. The printing of the title conveys the impression of a 'hybrid' script: semantically, it reads in Arabic, but it alludes to Devanagari by being embellished with certain elements reminiscent of this script. In Arabic, it is spelt 'al-Mahabarata', dropping the second 'h' from the initial Sanskrit title, which characteristically produces the 'bh' sound (also in Hindi and Urdu). Visually, it alludes to the Devanagari script commonly used to write Hindi and other South Asian languages. A top horizontal line is indicated by elongating the two *alif*s and the *lam*. The diacritics of the *tā'* and the *tā' marbūṭa* follow on the same level. At the same time, the two *alif*s and the *lam* underscore the vertical elements in the Devanagari script. The letters *hā'*, *rā'*, and the *tā' marbūṭa* are further embellished to make them resemble the Devanagari script. Still, the Arabic orthographical rules are fully observed; the title is fully legible in Arabic.

Romesh Dutt's versified English translation of 1898 fulfilled the role of both a linguistic and a cultural mediator in transmitting the Mahabharata from Sanskrit to Arabic. Recent scholarship has emphasized 'the historical and often power-laden settings of enacted translations'.[51] Assumptions about readership guided Dutt's choices in his selective translation from Sanskrit into English, just as much as Wadiʻs intellectual journey through Indian culture was structured by what intellectuals such as himself from the Levant imagined India to be at that·time.[52]

Wadiʻʻs Arabic translation of Dutt's English selective retelling of the Mahabharata was the product of the imperial confluences that prevailed and expanded from the late nineteenth to the mid-twentieth centuries. Both Wadiʻ and Dutt were preconditioned in their education by a search for the 'authentic', the 'traditional', an antique cultural heritage that could withstand the powerful political vicissitudes of their own times: British imperialism in the subcontinent for Dutt and British (and later Israeli) occupation of Palestine for Wadiʻ.[53] As recent scholarship has begun to highlight, the effects of British rule in India and in West Asia, especially in Palestine, need to be examined through the optics of 'connected history' (a term developed by Sanjay Subrahmanyam).[54] The synergies between Dutt and Wadiʻ were overdetermined by European dominance in Asia, and they felt the need among Asian nationalists to produce alternate cultural-nationalist hegemonies.

In India, as Milinda Banerjee has emphasized, the Mahabharata became, in the course of the late nineteenth and the early twentieth centuries, a major ideological template for imagining a unitary righteous nation state. The Sanskrit concept of *dharmarajya*, or righteous polity, was now used to imagine the nation.[55] However, this implied that the Mahabharata would also have to be updated for modern Anglophone, Western-educated Indian elites. Dutt, a key nationalist writer – and, eventually, president of the Indian National Congress, colonial India's most important political party – played a seminal role here.

Dutt explained in his 'translators's epilogue', which Wadiʿ fully translated for his edition, how he went about cutting down 'a poem of ninety thousand couplets, about seven times the size of the Iliad and the Odyssey put together'.[56] He excavated what he considered the 'leading narrative of the Epic', the battles between the Bharatas and the exposition of its main cast of characters.[57] He left out several portions of the epic, which he considered as digressions.[58] Apart from a few exceptions, his versified English translation told the story as 'a series of eighteen battles, fought on eighteen consecutive days' and thereby condensed the 90,000 Sanskrit couplets into 2,000 English couplets.[59]

In thus structuring the narrative, Dutt was guided by several considerations: first, by his intended Anglophone audience, who were expected to be well versed in the epic genre and to be familiar with English and, more broadly, with European literary classics; second, in creating a binary between a core narrative and digressions, Dutt was influenced by contemporary Indian nationalist writers such as Bankimchandra Chattopadhyay, who similarly sought to create a streamlined epic that would be fit for Indian nation-making.[60] In this enterprise, the martial tenor of the epic was necessarily emphasized over other sections and styles, as it was seen to be contributing to the project of politically unifying India. Ultimately, for many nationalists, 'the *Mahabharata* functioned as the constituent moment when the Indian nation's juridical being had taken shape in the (legendary) past' – the classic document of the formation of Indian national sovereignty.[61]

Esmat Elhalaby has discussed Wadiʿ's oeuvre as involving 'a vision of Eastern unity and pluralism…. His life and work reflect a history of imperial connections beyond those of administration and exploitation: an intellectual history of philology and solidarity.'[62] This necessitated taking a longue-durée view of cultural connections between India and the Arab world. Hence, in the introduction to this translation, he remembered how the Arabic text of *Kalila wa-Dimna* constituted the first literary link between these two worlds.

Wadiʿ had travelled to the South Asian subcontinent repeatedly between 1912 and 1916, had met Tagore, and engaged with a variety of literary works of South Asian provenance.[63] These included the Ramayana, the Gita, and *Shakuntala*.[64] In *Qissat al-muʿarrib* (Life of the Arabic Translator), his son Fuʾad recounts Wadiʿ's study of Indian literature (*dirasat al-adab al-hindawi*).[65] Fuʾad suggested that Wadiʿ became a 'prisoner of her [India's] imposing wonders and bewitched'. He immersed himself in the literature of al-Hind, read what he could find, the old (*talid*) and the new (*tarif*), and was never struck down by 'tiredness' or 'boredom'. He Arabized India's 'holy gifts of the Indian antique heritage' (*min turath al-mutahannida al-qudama*). According to Fu'ad, his father had learned Sanskrit to engage with its forms of versification and had compared English and French translations of the Mahabharata until he discovered Dutt's translation and thus based his work on Dutt's foundation.

The Arabic Mahabharata eventually gained wide transnational circulation. Exemplars of Wadi''s al-Mahabarata ended up in several university libraries, such as that of the University of California, Berkeley, and the British Library, London. With its initially limited print run and the two different sets of print editions, however, the editors presumably already had different ways of distributing the book in mind. We can assume that the 50 copies served social networking purposes and outreach to a selected community of readers. One version was given to Jawaharlal Nehru as a present and well received.[66] More versions probably ended up in private collections and would need to be explored further.

One copy derives from the collections of the Orient-Institut Beirut, Lebanon, and helps us visualize a trajectory of transnational circulation early after the publication. Two ownership marks and transmission notes on the title page document the movement of the book. The first note states that this copy was handed over to a certain 'K.B. J(I)andan of the Indian Embassy with the Translator's compliments'. The signature could be the one of Wadi', but it is not easy to decipher. The book changed hands on a special occasion: the date given in the transmission note is 28 February 1953, which back then marked the Hindu religious holiday of Holi, a fact that the presenter noted as '"Holy" day'. About a year later, on 24 March 1954, a certain M. Nizamuddin (presumably) inscribed his ownership mark and transmission note, detailing that the book was 'presented to me by Mr. Tawson [?] personally at the time of my visit to Cairo on 10th January 1954'.[67] M. Nizamuddin, the later owner, glued a note on the inside of the book cover, which stated that he (a Cambridge graduate) donated the book to the Orient-Institut Beirut, where today it is held in the library collections. While there are no further reading traces, the multiple people involved in the movement of this copy of the Mahabharata's printed edition indicates the opportunities of network-building the edition offered among actors who crossed national boundaries in this period, among them professionals, academics, and diplomats. This case provides at least one example of gift-giving practices between Indian, Arab, and British protagonists.

More research is needed in future on such paratexts, including reading traces, endowment notes, and dedicatory statements on different copies of the printed book. This will help us learn more about the readership of the Arabic

Mahabharata and enable a fragmentary but nonetheless important bottom-up approach to the history of reading this Arabic translation.

Conclusion

This chapter has studied some aspects of the first Arabic-language translation of the Mahabharata, produced in 1952. While the epic was cast into a nationalist political text in colonial India, it entered the Arab world as an exemplar of the epic form – a text of world literature. Despite these different trajectories, there were connections and intersections as well. Wadiʿ al-Bustani and his uncle Sulayman al-Bustani wanted to expand the Arabic literary canon by engaging with the epic form, where they saw narrative forms reminiscent of Arab ways of life. The uncle translated Homer's Iliad, while the nephew translated the Mahabharata. Given the Indian nationalist origins of the English translation that Wadiʿ used for his translation into Arabic, it is not surprising that cultural nationalism would inflect the Arabic translation project as well. Wadiʿ's engagement with India was certainly shaped by the desire to emphasize Asian literature in an age of European colonial dominance. Simultaneously, operating in West Asia where European colonialism had only aggravated sectarian conflicts, the translator sought in the Mahabharata pathways for overcoming sectarian differences. The literary classic pointed to common ways of realizing divine presence that was apparently shared by the Abrahamic as well as Indian intellectual traditions. The Mahabharata was thereby reshaped into an Arabic text – a text that resonated with Arab expectations about epic literature and monotheistic theology.

Notes

1. See Wadiʿ al-Bustani's biography at 'Wadiʿ Faris al-Bustani', Interactive Encyclopedia of the Palestine Question, https://www.palquest.org/en/biography/9843/wadi%E2%80%98-faris-al-bustani (accessed on 11 February 2024). The Lebanese order of merit was established on 16 January 1922. It has six grades (extraordinary, grand, first, second, third, and fourth). Wadiʿ received the second grade medal. Some of the most important Lebanese poets (such as Saʿid ʿAql), writers (such as Saʿid Taqiyy al-Din), scholars (such as ʿAbd Allah al-ʿAlayili and Fuʾad Ifram al-Bustani), and politicians (such as Kamal Junblat) attended the events. See Saʿid Taqiyy al-Din, *Sayyidati Sadati* (Cairo: Muʾassasat Hindawi, 2017 [published originally in Beirut, 1955]), 77–82.

2. For this and the following, see 'Wadi' Faris al-Bustani', Interactive Encyclopedia of the Palestine Question; Fu'ad Wadi' al-Bustani, 'Introduction' to his father's translation of the Mahabharata, in Wadi' al-Bustani, *al-Mahabarāta* (Beirut: Jam'iyyat Mutakharriji al-Jami'a al-Amiirkiyya fi Bayrut, 1952), 1ff.; and the encyclopedia entry 'al-Bustani family'.

3. For the term 'telling', see Ronit Ricci, *Islam Translated: Literature, Conversion, and the Arabic Cosmopolis of South and Southeast Asia* (Chicago, IL: Chicago University Press, 2011).

4. Esmat Elhalaby, 'Empire and Arab Indology', *Modern Intellectual History* 19, no. 4 (2022): 1081–1105.

5. Jens Hanssen and Max Weiss (eds.), *Arabic Thought beyond the Liberal Age: Towards an Intellectual History of the Nahda* (Cambridge, UK: Cambridge University Press, 2016); Jens Hanssen and Max Weiss (eds.), *Arabic Thought against the Authoritarian Age: Towards an Intellectual History of the Present* (Cambridge, UK: Cambridge University Press, 2018); Peter Hill, *Utopia and Civilisation in the Arab Nahda* (Cambridge, UK: Cambridge University Press, 2020).

6. Elhalaby, 'Empire and Arab Indology', 1086.

7. Elhalaby, 'Empire and Arab Indology', 1083, 1088.

8. Elhalaby, 'Empire and Arab Indology', 1102.

9. Elhalaby, 'Empire and Arab Indology', 1103.

10. Elhalaby, 'Empire and Arab Indology', 1105.

11. See, for example, Christopher D. Bahl, 'Transoceanic Arabic Historiography: Sharing the Past of the Sixteenth-Century Western Indian Ocean', *Journal of Global History* 15, no. 2 (2020): 203–223; Mahmood Kooria, *Islamic Law in Circulation : Shafi'i Texts across the Indian Ocean and the Mediterranean* (Cambridge, UK: Cambridge University Press, 2022).

12. Nile Green, *Bombay Islam: The Religious Economy of the West Indian Ocean, 1840–1915* (Cambridge, UK: Cambridge University Press, 2011); Sugata Bose, *A Hundred Horizons: The Indian Ocean in the Age of Global Empire* (Cambridge, MA: Harvard University Press, 2009).

13. Seema Alavi, *Muslim Cosmopolitanism in the Age of Empire* (Cambridge, MA: Harvard University Press, 2015).

14. Milinda Banerjee, *The Mortal God: Imagining the Sovereign in Colonial India* (Cambridge, UK: Cambridge University Press, 2018), 259–60.

15. Samuel Moyn and Andrew Sartori (eds.), *Global Intellectual History* (New York: Columbia University Press, 2013).

16. Gerard Genette, *Paratexts: Thresholds of Interpretation* (Cambridge, UK: Cambridge University Press, 2009).

17. See Milinda Banerjee and Julian Strube's introduction to this volume.

18. Genette, *Paratexts.*

19. Wadiʿ al-Bustani, 'Introduction', in *al-Mahabarāta* (Beirut: Jamʿiyyat Mutaḥarriǧī al-Jāmiʿa al-Amiirkiyya fi Bayrut, 1952), 18–21.

20. Wadiʿ al-Bustani, 'Endnotes', in *al-Mahabarāta* (Beirut: Jamʿiyyat Mutaḥarriǧī al-Jāmiʿa al-Amiirkiyya fi Bayrut, 1952), n.826.

21. Wadiʿ, 'Introduction', 1.

22. Sulayman al-Bustani, 'Introduction' to his translation of the Iliad, in *Ilyādhat Hūmīrūs* Cairo: Matbaʾat al-Hilal, 1904), 165–67.

23. Sulayman, 'Introduction', 69.

24. Fuʾad, 'Introduction', 3, 5.

25. Wadiʿ, 'Endnotes', §§825–26.

26. Sulayman, 'Introduction', 38ff.

27. Sulaymān al-Bustānī, 'Footnotes', in Wadiʿ al-Bustani, *al-Mahabarāta* (Beirut: Jamʿiyyat Mutaḥarriǧī al-Jāmiʿa al-Amiirkiyya fi Bayrut, 1952), §§449–50.

28. Sulayman, 'Introduction', 94–95.

29. Sulayman, 'Introduction', 95.

30. Sulayman, 'Introduction', 89–94.

31. Sulayman, 'Introduction', 169.

32. Sulayman, 'Introduction', 169.

33. Sulayman, 'Introduction', 193.

34. Sulayman, 'Introduction', 176–88.

35. Sulayman, 'Introduction', 193.

36. Sulayman, 'Introduction', 193.

37. Sulayman, 'Introduction', 167–68.

38. Sulayman, 'Introduction', 170–72.

39. Sulayman, 'Introduction', 171.

40. Sulayman, 'Introduction', 69.

41. Wadiʿ, 'Introduction', 22.

42. Wadiʿ, 'Introduction', 22; Wadiʿ, 'Endnotes', §257.

43. Wadiʿ, 'Introduction', 23; Wadiʿ, 'Endnotes', §§257, 259.

44. Wadiʿ, 'Introduction', 23–25; Wadiʿ, 'Endnotes', §§257, 259.

45. §900.

46. Wadiʿ, 'Introduction'; Wadiʿ, 'Endnotes', 16.

47. Wadiʿ, 'Introduction', 25.

48. Wadiʿ, 'Endnotes', §807.

49. For this and the following, see the title page of Wadiʿ, *al-Mahabarāta*, 1952. Unfortunately, it was not possible to get permissions for a visual reproduction of the title page here.

50. See the note next to the portrait drawing of Wadiʿ on the pages before the title page in Wadiʿ, *al-Mahabarāta.*

51. Samuel Moyn and Andrew Sartori, 'Approaches to Global Intellectual History', in *Global Intellectual History*, ed. Samuel Moyn and Andrew Sartori, 3–30 (New York: Columbia University Press, 2013), 12–13.

52. On 'Western' depictions of India, see Ronald Inden, *Imagining India* (London: Hurst & Co., 2000).

53. We thank Milinda Banerjee for his interpretation here.

54. Faisal Devji, *Muslim Zion: Pakistan as a Political Idea* (Cambridge, MA: Harvard University Press, 2013); Arie M. Dubnov and Laura Robson (eds.), *Partitions: A Transnational History of Twentieth-Century Territorial Separatism* (Redwood City, CA: Stanford University Press, 2019); Milinda Banerjee, 'The Partition of India, Bengali "New Jews", and Refugee Democracy: Transnational Horizons of Indian Refugee Political Discourse', *Itinerario: Journal of Imperial and Global Interactions* 46, no. 2 (2022): 283–303. Sanjay Subrahmanyam, 'Connected Histories: Notes towards a Reconfiguration of Early Modern Eurasia', *Modern Asian Studies* 31, no. 3 (1997): 735–62.

55. Milinda Banerjee, '"One Law, One Nation, One Throne": Debating National Unity', in *The Mortal God: Imagining the Sovereign in Colonial India*, by Milinda Banerjee, 162–288 (Cambridge, UK: Cambridge University Press, 2018).

56. Romesh Chunder Dutt, *The Maha-Bharata: Epic of the Bharatas* (London: n.p., 1898), 371.

57. Dutt, *The Maha-Bharata*, 372.

58. Dutt, *The Maha-Bharata*, 373.

59. Dutt, *The Maha-Bharata*, 373–74.

60. See Bankimchandra Chattopadhyay's essays 'Krishnacharitra' (1886, 1892) and 'Dharmatattva' (1884–86, 1888), in Bankimchandra Chattopadhyay, *Bankim Rachanavali*, vol. 2 (Calcutta: Sahitya Samsad, 1954).

61. Milinda Banerjee, 'Sovereignty as a Motor of Global Conceptual Travel: Sanskritic Equivalents of "Law" in Bengali Discursive Production', *Modern Intellectual History* 17, no. 2 (2020): 487–506, 493.

62. Elhalaby, 'Empire and Arab Indology', 25.

63. Fu'ad, 'Introduction', 2–3.

64. These appear in the list provided by Fu'ad al-Bustani of works prepared for publications. Fu'ad, 'Introduction', 5.

65. Fu'ad, 'Introduction', 2–3.

66. Marun 'Abbud, *Adab al-'Arab* (Cairo: Mu'assasat Hindāwī, 2014 [published originally in Beirut, 1960]), 345.

67. This is a copy of the book which is held at the library of the Orient-Institut Beirut, Lebanon.

About the Contributors

Christopher D. Bahl is an assistant professor of South Asian History at Durham University. His research focuses on early modern South Asia and the subcontinent's links with regions and communities across the western Indian Ocean. He is currently working on his first monograph, which traces shared cultural histories between the Red Sea region and western India through the circulation of Arabic manuscripts from the fifteenth to the seventeenth centuries. Before coming to Durham in 2020, he was a research associate at the Orient-Institut Beirut, Lebanon (Max Weber Foundation). He received his PhD in History from the the School of Oriental and African Studies (SOAS), University of London (2018). Previously, he completed a Master's degree in Historical Research Methods at the SOAS (2014) and a Master's degree in Islamic Studies and South Asian History at the University of Heidelberg (2013). In the academic year 2010–11, he studied at Damascus University and at the University of Hyderabad.

Egas Moniz Bandeira holds a PhD from Tohoku University, Japan, and is a researcher at the Friedrich-Alexander University Erlangen–Nuremberg, Germany. His main research interest is the global history of political ideas with a focus on East Asia. He has published in leading journals, such as the *Journal of Transcultural Studies*, *Global Intellectual History*, and the *Journal of Eurasian Studies*, and is the co-editor of several volumes on global political history and historiography, including *Planting Parliaments in Eurasia, 1850–1950: Concepts, Practices, and Mythologies* (2021) (co-edited with Ivan Sablin) and *Parties as Governments in Eurasia,*

1913–1991: Nationalism, Socialism, and Development (2022) (co-edited with Ivan Sablin).

Milinda Banerjee is a lecturer in Modern History at the University of St Andrews, Scotland. He is the author of *The Mortal God: Imagining the Sovereign in Colonial India* (2018), published with the Press, and the co-author (with Jelle Wouters) of *Subaltern Studies 2.0: Being against the Capitalocene* (2022). He has co-edited the volume *Transnational Histories of the 'Royal Nation'* (2017) as well as several special issues of journals on intellectual and global history.

Arkamitra Ghatak is a doctoral candidate in the Department of Klassische Indologie, South Asia Institute (SAI), Heidelberg University. Her PhD project is titled 'Female Gurus as Jagat-Janani: A Transcultural History of Universal Motherhood in the Nineteenth and Twentieth Centuries'. She completed her Bachelor's and Master's degrees in History from Presidency University, Kolkata. Her research interests include transcultural studies, global intellectual history with a focus on gender and religion, female religious and spiritual agency, articulation of piety in folk performance, and so on.

Paulus Kaufmann is a senior lecturer at the Japan Centre of the Ludwig Maximilian University (LMU) of Munich and at the Institute of Asian and Oriental Studies, University of Zurich. In 2010, he completed his PhD with a thesis on a problem in contemporary moral philosophy. Since then his research has focused on the conceptions of truth and meaning in the writings of the Japanese monk Kukai (774–835). His field of expertise is Japan's history of ideas, with a special focus on early Japanese Buddhism and on the political discourse of the Edo period (1600–1868). Philosophically, he is furthermore interested in ethics, the philosophy of language, and metaphilosophy.

Amanda Lanzillo is a lecturer in South Asian History at Brunel University London. She was previously a Cotsen postdoctoral fellow in the Society of Fellows in the Liberal Arts, Princeton University, New Jersey, and holds a PhD in History from Indiana University (2020). She is the author of *Pious Labor: Islam, Artisanship and Technology in Colonial India* (2024), which is her monograph. Her research on Muslim artisan communities, labour, technology, religion, and translation has also been published in *Modern Asian Studies, South Asia: Journal of South Asian Studies,* the *Journal of Social History,* and *South Asian History and Culture,* among others.

David M. Malitz is a senior research fellow with the German Institute for Japanese Studies (DIJ) in Tokyo. Prior to joining the DIJ, he taught at the Faculty of Arts of Chulalongkorn University, Bangkok; he remains affiliated with the university's History department. Additionally, he is a member of the Modern Monarchy in Global Perspective Research Hub at the University of Sydney. In Tokyo, his research focuses on Japan's relations with South-East Asia, as well as on the modern histories of Japan and Thailand, the history of their relations, and, particularly, both countries' monarchies.

Melanie J. Müller completed her Bachelor's degree in Buddhist and South Asian studies and her Master's degree in Religion and Philosophy in Asia at the Ludwig Maximilian University (LMU) of Munich, focusing on Sanskrit and Hindi on the one hand and also on modern India on the other. After completing her studies in Munich in 2016, she pursued a Master's degree in Culture and Literary Studies at the University of Santiago de Compostela in Spain. She then returned to Munich as a research assistant and taught several Sanskrit and feminist literature courses. Since 2021, she has been working at Heilbronn University, where she is currently a project manager in the Department of Equality and Diversity. Her research interests are in the area of gender and diversity.

Alok Oak is a postdoctoral fellow at the Institute for Advanced Studies in the Humanities (IASH), University of Edinburgh (2023–24). His research project is titled 'Dominion Status as a *Fait Accompli*: A. B. Keith and the History of Commonwealth Constitutionalism in British India (1919–1942)'. Previously, he was a visiting research scholar and tutor at the School of History, University of St Andrews (2022–23). For his PhD (2015–22, Leiden Institute for Area Studies [LIAS], University of Leiden), he wrote an intellectual biography of the Indian anti-colonial leader and conservative thinker Balgangadhar Tilak (1856–1920). His recent publications include the article 'Saving Indian Villages: British Empire, the Great Depression and Gandhi's Civil Disobedience Movement' in the journal *Studies in Indian Politics* (2022).

Abdallah Soufan is currently an independent scholar investigating dichotomies in classical Islamic thought, including the dichotomies of *sunna–bid'a*, veridicality–tropicality, reason–tradition, word–meaning, and exoteric–esoteric. He received his PhD from Georgetown University, Washington, DC, and taught at the American University of Beirut; Lebanese American University, Beirut; and Université Saint-Joseph de Beyrouth (Saint Joseph University of Beirut); and was a researcher at the

Orient-Institut Beirut. His previous publications include *The Call to God: An Arabic Critical Edition and English Translation of Epistle 48* (2019) (co-edited with Abbas Hamdani).

Philipp Sperner studied comparative literature and South Asian studies at the University of Innsbruck and at the School of Oriental and African Studies (SOAS), University of London. His PhD dissertation at Ludwig Maximilian University (LMU) of Munich explored narratives of friendship in Indian literature and the political imaginary of democracy under the conditions of post-coloniality. His research interests include global intellectual history, the rhetoric of literary forms and modes of knowledge production, post-colonial and political theory, deconstruction, and twentieth-century literatures in German, English, and Hindi.

Julian Strube is a professor of Religious Studies at the University of Göttingen. He works from a global historical perspective on the relationship between religion and politics, as well as on debates about the meaning of religion, science, and philosophy since the early modern period. His current research focuses on the relationship between Orientalist studies, religion, and nationalism; religious comparativism; esotericism and alternative religiosity; and exchanges between India, Europe, and North America, especially regarding reform, tradition, and modernity. His publications include his third monograph, *Global Tantra: Religion, Science, and Nationalism in Colonial Modernity* (2022); *New Approaches to the Study of Esotericism* (2021) (co-edited with Egil Asprem); and *Theosophy across Boundaries* (2020) (co-edited with Hans-Martin Krämer).

Index